TRANSFORMING YOUR *Life*

VOLUME II

Transforming Your Life II

Sai Blackbyrn

With

Co-Authors from around the World

Transforming Your Life II

All Rights Reserved

Copyright 2019

Transforming Your Life II

sai@sai.coach

ISBN 978-1-5272-4137-4

Edited by Surbhi Sanchali Gupta
Interior Design by Jeanly Fresh Zamora
Project Management by Antonetta Fernandes

Anila Kaba-Bashllari
Transformation Coach & Mindset Enhancer

Brielle Franklin
Author, Executive Recruiter, Holistic Career Coach

Clare Ford
Author, Speaker, Healer, Life Coach, Teacher

Corinne Steiner
Personal & Prof. Development Coach, Trainer, Mentor

Gregory Reece-Smith
Shamanic CEO

Gus Southey
Energy Healer, Author, Speaker

Iain Acton
Entrepreneur, Coach, Author, Teacher, Artist

Ignacio Perez
Aerospace Engineer turned Champion of Coaches

Justine Robbins
CEO, Growth Strategist, Coach, Board Chairman, Author

Kaley Zeitouni
Marriage and Family Therapist, Speaker, Coach

Kirsten Ward
Certified Diabetes Educator, Coach, Motivational Speaker

Lissa Pohl
Global Expert in Somatic Intelligence and Engagement

Mark Mudford
Coach, Author, Security Tactician, Business Strategist

Michael Golowyn
Relationship Grief Coach

Nikki Sinclair
Business Owner, Mother, Editor

Paul Hunting
Horse whisperer, 'maverick genius', Paradigm-Busting coach

Rob Wherrett
Executive Leadership Coach, Management Consultant

Sai Blackbyrn
Multi-Millionaire, CEO, DotCoach

Sampo Manninen
CEO, Spiritual Coach, Meditation Teacher

Sasha Raskin
Author, Life Coach, Psychotherapist

Venerando Cortez
Physique Transformation Coach, CEO, Author, Veteran

Vikki Coombes
Transformational Coach, Public Speaker, Author

This book is dedicated to Myles Sinclair and all those who, like him, live intentionally to positively impact others and the world we live in.

FOREWORD TO 'TRANSFORMING YOUR LIFE'

BY NIKKI SINCLAIR

"Life is not about waiting for the storms to pass
it's about learning to dance in the rain."
(Vivian Greene)

No one is immune to the challenges life throws at us. It's how we handle them, and the mistakes we make, that will determine the extent of our happiness, contributions, and success in life. This book is a result of decades of experiences and lessons learned from the hardships, pain, fears, and struggles of real people who share their stories and knowledge from which each of us can learn.

It is a privilege and honor to be asked to write the foreword for a book I know will impact many lives.

This book is filled with wisdom, inspiration, and life-changing ideas. If you are ready to make changes in your life that will help you rise to a new level of performance, clarify your vision, overcome your fears, unlock your source of happiness, become a more authentic leader, find joy, love again, and lead a more purposeful life, then this is a book you should not be able to put down. Each chapter brings insights that could change your future and make the world a better place for you and those around you to live in.

This diverse group of authors have opened up to share a wealth of information and tools and offer answers that can help us reach our full potential in our changing and challenging world. Reading is one thing, but transformation comes from making an effort to apply the concepts or principles that speak to you personally. The real reward, however, will come from sharing this with others and knowing that you have made a difference and perhaps helped someone else build something magnificent.

We think we have our whole life ahead of us, but the reality is that we don't know when we will take our last breath. I grew up being told that "Life is not a dress rehearsal," so make each day count. There is no time like the present to make the changes you need to make in order to achieve more – whether it's physically, mentally, relationally, or spiritually. As Zig Ziglar says, "You have to be and do before you can have." Transforming your life is a process that starts with having a vision or goal that will drive you to take action and motivate you to make the right decisions and wise choices to take you from where you are today to where you want to be. It's a journey that will require discipline and courage, but making small changes consistently will lead you to live a more fulfilled life characterised by hope, joy, and purpose. You have a choice to thrive or to just survive and to shove or to love. Wherever you are in your life right now, this book will inspire you to take control, serve others, and build the life you dream about.

TABLE OF CONTENTS

Going Beyond Limits

Anila Kaba-Bashllari

"Who are you?" are the three words still echoing in my ears from that sunny afternoon in the beautiful Tao garden in Chiang Mai, Thailand. Mary and I were sitting in front of each other in one of the most beautiful and quiet gardens I had ever been to. The only sounds were those of birds, but I wasn't able to recognize which ones. The only thing I can recall is the stillness.

"Who are you?" she asked again in order to bring me back to the present moment.

Very proudly, I started to mention all of my achievements: being married, having a great family and the most loving son, being graduated as an economist, MBA, Ph.D. in economics… and before I could continue further, Mary interrupted me kindly by articulating very clearly this time, "I am not asking what you have achieved or possess, but I am asking you, Who you are?"

I looked straight at her to ascertain if she was ridiculing me or trying to fool around with me. My face probably had a weird expression, and so Mary asked again, "Has nobody ever asked you that question before?"

I don't remember how long my pause lasted. I broke the silence by trying to sound smart. "What do you mean by this question?" I quipped. I am giving you all the answers and yet you keep asking me "Who I Am?" I don't know how to answer this anymore.

That was my first experience with a coach. I smile now when such memories are put into words, but it was the weirdest question I had heard at that time. I wasn't even able to respond to it properly.

Part 1: Everything happens for a reason: I can see clearly now

I cried all night long. When morning came, I was hiding from my parents as I did not want them to see my swollen eyes. My dream to become a doctor was blown up by the very *people*[1] who had a right to decide my future—regardless of my high-school results. I was desperate and didn't want to talk to anyone. I was an 18-year-old, struggling to understand why the youngest child of the family couldn't choose the faculty branch she wanted[2] to because the eldest one was studying for natural sciences.

My parents couldn't decide who should start talking to me. My father's first words made me cry harder.

---

[1] Communist governments were in charge of deciding the rights and academic paths for university students and even decided if one could continue further studies.

[2] I had applied for Medicine, Law, and Philosophy.

"Dad, I read the announcement and my name was at the Economy Faculty,[3]" I said sobbing and taking the handkerchief my mother was giving me. My father started to talk, but I wasn't in the mood for any explanation. It seemed as if the sky had fallen over my head. There was nothing he could say to give me a better perspective of what was going on.

Soon summer was over and my complaints, too. I had to prepare for University. I was calmer than before as a few of my high-school friends were in the same faculty like me. In the blink of an eye, I graduated as an economist with high grades. However, another 'storm' was approaching me—a job assignment outside my hometown.

It was already fall, and the colors were everywhere. But that fall was different. I had been assigned[4] to work outside Tirana[5] and had to go. Those days, the Communist regime was in its first sting.[6]

It was a cold morning but rarely could you see someone

---

3   It was year 1982 and Economy Faculty was not prefered at all for university studies.

4   During Communism, the assigned structures decided where the graduates would go to work.

5   Tirana is the capital of Albania.

6   For all those not having lived under the communist regime, I must explain that the right to education and job were assigned by the structures in charge. Fortunately, today, in the conditions of the market economy, everybody is free to get the education he/she wants and decide a career by themselves.

wearing an overcoat.

People were recognizing and acknowledging that summer was almost over, but nobody wanted to accept it. My father pointed toward the train wagon we were about to embark. I was literally dragging my feet. I do not recall the conversation we had up to Lushnje (the city where I was assigned to work as an economist, 90 km from Tirana), but I remember my father's blurred eyes. It was the first time I was leaving my family behind, and my 'wings' were fragile for the first flight. I was not prepared for life.

I was twenty-two then and felt like an abandoned child. I was extremely desperate.

Meanwhile, my fiancé Arjan had been assigned to work in Gramsh, a small military city, 100 km from Tirana. After three years, we got married; when our son Keltin was fifteen months old, I joined Arjan and three of us were traveling to Gramsh. It was fall again and while crossing the '3 steps bridge' at the city's entrance, I felt isolated from the rest of the world. At that time, the sole way to travel was public transport and it would take about nine hours by car with stopovers[7] from Gramsh to Tirana or vice-versa. Regardless of all the difficulties, I was happy.

Those were the last months before the fall of Communism. Being outside my dear Tirana was extremely difficult for me. Nevertheless, today I believe that those years were the most valuable experiences I had in preparing for the life ahead.

---

[7]   We had to stopover in another city and wait for random cars to pick us up to Tirana.

The last Communism bastion[8] in Europe fell down, but the transition period to which we were oblivious was taking longer—much longer than we expected it to be.

We returned 'home' after five years of experience outside Tirana, facing difficulties in finding a job. Arjan started working in another field, and I was still looking for a job.

I was passing the courtyard of the Ministry of Foreign Affairs, feeling tensed in the body. I was applying for diplomacy, and the majority of the applicants were from the Foreign Language Faculty.

"Goodmorning," I greeted the panel and settled down. Everything went well, and while leaving the room, I started to dream about my new job.

But the universe had a different plan for me. I was selected in the Ministry of Foreign Trade, and the job[9] was rather appealing. Soon, I started working as an assistant to the Deputy Minister, which was a coveted position. One day, as I was immersed in paperwork and was trying to arrange them, I heard someone talk to me in English. I turned my head to find a tall and handsome man entering the office. A few minutes later, the con-

---

8   Albania
9   I admired the people working in these institutions since I was a kid. And I used to tell my parents, I would like to work there when I grow up. What I did not know was how difficult it would be to get a job in these institutions without proper conections. It was still the era of Communism.

5

versation got extremely interesting, this time in the Albanian language. Regardless, I could sense that this person did not live in Albania.

"You speak English well," he said and this was followed by a brief silence as if he was weighing what he had to say. "Why don't you apply for an MBA?" he continued. It was 1992, and Albania had just done away with Communism, but perhaps only in surface.

"What is an MBA?" I asked hesitating since I was embarrassed at not knowing.

"It is a post-university degree, and I can get you a full scholarship," he said. He was watching me again as if trying to make sure that his suggestion was the right one and well-received.

"I would like that very much," I responded, holding my breath. "When is the deadline for submitting the application?"

It was January 1993, and I had been selected to attend one of the best business management schools in Europe. Excited and worried at the same time, I took a deep breath, and the clean air brought me to my senses. I was feeling concerned. Keltin was only five years old, and I knew it was going to be difficult for both of us. But we made it.

Touching the rough surface of my MBA certificate, I felt I had something precious in my hands. But I did not know its worth yet. Only years later would I be able to say that it had been one of the most important decisions in my career. Every moment of sacrifice had been worth it. Tears start to well up in my eyes even today when I remember those beautiful, curious eyes of my son waiting for me after the passport control cabin at the Tirana airport.

If the person who helped me attend a business school is reading this, I would like to express my sincere gratitude again since it was a turning point in my career.

Everything that followed seemed to be helping with my career advancement—projects, applications, and managerial positions. And as I was climbing my career ladder, the stress levels also went up. To manage people was the most difficult task. Every job that I was applying for got me more and more concerned about its technical aspects But, it was later when I realized that working with people was the most difficult part.

When I turned forty, a circle of 'health' problems hit me, out of the blue. And I sensed that these could continue for a long time.

Professionally, it was one of the most stressful periods of my career. As the Country Manager[10], I had to spend a lot of energy and time settling communication issues between the technical and support staff.

I began growing weary and deprived of energy and did not wish

---

[10]   Country Manager of one large donor financed programs in Albania

to be in office. Not only did I feel physically tired, but I was also mentally and emotionally drained. I could not fathom what was happening in my life. I blamed others for the situation I was in, failing to understand that I was in need of a change. And to do that, I had to work on myself, manage my emotions.

I felt a wave of pent up anger toward people I had been kind to and helped a lot—people in office who caused me that stress. The resentment and anger stayed with me for a while, until I started working on myself to understand forgiveness.

"As I walked out the door towards the gate that would lead to my freedom, I knew if I didn't leave my bitterness and hatred behind, I'd still be in prison."

Nelson Mandela

It took me a while to understand that forgiveness is not about the other person but about the negative energy within me.

The years that followed were an emotional and professional roller coaster. It seemed that I was trying to get the answers from within me, but nobody understood what I was going through.

It was 2011, and I had just returned from a long trip to China. I felt completely different. For weeks, I had watched no TV. I was eating healthy and felt energized and full of confidence. I had met new people who had a different perception about life, and contact with them opened many knowledge doors for me. The months to come were intense. Soon the trip to Thailand came, and it was one of the most impressive trips in my life. However, at that moment, I did not know that this trip to Thailand would change my personal and professional life and go on to define me.

On April 3, 2012, my memories of Thailand were still fresh and occupying my mind. While thinking about what I should do next, I was scrolling down a long list of emails. My eyes stopped at this particular email that I had seen about some six months ago, on my return from China. "This might be a sign," I thought and opened the email again. It was the same program I had read about a few months ago. The deadline was within a week, and I needed to contemplate upon it, especially the course fee. I had spent a lot in the past three years and was feeling guilty. Instead of deleting the email, I went through it several times with an inner voice supporting my choice to apply. The last hour of the deadline was decisive. I applied for the course and took the first class on May 1st. But I had no clue about what was in store for me.

When I got my certification as a life coach, I was thrilled. All doubts and worries about going through the intensive program faded away. But it is still vivid—the memory of my very first practice coaching session with a certified coach.

"Hi Catherin, nice to talk to you," I began. I had prepared a lot prior to the session, reading all instructions and repeating the questions I needed to ask. I was sweating and my voice was breaking. I was trying to remember everything

that I should talk about but at that moment, my mind was like a whiteboard. Catherin smiled in a way that was soothing. "I have been in your shoes years ago, and I know how it feels. Through practice, you will understand exactly what coaching is about but it will take years to get into it. However, you are doing great my dear," she said.

It was an intensive year, yet it lives on in my memory as one in which I practiced self-management and systematic planning persistently. It was then that I realized each experience in life is unique. And more than anything, I was feeling happy and fully charged.

At that period, it all seemed to happen by chance. But now I see it clearly. It was leading me toward a holistic life, on a journey from the unknown to being at peace with myself and my surroundings. I was searching and seeking answers from within, living in the present, and most importantly radiating confidence and happiness.

I trained and reprogrammed my brain through the years to see and live life intelligently, prioritizing but never compromising the four inner pillars of personal strength: Health & Fitness, Emotional, Mental and Spiritual.

The rest is history. There were many opportunities showing up, and I did what was best for me—following my dreams, passion, and intuition.

I have had my own business for five years now, and it is steadily growing. When I look back at all those coincidences, I realize that it all happened for a reason. I CAN SEE CLEARLY NOW!

- I was meant to study Economics as it opened doors for me in different managerial positions.
- My previous struggles and pain while working outside Tirana strengthened me and prepared me for the future.
- I couldn't wait to start a career as a diplomat, but the opportunity to pursue an MBA appeared when I started working at the Ministry of Foreign Trade. MBA was the key to opening several other doors for me. Sometimes, what we are seeking might not be the best thing for us.
- My emotional roller coaster ride was a blessing. All the people who showed up in my life were there for a reason—my personal growth. I learned that by taking care of my own needs and body, I could live holistically.
- The coincidences were meant to happen so that I could end up at the 'right' place.

Part 2: Do it afraid! Developing a growth mindset toward success

"Don't be afraid to give up the good to go for the great."

John D. Rockefeller

"What?! You are going to throw away 30 successful years of your career?" Arjan[11] asked in a condescending tone, trying to understand what was going on in my head. For several days, it had turned into a 'hot' topic. Our conversation would start with a small remark on my end, followed by his doubts. I would then try answering his questions, even though I knew that I wasn't convincing enough. It seemed like we were both avoiding an

---

[11] Arjan Bashllari, my husband of over 30 years.

11

unpleasant conversation.

Throughout my career, Arjan has played an important role. He has always been supportive and talked me through my fears and insecurities. I feel that he has had more confidence in me than I did in my own capabilities. But this time I was concerned.

The project that I was working on was coming to a close in a few months. Meanwhile, I had already been certified by QSCA as a Life Coach and had started taking some clients in the afternoons. I enjoyed working with different individuals, and my confidence and enthusiasm were growing. I thought that it was the right time to talk with Arjan about my future as a life and business coach in personal & professional development. I had even found the name for the company, but it turned out to be extremely difficult to explain to him that my business has a future. I recognized that it is hard to put your intuition into words.

Days passed, and my birthday was approaching. It was an important anniversary. Arjan is not a typical flower or presents man, but he loves traveling, a lot.

"If you really want me to be happy and remember this for a long time, a trip to Bali together would be the best gift for my birthday and our silver wedding anniversary," I demanded. I stood there in anticipation, waiting for his response.

"Yes, we can go," he said. The answer was brief, but enough to get me excited. I would take care of the rest.

Autumn had already set in, with its lovable colors. I noticed this while I was looking out the window of the plane. I felt so good. I did not have a clue what was to follow and immersed into the unknowing. I instinctively took out the books for both of us to read. The flight to Bali was long, but I was filled with enthusiasm and joy. Above all, we were together on this spiritual trip. Later on, I understood that it was the right decision to live together through experiences, where words to describe them are always not enough.

Upon our return from Bali, I felt more relaxed to talk about my new business. I began explaining to Arjan how I looked at myself in the future and what I wanted to do. He did not object but added, "You had made up your mind a long time ago. And I know it is in vain to discuss this any further. Don't expect me to understand what you are going to do, but count on my support, always." I was somewhat relieved. Years later, I helped him understand what I really wanted to do, but for what it was worth, I knew that I was not throwing away my 30+ years of experience. I was building upon it.

It was a period of hard work and playfulness, fears and courage, getting stuck and accelerating, bad and great decisions, demotivation, and inspiration, failures, and successes. I was growing every day but was also learning that success is a state of mind.

"Success is not final; failure is not fatal: It is the courage to continue that counts.

Winston S. Churchill

I found it hard to keep my business and my personal growth in harmony, then. I was wearing several hats and needed to juggle between a lot of things. In the beginning, I would do everything by myself, and it was overwhelming.

I was playing out of my comfort zone.

What I was feeling then is not easy to describe and explain today. Today, I feel confident as a coach, mentor, and trainer in personal development and have a stable business that is growing. But in those days, coaching was not even articulated as a word in my country. Some of my friends and family members might have thought I was crazy (and I am sure they did) to dedicate all my time, energy, passion, and finances to something that could not be understood by the majority of the population.

I chose another career path and was persistent even though few things appeared to work at the beginning.

It seemed vague that the surroundings and people around me to see my vision and efforts. I felt tired and exhausted beyond words. Having my personal coaches and mentors at that time and being a part of different personal development international networks and programs supported me to maintain a positive outlook.

I did invest myself fully in developing a growth mindset through different personal development programs and my own work.

Sure, I had my own fears. They appeared at moments when I decided to move ahead. And amongst the strongest of them all was the fear of criticism.

"When you are afraid, do things you are afraid
of and soon you will lose your fear of it"

Norman Vincent Peale

I feared criticism and judgment, especially when I decided to create an online program on living life holistically. I had invested enough to prepare the content, but I was frightened to death to register myself on video. That was beyond what I had ever conceived before. Even though I wanted to achieve that goal, my mind started to list excuses. The excuses were telling me that the job was difficult and I did not have enough expertise to do it. I felt that it would take me a long time to complete the task. I might look bad on camera. "Who are you, anyway to teach others how to live life intelligently?" I kept asking myself.

Eventually, I took an important decision and let my fears die. I decided to shoot videos regardless of my fears. It was painful, but I did it afraid. I learned and tattooed it in my mind that I can reach whatever goal I dream of and committed to achieve.

I was aiming to reach my mentors.
The reason most people fail is because they lack clarity, have indefinite goals, and don't know what their big action plan is. I learned that I couldn't grow higher than my level of awareness. *In order to rise above my darkness, I hired coaches who would help me grow personally and professionally.*

And to develop my coaching and mentoring business, I had to maintain my growth mindset and create a new money story[12].

---

[12]   We grew up with a money story that learned in childhood. We never questioned if it served us or not at the present moment.

I paid money beyond my financial edge for personal coaching, savoring deep inside me the value of what I learned. It helped me develop confidence. As a coach, you cannot dive others deeper than you dive yourself.

"The two most powerful warriors are patience and time"

Leo Tolstoy

Most people seek quick answers and choices but do not learn the lesson that is a universal law that applies everywhere—The Law of Gestation. Everything has a cycle of incubation. There are no exceptions. Watch nature and you will see it everywhere. In this context, I find the bamboo story to be quite fascinating. The bamboo plant takes five years to grow its roots, but in the sixth year, it shows up 90 feet tall. I learned not to give up, regardless of results. The bamboo story surfaces every time I get upset or impatient to see results.

I learned to be patient and focus on the process itself, not the destination.

I understood that the only way to move toward my goal was to take small simple steps in the right direction. I had realized that amazing things happen when you take that small yet significant step. Napoleon Hill talked a lot about persistence and wisely said, "That quality is to the character of man what carbon is to steel."

I developed a new habit: PERSISTENCE

If I was able to start and develop my coaching business in an environment that was not open and friendly at all for such services, YOU CAN DO IT, TOO. You can achieve whatever it is that you wish for and are committed to achieve.

Part 3: Five Neurowisdom[13] – Brain proven strategies to enhance your growth and development

It was February, and it seemed as if spring was knocking on the doors. Being deeply immersed in thoughts about writing my chapter in a book, I felt hollow. Nothing would come to my mind. In that stillness, I didn't notice that Rudina was greeting me from the zoom window. I smiled at her, but her watery eyes got my attention. I had no doubt that the session would be very emotional.

Rudina is a very intelligent and accomplished woman. But the arrival of her second daughter, after several months of a difficult pregnancy, had made it difficult for her to manage herself and her time. Her role in the company, which was established with her husband, was important, and at that moment she wasn't able to handle everything. It caused her a great deal of stress.

We had been working together in personal coaching for three months, but I had never seen her like that before.

"What wins would you like to share with me from the previous two weeks?" I asked, compassionately looking at her. She gave me that rhetorical look, and so I continued, "Nothing positive

---

[13] Neurowisdom: Neuro relates to the brain and nervous system, and Wisdom relates to the ability to use knowledge and experience to make good decisions and living life intelligently.

in these last two weeks?" I stopped in order to give her the time to contemplate. I knew she was an emotional wreck at that moment since we had spoken on the phone during the week.

"I need some peace of mind," she said in a soft voice. "I have been overwhelmed by my thoughts in the last two weeks to the point that I don't even want to think about it."

I let a longer pause than usual, on purpose, and we were just exchanging looks. The pause seemed like a key to the gate, and words started pouring out of her, like an explosion.

"Do you hear what you are saying?" I asked. I knew that my question went unheard since she was so lost in her thoughts and words.

"Can you listen to what you are saying?" I asked her again quietly but firmly so that Rudina would stop talking so negatively. Intuitively, I was trying to engage her in a mix of traditional coaching with neurocoaching techniques.

"Do these thoughts help you?" I asked her again, waiting for her to put herself together.

"Of course not," she said sobbing and continued, "But I don't know how to stop them."

"This is the right moment," I thought to myself and started talking to her slowly. I began to teach her some simple but very effective neurocoaching techniques, which I would also like to share with you. I brought this experience up because we all find ourselves in such situations and often get lost in an abyss of lack of awareness and choices.

There are many ways to thrive in life. Here, I will focus on some simple yet proven strategies that can help you release stress and free your mind from negative inner chatter. These strategies will increase your confidence, heal your cells instead of killing them, and help you reflect on your current situation. They will aid you to evaluate and take steps to accelerate your personal growth, developing new habits through persistence, and utilize brain faculties to self-motivate and take actions.

1) Free your brain by questioning what you know as 'true'

We see reality through our five senses and understand it through our learning experiences. As the years go by, we create our *Inner Map of Reality*. Some of the learning experiences might be true, while some might be not. It all depends on the environment we grow up in and our parents or caregivers. We experience emotional responses based on our inner filtering (learning patterns) or our Inner Map of Reality. Then we take actions and achieve results.

Schematically, it would look like this:

Only when we realize this process does it give us freedom of choice. We can change the results that we don't like by going back to its origination: our thoughts[14].

---

14   A thought for more than 17 seconds becomes a dominant thought and imprisons us the same way in which an avalanche is created by a mere snowflake.

Our thoughts and feelings reflect our Inner Map of Reality, or our learning patterns, which are created early on in our lives. That map makes our thoughts and feelings appear as real[15]. Sometimes our thoughts, which are mere fantasies, can drive us crazy if left unobserved[16].

So, when you feel bad, understand that it is the reflection of your thoughts in your body. If you want to feel better, question your thoughts and observe if your thoughts are rational or irrational. Our brain is very smart and tricks us through its games. Reframe your thoughts until you are comfortable with them.

I know it is not easy, but it is also the best way to change your feelings. When you learn to distinguish between your rational and irrational thoughts, you begin to see reality for what it really is.

2) Yawn and stretch for fast relaxation of the brain by lowering mental stress

Our lives today have become volatile, complex, and extremely uncertain. We get stressed very easily, and it takes a lot to release that stress, if at all. We are putting our brains in a state of ambiguity, the consequences of which can be catastrophic. We are tired most of the time, lack energy, are in conflict with ourselves, and are perpetually anxious.

---

[15] Woolley & E Ghossainy, *'Revisiting the fantasy-reality distinction: children as naïve skeptics'.*

[16] Rimes & Wingrove, *'Pilot study of Mindfulness-Based Cognitive Therapy for trainee clinical psychologists'.*

As various studies have shown, meditation is a proven solution for calming the brain and settling the body and its energy. And it's amazing if you are regular at it. But can we afford to meditate thirty minutes to one hour daily? It will be great but is not possible, owing to various personal and professional obligations. So, what can we do instead? I will share with you a secret—something that you can do in the long run and is extremely beneficial.

If I tell you that you need only sixty seconds to relax your brain every hour, which ultimately equals twenty to thirty minutes of daily meditation, will you believe me?

Through several studies and experiential groups, it is proven that yawning might be considered the fastest way to lower neural stress and increase one's attention span.
Athletes and artists naturally yawn before taking up a new challenge. Haven't you noticed that when you are stressed out, you yawn without being aware that through this mechanism your brain is releasing neural stress?

Different scientific studies have proven that yawning helps to cool the brain in part due to counter-current exchange with the deep inhalation of ambient air[17]. It enhances attention and mental efficiency by clearing away fogginess of sleep or tiredness and enables one to have a heightened level of awareness.

What are the benefits of yawning?
1. Lowers stress and relaxes the upper part of the body

---

[17] Massen et al., *A thermal window for yawning in humans: yawning as a brain cooling mechanism*.

2. Cools the brain by stimulating focus and heightened awareness
3. Improves cognitive functions and increases memory recall
4. Helps to be in the present moment and fine-tunes one's sense of time
5. Activates the circuits in the brain that relate to social awareness and empathy

Are you still skeptical about yawning[18]? Whether you are aware or not, you yawn all the time. What if you yawn mindfully to get all these benefits?

Yawning mindfully means that while you yawn, you observe any sensation in your body, any thought, feeling or memory. You simply observe them without judgment. It might not lead to results in the beginning, but don't get discouraged. Even if you have to fake yawning when you start, just do it. If you continue, the real yawning will come (if you find it difficult you can watch in youtube videos with animals yawning). Yawn eight to ten times when you are stressed, and over time you will notice great changes. Just give it a chance. It works if you work it up.

3) Slow down to speed up

How often do you find yourself in the 'express train' without any stopover station? And how often do you want to go faster because there is a lot more to do and achieve? How often do you feel anxious because you are not good enough or do not have the right skills? How often do you struggle with negative

---

[18] Gallup et al., '*Yawning, sleep, and symptom relief in patients with multiple sclerosis*'.
Gallup & Gallup, '*Yawning and thermoregulation*'.

feelings about yourself which you can't escape?

Don't worry. You are not alone!

For most of my career, I was in such a train myself and for years I could not escape it, owing to a misunderstanding about the notion of speed.

In Physics, we know that to reach the same distance in a lesser time, we have to increase the speed. But physical laws do not take into consideration human beings as a whole. We are not machines.

I was in a group coaching when I heard, for the first time, the concept of 'Slow down to Speed up.' It completely blew my mind.

It took me some time to understand the concept and then apply it. It was amazing.

When we slow down, we calm our brain and get clarity as to where we are and where we want to go. When we slow down, we allow our executive brain to switch off and relax. This helps to regulate our emotional state by calming down all our systems. We get aligned again with our core values—the values we are mostly unaware of when we are in the 'express train.' Thus, by slowing down, we are preparing ourselves to speed up again, but this time with more energy and focus.

Where are you at this moment? Start from wherever you are, and if you find yourself moving at an unstoppable pace, intentionally decide to slow down and prepare to speed up. You will not regret it.

4) Positive /Negative ratio

It seems that by default our brain is focused more on the negativity than the positive things. I remember one of my first sessions with Xhoi. It was the beginning of my career as a coach.

They had just reached the house of Ledina, driving when suddenly Xhoi began to sob.

"I can no longer take this situation. I feel drained. My mom needs a psychologist," she wept.

Ledina was taken aback by this abrupt outburst of Xhoi. She understood her friend needed to talk. She stopped for several seconds to listen to the muffled words of her and the sobbing that was becoming harder and faster and then she said, "Maybe you need to see a coach." She was sure about what she said. Xhoi remained silent for several seconds, and then added, "Maybe."

They set the meeting time with a coach[19], the next day, somewhere in the Bllok area[20], in one of the cafes where they knew they would not be disturbed.

I immediately noticed from the deep circles around her eyes that she had not a good night's rest. We talked for a long time. Xhoi seemed to relax and was talking freely. We decided to start working together the next day.

Xhoi had never thought she would need a coach, let alone to

---

[19] You can guess that I was the coach.

[20] It is the area in Tirana where ex communist leaders had their residences guarded by soldiers, and citizens were not allowed to pass by.

address problems she wasn't even aware of.

It was the third session, and Xhoi was talking incessantly. She had been through a tough day, and in particular, a dispute with her supervisor had really triggered her emotions.

"What's up?" I got straight to the point. Xhoi is a very courageous woman and appreciates when I am bold. Her voice was cracking and tears showed up almost immediately. She continued to look at the ground feeling insecure to share what was going in her mind.

"She is insane," Xhoi said with a strong voice. "She is making my work a mess."

"A mess?" I asked with a calm voice.

She nodded, wiping her tears away and repeating what she had said, "She drives me nuts."

She rolled her eyes and was looking at me skeptically when I asked her, "Is there anything positive about your boss?" I had not finished my sentence before she said, "No."

I could sense the anger in her tone as if she was asking me, "How dare you ask me to find something positive in her?"

We remained silent for several seconds, and Xhoi thought I delicately gave up on my question when she frowned, as if begging me to stop with the questions.

"Xhoi," I persisted with a warm, calm voice. "Do you think there is something positive about your boss?." Looking at her face and expecting a no again, I went on, "For example, does she have beautiful hair?"

Xhoi gave me that knowing look, "How do you know?" and then nodded. "Yes, her hair is beautiful."

That's all I needed and then asked her to write it down.

Xhoi was reluctant, but I managed to get her to write down a couple of positive things. To say that it was extremely difficult for her is to put it mildly.

We kept on talking, and Xhoi pointed out some twenty positive features about her boss. From the stems of her lips, I could feel a different energy radiate.

After writing down the twentieth positive feature, she said, "Okay, stop. No more now. My boss seems more than okay."

And then EUREKA, I thought! This was a good beginning.

I asked her to go home and make a list of fifty positive things, and Xhoi promised me to do that.

And then I asked her, "Do you want me to make the exercise a bit more difficult?"

"Let's see," was her energetic answer this time.

"Once you are done with the list, meet your boss, and give her this letter."

I had asked her to write neatly and in a certain style. "Tell your boss that this is what you think about her."

I am sure you are all curious to know what happened later.

The boss was extremely surprised to get the letter from Xhoi. She opened and read it. What Xhoi saw after that was a different face altogether.

We need to understand that negative things happen because of a monologue that goes on only in our heads. In that state of negativity, not only do we damage our relations with others, but also let it affect our mental health. This can interfere with memory storage and cognitive accuracy, and it can disrupt the ability to properly evaluate and respond to social situations[21]. It interferes with making rational decisions and makes us feel judgmental toward others[22].

Different studies show that there are several ways to deal with negativity, but the best way to deal with it is to observe it mindfully[23]. This means to observe yourself, your thoughts, and feelings without any judgment.

Another very effective way is to reframe it in a way that you feel most comfortable with and something you believe to be true. 'Reframing storming' is a powerful technique that can help you learn how to get rid of negativity.

---

[21] Words can change your brain: Andrew Newberg and Mark Waldman.

[22] Fredrickson & Losada, '*Positive Affect and the Complex Dynamics of Human Flourishing*'.

[23] Raffone et al., '*Toward a brain theory of meditation*'.

The following are simple but underestimated techniques. They work if you work upon them.

- Put your negative thoughts, feelings or statements in ratio with positive ones. Initially, start with one negative and one positive. Then extend to 3:1, three positives versus one negative. The best would be a 5:1 ratio. Be intentional and make efforts to apply them daily, either in your family or at work and your social life. You will see that things will change for the better and people will love to stay around you.
- Learn to be grateful.
- Express comments of appreciation and compliments frequently, and ensure you also mean them.
- Stop complaining. Go one week without it. Pair with your partner, friend, or someone in the family.

Personal development is about your experience in life. Knowledge is important, but it is worthy only when you take actions.

5) Increase productivity by shifting from focused attention to relaxation and back

In order to have a healthy and highly function brain, we need to maintain a balance between focusing our attention on important goals and regular 'daydreaming' moments. Our body needs a break of at least one minute every hour.

This might be considered easy but most people fail to do so. Studies show that people fall under these two categories:

- Spending a lot of time daydreaming, being playful and having fun, relaxing or engaged in highly creative or imaginative activities. For this category, it is very difficult to remain focused.

- Being in a highly focused state, some people are very capable to accomplish their daily tasks and goals but risk an emotional burnout creating problems in their professional and personal life.

Neuroscience different studies are showing that in order to create the 'golden point' of balance, the easiest and fastest solution is to train your brain to relax but in a mindful way[24]. What do you need to do?

- You can mindfully be focused on your breathing, without thinking or judging. This will help raise your focus levels.
- You can mindfully observe your thoughts and feelings that are mostly outside your state of awareness. In other words, it can be called the default mode network or autopilot mode.

You can either relax and observe your thoughts or focus on the desired goal, the choice is yours.

By doing so, you are stimulating a very important area and circuits of the brain recently named as Salience network. This is the newest revolutionary part of the brain. Applying mindfulness is the best-recognized training strategy to stimulate the salience area that creates that balance between focusing on a task and relaxation, leading to intuitive problem-solving skills.

Neuro tip: I would recommend practicing going back and forth between being highly focused, deeply relaxed, and mindfully

---

[24] Tang et al., *'The Neuroscience of mindful meditation'*.

observant. You can use your Android to set a timer every 30 minutes or an hour? Why? Because most of the time, we lose awareness and need a reminder until we create a new habit. In order to increase its efficiency as an exercise, add yawning and slow stretching, allowing your brain to reset in a fresh mode. When you stay focused for more than an hour, daydream for one to five minutes or do something that you like very much. To your surprise, you will find out that at the end of the day, your productivity has doubled or tripled, and your stress levels have drastically dropped down.

I was invited to speak and share my story in front of 150 women on March 8th.

With my first words claiming that, "I can see clearly now," I brought silence in the room. Having achieved the level of attention that I wanted, I continued.

"After several years of ups and downs in my life, I was forced to open my eyes and mind and see the reality for what it was. I was struggling and blaming everything outside me for what was happening. I learned that either you take the lesson and improve it or accept the loss with grace and ease. I had stored in a lot of resentment, anger, and hatred that only brought imbalance to my body energy and were the reasons for my 'burning out'."

I learned the hard way that there are several dimensions to life,[25] and it is our duty and responsibility to take care of them and bring them into harmony. I learned to take care of my physical

---

[25] I have now developed a program in Albanian about how to live life holistically. Everything that has happened to me in the past was for a reason: for me to come up and share my experience with others and help them the same way as I helped myself.

body, expand my mental capabilities, recognize and manage well my emotions through Emotional Intelligence development, and tune deep into my spirituality.

I learned that if I have to move ahead and prosper, I must train my brain and develop a growth mindset. There is no other way.

"You cannot solve the problem with the same level of awareness you created it"

Albert Einstein

I did things I was afraid of. I was terrified. But, I was mentored and coached by the best professionals.

I learned that we have choices in life and how we decide and what we do, is important. I chose to thrive in life, live it holistically, and feel in peace and harmony. Stay in your path of faith, believe that you are loved, and everything will conspire for your growth.

If I did it, you CAN DO IT, TOO!

Anila Kaba - Bashllari

Anila Kaba - Bashllari is a certified Neurocoach, trainer, and mentor who helps entrepreneurs, managers, executives and individuals achieve more in less time. She aids them to reach high efficiency and create time for themselves, their families and social life.

Anila holds an MBA in Entrepreneurship. Her 30+ years of experience and continuous education in personal development brings a unique holistic approach for her clients to develop a growth mindset in their personal and professional life. She is educating and influencing thousands of people find their passion and direction for a purposeful and meaningful life.

She advocates for a high quality of life, which is worth living and remembering. Her passion to motivate, inspire, and encourage others to explore their potential and unleash their inner power toward a better life has positioned her as an experienced coach, mentor, and trainer, both locally as well as internationally.

She is a licensed Think & Grow Rich trainer and brings a holistic approach while working with her clients.

References

Fredrickson BL, Losada MF, *'Positive Affect and the Complex Dynamics of Human Flourishing'*, Am Psychol. 2005 Oct, Epub.

Gallup AC, Gallup GG Jr. , *'Yawning and thermoregulation'*, Physiol Behav. 2008 Sep 3, Epub.

Gallup AC, Gallup GG Jr, Feo C (2014), *'Yawning, sleep, and symptom relief in patients with multiple sclerosis'*, Sleep Med. 2010 Mar, Epub.

Massen JJ, Dusch K, Eldakar OT, Gallup AC, *'A thermal window for yawning in humans: yawning as a brain cooling mechanism'.* , Physiol Behav. (2014), Epub.

Raffone,Marzetti, Del Gratta, Perruci, Romani and Pizzella (2019), *'Toward a brain theory of meditation'*, Prog. Brain Res. 2019, Epub.

Rimes KA, Wingrove J. *'Pilot study of Mindfulness-Based Cognitive Therapy for trainee clinical psychologists'*. Behav. Cogn. Psychother. (2011), Epub.

Tang YY, Holzel BK, Posner MI (2015), *'The Neuroscience of mindful meditation'*, Nat. Rev. Neurosci. 2015 Apr, Epub.

Woolley JD, E Ghossainy M. (2013), *'Revisiting the fantasy-reality distinction: children as naïve skeptics'*, Child Dev. 2013 Sept-Oct, Epub.

Anila loves energy and is a Qigong, Reiki, and Reconnection practitioner. She lives what she teaches. Her motto in life is Learn, Live, Lead.

Contact Information

Website: https://www.anilabashllari.com
Email: anila@anilabashllari.com
FB: https://www.facebook.com/anila.bashllari
Linkedin: https://www.linkedin.com/in/anila-bashllari-294a4b7/
Instagram: https://www.instagram.com/anilabashllar

Uncomfortably Numb

Brielle Franklin

As I run to catch the train, I'm acutely aware of three things: the time (I'm definitely going to be late again), the wind (it feels exceptionally nice against my skin), and my abs (I'm pretty sure I pulled a muscle laughing last night).

To most people, this list wouldn't be particularly noteworthy; however, to me, it's a pretty big deal. The ability to laugh openly, to appreciate the weather, to get so caught up in my new website copy that I totally lose track of time: these are the things I live for these days, they are the moments that fill up the pages of the gratitude journal that sits on the nightstand next to my bed. A few years ago, the only things on that nightstand were a lamp and a bottle of over-the-counter sleeping pills to counteract the mega-dose of prescription stimulants coursing through my veins. While I still suffer from the occasional bout of insomnia, on the whole, my life looks completely different than it did back then.

I finally get on the subway (just in time) and allow my brain to decompress (also a relatively recent development). It was a great day, but I'm ready to get home and see Kevin. I know he'll be waiting anxiously by the door, as he does every day, ready for my arrival and his next meal. I smile, thinking about how much that dog loves his dinner and how much joy he brings to my life.

As the train starts moving, so too does my mind.

I lose myself in a memory.

It had been 72 hours since I last heard the sound of my voice. I briefly pondered saying something, maybe "testing 1-2-3," just to see if my vocal cords still worked but thought better of it. It had been 24 [or was it 48?] hours since I last brushed my teeth, and keeping my mouth closed seemed a good way to avoid the issue of my less than stellar dental hygiene. At this point, I had all but mastered the art of avoidance.

I didn't get out of bed, so I avoided showering or changing my clothes. I didn't check my phone, so I avoided the 62 unread texts and 20-odd missed calls that awaited my response. I didn't tell my best friends I was bailing on the trip we'd been planning for six months, so I avoided their disappointment.

Avoidance is pretty much your default state when you can't feel anything at all—an inevitable consequence of being uncomfortably numb.

It wasn't that I wanted to die, because I didn't. I just didn't particularly care to live. I knew from experience that in a few days, maybe a week at most, I'd drag myself out of my self-imposed exile, go through the motions of becoming a presentable human being, and let my friends and colleagues know that the worst of my "flu" was over (and "of course I checked with the doctor, he assured me I'm no longer 'contagious'").

But this was only day three.

I was deep in the throes of Adderall withdrawal. It wasn't the first time, and unfortunately, it wouldn't be the last.

My relationship with this little blue pill started during my sophomore year in college. Against my doctor's and advisors' well-intentioned protests, I was back on campus after a severe bout of mono and was struggling to catch up on all the work I missed while I was bedridden. Could I have taken a leave of absence? Requested an extension? Maybe settled for something less than an A?

In retrospect, I absolutely could (and should) have. However, being the Ivy League perfectionist I was, the thought of sitting back and 'relaxing' (recovering seemed far too strong a word) while my peers finished the semester was unconscionable. I had papers to write, exams to take, parties to attend, a reputation to uphold, so here I was—falling asleep in class, living on Au Bon Pain chicken noodle soup, and cursing myself for being so lazy.

After one particularly long and unproductive day at the library, I went to a friend's apartment to study for an upcoming final. His roommate, who would go on to become an orthopedic surgeon at Stanford Med, had just picked up his 'study buddies' and had a few to spare. I knew plenty of kids on campus took Adderall to pull all-nighters and cram for exams, and if this brilliant pre-med was offering (I mean he was basically a doctor, right?), who was I to decline?

Even as I write this, I want to yell at the screen, as if I'm watching a horror movie and know the killer is around the corner—an exercise in futility but a reflex nonetheless. However, there was no older, wiser version of myself to step in and prevent the inevitable. I was introduced to the love of my life that night—in the form of a little blue pill—and we were invincible together.

Or so I thought.

Looking back, it's not surprising that Adderall and I were a match made in heaven. It provided one of many masks that I used to hide my crippling fear of being 'ordinary,' or worse, boring. Adderall hindered my anxiety but fueled my work ethic—the two things I needed to achieve my lifelong goal of success.

The first recollection I have of my unhealthy relationship with success was when I was five years old. My paternal grandfather had just passed away after a long battle with cancer, and to say I was devastated by this is an understatement. There are conflicting opinions in the scientific community about the age at which a child fully grasps the concept and finality of death, and like most things in life, I was precocious in that regard. I knew at that moment that my life was irrevocably changed, and I cried with the unabashed sense of grief reserved for a child experiencing his or her first true loss.

While my reaction may or may not have been atypical for a five-year-old, what stands out from this particular memory is not my response to grief but my response to missing school the next day. In my Kindergarten class, every student had a chance to be the weatherman (or weatherwoman), a highly esteemed job that involved finding a sticker that reflected the weather of that particular day (a sun, a cloud, a raindrop, or a snowflake) and placing it on the day's date on our giant homeroom calendar. Understandably, some students fumbled when finding the right date or choosing the correct decal; however, I knew when my time came, I was going to be the best weather girl our class had ever seen. It just so happened that my big day fell on the day of my grandfather's funeral. If I felt my life had ended with the passing of my grandfather, I knew for sure it was over when I failed to report to duty.

Due to the extenuating circumstances of my absence, my beloved Kindergarten teacher allowed me to be the weather girl the following day, and my world returned to order. Though I still missed my grandfather terribly, I understood that nothing I said or did could bring him back. What I could do was continue practicing my weather girl responsibilities so that when it was my turn again the following month, nothing would stand in the way of my succeeding.

Some well-intentioned psychologists would likely say that at the ripe age of five years, I found a way to mask emotional pain by fixating on achievements that I knew were in my control. And who knows, perhaps they'd be right. What I do know for certain is that as I got older, my need for control and external validation deepened—with or without the catalysts of loss or emotional pain.

To the best of my recollection, the majority of my childhood was nothing short of idyllic. My mom took time off from her blossoming career as an Interior Designer to stay home with me, my sister, and in time my little brother. My dad coached all of our little league teams, and despite my complete lack of hand-eye coordination, he never discouraged me from playing team sports. I was naturally a great student, and despite being a bit obsessive about my homework, I was never bullied for being a 'nerd.' There were sleepovers, carpools, dance recitals, and first crushes. My best friends from growing up in my tiny suburban hometown are still my best friends to this day. Sure, there were moments of 'trouble in paradise,' but nothing that explained why I never quite felt I was 'good enough.'

This feeling persisted throughout high school; although from the outside, you certainly wouldn't know it. I got in just enough trouble to be considered a 'normal teenager' but never let my grades suffer as a result. I was certainly no angel, but it was hard to punish a 16-year old who went out drinking with friends only to sneak upstairs to finish her calculus homework when her friends fell asleep. Freshman year turned into sophomore year. Junior year turned into senior year. Senior year turned into a frenzy of AP classes and SAT courses—all in preparation for college applications, eventually paving the way for college acceptances, and in my case, early admission to the University of my choice. Finally, I was on my way to the Ivy Leagues. Surely I would find this elusive feeling I had spent my life searching for—the feeling that I was enough.

College brought with it a new set of challenges—the top of which was being the proverbial small fish in a big [incredibly well-educated] pond. I was away from home for the first time and despite being in the school of my dreams, felt utterly lost, unprepared, and alone.

While I made friends easily that first year, I quickly realized that new friendships are born according to the person you are today, not the person you've spent the past 18 years becoming. Years of history were replaced by first impressions. Unbreakable bonds were replaced with tentative, hopeful connections.

As my sense of self got smaller, everything around me became that much larger. Small classrooms were replaced with massive lecture halls. Tiny basements were replaced with giant frat houses. My house of five was replaced with a dorm of thousands.

I was desperate to fit in, yet longed to stand out; somehow, neither seemed possible.

Looking back, I know I wasn't the only one who had a difficult time adjusting to freshman year of college. It just felt that way at the time. I kept my pain and confusion to myself and set out to control the only thing I felt *was* in my control—my projection to the outside world.

After a rocky start, I eventually hit my stride. I moved into a house off-campus with seven amazing girls and solidified my reputation as a carefree girl who worked hard but partied harder.

Everything was going well.
Until, of course, it wasn't.

A recent national study of 10,000 students found that approximately 7% had abused 'study drugs,' although the percentage varied at different colleges[26]. Another study of students at Bates College, a small liberal arts college in Maine, found that one in every three students had abused Adderall at some point[27]. Whether the typical abuse rate is 7% or 33%, or something in between, the extent of the problem is alarming.

The day I became part of the statistic, the first time I ever took Adderall, I was euphoric. I was more confident, more engaging. My work was easier. Formerly dry textbooks were now fascinating. I was laser-focused and in a state of peerless ecstasy. Fresh off the heels of a two-month-long battle with mono, I was suddenly catching up on classes, spending 14-hour stretches in the library, and then meeting up with friends at the bar on campus or the frat house next door.

I didn't notice at the time that my personality was slowly changing. My best friends from freshman and the majority of my sophomore year knew something was up, but I was in my own world of blissful intensity and oblivion.

---

[26] McCabe, Knight et al. *"Non-medical use of prescription stimulants among US college students: prevalence and correlates from a national survey."*, 99,96-106.

[27] Graff Low, Gendaszek, *"Illicit use of psychostimulants among college students: a preliminary study."*, 7(3),283-287.

Adderall quickly found its place in my daily routine, and there was no shortage of places to get it. Plenty of friends had prescriptions and there were a handful of doctors who were more than willing to prescribe it. There was even a section of the library where I knew I could go and be with 'like-minded' individuals who were always willing to spare a pill or two with a friend in need.

Willpower was no longer a struggle. I could study all day and then spend two hours at the gym. I could stay out later without guilt; after all, I'd be back in the library by eight in the morning. The question of my identity no longer haunted me because I could be anything and everything at once. Adderall expanded time.

By the time junior year rolled around, I had my very own Adderall prescription that supplemented the pills I bought from friends and casual acquaintances. By this time, I started to notice that when I didn't take my precious blue pills (which by now were not exclusively blue), I'd fall into a slump and just want to sleep, eat, and be left alone. I thought nothing of it—after all, I was working hard, partying hard, sleeping little, and surviving on nothing but rice with butter (which was pretty much the only food I could stomach at that point). And I knew that once I refilled, I'd be fine and ready to go again.

By senior year I could be found in one of two states: high on 100 mg + of Adderall at the library or drinking at a bar or frat house. Still, I didn't believe I had a problem. In the eyes of pretty much anyone who *didn't* know me well, I was thriving.

At this point, my younger sister had joined me at Penn and

sensed something was amiss. As a freshman in the incredibly demanding Engineering school, she had plenty of her own work and a budding social life to worry about, but by the end of the year, she had become a stand-in babysitter. The night before my last final, I was on my fourth straight day at the library with nothing but amphetamines and Red Bull in my system. Terrified by my appearance and my overall demeanor, my sister dragged me to a restaurant nearby and walked me to my house off-campus, where I proceeded to open up my textbooks and finish cramming for my last exam.

I'm not sure how much time passed, but eventually I was woken up by an alarm clock that had apparently been going off for the better part of two hours. I begrudgingly checked the time, thinking I could get in a few extra hours of studying before my exam, and the clock read 11 am. At first, I didn't know what day it was… maybe I still had a full 24 hours and could embrace the slumber that was so desperately calling my name. However, I knew in my gut something was wrong. A series of missed calls alerted me to the fact that I had slept through my last final of college.

In a cold sweat, I called my professor—who thankfully had been one of my professors for the past three years—and told him I was sick. He graciously allowed me to take my last final the following week, two days before my graduation, and I swore to myself that after I secured a job, I would never take Adderall again.

I spent the following week withdrawing from Adderall cold turkey, securing a roommate, and more determined than ever to prove myself in the 'real world.'

Though I graduated college with an impressive GPA, a handful of awards, and a sufficient number of extracurricular leadership positions (which I knew would bolster my resume for any potential employer), I still had no sense of direction about what I wanted to do with my life. Perhaps if I had taken the time to truly do some soul searching, which is virtually impossible when you're high on Adderall, I would have had a more sustainable plan of action. To be totally honest, I got lucky when I landed my job as an Executive Recruiter at a boutique executive search firm—not only because I enjoyed the job itself but also because I loved the team who worked there. I wasn't worldly enough to spout phrases such as corporate culture and job fulfillment, but in retrospect, that is exactly what I got.

I embraced the goals that measured my performance and the pressure of having a quota, as they filled the void of grades as markers of success. What's more, I was actually good at recruiting. In spite of it being a sales job, the environment wasn't nearly as cutthroat as I was accustomed to in college. If I worked hard enough, I could stand out and be praised for my achievements.

The work was new enough for me to feel challenged but straightforward enough to feel manageable, and the adrenaline and excitement that accompanied my new job were stimulants strong enough to replace Adderall.

For a while.

It wasn't until a year and a half into my new adult life that things started to slide. Until then, I had been able to burn the candle at both ends and maintain my reputation as a party girl who could chase the sun four nights a week, yet still work 14-hour days and excel in a fast-paced, highly demanding job.

I was so absorbed in my exhilarating NYC existence that I had turned a blind eye to the tragedies looming at home. My parents' divorce, which had begun the day after my college graduation, was getting more brutal by the day. My grandfather, who was and continues to be my greatest role model, was losing his battle with Alzheimer's faster than we ever anticipated. To top it all off, my first serious relationship as an adult was coming to an end.

Try as I might to ignore these external stressors, I was blindsided by their devastating reality and in turn, was struggling to stay afloat. While alcohol was a sufficient analgesic at night, the relief it provided was temporary and often impacted my performance at work the next day. The stress of my job, which I normally found palliative in and of itself, was quickly becoming overwhelming and my inability to concentrate only added fuel to the fire.

Figuring it would just be a crutch to help me through these 'turbulent times,' I justified refilling my Adderall prescription and 'just taking it until things get easier.' After all, I had already come off the drug once. I could easily do it again.

Or so I presumed.

My addiction picked up right where I left it: with a vengeance. While I was back to being a top performer at work and juggling a very active social life, I was entirely dependent on my prescription to get through the most basic tasks. I relied on it to check my emails, to make phone calls, and to sit through meetings. I relied on it to get to warehouse parties in Brooklyn, to get to happy hours, and to have dinner with friends. I even relied on it to write my grandfather's eulogy, which I gave after popping a handful of little blue pills. To this day, that moment is one of my biggest regrets.

Three years into my job, I was crumbling once again—I wasn't sleeping, and I wasn't eating. As opposed to college, where this behavior was acceptable, if not encouraged, in the 'real world,' these all-nighters were an anomaly. I was on my own, and I knew that the only way I could recover was by kicking this 'habit' for good.

My employer, to my undying gratitude, was more than understanding when I requested a month off from work. They had been watching me wither before their eyes, and being just as much of a family as they were colleagues, they were more than willing to give me the space and the support I needed to recuperate. After tying up some loose ends (finishing the last of my Adderall prescription), I took a full month off work and went off the drug, cold turkey. To this day, the experience still haunts me.

When I wasn't crying or sleeping, I was staring blankly at the wall, willing time to pass. I stopped speaking, I stopped bathing, I stopped caring about anything and everything. When the worst was over and I had the energy to at least get out of bed, the world around me felt duller, the colors dimmer.

After four weeks, I came back to work; however, I was a shell of the person I once was. The work no longer interested me; the money no longer motivated me. No matter how many hours I worked or deals I closed, I still felt like I was failing. A few months after my return, I decided the job must be the issue. Without much notice or consideration, I left the company and the family I had grown to love and accepted an offer from a prestigious media consulting firm. Perhaps I could find this supposed work-life balance I had heard about.

Perhaps I could find myself.

It never occurred to me that the job wasn't actually the problem.

Although I had sworn to myself that I was done with Adderall for good, my pill-free period didn't last long.

Due to a clerical error, I started my new job three months later than I was supposed to, and with each day that passed, I fell deeper and deeper into a depression. By the time I finally started working again, I was vacant.

Around this time, a friend of mine—who had been diagnosed with ADHD as a child and took her medication as prescribed—was staying at my apartment and seeing her bounce from meetings to spin classes to her second job and the occasional happy hour, I was nearly green with envy. Eventually, I asked if I could 'borrow' a Vyvanse or two for a 'major project' I had to get done and she readily acquiesced. "Her doctor prescribed her too many anyway," and she "didn't like taking it on weekends."

"Is she out of her mind," I thought to myself. "You have a prescription! You could double your dose and get even MORE done!"

One pill and I was back to where I started.

Within a week I had my own prescription refilled, and within two I was searching for a reason to use it.

I took the opportunity to join a growing startup as a form of redemption. The hours were long, the work was tough, and the opportunity gave me a chance to reinvent myself. I could drink the proverbial Kool-Aid, devote myself to a 'cause,' and truly feel like I was a part of something again. In retrospect, it also gave me a reason to hold on to my Adderall prescription, which at that point was all the convincing I needed.

I threw myself into the job as if my life depended on it because in a way, it did. I worked around the clock, sacrificed weekends, added Vyvanse to my cocktail of stimulants, and never saw a reason to slow down. I ignored the sleep deprivation, I ignored the pain in my stomach that never seemed to go away no matter how many Tums I took, and ignored my friends' pleas to 'take a break' and spend time with them. As if the job wasn't enough, I also threw myself into the second serious relationship of my adult life, so whatever work wasn't able to cover by way of distraction, my new boyfriend did.

I was burning the candle on both ends and wore my workload like a badge of honor. I knew that physically I might be struggling a bit, but the sacrifice was worth it.

Or so I thought.

Six months in, everything came to a head. Without warning and much to my dismay, I lost my job. Consequently, I lost my entire identity.

In the grand scheme of things, spending two months unemployed is a blip on the radar; however, for someone who doesn't know how to spend time alone, it can feel like an eternity. The Monday after my termination, I had a doctor's appointment at a new practice, which meant I had to fill out intake forms—a somewhat dull but necessary task that I had done countless times in the past without incident. When I reached the part about my 'Current Occupation,' my heart skipped a beat and bile rose up my throat. Feeling a wave of panic come over me, I headed back to the receptionist to let her know I wasn't feeling well and would need to reschedule my appointment.

The irony of my cancelling a doctor's appointment because I 'wasn't feeling well' is not lost on me.

Shortly after that incident, my then-boyfriend and I decided to take a trip to Mexico, which in retrospect was his way of trying to pull me out of the funk I had rapidly been succumbing to. We stayed at one of those all-inclusive resorts, where the service more than compensates for the subpar foor and the watered-down drinks.

After a tour of the place, our animated guide walked us to our room and indulged in some well-meaning small talk. After we covered the usual topics, he asked us what we did for work. Much to his dismay, I responded by bursting into tears. I spent the rest of the evening with the hotel-issued notebook and pen determined to find a more suitable answer to that dreaded question, should it come up again.

While I cycled through countless possible iterations of my next 'identity' during those two painstaking months (which included going back to school for my Ph.D., selling skincare products for Rodan + Fields, and learning the telecommunications business so I could beg my father for a job), I never once considered coming off my beloved Adderall. To my chemically-altered mind, this drug represented the only constant in my life. I had just lost my job and felt fundamentally useless. I had chosen work and Adderall over my friends and family and was too ashamed to ask for their forgiveness, so I felt alone and more than a little pathetic. I had no income coming in to pay off the mountain of credit card debt I had accumulated from stimulant-fuelled shopping sprees, let alone pay the rent; so I was surely going to lose my apartment. My sense of self-worth was at an all-time low, and I was certain my equally ambitious boyfriend would soon leave me. No, I had lost—or in most cases, anticipated losing—far too much already. Adderall would stay.

After two months, with nowhere left to go, I returned to the

only other constant I had come to rely on in my adult life: my first job. To my eternal gratitude, they welcomed me back with open arms and I was determined to prove—if not to them, then to myself—that I deserved it. I thrived at this company at the ripe age of 22, so surely I could excel at 27. It never occurred to me that my seven-year struggle with stimulant abuse and my non-existent sense of purpose would stand in my way.

More often than not, I felt like I had paused a movie I was completely absorbed in, only to hit play and realize I had lost interest. No matter how many articles on motivation I read or how many milligrams I increased my Adderall dose, I couldn't find the work ethic I had prided myself on for my entire academic and professional career. I couldn't sleep, yet I constantly felt exhausted. I woke up feeling sick every morning but never spiked a fever. My relationship with my boyfriend was suffering, my friendships were dwindling, and my performance at work was rapidly declining. Both my personal and professional lives were coming apart at the seams, and I had neither the willpower nor energy to save it. I was failing on all fronts.

In a last-ditch effort to salvage my mental and physical health, I began researching alternative remedies for my 'symptoms.' I was sick and tired of being sick and tired and had finally, albeit reluctantly, accepted the fact that no amount of affection (romantic or otherwise) or achievement could help me. With the enthusiasm of a junkie searching for her next fix, I devoured articles on therapies for Adrenal Fatigue and the wonders of Eastern Medicine. I tried acupuncture, visited infrared saunas, drank bone broth, and for the first time in nearly ten years, began to feel a niggling sense of lightness—a feeling I now recognize as hope. Little did I know that my succession of professional and personal failures was about to lead me on a journey of self-discovery, toward that elusive, authentic sense of purpose that I had sought for so long.

After exhausting all articles and books on alternative healing that I could find, I decided to take my education a step further and enroll in a year-long program to become a certified holistic health coach. At the time, I simply wanted to get my hands on as much information as possible and admittedly feed my damaged ego with another accomplishment to add to my CV. What I got in return was so much more.

Six months into my training program, I received my partial license to start coaching. Although I never intended to use my education for anything other than my own recovery, I knew that one of my graduation requirements was to actually coach, so I timidly called in some favors and got to work. By this time, my diet was transformed. I was sleeping better, and my performance at work was improving. However, it wasn't until I started coaching that I found the strength to address the biggest problem impacting my mental and physical health: my Adderall addiction.

Addiction is a terrifying word that often evokes images of homelessness, hopelessness, and desperation. While I didn't 'look like an addict' and hated the stigma attached to the word, I knew that I had long abandoned the ability to get off this drug on my own. According to Dr. Raju Hajela, former president of the Canadian Society of Addiction Medicine and chairman of the American Society of Addiction Medicine (ASAM), "simply put, addiction is not a choice. Addictive behaviors are a manifestation of the disease, not a cause[28]." Though the decision to take Adderall in the first place was undeniably my own, I never could have predicted the implications the drug would have on my life in years to follow. Highlighting the potential risks associated with Adderall, the government classified prescription stimulants as a Schedule II controlled substance, a designation it shares with drugs such as cocaine, crystal meth, oxycodone, and bath salts. While not everyone who takes the drug will become addicted, there are definite risk factors that increase the likelihood of abuse. Ease of access (check), perfectionist behavior (check), and high academic rank (check)[29] are just three of them.

There were a handful of times I made a rash, theatrical attempt to come off Adderall—which included flushing most of my pills down the toilet, stashing the rest as an 'emergency fund,' and then calling any source I had (legal or otherwise) in a panic to refill my supply. However, the times I 'seriously' committed to giving up the drug were well-intentioned but poorly executed. For starters, I didn't put a support system in place (a psychiatrist, a therapist, and a coach who specializes in addiction) that could not only safely wean me off the drug but also hold me accountable for staying off the drug. More importantly, I never had a 'good reason' for getting off Adderall in the first place. It was always a decision made in haste, and in fear, based on how I felt at the time and who I thought I was disappointing. I never thought about what I truly wanted for myself and my future. Coaching opened my eyes to a life I wanted to feel, and

---

[28] Nordqvist, *"Addiction Has A New Definition - It Is A Disease, Not Just Bad Choices Or Behaviors"*. https://www.medicalnewstoday.com/articles/232841.php.

[29] Baldisseri, *"Impaired healthcare professional"*, 35 (2), S106-116.

I knew with Adderall in the picture, that dream would never become a reality.

The decision to come off Adderall for the last time was one of the most terrifying decisions I have ever made. This might sound a bit dramatic, but I was giving up a huge part of my identity: I had no idea who I was beneath the stimulant-fuelled haze. All I knew was that this drug was hell to withdraw from. I couldn't afford to physically miss an entire month of work—not to mention the subsequent six months that I knew from experience would render me mentally absent. So, going cold turkey was off the table. This time I was in for a slow and painstaking taper.

Fortunately, by this point, I was working with one of the most amazing holistic psychiatrists in the country—who had somehow seen beyond my chemical shield of armor and gotten to know me better than I knew myself—and an incredible holistic health coach, who at one point had struggled with Adderall herself. Together, they crafted a plan for me to slowly taper off the drug, which included a nutrient-packed diet (a concept I was now intimately familiar with) and an abundance of mental and emotional support—two crucial components to successfully withdraw from Adderall that I sorely lacked in my previous attempts.

Despite my fantastic support system and burning desire to free myself from Adderall's reins, the process was far from easy. The only thing worse than the physical withdrawal was the anticipatory anxiety that plagued me every time I was about to lower my dose, which left me doubting my ability to do so at all. When I finally reached the lowest dose, the penultimate step before saying goodbye to Adderall for good, I was more distraught than I was triumphant. The final push came in the form of the most alternative therapy I've tried to date—two weeks of intravenous NAD therapy.

NAD, or nicotinamide adenine dinucleotide, Therapy is a relatively new addition to the realm of addiction recovery. To summarize, NAD is a naturally occurring co-enzyme that helps cells in our bodies produce energy through the conversion of food. As a person abuses drugs or alcohol, in my case Adderall, his/her natural amount of NAD is depleted, which severely impacts brain functionality and in turn, the production of the neurotransmitters critical for mood regulation[30]. The science behind NAD therapy is complex and has not been assessed by the FDA, so its application is not widely known. For me personally, NAD therapy was an instrumental part of my recovery; however, it was not a miracle cure. I was finally off of Adderall, but in many ways, the work was just beginning.

The months that followed my last dose of Adderall were ripe with new experiences, unfortunately not all of them were positive. In many ways, I was seeing my life and the consequences of my actions for the first time, which often was equal parts humbling and heartbreaking. I had tested the boundaries of my family and my friends who showed me that their love had no bounds, despite the inevitable pain I caused them. I had relied on stimulants

---

[30] "*NAD Therapy*" AddictionCenter. https://www.addictioncenter.com/ treatment/nad-therapy/.

to succeed academically and professionally, which made it impossible for me to perform at the level I was accustomed to on Adderall but enabled me to feel genuine pride about the success I eventually saw without it. I learned how to feel joy and excitement but also sorrow and disappointment. There was a whole world of conflicting emotions out there waiting to be felt, and whether I wanted to or not, I felt every one of them.

One of the most surprising pairs of reciprocal emotions that I encountered in my life after Adderall was that of passion and pain. On the surface, passion is inspiring; it's uplifting, and it's the motivation needed for growth and positive change. However, at its root specifically, its Latin root, is 'passio,' or suffering. Both literally and figuratively, you cannot have one without the other.

Ironically, I spent my life searching for this nebulous idea of passion and purpose but anesthetized myself from ever truly feeling it. Without Adderall in my life, I was able to feel passion for the first time and it was more than worth the pain and suffering it took to get there.

Building a coaching business has undeniably been one of the most exciting and rewarding experiences I've had to date; however, it has not been without its own unique set of challenges. Any entrepreneur worth her salt will have a story about the failures and rejection she faced while starting her business. What separates the ones who succeed from the ones who don't is that they see failure as an opportunity for growth. As someone who is intimately familiar with failure, I'd like to think I fall into the first category.

I'd be lying if I said there were days I didn't miss my little blue pills, or more specifically, their ability to turn me into a superwoman. However, the thought of losing my ability to feel passion, even at the expense of pain, is enough to nip those thoughts in the bud. If I've learned anything from my struggle with Adderall, it is that a life worth living demands to be felt. And after spending nearly a decade of my life uncomfortably numb, I intend to feel every second of it.

Addendum: Resources for Adderall Addiction

If you or someone you love is struggling with Adderall addiction, it is never too late (or too early) to get help.

- For 24/7 access to trained specialists and addiction resources, visit the <u>Addiction Center Website</u> or call the Substance Abuse and Mental Health Services Administration (<u>SAHMSA</u>) National Helpline: 1-800-662-HELP (4357)
- For more information on NAD Therapy, visit <u>https://www.addictioncenter.com/treatment/nad-therapy/</u>.
- For more on my personal tips, visit: <u>www.thewellthstudio.com/blog</u>.

Brielle Franklin

Brielle Franklin is an Author, Executive Recruiter, and 'Holistic Career Coach' who has spent the majority of her career working with senior executives in the Media, Emerging Tech, and Health & Wellness industries around the world. She graduated from the University of Pennsylvania with top honors. After spending seven years recruiting at a boutique search firm, she went onto become a Certified Holistic Health Coach and Executive Career Coach. Brielle founded The WELLth Studio with the mission of helping individuals find meaningful, purpose-driven careers.

When she's not juggling her two full-time jobs, Brielle can be found reading British crime thrillers, searching for flight deals, drinking the occasional extra-extra dirty vodka martini, or hanging with her Mini-Newdle, Kevin.

She offers both online and in-person private, group, and corporate coaching and is currently based in NYC.

Contact Information

Website: www.thewellthstudio.com
Facebook: https://www.facebook.com/brielle.franklin.5
Linkedin: https://www.linkedin.com/in/briellefranklin/

PHOENIX RISING FROM THE ASHES

CLARE FORD

Are you tired of living a life that doesn't really fit? Like a jacket that is too small? Or perhaps you feel that you are not being heard – that your message and voice fades in the wind? Or that your contribution counts for nothing?

This is a story about <u>Rising up.</u>

Rising from the ashes is the story of a woman who felt like she had lost everything and that life was not worth living. This is the honest story of how she overcame depression, anxiety, and grief in order to make difficult decisions with far-reaching consequences.

The important thing to understand is that this woman is just like you: an ordinary parent with an ordinary job, but now she lives an extraordinary and purposeful life full of passion and meaning because she is true to herself.

Have you ever turned up somewhere, only to look around you and wonder - how on earth did you arrive here? Perhaps you've experienced a car journey where you suddenly arrive at your destination without being aware of the journey at all?

Well, this is exactly how I felt when one day I 'found' myself at a nearby beach. I remember that I had gone there for some important thinking time, but I do not remember driving there or walking up the dunes or any part of the journey of getting there. I realized that I felt nothing. I was numb.

You see, a few days beforehand, I was considering taking an overdose while imagining drifting off into a drug-induced sleep, finally free from pain. I was sitting in my lounge with sleeping tablets in my hand and anti-depressants in my bloodstream and was convinced at that moment that everybody's life would be better off without me. This may sound shocking, but it's absolutely true. Depression can do this, and more, to a person.

At that time, I felt that I was a failure. In my head, I had failed as a mother, as a wife, even as a teacher; so who would really lament my passing anyway? On some level, I understood that all this wasn't strictly true, but this was how I FELT and I just couldn't shake it off.

I felt so disconnected from all the people around me like I was swaying this way and that on the tide, completely adrift. Along with the alienating feeling of disconnection, I no longer felt like I could recognize myself. I couldn't find the dynamic fun-loving person I had been within the shell of the person I was now, and while sitting forlorn and lonely on that beach, a part of me didn't even care. I had lost all sense of myself.

I couldn't believe that, at one point in my life, I had been traveling the world solo, trekking the Golan Heights, camping in the Sinai desert, riding on camels, drumming in Martinique and so many more things I could no longer imagine doing. Now all I could think is *how did I DO that? I can't even get out of the bed to get dressed!*

On really bad days, I had to even ask a friend to walk my boys to school. I just couldn't face the chirpy "good mornings" and the pitying stares. Have you ever felt like that? When you have wondered where the essence of *you* has gone?

Now, the reason that I say I *found* myself that day on the beach is because, at that time, I didn't know what I was doing! I found that things happened without my knowledge. Somehow, the chores were done, yet I wasn't really fully present for any of it. I was showing up but not connecting with my work, family, or friends. I struggled to get up, to get dressed, to wash my hair, or basically anything. On what I would call better days, even though people didn't know how low I was, I knew that I was really only playing a part.

I felt like there was no-one I could turn to. No-one I could talk to. You know that feeling of being surrounded by people but feeling so incredibly alone and isolated? That feeling became my new normal.

I was tired of struggling and trying to please people, all while being someone I wasn't. I tried to talk to people, but I got the sense that nobody really *got* what I was trying to say. So, I stopped talking.

Even though silence seemed like the best option, it created situations or problems unintentionally. I felt like I was getting everything wrong. Eventually, I lost my voice and couldn't actually talk at all for what seemed like ages. Now, this is not ideal for a teacher as you can imagine. On top of it, it was difficult to take time off when I was already working part-time, so the guilt piled up.

Consequently, I kept returning to work too early, not really allowing myself the time I needed to heal properly and to build up my stamina. This also meant that I wasn't really *there* for my boys. All my energy went into work, and then what little I had left, went to my boys. I literally was unable to speak to my husband during this period. Even when I did find the energy to speak in a voice louder than a whisper, no one seemed to hear me. People constantly interrupted me, spoke over me and finished my sentences for me, so I began to feel more and more disempowered, invisible, and irrelevant.

Was this Nature's way of telling me to stop banging my head against a brick wall? These feelings of hopelessness and invisibility had led me down a deep dark tunnel of depression and despair. All of it came to a head in my lounge that evening, with pills in my hand. That moment was when I had my light-bulb moment. Something had to change.

Ultimately, it was up to me to fix this. So I had to reach out. I put down the tablets and rang a friend, a nurse, who luckily had finished her shift. She knew of my situation and how difficult it was living in the same house while being 'separated' from my husband. She knew about the work-related stress and depression. I told her about the tablets. I described how I longed for the peace and fuzziness to descend so that I wouldn't need to make any more difficult decisions. She told me that my boys loved me. She told me they needed me and that I could do it.

I listened and I allowed myself to be heard, helped and held.

That was all I needed at that moment and thank goodness I was given the opportunity to weigh things up for just a moment longer.

It is true that we are indeed creators of our own lives, but we are the destroyers as well.

Then I realized that I HAD to come back to me. I had to find my true essence. I had to reconnect with myself. I had to learn to love and forgive myself. No one else could do it but me. In order to do that though, I needed to create a bigger version of myself – something greater – a version where I could find strength and courage. I needed to feel connected internally to a greater source of strength. I had to do it for myself so I could live! I am very aware that I actually made a choice between life and death that day. I'm not saying that to be overly dramatic or to elicit sympathy; it is simply what I realized at the moment that proved to be the turning point in my life.

I understood that in order to survive, I could no longer play the part that I had been assigned. The words were getting stuck in my throat for a reason, and my feet could no longer traverse the well-worn stage. I was tired of plodding and running into dead ends. I was created for a different stage, with different actors and a different story. I had to change what I was doing, thinking, and accepting. BUT I WAS TERRIFIED!

Because I understood emotional abuse and had been practising my response to it since childhood, I understood my role and what I was expected to say. I understood narcissistic behavior, and I understood how it affected people. Understanding this kind of thing makes you feel like there is power in knowing what's coming and what's possible. It makes you feel like you are wearing a coat of armor. It was a coat that I had worn well.

It was a role that I knew by heart.

I understood that even though I was very good at playing the *'middle class, living-in-the country, husband-in-the-city, teaching-in-a-village-school, being-a-member-of-the-tennis-club'* game, it wasn't really who I was. The cap didn't fit. The jacket was too small.

With realization comes fear, because with it comes the need for action and stepping out of comfort zones. For now, it was crossing new thresholds, opening new doors, and taking the dreaded "leap of faith". I remember with absolute clarity the image of seeing myself balanced precariously on a vertiginous cliff top. I haven't abseiled, but I think that is what I was imagining. I could feel the space around with a sense of wonder and fill my whole body with the blue sky. It seemed like I had not felt so much space for the longest time. In my mind, I breathed it in, I prepared to jump and that's when the voices started.

"What if..."

What if I don't make it? What if I fall and break something? What if I'm too weak? What if it's safer to stay where I am? What if I can't play the new role? What if I fail the audition?

Have you heard them too? These voices that try to keep you *'safe'*? If you aren't careful though, your safe zone would become too toxic for you to survive.

NO! I knew that trusting the voice that was telling me to stay put was no longer an option. I had to jump into the void. I had to take a leap of faith. I had to understand and TRUST that I was being supported in my actions by a divine force. I HAD to say YES to myself. I had to learn from the lessons of the past, otherwise I knew that they would keep repeating themselves. I had almost died, and I couldn't take that risk again.

So, that's when I decided to embrace essential change. I decided to leave my husband and to raise my boys on my own, on my terms, so I can model authentic relationships for them. I also decided to get a better work-life balance and in doing so, I could put my spiritual, emotional, mental and physical health first. I had no idea how I was going to manage any of this, but I knew I had to survive. I knew that I had a reason to be here – a calling, a mission – and I was going to discover it.

I was SO SCARED, though! I kept having nightmares that I would be homeless and would end up begging on the street with my boys, just another bag lady.

Once I had made my decision, it felt like the world around me was amplified – the sky seemed bluer, the gulls louder, the sand whiter. I felt a rushing in my head and a lightness in my chest because what I had decided to do was going to change everything. It was going to turn my family's world upside down. I was under no illusion that my journey was going to be an easy one, but at least it was going to be one of truth. My truth. I also knew that I couldn't make this journey on my own. I knew that I was going to need help and that I was going to have to ask for it. These were two quite new observations – ones that didn't feel very comfortable if I'm being honest.

My journey to wellness began with healing.

I had heard of 'healing' and had realised that anti-depressants and sleeping tablets weren't healing me. They were only numbing the pain (for which I was grateful at the time, I won't lie). I had even been told that I was a natural healer, but I had ignored that for some years. Out of a mixture of curiosity and desperation, I located my nearest healer and paid (what I considered back then) a lot of money for my first energy healing experience. Since then, I haven't looked back. The treatments were so effective! The easiest way to explain my transformation is to use the metaphor of a flame. When we numb the darkness, we numb the light. It was time to start fanning the flames.

Before the healing session, I was broken, vulnerable, depressed and grieving. The flame in my belly was small and blue, barely burning at all. In fact, it had almost been extinguished. Through a nurturing combination of healing treatments, massages, acupuncture, reflexology, osteopathy, counseling and life-coaching, my flame grew brighter. I was adding the fuel I needed; I was adding compassion, forgiveness, kindness; and I was adding self-care, self-nurture, and self-love. I was taking my time.

I was also having fun, but I'm sure that some mums at the school gate possibly thought that I went a bit crazy! I learned to fly a light aircraft – to see life from a different perspective. I started walking regularly, and then I started running. This re-acquainted me with nature and helped my perspective. I understood how I was connected with the rhythms of the seasons and the Universe and how the seasons would come and go, whether I took action or not.

Since that time, I meditate and walk every day, and for me, this connection with Nature is crucial and beautiful. Through this process of rediscovery, I reinvented myself. I had to get used to going out and meeting new people who could relate to what I was going through. So I re-ignited my interest in music and the gigging scene. I started drumming and dancing again. I started doing activities that gave me joy and made me feel fulfilled. Now, I make a point of doing these activities regularly and consistently, because I need them in order for me to be the whole me (not the flying though – that was a one off!)

Eventually, I decided that it was the right time to train as a Reiki Master, so I could help others the same way I was helped. I was able to set up my own practice, and I have been able to help countless women and children over the years with anxiety, panic, grief, and stress, just as I had hoped.

Certifying as a life coach turned my life around. I was able to leave my job and set up my coaching practice. In doing so, I finally had the flexibility I so craved. I am able to serve others, and I especially love helping pregnant couples connect with their baby and help them master their mindset before the birth. To this day, I continue to support stressed-out mums and anxious children.

I use the mentoring, teaching, coaching, and healing skills I have honed over the years to help these couples operate from a place of expansion and love so they can become a strong, loving unit that can support each other as a team and give their baby the best start in life. I am able to support my boys emotionally, financially, and practically, and I am at home with them when they need me there. No guilt. NO GUILT! As a single mum, that takes some saying!

It is said that our children are a reflection of us. How wonderful then that my sixteen-year-old son said to me that he was glad that I divorced his dad. To say I was surprised is an understatement, but my son went on to explain how both of us seemed happier to him. His dad has moved on and is in a healthy relationship with a lovely person and so am I, but more importantly, our boys can sense and see that. They can see that relationships can become different.

They have understood that there is a way through. They know that to compromise oneself is not an option. My boys are supported and encouraged by me to become who they really are and to go for their dreams, and that is the greatest gift that I think I can give my children. I harbor no ill-will toward their father, and I have forgiven my mother for her harsh treatment of me as a child. I understand that everyone is just doing their best with what they have and what they know, and we are all on this journey called life.

During my recovery, I was prepared to do whatever it took to regain my health, vitality, and zest for life, so I immersed myself in the study of meditation, mindfulness, NLP, and healing modalities. Later, I became fascinated by modern neuroscience, the energy of the universe, the power of mindset, and focus and even quantum physics. I followed my gut instinct, and solutions and opportunities started to present themselves as I kept following my path. Because of this, I am able to use all the knowledge I have to help and serve others.

Of course, there are still bumps in the road, hiccups along the way, and a fair few mistakes – but it's all good. This is the beautiful journey of self-discovery, in all its imperfect glory.

I reach out for help when I need it. I know what I don't know (which is a LOT!) and I accept help and advice when it is offered with genuine intention. I choose not to dig so deep that I wear myself out. I am my business. My health and wellbeing is me. So, my health is my business.

Now, when people see me, they see that I live an authentic life – a life where I am ME with all my glorious imperfections. A life where I embody my spirituality instead of hiding it; a full and abundant life; and a life where I am an active participant connecting with people from a place of unconditional love. It is a life where I can speak my truth, and I am heard, acknowledged, and appreciated.

Many people ask me if there are any things I would have changed about my situation, and I always reply with the same answer: absolutely not. I spent much of my life in a strange, bewildering, and irrational space where my soul was consumed by my edgy nervousness. I used to tread on eggshells and I spent my life living with continual confusion of inexplicable episodes of cruelty. It all left me feeling bereft and confused as well as inadequate and hopeless. Do I wish that I'd never met him? The father of my children? Of course not. I don't regret that part at all. I sometimes grieve for the loss of the relationship that might have been, but I am so grateful to have had this incredible human being in my life.

Now I have met my true soulmate, but I also see that I wasn't ready to meet him earlier in my life because I wasn't whole. He and I have been through very similar journeys, and as a result, we treat each other with utmost respect and care. It was almost as though we recognized the essence of each other immediately. He, too, has grown through his experiences and has had to reassess a lot of things. Our values are intrinsically the same, and we are on the same page, reading the same script. We can relax now.

My circumstances, situations, and crises have played a crucial role in creating the person that I am today. So, how I have chosen to perceive these experiences, and what I have chosen to learn from them is entirely within my control. I chose to rebuild myself. I chose to plug the holes that were there from the aches in my heart. I chose to become whole so that I could unconditionally love myself before loving others. We cannot give to others what we don't have. In fact, that little sentence is so crucial that I am going to be indulgent and repeat it! <u>We cannot give to others what we don't have.</u>

I have struggled with feeling different for so many years, feeling as though I was on the outside of everything, feeling trapped, suffocated, misaligned, and misunderstood. It was a really important part of my life journey to reach out for healing in order to become a healer myself. I could finally bloom! I came home to myself and to my reason for being here in this lifetime.

Perhaps, like me, you too have always felt as though you had to do certain things and be a certain way to be accepted. I felt so much pressure in school to have good grades and then get accepted into University. I would be the first person in the family to do so, after all. Then, I wanted a safe, secure and steady job and thought that that was the ultimate measure of success. What it really was, was a way of pleasing my mother to get love, attention, and praise. As a result of academic pressure, I suffered from depression during my teenage years, which resurfaced again after the birth of my first son.

As it turned out, the Universe had bigger plans for me, but I actually stopped to listen only after years and years of misery, and only when I was forced to listen against my better judgment. I finally listened to my heart and my intuition, and then my purpose revealed itself! It was like having permission to embody all my quirks, curiosities and magic and permission to understand life, people, and emotions at the deepest level.

I could have allowed my lack of self-worth continue to keep me trapped in a miserable existence; instead, I have chosen to turn my life around and inspire others, like you, to feel empowered. So, spread your wings and fly. I believe that every person is entitled to create a destiny that gives them the confidence to be themselves and to live a life with happiness, ease, and abundance. To live with peace in their heart.

Dear reader, please know this:

If you feel worthless and alone, know that you are not. We are ALL connected in an intricate web of life. I feel your pain. I hear your soft crying. I see the effort it takes to smile. Know that you have incredible power inside you and amazing gifts to share with the world. Know that you are here, in this lifetime, on this planet for a reason. Know that you have a purpose, and it is time to live it. YOUR time is now. Your time is NOW!

It's time to shine. It's time to rise out of the ashes like a Phoenix and reinvent a new, bigger, bolder, shinier version of YOU! It is no coincidence that you are here now, reading these words. It is no coincidence that I have been on a journey so that I can write about it. Coming out of a dark place is not easy, but I can assure you that it is so worth it. Give yourself permission to step away from what your parents, society, families, and communities say you *should* do and step into your heart's desire – your higher calling.

Yes, I know, it is a big ask. It feels like a big step, and it is!

Possibly the biggest, bravest, boldest step you have ever taken in your life. So, find a life coach whose story resonates with yours and with whom you are energetically aligned. No-one has to go through this life struggling on their own. I KNOW that you can change your life around.

Here are some ideas about how you can turn your whisper into a roar; how you can ignite your small blue flame so that it becomes a burning furnace of passion, desire, and creativity. Do you want to reclaim your power? Would you like to be in control of what you think, feel, and do? Well, you can. This is all possible.

When you establish a center of peace within your core, you empower yourself to act rather than react in distressing situations. And this is the MAGIC KEY: learning to act from a space of empowerment.

When I was living with my ex-husband, a narcissist and a controller, I gave my power away, and there is no-one to blame for that but myself. I used to dread him coming home because I knew that I would feel small and weak, but now I understand that although he may have been playing mind-games, it was – and still is – upto ME to decide how I FEEL in any given moment.

It is important, firstly, to locate where the negative emotion, feeling, or pain is in your body.

For many people, apprehension manifests itself as feelings of heaviness or nausea in the depths of the lower abdomen, and it is there that we must lovingly and deliberately confront the anxiety.

By reaching down into the deepest parts of ourselves, we can cleanse ourselves of unease and replenish the space it leaves behind with tranquil awareness. You simply have to ALLOW yourself to let go of the feeling, and then ALLOW yourself to receive a much higher, better-feeling feeling. You will know it when you have done this successfully because you will feel relief; you will feel grounded and strong, like a mountain.

There are many ways to restore your strength and clear negative energy from your core. To ground yourself and regain your emotional equilibrium, concentrate on the area just above your pelvis, picturing it as a funnel of vivid orange light. Reach down toward that light with your awareness and channel your breath into space it occupies. You can channel healing energy into your core by visualizing the area below your belly button as an open space into which you channel white, loving light.

Often in our daily lives, we are in situations that make us feel nervous or out of control.

A situation that seems hopeless when viewed from a perspective colored by fear may become easily manageable when approached with a serene heart and mind. As you root down into your core, you'll discover that the trepidation and helplessness you feel within you is not invincible. Rather, it will respond readily to your efforts to eradicate it, leaving you feeling peaceful and capable of calmly handling any challenging circumstances that arise.

As an author, mentor and teacher, I practice what I preach. I hold myself accountable for the lessons I share and I make sure I'm walking my talk. When I find myself feeling out of sorts, I reflect on what I've been sharing with my clients and then follow my own advice! (Easier said than done!)

This is sometimes uncomfortable because I feel like I am always working on myself, but it is also deeply rewarding.

There is nothing more rewarding and humbling than teaching children because they are our best teachers! Being a teacher keeps me committed to being a student.

Writing this chapter has been a wonderful spiritual learning opportunity – not only to see how far I have come and to acknowledge and celebrate that but also to fully surrender to the process of writing, sharing, and being vulnerable.

My Wish for You and Some Top Tips

It is my deepest wish that you find some meaning and relief by reading my story and that you find guidance, strength, and inspiration to do what needs to be done to become the very best version of yourself—with what you have and what you know. That, dear reader, is your soul's purpose, and indeed, your sole purpose.

Here are top twelve tips that I recommend:

1. Live fully and with passion.
2. Never be afraid of making mistakes.
3. Do the best you can, with what you have, and what you know. No one can ask for more than that.
4. Master the power of daily Gratitude. Be grateful for every person and every experience, however you perceive them. They are your teachers and your mentors. They carry the messages and lessons that you need to hear and learn to help you reach your full potential.

5. Acknowledge negative thoughts, emotions, and feelings; choose to allow yourself to get rid of them, and replace them with something better.
6. Ask for and receive help, guidance, and support. We're all in this together!
7. Allow yourself time to become whole again. It is not someone else's responsibility.
8. Spend some time every day being silent.
9. Express yourself fully in spite of perceived judgment.
10. Express love, gratitude, and appreciation.
11. Be kind to yourself.
12. Choose to be happy.

Here's to your fearless life! Thank you for reading my story.

Clare Ford

Clare Ford is an author, speaker, healer, life coach, and teacher.

Founder of Beautiful Souls and creator of the 'Mastering Your Mindset in Pregnancy' coaching programme, Clare is mum to two boys, Alex and Oskar, a Dreambuilder Life Coach, Master Usui Reiki healer, and Wasui® practitioner and teacher. Her best-selling book, **"How to Have a Positive & Empowering Pregnancy"** is the first in Conscious Parenting Series. Clare has inspired and worked with parents and children for over 15 years, facilitating various workshops and private sessions.

Her passion and specialties lie in working with pregnant couples to connect them with their growing babies; by preparing them mentally, emotionally, and spiritually for labor and for the transition into parenthood.

By combining Reiki healing practices and water flotation therapy, Clare has created a new healing modality Wasui® to create the ultimate relaxation and deep healing experience for couples, parents, and children.

As a sought-after transformational coach and conscious

pregnancy and parenting coach, Clare regularly offers inspiring workshops as well as in-depth coaching programs that help clients achieve new heights of success, awareness, and spiritual consciousness. Clare is on a mission to create a ripple effect of global transformation by breaking the stigma and offering solutions to mental and emotional health issues. Having overcome emotional abuse in childhood and marriage, severe depression, anxiety, perinatal and postnatal depression, she is more than qualified to walk this path and guide others to greatness

Clare says, "I have come to believe that pregnancy is a sacred journey and that birthing new life, a baby spirit that has been nurtured and nourished, by a mother who embraces the connection between mind, body, and spirit, is wondrous to behold. It is my passion and calling to support women at this incredible time in their life."

Contact Information

If you would like to work with me for transformational coaching, parenting and pregnancy coaching, or Reiki healing, please contact me on: support@beautifulsouls.co.uk

You can find out more about me here: https://www. beautifulsouls.co.uk/ or read more here: https:// www.beautifulsouls.co.uk/reiki-healing/

Alternatively, you could get in touch with me on social media:
Facebook: @beautifulsoulscoaching
Twitter: @ClareSouls

Instagram: @Beautiful50uls
LinkedIn: in/clare-ford-92780850

A Healthy Way of Dealing with Yourself

CORINNE STEINER

Everything is perfect, but nothing is.

D o you know the situation where you think you should be happy, satisfied, or content but you aren't? Instead, you feel guilty. Or when you try to convince yourself that everything is okay, but on the inside, you know it's not? Have you ever consciously influenced yourself and your life for the better?

I grew up in Switzerland, a country of high standards, where everything was available to me to lead a good life. Despite my successful career and my positive environment, I didn't feel happy. I was searching for purpose and fulfillment in my life and jobs for years. Emptiness and senselessness were constant companions. Life felt like a continuous fight without knowing what it is that I was fighting for.

This chapter is intended to inspire you to review your focus on your life, and, if desired, to redirect it. In the best case, you will see your potential for a healthier way of dealing with yourself and how you can make better use of it. This can lead to you cultivating (even more) actively and enjoying what is special in your life.

We service and maintain electronic devices so that they are functional for as long as possible. Before the battery of our mobile phone is completely empty, we charge it again. Do we do the same with our batteries? Many people don't take preventive care of their well-being. As long as their engine—their body—is running, they see no need for maintenance or repair.

My own journey was different. I have manipulated myself for many years, which has led to inner conflicts, and a double life. I was well aware of it but not capable of changing it. I felt that I had lost myself. Fortunately, I have never experienced going beyond my physical limits and being completely out of action. But the constant struggle against myself and the hope to be happy again is not a state that I wish to be back in. I wouldn't wish it for anyone else.

From working with different people in the corporate world, over the last 20 years, I know that there are many of them who show exactly this self-manipulative behavior, mostly without being aware of it. By "exactly this," I don't necessarily mean an eating disorder. There are many other types of self-manipulation, such as overwork or activism followed by sleep deprivation or excessive sports training.

My experience with the stumbling blocks I have encountered by my bad dealings with myself and my knowledge of how to avoid them should show you and these people the opportunities to do things differently in time. It should serve as motivation to change the way of life for the better. I will show how easy and helpful it is to integrate new habits into everyday life in a sustainable way. As examples, I mention the habits with which I have managed to get out of the vicious circle of my eating disorder and the hamster wheel of my demanding job. Finally, I reveal the most important skills that can lead to a healthy, fulfilling, and self-determined life.

Throughout the chapter, you will find thought-provoking questions. Consider them an offer to reflect on your own situation. Get inspired and feel free to take notes. Under the following link, you can download a free printable file with all questions and space for your answers: Http://corinnesteiner. com/key-questions-for-a-healthier-way-of-dealing-with-yourself

Before you continue reading, here comes the first question.

Do you have any situation in life that you'd like to improve? If yes, which one is it? If not, are you being honest with yourself?

A ray of sunshine that couldn't shine anymore. This was me, constantly fighting against myself, in a world I felt I didn't belong to and at a workplace I didn't want to be in.

It all began in my adolescence with the choice of my career. Sports was my passion, and I wanted to become a sports teacher. But, my grades weren't good enough for a sports school. My plans were over even before they began, and I had no more dreams left to pursue.

I didn't know what else I wanted to do. This is how I ended up doing a commercial apprenticeship, which was a compromise with my parents. Simultaneously, with the start of my apprenticeship, an eating disorder developed. I tried to avoid eating, whenever possible. There were days when I would only consume one apple in a day. When I realized that I didn't have enough energy even to climb the stairs, I forced myself to eat again. At first, I was proud of outsmarting myself. Then I was afraid of gaining too much weight. That was when I deliberately started vomiting after dinner. It was a vicious cycle of eating and vomiting and the start of a 15-year-struggle with Bulimia[31].

My thoughts constantly revolved around food, and even if I tried to not think about it, I was steered in that direction. Eventually, I had to eat something. And I ate, but the fear of gaining too much weight made me vomit. I felt shameful about it. At some point, going to the toilet frequently to throw up became a routine.

You might probably wonder why someone would do this to themselves or why I wouldn't just stop. Believe me, I had asked myself the same questions, over and over again. Even though I wanted a healthier way to deal with myself, my strong willpower and my innumerable attempts to stop were not enough to change my deranged behavior. On the contrary, the constant thoughts about it had intensified the vicious circle.

I made an effort to get my life back on track by undergoing countless therapy sessions and seminars, which cost me a fortune. Self-help books and mental training were also a part of my desperate attempt to a healthier lifestyle. However, my little accomplishments would always be followed by a setback.

These struggles didn't stop me from continuing to strive for an

---

[31]   Bulimia is a mental illness in which those affected are trapped in a cycle in which they eat large amounts of food and then try to compensate for that overeating by vomiting, fasting or exercising excessively.

improvement in circumstances and believe me, I worked hard for it. A positive outcome of these efforts was my professional success which was reflected with a higher salary and promotions. It was at the age of 27, when I worked for a global corporation, that I was promoted from the Assistant level to the Directorial level. This called for more hard work on my part but brought no fulfillment and certainly no solution to my self-sabotaging behavior.

As the youngest leader in my department, I was about 15–20 years younger than my peers. Because I was a new manager, very young, and the first female team-lead in this department, I was under constant control from my supervisor, my colleagues, and my employees. Suddenly, it was up to me to lead and to manage. I had to learn what it means to not be popular with everyone and to not be able to do all the work alone. Without experience and a tendency toward perfectionism, it was all quite a challenge for me. But, I was willing to accept it because I had nothing to lose and a lot to learn. With the success, the expectations grew, not only from my environment and the people around me but also from myself. I wanted to do a great job to the contentment of everyone. I still believe that I have successfully mastered my job.

What I didn't do best was to deal with myself.

I demanded more and more from myself and my own body. In my main job I was employed on an 80% workload so that I could further my knowledge in the field of adult education and coaching. This was the area where I had found joy again and could do what I enjoyed doing. But I couldn't earn enough money with it to make my living out of it.

Since it was not possible to do my management job in four days, I continued working from home after work. As a result, my workload was at least 100%. In addition, I worked twice a week, in the evening or on weekends as a fitness instructor. This meant that at peak times I was 150% occupied with work and further education. I also needed two to three hours a day to get to work and back home. I was always on the road, had little time to sleep and almost no time to rest. First, I played sports six to seven times a week. I participated in swimming, road racing, jogging, diving, strength training, boot camp, and a couple of other things. Then I stopped completely. Also with further education and the part-time job, I had to save my energy to get through the week. I was always at the limit but on the weekends, I could recharge my batteries for the following week. That 'actually' worked out quite well. I say 'actually' because I became more and more dissatisfied, unbalanced, and unfulfilled.

Others admired me for my ambition, courage, and professional success. I was envied for it and got many compliments. However, I didn't feel outstanding at all. For me, the external challenges at work were nothing compared to the internal struggles—of which nobody knew anything, except for a few close people. This double life was a burden. It felt more and more difficult to find my motivation and energy to get up in the morning, and to take on new responsibilities. I started questioning myself. What was it that I didn't understand? Why couldn't I stop vomiting and feel fulfilled and happy instead? I tried hard, but the only success I had was my career, which felt more and more like a failure to me because it didn't fulfill me. I was wondering what this was all for.

How self-awareness and focus serve as resources for everyday life

To overcome my eating disorder and escape the stress at work, I had to understand what I was missing and what was preventing me from changing my situation. This required an improvement of my consciousness and a shift in focus.

I am happy to share my most valuable learnings with you in the following lines, in the hope of giving you food for thought, with which you can make a positive contribution to your own everyday life.

If, at the moment, you expect something extraordinary to come to you, something that you may have never heard of before, then you might be in for some disappointment. I won't tell you any new and extraordinary tools or unprecedented insights. Instead, I will focus on something much more valuable. We can make our lives special instead of constantly striving to be someone special. I have learned that the answer lies within myself. I should simply be more aware and focus on what is there in my life, not what is missing.

Getting clarity about my challenges and possibilities was the first step in my consciousness development.

This was a complex process with countless questions that I had to answer every day to my coaches and to myself. It was like the Onion Principle. First, comes the outermost layer, which is the most obvious challenge I had at that moment—the eating disorder. Then the next layer where I tried to find out what the underlying need was by asking questions such as, "What was

I missing?" As soon as I got clarity, I went to the next layer to figure out what hindered me to fulfill that need and so on.

This is what I found out about myself by asking the right questions.

- **I had distanced myself from my being by making others and their expectations a priority in my life.**

Since it is in my nature to listen to others and do what pleases them, I wasn't able to take care of myself. I would easily forget my own needs, placing those of others above mine. My career choice, as I mentioned earlier, was a compromise with my parents. It wasn't the first compromise that I made, and it definitely wasn't my last. I did it many times. More and more of my decisions were based on what others said was good for me. Granted, most of the time they were right. I ended up having a great life. But there was another side to it. I had completely forgotten myself.

Consequently, I lost the natural access to myself and my intuition. I was completely driven by the expectations of others as well as by my everyday tasks and could no longer be a master of myself. The result of all this was muffled feelings through which I perceived experiences and successes. I felt guilt and shame for not being in control of my life.

- **Doing everything but nothing right led to disorientation.**

Wanting to do everything right and being strongly involved everywhere made it difficult for me to switch off. I was constantly busy with something, either in my mind or with physical activity. It was extremely difficult for me to relax and do nothing. I had been everywhere but wasn't really involved in anything, and this led me to experience things only half-heartedly. I felt as if everything was passing me by.

Now, pause for a moment and think about yourself.

What are your most important drivers in life? And where do you notice that these drivers influence you negatively, slow you down, or even prevent you from reaching your goals?

According to Anthony Robbins, an American bestselling author, NLP[32] trainer and coach instructor, there are six human needs that can be considered as the main drivers of your life. Which one of these applies to you?

1. Certainty/security
2. Uncertainty/variety
3. Significance
4. Love
5. Growth
6. Contribution

Everyone is going to measure themselves differently because everyone values things differently. You can think of your existence as a measuring scale, which is the indicator of your balance in life. On the left side of the scale, you have the weight of everything that burdens you and demands energy, and on the right side, you have the weight of everything that strengthens

---

[32] NLP = Neuro Linguistic Programming is an approach to personal development, communication and psychotherapy developed by Richard Bandler and John Grinder in California, US, in the 1970s.

you, offers personal development, and gives you energy. Everything that comes to you from outside (job, relationships, expectations, health, etc.) as well as what comes from inside (your thoughts, expectations, and emotions) can be found as weight on one side or the other of the scale.

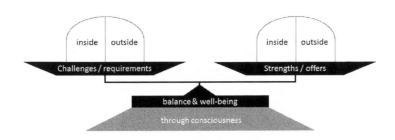

Both sides of the scale—the left side that challenges you and the right side that strengthens you—are needed for your balance, well-being, and personal development. If the side with the burdens is heavier and therefore predominates, it is likely that you feel slowed down. In case you are exposed to too much stress, you will eventually experience excessive strain and stagnation. However, if the challenges match up to your strengths, you may feel driven and encouraged. If your strengths side is heavier and dominate, you will experience personal development, positive energy, and satisfaction. However, in this situation, it can also happen that you get stuck in your comfort zone. You become sluggish and do not develop further. This can also become a burden. Only with some challenges, you will receive a stimulus that will make you maintain or change something.

How balanced is your life considering what life offers and asks from you?

It wasn't just my thoughts that contributed to a better understanding and clarity about my situation. Thinking about it alone left me confused. How can we know something we are not aware of? How could I know, for example, that I had obstructive thoughts or behaviors if I did not realize them at all? Therefore, it was essential for me to promote further levels of consciousness, which enabled me to gain new perspectives.

Thanks to different training in the areas of well-being and coaching, I have developed self-awareness on different levels. This consciousness has shown me how I think, feel, and behave. With this access to myself, I discovered a new resource that I could use for myself and my everyday life, especially when it came to gaining clarity about a certain situation.

The following list shows the most useful methods I discovered for myself, most of which I have integrated into my daily routine. They are not the only possibilities of course but can serve as inspiration, if you are looking for effective training approaches for your body, thoughts, emotions, feelings, and actions.

- Body: Massages, eating with closed eyes, walking barefoot, doing things with your other hand, cold-warm showers, progressive muscle relaxation according to Dr. Jacobson[33], juice fast for one week, and playing moderate sports

---

[33] PMR is the progressive muscle relaxation method of Dr. Eduard Jacobson, in which a state of deep relaxation of the whole body can be achieved by the deliberate and conscious tightening and relaxing of certain muscle groups.

- Thoughts: Watching your own thoughts without judging others and yourself, doing mental and autogenic training, writing a gratefulness diary or a diary with the top three experiences of the day, and what to do better next time

- Emotions and feelings: Watching your own emotions and feelings without judging, creative painting or writing in which you let your thoughts run wild, mindfulness meditation, and breathing exercises

- Actions: Keeping a training plan and an eating diary and reflect on the implementation, asking for feedback at work and from friends to understand how others perceive you

I assume you already know these methods or other similar ones. However, there is a high probability that you're only doing a fraction of what you want to or could do. Why is that?

Whenever I wanted to change a behavior or become aware of my challenges, I focused and tried to solve them. But it hardly ever worked, no matter how hard I tried. It was later that I got to know why. This was one of the first insights I gained during my coaching education.
Once we gain clarity of our challenges, it is important that we do not remain focused on them but focus on where we want to go. Because what we focus on is what we aim for.

Therefore, from where you are right now, get clarity about what distracts you, your challenges, and <u>focus</u> on your aims, needs, and desires. (See the graphic next page.)

That's why the next important milestone on my path was to become aware of my needs, aims and desires in order to set conscious, realistic, and above all, attractive goals.

There are innumerable methods that I got to know and used, which go beyond the scope of this chapter. What I would like to share with you are questions that have brought me forward—questions that you can ask yourself again and again.

What are your challenges and what do you want instead? What keeps you from getting it?

If you want to look at it from a broader perspective, here is another question for you.

If you had a chance to get a new life, what kind of life would you wish for?

Everyone has different priorities and their own techniques for prioritizing. The following eight steps help me best to focus on my priorities.

1. I keep my own overall goal, needs, and desires in focus.

2. I get an overview of all my priorities, regardless of their importance. You can do this in your mind, but it is better

to do it in writing or, if possible, spread them out visibly in front of yourself.

3. I focus on what really matters either for myself or for what I am doing at the moment and make it my priority.

4. I watch my own and other people's expectations that might stand in my way. Here are some helpful questions.

   Are all my priorities really a priority? Why?

   Do I allow myself to concentrate on my priorities, or what prevents me?

   Do I say 'No' to the expectations of others if they interfere with my priorities? If not, why not?

5. I set myself a clear time limit. Until when will I do what? Imagine having only one month, one day, or one hour for all my priorities. How am I going to do that?

6. I do not let myself get distracted by anything that has nothing to do with my priorities. Unless something else becomes a priority due to unforeseen circumstances. Then this will be my new priority.

7. I communicate my priorities to my immediate environment so that I am not distracted by them.

8. I get help when I realize that I am losing time, concentration or energy for my priorities, either to find out how to do it best or differently or to get some motivation and inspiration.

By becoming aware of my destructive and self-manipulative thoughts, sensations and behaviors, I knew that I could also change them. However, mere awareness was not enough to bring about a change. I knew that too little sleep disturbed my equilibrium; that frequent ignoring of my inner voice, which among other things expresses my needs and desires, led to dissatisfaction; and the self-doubting thoughts made me feel small and insignificant. I could not do anything about my eating disorder and still did not pursue my needs—for more sport, relaxation, and balance—because after all the work I did, there was no time or energy left for all this.

Life felt like a constant struggle—an endless loop that I couldn't get out of. Every time I tried to take a step ahead, I was pulled back in and thrown around. Something held me back. I managed it anyway, and I will share how I did it.

What you need and can do to lead a healthy and self-determined life.

Have you ever tried to control life or to get a hold on it? And have you experienced how much energy, will, and motivation that requires? What if life isn't a fight but a game? A game that is not about war and struggle but about taking it to the next level, while having some fun.

I started to compare my life to an adventurous computer game, where I must master one level to get to the next. Each level brings new challenges. Trying out new things makes it interesting but sometimes also more difficult. I can have fun or get angry about the obstacles along the way. I will probably fail several times before I complete the level. With each level I complete, my conviction grows that I can do it again. I don't quit the game because I want to get ahead, become stronger and win.

With the idea that life is a game and I am the captain of it, I no longer see challenges as a problem but as an opportunity for personal development and to have fun.

Of course, life is not quite like a game. I don't have several chances at my disposal. That makes it all the more important that I take care of the one life given to me.

An effective self-leadership is what I needed. My self-leadership skills largely decide to what extent the given life situation can influence me. In other words, it means that I can consciously control my thoughts, feelings, and actions and increase my personal effectiveness in dealing with the challenges of everyday life, while feeling happy and satisfied. Yes, with self-leadership I can consciously set the right actions. And you can do that too.

However, our awareness of our thoughts, feelings, and actions, as well as our goals and desires do not yet lead us to do what we actually want. From my own experiences and as part of my master's thesis, in which I conducted extensive literature research of well-known authors in the field of self-leadership, such as Charles C. Manz, Günter F. Müller, and Marco Furtner, I have learned that besides self-awareness, these three components lead to an effective self-leadership:

1. Self-responsibility
2. Self-efficacy conviction
3. Self-development

I will now describe these skills in detail and how I have developed them over time.

1. Self-responsibility

You can only lead yourself if you are willing to accept leadership responsibility for yourself. This requires the curiosity to know yourself better. It can be triggered by a necessity, for instance, dissatisfaction with your own work situation. In my case, it was the eating disorder. It also requires your willingness to commit yourself to your personal development, achievement of goals, and your own values. You must also face unpleasant situations, break away from habits, and actively steer and control your own feelings, thoughts, and actions. External influences must not play a role. You need to be willing to accept change and look for development opportunities within it. Further, a positive attitude and your understanding of fellow human beings and situations will make it easier for you to deal with your environment.

It is important that you stand up for yourself and overcome the resistance you encounter. By being aware of your personal limitations, weaknesses, and needs, you can consciously distance yourself from them and avoid unwanted situations.

I dealt with my eating disorder openly from the first moment. I became aware of it, got help and constantly looked for new solutions. No effort was too great for me, neither financially nor in terms of time or personal challenges. Professional challenges, in my leadership role, were addressed with my supervisor and employees. I gave my challenges the necessary attention, which led me to change the situations.

Only by admitting my own weaknesses and developing the willingness to change something about it could I change it.

Ask yourself:

> **How willing and ready are you to take on self-leadership for yourself and your aims, dreams, and desires on a scale from 1 (not at all) to 10 (100%)? If you are not on a 10 yet, what else do you need to get there?**

You can also break it down and ask yourself these questions for a very specific intention. For example, how willing are you to stop smoking?

It's up to you to declare yourself ready for this!

2. Self-efficacy conviction

In order to consciously take responsibility for yourself and be able to act purposefully, you require a need for action. This is accompanied by clarity about your needs, values, and goals, but most importantly the conviction of feasibility.

Your self-image offers clarity about your own personality traits (e.g., values, beliefs, resources, limits, needs, and experiences). Your life concept (mission, vision, goals, and roles) serves as a signpost for orientation and for choosing the desired direction.

This you get with self-awareness, as I mentioned in the previous section of this chapter. Focus your attention on the circumstances inside (thoughts, emotions, body signals) and outside of you (environment and your own actions). For me, coaching was very helpful to open up new perspectives and ways of looking at things through which I could recognize my blind spots.

What helped me maintain a strong will was the desire to be healthy and feel fulfilled again. I knew exactly how I wanted to feel when I reached my goal, how it would look like and what will be better and different. I had with me these strong and positive memories of my happy childhood and different moments of flow and success in sports. I did combine these with light-heartedness, happiness, and endless joie de vivre. I knew these feelings were still inside me, and I longed so strongly for them, that over the years, they gave me the will to persevere.

Do you know what exactly it is that you want to achieve?

Once you know what you want, you do not need any superpowers to achieve it. What you need is high self-efficacy and faith in yourself.

For me, it was again my very strong inner feeling of happiness and contentment that encouraged me to go on, persist, and do everything to get there again. I didn't know if I would ever be able to do it, and I didn't know what it would take to get there, but I believed in it.

What makes you strongly believe that you can achieve your goal(s) no matter what?

With the answer to this question, you can activate your inner and outer resources. Therefore, you need to believe in yourself and your possibilities and be ready and willing to use your knowledge and experiences in uncertain or challenging situations. If you plan the individual steps of implementation in advance, the implementation runs almost automatically with the necessary energy and without great will activation. You then stand up for yourself and overcome resistance. With the awareness of your personal limits, weaknesses, and needs, you can consciously define yourself and avoid unwanted situations.

Are there any other doubts that need to be dispelled?

If this is the case, it is important that you find a way around and that you don't feel guilty and punish yourself for what is not working but acknowledge your personal value and your own achievements. Hold on to your strengths and successes and always remember what you are capable of and what you have already achieved.

3. Self-development

Self-development can take place through targeted self-control and self-regulation (i.e., self-motivation and self-calming) in the case of negative feelings, uncertainties, setbacks, and internal conflicts. Flexibility for changes in your own way of thinking and intentions can also arise.

This enables you to regenerate quickly, develop positive thoughts and—despite inner resistance and habitual thinking—to act in a goal-oriented, self-confident, and situation-adapted way. It is essential that you maintain your inner balance through self-care. If you manage yourself, i.e., if you eat a balanced diet, take care of sufficient recovery and movement, cultivate an appropriate approach to internal and external causes of stress, and use appropriate working techniques—such as problem-solving strategies to cope with life's tasks—you will create a good basis for balance and resilience.

Control and steer the thoughts of the moment, by conducting an inner dialogue, activating your willpower, and thinking in terms of opportunities and possibilities. You can influence feelings and actions positively in order to concentrate on your own actions and still be open for contributions from outside.

Dealing with feelings and emotions allows the control of attention, emotion, and motivation. This requires the development of emotional and physical awareness as well as the recognition of positive situations and intrinsic motives. Emotional control even makes it possible for you to find a suitable solution to conflicts. So, for example, automatic and apparently uncontrollable emotional reaction can be steered by pausing and noticing the external effect on one's sore points. If you recognize your own behavior, as well as negative interactions with others, you get the possibility of self-regulation and can thus change hindering automatisms and behavior patterns. This requires an understanding of the nature and dynamics of conflicts as well as of one's own conflict behavior and the ability to differentiate oneself and clarify the conflict through communication.

The control of actions makes it possible to satisfy your own needs as well as to pursue life in a self-determined way and in the desired direction. It helps you to tackle what you have imagined and make it happen—quickly, easily and in the most appropriate way.

For this purpose, it is necessary to activate unused potential and to strengthen your own behavior through appropriate postures, gestures, and facial expressions.

Discipline, diligence, and stamina are essential for effective self-leadership. This is supported by written SMART goals: Specific, Measurable, Attractively Realizable, and Time-bound.

Clear, purposeful, continuous, and flexible actions need organization. Organization means a systematic and goal-oriented approach to the completion of tasks. It is guaranteed by lived self-management, such as concentration on the essentials, setting priorities, decision-making, and implementation planning.

With a sustainable productive behavior, you can achieve clarity, security, and attention for all challenges without having to think about it.

Self-development includes an honest approach to yourself.

> **Are you honest with yourself and do you admit to yourself where you need to act? How often do you pay attention to your consciousness? How often do you really think about your well-being (not your health or the absence of it)? Can you feel tension or**

stress before it starts to hurt, or do you feel stressed out?

Are there perhaps situations in which you are no longer the master of your conscious and intended actions? How do you deal with yourself in these moments?

Here are some examples.

If you are tired, do you go to bed? How often do you play sports? How healthy is the food that you eat? When you make a mistake, what do you think about yourself? If you want some time for yourself but your friends ask for a favor or want to go out, what do you do? If you say no, how do you feel?

If, when answering these questions, it came out that you are not treating yourself well, don't worry, that doesn't mean you have a problem. It just shows you that you have the potential to work on yourself. If everything runs smoothly for you, there might still be options for optimization.

Often, we assume that we have no problems and no stress, apart from the one obvious problem. This, however, we cannot change and somehow, we can deal with it quite well. On closer inspection, we can notice that this one problem is only the result of the actual cause. It serves as an indication that something is not okay and helps to deal with the cause in the meantime.

Example: You eat unhealthy food and gain weight because of it. Being overweight and getting tired is a problem for you. If you now become aware that you are eating badly, you will notice that this is not an optimal and natural behavior on your part. By reflecting on it, you will realize that you have not always eaten unhealthy food but have only begun to do so recently since you have a new boss with whom you are in constant conflict. That's the root cause of your problem—you eat to overcome the conflict. The more you eat and the more weight you put on, the greater the indication for you that something is wrong. In the meantime, you eat to solve the conflict (your problem helps you to eliminate the cause).

Today, my eating habits serve as an indicator of my well-being and as a general guide to life. When I eat without enjoying it or being hungry, I know that something is not right. This is a sign for me that I have to act, sit down, and reflect in order to understand what is going on. Of course, I can overrule this indicator and just eat, but I know that in the long run I will suffer and be disappointed with myself. And that's why I take this indicator seriously and pay attention to it.

I can just recommend you become aware of your indicators in life. If you don't know them already. Indicators can be very different things. For example, your state of anger, motivation, or an unwanted behavior. To become aware of it, regularly reflect why you feel how you feel and why you behave the way you behave.

That's why time-outs are so important. Time-outs create distance from everyday life to find out where we have a need for action. This can be experienced, among other things, during the exercise of passion activities (e.g., sport, painting) by experiencing a 'flow' state (i.e., the complete absorption into an activity and the fading out of time and one's own self) or through a change of place as well as meditation.

In order to change obstructive behaviors, it is helpful to replace them with conducive behaviors in the form of habits. This can be on the level of thinking, feeling, or acting. At best, at all levels.

Healthy habits lead to a healthy way of dealing with yourself and promote personal well-being. They bring more self-confidence, motivation, energy, and satisfaction and lead to a self-determined, fulfilled life.

A healthy way of dealing with yourself can be understood in different ways, but it essentially means that you can use your time and energy optimally for yourself by carefully handling your thoughts, emotions and your body.

I integrated such habits into my everyday life and focused on three key areas to keep myself in balance: Nutrition, exercise, and relaxation.

In the next section, I will share with you helpful habits I tried out and that can be easily and sustainably implemented in everyday life. With these habits, I have managed to motivate and positively influence my thoughts, feelings, and actions despite the 15 years of struggle with Bulimia and the very demanding jobs I had. I also managed to leave the eating disorder behind and focus on my needs, goals, and dreams again.

Nutrition

- Decide before shopping what you will eat.
- Cook with fresh ingredients.
- Prepare healthy food the day before or for several days.
- Prepare healthy snacks in case of cravings.
- Focus on what you are allowed to eat and not on what you are not allowed to eat.
- Make a list of healthy foods and recipes you like.
- Observe what emotions you feel when you eat or think about it.
- Create a pleasant and cozy atmosphere to eat.
- Present the food attractively because it should be a feast for the eyes, too.
- Eat slowly and chew food at least 30 times before swallowing.
- Ask a friend or partner to remind you that you want to eat healthy if you should ever abandon your plan.
- Get together with friends and cook healthy food for each other.

Exercise

- Find and do things you enjoy.
- Think about how fit you will be after training and not how hard it will be during the training.
- Try out endurance sports with moderate performance. For example, Nordic Walking, snowshoe hiking, swimming, dancing, stand up paddling, or rowing

- Do sports where you can strengthen the awareness of your body like with dancing, Pilates[34], or Yoga.
- Combine the useful with the ordinary. For example,
    1. Travel to work by bicycle or on foot instead of taking the train.
    2. Use the stairs instead of the escalator.
    3. Connect the meeting with your friends with a round of jogging, cycling, or rollerblading.
- Look for new and exciting experiences such as diving, canoeing, city trips with sightseeing on foot or by bike, or prepare yourself for a sporting goal depending on your fitness level.

Relaxation

Allow yourself to do nothing and enjoy it. Best to relax is with something to let your mind go. Listen to music, read a book, write or paint, do breathing or stretching exercises, take a leisurely walk, take a candlelit bath, take a footbath, or make yourself a face mask. Sit in the sun, do simple work in the garden like weeding out, drink a cup of tea, or call a friend for some positive small talk. Sometimes it helps to do something active first to get rid of the tension and then to relax better.

Now it's your turn.

---

[34] Pilates, developed by Joseph Pilates, is a form of strength training in which you focus primarily on your breathing and body center (Powerhouse) consisting of abdominal, back and hip muscles. The development of a strong Powerhouse leads to better body control, improved coordination and balance. In addition, Pilates can improve your mobility and endurance.

Think of what you need or even miss in your everyday life. What have you always loved or wanted to do? What is fun and gives you energy?

It is as simple as that—take the next step.

Life is not always positive and not perfect at all, and that is okay. Every problem is a potential possibility to learn and create a positive experience. When we experience difficult times, we can be sure that there will be more such situations, just as there are more pleasant ones.

I remembered a wonderful time and wanted to have it back again. I worked hard on myself for over 20 years and didn't lose the courage to live a healthy and fulfilled life. I can only encourage you to create wonderful moments in your life as well, and if this means primarily remembering or picturing a situation as you would like it to be, then so be it.

Make yourself and your desires, goals, and dreams the focus of your attention. Use your consciousness as a resource for your thoughts, feelings, and actions to shape life accordingly. Be ready to take on responsibility. Knowing how you can overcome hurdles and achieve goals will bring you the necessary willpower and self-conviction.

Healthy habits (balanced diet, moderate exercise, and relaxation) lead to healthy interaction with yourself, which includes conscious perception and interaction with

your thoughts, feelings and actions. This enables you to focus and achieve your goals in order to lead a balanced and fulfilled life.

When you consider this, more wonderful moments will definitely find their place in your life. All this cannot be achieved overnight but they can be mastered step-by-step, over time. It is better to do one step than no step at all.

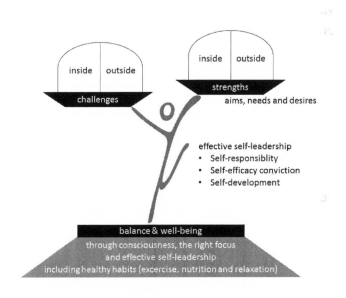

What's your next step?
What are some of the things that you can apply for the biggest challenges in life?

Be SMART (Specific, Measurable, Attractively Realizable, and Time-bound) about it.

Corinne Steiner

It is no surprise that Corinne Steiner is a highly valued coach, trainer, and mentor.

By shaping the everyday life of her clients, she empowers them and helps them live a purposeful and fulfilled life.

Corinne's exceptional skills ensure that her clients realize their untapped potential, taking with them truly tangible and effective tools, strategies and a new mindset for time and health management which they can use to master and accelerate their own personal success and achievements.

Do you want to get back in the center of your life, treat yourself well, find your own drivers, and experience motivation, energy and meaning in your daily lives? Then Corinne is the person to go to.

Contact Information

Website: www.corinnesteiner.com
E-mail: corinne@corinnesteiner.com

CEO TO SHAMAN

GREGORY REECE-SMITH

"To manifest wisdom means simply to step back and see—to reflect, inquire, be aware, be disciplined, and be focused not once in a while, but all of the time, moment to moment. This life is precious and fleeting. Pay attention."

Seido Ray Ronci, *The Examined Life*

The beginnings of this story go back to when I was seven. It was this event that influenced the choice I made to become a businessman—not consciously knowing what I was deciding even though I believed that this was necessary to attract the love of my father.

What was the event?

It was one of those traumatic moments that make our lives—though we are not aware of it at the moment. For me, this was when I was taken to the hospital to have my tonsils removed. This was a period when it was a routine procedure for those experiencing severe bouts of earache.

I remember being taken to the hospital by my mother and a neighbor as my mother had yet to learn to drive. At the hospital I was left with my small suitcase, a big hug and an *"all will be well*" comment.

At the hospital, there were no other children to play with or talk to. My bed was in the men's general ward since there were none free in the children's ward.

The men in the ward were very friendly, and once my mother had left, they came up to my bed and spoke to me as they wandered around the ward in their dressing gowns—often carrying with them bags of what looked like water connected by a tube to their body.

The nursing staff were also friendly, though they seemed to spend most of their shift dispensing pills or seated at their desk completing paperwork. The night after my operation, I remember being woken up by the noise of nurses rushing around. In the morning, I noticed a bed was empty and curtained off. My meal that day was mashed potato and gravy, with warm water or milk to drink. The energy of the entire ward was subdued.

I do not recall leaving my bed, preferring its warmth and comfort to the stark nature of the ward.

And the event?

Even though I was in the hospital for no more than four days, not once did my father visit me. And my mother only visited me once, with a neighbor. Yes, she had my younger brother and sister to look after, and she couldn't drive either. However, this event created a persistent belief that to attract my father's love, I had to be a successful businessman—for this was his focus! I believed only then he would show his love for me. It was this choice that then directed the events in my life.

The First Step(s)

As I came to my final year at University, I had a choice to make.

Which profession would be the most effective route to becoming a successful businessman? Was it accounting and finance or the law? I chose the former, primarily because a close family friend was an accountant and had offered to make some inquiries.

This led to an interview with Peat Marwick (the PM in KPMG) in London as they launched their first university graduate training program.

Three years later, I qualified, and the work had already taken me to various other European countries. Over the next ten years, I worked in many more countries, including the USA and advised a wide range of businesses on how to grow and re-structure.

The moment had finally arrived for me to become the corporate executive. The choice came down to which client to join— Citicorp or a public electronics group. I chose the latter because the salary was higher, I would have the title of Chief Financial Officer, and it meant relocating my family to the New York area.

At the end of a year, I calculated I had spent only one week in my so-called office on Long Island. I was being pushed and pulled by the demands of the Chairman and CEO as they sought to fight the fires created by the expansion strategy that had first brought me into contact with them. You can be sure I was not enjoying my role as a corporate executive!

My direction was decided for me by boardroom changes that led to the Chairman's departure and subsequently mine, too.

After our family's return to England, I began to build my coaching business. My offer was to help owners accelerate their business though my underlying intention was to come to know its management and perhaps be asked to join them as an executive.

One such opportunity came when the CEO of an application developer asked me to join them as the Group Finance Director. Doing so meant re-locating from the South East to the South West of England. This move provided us with a rural property where our children could disappear into the surrounding fields and woods and only re-appear when they were hungry or wanted to chill out.

Two years later, a sale to a fast-growing public company had been arranged, so control passed to others. A year or so later, a new group CEO was appointed; not long after, the parent company filed for bankruptcy. I effectively became the CEO of the application business and assisted in engineering its sale, though at the cost of my own job!

What had I learned from these two episodes? Not a lot since I was still motivated by the childhood belief I needed to be a successful businessman for my father to notice me. Though, by now, I was aware of some bouts of pain and discomfort in my body. My gallbladder was removed before I was thirty.

Yes, I had continued to play rugby until I was forty for I believed this was an essential means of releasing physical stress. Now, I was aware of issues within my digestive system; there were occasional twinges in my lower back preventing me from enjoying nature gardening, and there was my right shoulder indicating it was beginning to freeze up.

Did I listen to any of these messages?

No. I carried on despite seeking alternatives to the prescribed medication at this point.

Returning once again to coaching, I revitalized a training company by broadening its offer to include coaching. It became one of the premier coaching and training services in the South West of England, serving entrepreneurs and executives of both public and privately-owned businesses.

And yes, it did lead to an invitation to work with an entrepreneur to commercialize a radio-based technology. On this occasion, I agreed to act as the CFO until venture funds had been received; then I would become CEO and the entrepreneur step up to Chairman.

This was completed successfully by means of a public offer. Over the next two years, the business was re-orientated from focusing on the security market to serving the global energy industry—leading to new opportunities for travel and engaging with different cultures.

New Horizons Beckoning

It was exciting to grow the business of the organization I was part of. However, outside of 'the day job,' broader horizons had appeared. I had begun to associate the pain and discomfort experienced by my body with the beliefs I held. I accepted a person's beliefs are energy, and if it does not flow, then it results in pain and discomfort.

This awareness accelerated after my wife came home and announced she wished to acquire a local shop selling whole foods and natural remedies. The focus of the shop was to serve those seeking awareness about the cause rather than the symptom of their complaint. We decided to bolster the reputation of the store by writing a newsletter outlining natural remedies as well as the latest scientific research in the field.

I was being drawn into a world outside of my limited experience—one where the flow of energy rather than intellect determined outcomes. It was a world where a connection to Spirit provided access to a broader perspective.

By now, my reading had altered to include esoteric and spiritual material. This helped me understand the link between our beliefs and our actions, no matter when and where we acquired them.

It is these beliefs the unconscious mind uses to direct over 95% of our daily thoughts, actions, and words.

And they determine whether or not we are successful and the quantum of that success.

To assist me, I had already become a Reiki Master and would shortly complete my training to be a Master of Neuro-Linguistic Programming, Time Line Therapy®, and its related

Creating Your Future® coaching as well as hypnosis and spiritual counseling.

Back at the Ranch

The group had just completed another successful fundraising to finance the acquisition of a complementary business with operations in the USA and Europe. We had exciting prospects, yet I was not content even though I had achieved the mark of success I believed would attract the love of my father.

By now, my back was troubling me so much I could hardly walk—which I now knew was not because I had strained it lifting a sack of oats for my wife or been digging too long in the garden. Some aspect of my life was not in balance with what my soul desired.

We all have defining choices to make—to live our passion or continue to follow the beliefs we have accepted for ourselves.

Unable to drive, go to work, attend the meetings, a space for reflection had been created.

One afternoon, moving slowly along a country path I had walked many times before, smelling the recent rain in the air, and looking at the large, fluffy white clouds moving across the sky, my head was full of *Position*: Purpose; *Position*: Purpose; *Position*: Purpose.

As I began the slow walk home, my choice had been made.

I decided to take the path of acknowledging my passion, my

purpose – helping others to transform and helping them to blossom and grow as they follow their own passions while living their full potential and leading the exponential life they have created and to guide them to their financial freedom to support this.

The Moment After

So began another phase of my journey. In a matter of weeks, the epiphany led me to resign—stepping out into the uncertainty of having no position, no job, and no means of supporting my family. With no certainty as to the next steps, I had taken the decision of leaving behind the *'security'* of a monthly salary and the other benefits of corporate employment.

Why? I chose to seek the flexibility and freedom every soul desires rather than the corporate position I had been striving for. My coaching since has included the realization that beliefs are not fixed. As Creation continues to expand, so can we— provided we are prepared to step out of our comfort zone. Being unwilling to move beyond their limits, most people never take action to create the dream they have or let go of the patterns that are limiting their life, including their business.

About one-third of clients we first meet have a limitation about their income and the wealth they can create. Around 40% are afraid of being visible. I believe these beliefs were created in their early years before the age of seven or in another life. These beliefs can be altered and removed, no matter where or when they were created.

Jena is one such client. Her belief was that if she was visible, then she would not attract support from those around her. To attract love, she needed to be invisible. Today she has launched her own healing business and is in the process of moving to a new location in Nature, away from city life.

I am waiting to hear how a prospective new relationship unfolds!

It is those who believe such patterns are fixed and immutable that limit their progress.

Safe in Your Comfort Zone?

All of us have beliefs for that is how we create patterns that enable us to cross the road safely, drive without being consciously aware of our individual actions, or avoid drinking a cup of boiling water. These are recorded by what I refer to as our 'Lifeguard', our unconscious mind. Its purpose is to keep us safe, and in this, it is a true master.

The only problem is that its definition of safety is based on our individual experiences. Hence, it seeks to keep us safe in our existing comfort zone, no matter how much we may dislike or wish to change it.

This is why so many entrepreneurs and executives never take action to accelerate the evolution of their lives and businesses—for their businesses reflect their inner world, whether limited or not.

The addition of my expertise in accelerating businesses when combined with that of shifting limiting beliefs is an unstoppable combination. To this, I add my perspective as a shaman to obtain insights from the unseen world.

A New Opportunity

Initially, I thought the focus of my coaching would be assisting fledgling start-ups and entrepreneurs break out of the stagnation they found themselves in, Spirit had other plans.

I was invited to join a team creating a new coaching program for IKEA. Its purpose to accelerate the business of a country, region, or individual store—each of which is considered a large or medium-sized business in itself!

After its launch, for nine years, I was one of the teams of coaches who worked with senior management to implement business acceleration. It was in this corporate environment I came to accept it was 'safe' to say *"This has good energy"* or *"Not so good energy"* when developing strategies and action plans. And, a jacket or business suit was not the required badge of office!

Another aside was that after my return from the nearly twenty countries I visited, my wife would ask what else I had been up to. She was asking whether I had once again been asked by Spirit to clear dense energy. We used to joke about who really set my travel agenda because there always seemed to be some extra-curricular activity involved. Whether it was releasing the energy of a Native American burial site or energetic debris in Hong Kong, Moscow, Warsaw etc., there was certainly a fulfillment at the end of each trip.

As my spiritual practice deepened and I became more open to receiving insights and guidance, I was called once more to be a shaman.

Being a Shaman

A shaman is someone who has been appointed and initiated by **Spirit and Nature** to look after the needs of his or her community.

Shamans believe all problems—physical, emotional or mental—have their root cause in imbalances between body, mind, and spirit. Healing this is achieved by accessing information in the unseen world to effect transformation.

The purpose is to **create an alignment** between the freedom and flexibility that our soul seeks and our personal beliefs, which limit what we can be, enjoy, and create in this life.

Despite my studies and certificates, I felt as though a part of me was missing. Although, I was unsure about what it was.

A friend contacted me to say she had been guided to take me to Avebury, in southwest England. This is another stone circle and part of a spiritual complex which includes the better known Stonehenge. Walking down the processional path away from Avebury, the sky became heavy with dark, grey clouds. Following the path up the slope and then down toward **Silbury Hill**, the rain became more intense.

Arriving at the base of Silbury Hill and looking up towards its peak, I remembered my last visit.

I had been leading a ceremony on the Hill when a participant had died. Swearing never to use my powers as a shaman again, I had renounced shamanic practice.

After completing a ceremony of forgiveness, release, and gratitude, we began to walk away from Silbury. Turning to say our last goodbyes to the Hill, a shaft of sunlight broke through the leaden sky, its beam passing straight over the peak of Silbury Hill—a confirmation that all was now complete.

Since then, I have used insights to guide many people regarding the real causes of their limitation and the optimal direction for them to take.

I use my unique abilities to combine insight with the practical experience of the business world to guide entrepreneurs and executives to *take action* to produce real success—being the Shamanic CEO!

Steven from Colorado Springs had a belief he would not be loved if he earned more than $175,000 or had savings of more than $10,000; yet his desire, his calling, was to create an innovative, multi-million dollar conscious business. He had a history of financial failure in his lineage. My insight was that his desire was never going to materialize, no matter what actions he took because of his personal beliefs and family lineage.

Today, with the limits gone, he is having fun accelerating the conscious business and has re-ignited the relationship with his wife.

Clare also had a passion to help others change their life; Although, her mental chatter kept telling her she was not good enough to do so. She had tried doing this without success—ultimately returning to a job she did not enjoy. After changing her beliefs and being provided with new approaches to gain clients, she returned to her business, which began to grow.

Her vision has now moved from surviving to financial freedom—allowing her to take exotic holidays! She has also allowed herself to open a new relationship with a life partner.

Big Steps

In 2010, my family moved to Central Portugal to be closer to

Nature and begin the next nine-year cycle of our development. The month before we caught the ferry was dominated by my very last bout of severe back pain. Friends helped pack all that we were taking as I could not bend, let alone fill boxes!

Every day, we look out onto the highest mountain in Portugal— Serra da Estrela (Mountain of the Star); some of our views can be seen by visiting www.quintadaluz.org. Here, along with my wife, we offer VIP days as well as retreats and workshops.

Prompted by this last back pain, The Seven Secrets to Living in Harmony was written during our first year in Portugal. Each of the Seven Secrets is linked to one of the prime seven chakras, or energy centers, in our body. Because I was afraid what others might think, there was no mention of a chakra in the book nor the fact I am a shaman even though shamanic practices are outlined!

To me, these concepts did not fit with the beliefs I had about working in finance and corporate management. They were worlds apart, and *"Never the twain shall meet."*

I was not being true to what I believed. As a result, the manuscript sat gathering dust until an event I hosted at the San Luis Rey Mission in San Diego.

The Saturday evening featured a fire ceremony as part of the event. Standing by the cooling embers while chatting to one of the participants, who had said he was a publisher, he pointed up to a hawk. It had come to perch at the top of the tall pine next to us. Returning to our conversation, we were suddenly aware of the hawk passing a few feet over our heads before turning upward and spreading its wings in the last light of day.

It was the moment after I asked if he would publish <u>The Seven Secrets</u>. The rest, as they say, is history.

When Ted McGrath sent me his foreword, I was taken aback by what he wrote, for the outsider often sees what we cannot. It confirmed to me that others could see my passion, as well as skills and expertise.

To quote it, *"The one thing you need in life is perspective and awareness of the right path for you. I can assure you that Gregory's principles and life experience will pass on the wisdom and knowledge you need to uncover your true path. Ultimately, it is the path of Joy, which Gregory has found."*

A Fire Ceremony

The fire ceremony is one of the shamanic practices I suggest to clients and participants in my challenges. The process is to:

1. Write down on a piece of paper as many of your beliefs you desire to release.
2. Write down on another piece of paper the outcomes you desire in your life.
3. Light a candle or a fire, and then tear the paper into strips, one for each point.
4. Then with due ceremony, read each point you wish to release and place the paper into the flame. Once complete, do the same for the outcomes. Be aware of any feelings as you watch each piece of paper burning in the flame.

Many ask why they should burn the positives. The answer is that fire brings transformation, and transformation is needed to create what is not yet present in your life.

As Steven reported after completing this, *"The candle exercise. In a word: potent! After burning the two sheets, saying a prayer... I felt free..."*

Some Conclusions

In reading through this chapter, you may have noticed a theme constantly appearing. It is one which underlies all healing and creation—no matter whether it is for your business or personal development. To achieve sustainable success, you need to be aware of:

1. Beliefs that are restricting your life—both business and personal
2. Recurring patterns that are directing your life through their stories
3. The inner conflicts they are creating—usually felt as pain and discomfort in your body
4. Your acceptance that you can change these and choosing to do so
5. Gaining insights as to your full potential and having the vision to create and live it

Surveying my students and clients over the past two years, I discovered almost 95% reported feeling burned out in some way. Additionally, everyone reported they felt resistance to taking a step because of a fear related to an unknown trauma.

Because of my own experience and work, my understanding of burnout is more refined than most sociologists and psychologists.

I also have a different definition of trauma.

To me, trauma is any **event, experience, or memory that creates inner conflict**—which in turn keeps us from loving and accepting our authentic self.

2019 marks the start of a cycle in which we are all asked to speak our truths and live our lives as ourselves rather than who we think we are. Each of us is being guided to make a **fresh start, turn over a new page, or take action on a new project/ venture**.

To do so, each of us must gain insights into the **grander, more inspiring personal vision your soul desires** of you. Only then can we nurture the ground in which they will grow.

However, very often, we do **not embrace new possibilities** for a very simple reason.

Our Lifeguard, our unconscious mind, prefers that we stay within our **existing comfort zone**—the one we know.

It is **your choice whether or not you do so**.

What I can tell you is that, in March 2019, **the Great Awakener—Uranus—entered the secure, grounded Taurus.** Uranus is about freedom, revolution, and tearing down boundaries—embracing those who think differently and going where you have never been before. It ignited a **transformative**

spark in us all that will change every facet of your life over the next seven years.

Derrick had experienced burnout as an M.D. In particular, he had difficulty aligning his awareness of the side effects of prescription drugs and the potential of other approaches in healing the cause and not the symptoms for his patients. He had the idea to launch an alternative holistic service to wealthy clients he knew.

He had attracted a like-minded team who were eager to support his idea. At the launch meeting, it was suggested he visit the prospective clients to confirm their interest. When he did, he found it was not a service they were interested in buying.

In rebuilding Derrick's trust in his vision, what emerged was an offer focused on serving the desires of recently retired couples who had chosen to move into serviced estates. Their desire was to enjoy life to the full—now they had the freedom to do so. Although they are very different clients, they are ones Derrick is excited to be serving!

For those of you seeking to grow your own business and accelerate your life, here is a link to download an E-book I have written 7 Mystical Ways to Accelerate Your Business and Your Life.

To Find True Contentment

True contentment will help you gain complete congruence **between your values and your purpose;** like a hand in a glove, you will feel strong, happy, healthy, and fully integrated as a person. This will also be reflected in your business. You will develop a kind of courage that makes you completely unafraid to make decisions and take action. You will see your whole life improve when you live by the values you most admire.

Never be afraid to be yourself in everything you do. When you **stand in your personal power and acknowledge who you really are, miracles happen**. Live your purpose and passion. That is the way to live consciously and accelerate your business.

For business is a vehicle for **healing all those places where you learned that you had to compromise who you are to create success**. It is the place where you craft your self-expression YOUR way.

Always remember to celebrate your wonderful qualities. You will soon discover, the more you love yourself, the more you will be able to give love to others—and the more others will be able to love you, thus creating more harmony in your life! You will achieve this by accelerating your business as it serves others.

If there is anything I can do to support you or add value to your life in any way or if you have thoughts on this chapter, please let me know—even if only to say hello. To send me a message, the easiest way is to go to www.gregoryreecesmith.com and click on the contact tab.

I look forward to hearing from you, hearing about your own successes, and exploring how we can help create harmony for all—together.

One last request. If this book has helped give you clarity in leading your life and living your passion, your purpose, then do something for others you love. Give them this book or let them borrow your copy and ask them to read it. Better yet, give them their own copy as a gift of love. Use words such as *"I love and appreciate you, and I want you to have the harmonious life of your dreams. Please read this."*

Then you may receive similar emails, like this one, from Kim, one of my Danish clients:

"Thank you for what you have helped me achieve on multiple areas in my life.

You are brilliantly talented and I loved our sessions and you still reside inside my heart. Thank you Gregory for the support, tutoring, help, teachings and your love.

I am not sure if you needed it, or I needed this...one thing is for sure, It feels great telling you this and be able to thank you with all of my heart."

Thank you for the investment you have made in reading this chapter and the book. **Blessings to you on your own journey through this wonderful life.**

> *"If you change the way you look at things,*
> *the things you look at change."*

> Wayne Dyer

Gregory Reece-Smith

Gregory Reece-Smith is known as the Shamanic CEO. A CEO and popular business and life coach with a Master's in Business Administration. As a coach, he brings to the table several decades of practical experience working with small businesses as well as international corporations like IKEA, to help people take action and produce real success in their lives.

Gregory helps executives and entrepreneurs accelerate their business and personal lives by providing valuable insights and perspectives from his shamanic practice and his experience in business. In helping people move beyond their fixed beliefs, he helps them achieve personal and financial freedom where none existed before.

Contact Information

Website: www.shamanicceo.com
Email: gregory@gregoryreecesmith.com
Facebook: https://www.facebook.com/gregoryreecesmith
LinkedIn: https://www.linkedin.com/in/gregoryreecesmith/
Twitter: https://twitter.com/grs2030
Pinterest: https://www.pinterest.pt/greecesmith/shamanic-ceo/

LIVE YOUR DREAM – ATTRACTING ABUNDANCE WITH E.F.T.

GUS SOUTHEY

Have you ever tried living your dream? Or perhaps you have a dream that seems completely unreachable? Or maybe your life feels like a nightmare where dreams don't exist? Before I woke up spiritually, so to speak, and became a certified Law of Attraction Coach, my life wasn't exactly satisfying. I was stuck in my own lonely and miserable world that was like the ultimate nightmare I could conjure for myself. In fact, it became so intense that it forced me to open my eyes and see the bigger picture. I finally realized that both nightmares and dreams are entirely self-created, and my awakening allowed me to choose exactly what sort of dream I wanted to live.

My career took a massive correction in 2014 when I decided to leave the corporate world for good. To be honest, I never knew what I wanted to do after high school and ended up completing a degree in Accounting in order to secure my future. The succeeding twelve years as an accountant and financial advisor provided me with almost no job satisfaction and an extremely volatile commission-based income. It was only once I completely let go of my painful past that I truly started thriving

—not just surviving.

I began attracting an abundant life of passion, including my ability to use and teach the Emotional Freedom Technique (E.F.T.). My suffering was a portal to self-realization—that my past was just an unhappy memory and a bundle of thoughts that I clung to and nothing more. Happy memories are wonderful to have; however, when we completely identify ourselves with our past, we can never fully appreciate life, which is always happening NOW. Similarly, the future is an illusion consisting of thought forms the mind creates and is the underlying cause for so much stress in our lives. The present moment is normally completely overlooked as a means to an end.

Our mind, also known as our Ego, always needs to achieve some future goal in order to feel satisfied. However, that satisfaction is always short-lived. Soon, something else is required to experience any sense of fulfillment. Our so-called happiness is fleeting, whereas real and eternal joy can only be found in the present moment. Everything occurs in the 'Now' and we are able to access that permanent joy at any moment. Living in the present is a wonderful gift because life itself is always now, and we are an expression of that life. Eckhart Tolle, the famous author, once said, "You are not separate from the whole. You are one with the sun, the earth, the air. You don't have a life. You are life." I totally agree with this statement because it's a perfect and beautiful summation of how I feel since transforming my own life. It also reaffirms my faith in life itself, rather than trusting my own illusory self, or me and 'my life'.

The foundation of my E.F.T. coaching is based on the universal 'Law of Attraction'. Since this law represents one of the 7 Spiritual Laws of Success, I've written a brief summary explaining how the other six Laws intrinsically accompany it. Essentially, it is a logical interpretation of how all of these powerful laws interrelate and affect one another as well as our own daily lives.

7 Essential Laws of Success

Are you worthy to be wealthy? **I. The Law of Pure Potentiality**

Ever since we were young, the subject of wealth has largely been looked at from an extremely negative perspective—mostly as a result of social conditioning. It was the cause of so much stress in my life and led me to believe that money was incredibly difficult to make. I was repeatedly told "It doesn't grow on trees," "Money is the root of all evil," and "Working really hard is the only way." After hearing this throughout my childhood, retirement seemed like that paradise where one could finally rest by attaining outright fulfillment, which often never arrives. On the other hand, as I proved to myself, if you are open-minded and are aware that you have the potential and ability to achieve anything, including an abundant life, then that is exactly what you will attract. A phrase I love to share while coaching is "You are Pure Potential by Nature." Worthiness is our birthright, yet most human beings are absolutely convinced that it is something we have to earn. The well-known cyclist phrase, a sport renowned for its suffering, is a befitting illustration—the winner is the one who suffers the most.

Are you mindful of your emotions? **II. The Law of Attraction**

This law is fundamental to my coaching practice, and it transformed my life once I realized that it affects every single one of us, regardless of our beliefs. If we are feeling negative emotions, we draw in and experience negativity. If we are feeling positive emotions, we draw in and experience positive life experiences. We can attract only those qualities we possess. This confirms the age-old proverb, "You reap what you sow." While I was a financial advisor with no salary, there was immense pressure for me to find new clients to generate a steady income. I lived in a state of perpetual anxiety and was trapped in my own stressful world. I finally realized if I wanted to experience freedom and joy in my life, I must feel that freedom and joy throbbing through my veins here and now. By living in the present moment, I enjoy and appreciate my life every single moment. This is also true regarding abundance. If you are optimistic and 'view the glass half full', you will attract an abundant life.

The term 'abundance' is often associated purely with wealth; however, money will never buy you happiness. Abundance should firstly be perceived and experienced as pure limitless joy by itself. This is why I first guide people to let go of all past financial trauma and related suffering. Once they are free from deeply ingrained negativity, abundance in all forms can begin to flow into their lives.

Can you achieve anything you desire? **III. The Law of Deliberate Creation**

Our thoughts create many of our emotions—both wanted and unwanted—and those emotions trigger the Law of Attraction into action. Conscious or aware thought, on the other hand, will invariably produce positive emotions and will always attract that which you seek. In other words, when you give thought to something you desire with an innate belief, you are in an optimal place to receive it. Therefore, you can achieve anything you want only if you truly believe that you can do it. For example, I only attracted success after letting go of all my doubt caused by past pain I accumulated throughout my corporate career, including the outrageous belief that my self-fulfillment was only achievable through endless struggle and toil.

So, how is this different from the Law of Attraction?

The difference between the Law of Attraction and the Law of Deliberate Creation is that the Law of Attraction is like a boomerang. Everything in our universe, including our bodies, is a form of energy. Our human emotions directly influence what level of energy vibrations we emit, which will determine exactly what we attract to us. The Law of Deliberate Creation is offering a vibration consciously and no longer creating by default. Unless we are aware of these laws, we are offering a vibration unknowingly or unconsciously. It explains why pessimistic people continuously attract negativity. They constantly suffer and are unaware that they are doing it to themselves. My prolonged suffering inspired me to coach others to become aware of this phenomenon and transform their lives.

You can create limitless abundance if you believe that you can do it. However, in order to truly believe anything, you need to feel positive about it right here and now. You must live in a state of optimism as though you've already achieved your goal. Otherwise, you will continuously rely on reaching that goal to find lasting joy or satisfaction.

Are you attached to your possessions? **IV. The Law of Detachment**

The Law of Detachment says, "In order to acquire anything in the physical Universe, you have to relinquish your attachment to it." You shouldn't have to achieve or acquire anything to give yourself a sense of fulfillment or completeness. This should not discourage you from being creative or no longer desire what you want to create. It means that you no longer identify yourself with it.

While I was still a wealth manager—striving to generate commission from new and existing clients—I was completely attached and identified with this endeavor. I spent almost every hour of every day worrying about it. This law simply taught me that to create abundance, I needed to detach myself from it. After I started coaching and living my passion, wealth was never an issue again. Besides needing money to survive, I never required it anymore in my life to find fulfillment. In fact, I began attracting a continuous stream of decent income soon after relinquishing my attachment to it.

Once you accept the way things are regardless of your wealth, you are detached from it and will feel a sense of freedom and relief. These positive emotions will become more familiar and soon become your normal experience over time. You will only stop worrying about your possessions once you detach yourself from them and consequently transcend any neediness.

Are you living in a state of allowing and acceptance, or, in a state of resistance? **V. The Law of Allowing/Acceptance**

This is the principle of least action and no resistance. Once you are accepting and allowing life to unfold, you are 'going with the flow.' I love using the analogy of 'life is a river' because it perfectly depicted my own journey as well. Instead of relentlessly paddling upstream to achieve one definitive goal, simply turn the boat around. Start appreciating the beautiful surroundings by becoming one with the stream, and enjoy the entire sojourn by floating effortlessly down toward the sea. Just as a river is destined to reach the vast ocean, so are we destined to return home to eternity. By applying the Law of Allowing, I naturally attracted absolute freedom and tranquility into my life.

This powerful law allows us to feel free in our relationships to be who we are; feel free in our career to do what we want; and feel free in our lives to create whatever we desire. There are two ways to apply this law. Firstly, accept others by allowing them to be as they are. Secondly, accept who we are by allowing ourselves to receive that which we truly desire. Life no longer feels like an uphill struggle because we've accepted and allowed ourselves to be who we really are. This means we no longer pretend to be someone we're not. Assuming various identities or playing different roles is simply a desire to argue with, or, resist what is. Shifting to our positive authentic selves allows life to be a wondrously sincere experience.

Are you giving without expectations? **VI. The Law of Giving & Receiving**

Applying the Law of Giving & Receiving is a natural desire after allowing yourself to become completely free. Appreciation and love, through alignment with the source, is the ultimate giving back. When we live a life of pain and struggle, we have nothing to give back. While I struggled relentlessly for so many years in the corporate world, my life was absent from all joy and peace. Essentially, I had nothing of value to offer because I was living an exact replication of what I was giving. I discovered that nothing could be more fair than life as you are living it. For as you are thinking, you feel and vibrate; and as you vibrate, so shall you attract. The powerful Law of Attraction confirms this, so you are getting back the essence of what you are giving.

Today, feel free to give whomever you encounter a gift, e.g., a compliment, a 'thank you', or just about anything. At the same time, receive gifts gratefully. Keep circulating wealth by giving and receiving care, affection, appreciation, and love. When you give without expectations, you will receive without limitations. You are giving without needing or seeking any reward from your action, and this attracts endless abundance into your life. It is the Law.

What is the purpose of your life? **VII. The Law of Purpose**

Finally, you seek your higher Self. Do not continue living without honoring the vocation your soul is calling you to pursue. Use your intuition, or gut feeling, to discover your unique talents and true passion in life. Ask yourself how you are best suited to serve humanity. In my case, I stopped following my head and began following my heart, i.e., I let go of my mental or egoic desire to achieve so-called 'success' and instead allowed my true sense of Self to guide me towards my life purpose.

Using your unique talents and serving others brings unlimited bliss and abundance. This basically means that your priority in life is to awaken, also referred to as Self-Realisation. Once you find your authentic Self, you are living an optimal life for you and everyone else! To experience your natural state of well-being, self-acceptance is essential. This firstly requires acceptance, rather than resistance, of the present moment, including yourself and your current life situation.

A prevailing lesson to take away from these 7 Essential Laws of Success is to accept the 'Isness' of your present situation at this moment to gain any clarity or direction in life. Eckhart Tolle's following quote also highlights the importance of 'Acceptance.' He says, "When you complain, you make yourself a victim. Leave the situation, change the situation or **accept** it. All else is madness."

Accepting the "Isness" of This Moment

Life is always experienced as the present moment. Our life situation 'is as it is' right now. Yet, countless people live in a habitual state of discontent and constantly complain about their life. This means they are resisting what is because they believe that true happiness and eventual fulfillment will only be found sometime in the future. However, the future doesn't exist because it cannot be experienced. It's a mythical thought form in the head. When the future arrives, it can only be experienced as the present moment.

What could be more ludicrous than denying or not accepting one's present life situation when the present moment is all there ever is. If we truly believe and associate real happiness with some future goal achievement, we spend almost our entire life missing out on the joys and wonders of life itself, which can only be experienced now. Therefore, acceptance of 'what is' is a fundamental step toward a peaceful life. Resisting, or non-acceptance, of what is will always lead to continual pain and suffering.

My life story epitomizes how essential this concept is. Since the age of ten, I started living in my own abysmal world of anxiety. I even began experiencing mild blackouts and was consequently diagnosed with epilepsy. My entire identity embodied this cruel image of myself. Instead of accepting my situation, I took pleasure in resisting it by convincing myself I was terminally afflicted for life. What I resisted, therefore, persisted. In fact, this resistance amplified my suffering, including regular seizures, to such an extent that by the age of thirty-four, I could no longer live with myself. I finally realized that 'myself' was an entirely fictitious identity I had created of 'poor little me.' My acceptance of this reality provided my own liberation and transformed my life. All my so-called burdens were transmuted into wonderful challenges.

Non-acceptance of What Is: A Real-life example

Let's consider the current state of the US economy as an example of non-acceptance of what is. It's still the largest economy in the world according to its GDP. However, if you delve a little deeper, you'll be shocked to discover that over the past several decades, US national debt levels have soared thrice its annual GDP. This means that the country's monetary borrowing and expenditure far outweigh its capacity to pay it back. It's also the reason why it has been able to boost and maintain its status as the global 'Super Power', in terms of its economy as well as its military strength, for so long. An economic collapse is highly likely because you cannot continually borrow more and more money without paying it back and not face the consequences.

I believe the core reason why the US has found itself in this predicament is because of its non- acceptance of the bare facts. Obstinate and indefinite over-borrowing is destined for a dire ending, and both the Government and Federal Reserve have successfully covered up this debt issue for a long time. Many Americans have also been socially conditioned to believe that the accumulation of large debt from excessive use of their credit cards is perfectly acceptable. This leads to overspending, which can become addictive because it allows you to live beyond your means. Indebted people then become even more reliant on borrowed money so they can continue spending it lavishly. They believe that money can buy them happiness, which it certainly can't. Happiness derived from material things is superficial. It's a fleeting happiness—not a pure inner joy that is unaffected by one's possessions.

Inner acceptance brings peace. Once you accept your life situation for what it is, a huge sense of relief arises within you because you're no longer resisting the truth and intentionally deceiving yourself. The power of acceptance applies to any life issue or situation. It provides the foundation for all joyful and successful endeavors. This is why the 'Law Of Acceptance' is included as one of the Seven Essential Spiritual Laws of Success. Life's so-called problems are then viewed from a more positive perspective and are called challenges.

Life is full of challenges. Even those resulting from personal devastation are incredibly valuable learning experiences. I avoid using the word 'problem' because it has negative connotations. All problems are created by the mind, whereas challenges are wonderful opportunities to express ourselves and evolve as beings. I experienced a life-altering challenge five years ago while I was a financial advisor. I was earning a solely commission-based income by selling various alternative investments, and I faced a stark reality. I had to either increase my sales or be forced to resign and start a whole new career, preferably one with a stable income. My entire wealth management career was hanging by a thin thread, and I felt doomed to fail.

Sure enough, this challenge rocked me to the core. After several more fruitless months, I had no choice but to leave. It was a harrowing experience. Nonetheless, I soon accepted my situation and was immediately consumed by a huge sense of relief. I realized that my greatest challenge in life had also become my greatest teacher. Instead of labeling myself and my situation as a 'failure,' I saw it as a massive opportunity. I felt free for the first time in my life because I let go of everything from my past. I had no job, yet I had no worries. My acceptance was my bridge to the non-physical source of energy, or pure consciousness, which was a revelation for me. Life then started working in my favor to pursue my passion and build my own coaching business. I had finally allowed myself to tap into my natural state of well-being.

It's also essential to understand that acceptance of 'what is' doesn't mean that you should continue to tolerate a painful situation or dwell in some form of suffering. It means that you accept, rather than resist, your current situation. This allows you to take appropriate action if required, because you have risen above your mind's judgmental labeling of everything. A painful situation often leads to further suffering because your mind believes it needs to continue doing something and suffers more to overcome its problems. The illusory future is where its only salvation lies; however, this can never manifest because your mind lives in a continuous state of denial or non-acceptance of what is in this moment. Once you let go of the painful past and the need for a fulfilling future, your suffering is no longer seen as a threat—but a blessing only visible in the present moment.

Suffering is a wonderful teacher. Ironically, it is actually a blessing and often a person's only spiritual teacher. If I had not suffered, I would not have written this chapter and built my coaching business. Most people believe that life requires great effort, from start to finish, to achieve their final goal of self-fulfillment—normally in the form of a happy retirement. I'm not denying that it can be extremely challenging at times; however, believing that eventual success is a reward requiring a lifetime of struggle, toil, and turmoil is absurd. This makes the entire journey an arduous and painful experience for various reasons.

Firstly, the pressure to pursue and reach this final goal continues to mount and is rarely achieved as intended. A tranquil retirement often never arrives. Yet people wear their life's scars like a badge of honor with immense pride. For instance, I clung to my endless suffering and it became an integral part of my identity.

Secondly, living with the intention of pursuing some fictitious idyllic future is completely nonsensical. I spent a large part of my life striving for my future success, which didn't exist except as a surreal thought of some form of utopia in my mind. But the future doesn't exist. It never arrives because life can only be experienced now as the present moment.

Finally, the present moment is treated as a means to an end and is hardly even noticed by many people. My need to find future fulfillment remained at the top of my life's agenda for years, and I almost completely overlooked 'the Now'. But life is never not now. It's all there ever is.

My protracted suffering became a blessing in disguise. It lead

to my salvation once I realized that all things happen for a reason. My mistakes helped me evolve as an individual and all the pain I previously suffered provided a portal to celestial bliss. It taught me that regret serves no useful purpose, because it denies how each and every life experience plays a vital role to help awaken and transform ourselves. In truth, we can never get it wrong because our world of polarities exists as a means for us to become consciously aware and realize who we really are— extensions of pure positive energy. Excessive use of the word 'wrong' is pessimistic and is normally judgmental. It originates from an emotional state of compunction or superiority, i.e., from our ego or false sense of self. Alternatively, once the glass is seen as half full, all events are viewed from an optimistic perspective and life is not so threatening anymore. Our little scruples and unpleasantries begin to dissolve, and they are no longer that unpleasant anymore.

Serenity does not have to be an idealistic thought formed in the head or come at the cost of one's own inner peace. It can become a reality in our daily lives. Why wait until a ripe old age to reward ourselves with our lifelong goal of serenity when we have the power to access it right now. This beautiful phrase from the Bible, as quoted by the Lord, provides an apt summation: "The kingdom of heaven does not come with signs to be perceived." Once fear is transcended, eternal love remains.

FEAR is an acronym for **F**eeling **E**xcited **A**nd **R**eady. Once you view it from a positive perspective, it is transformed from a negative emotion to a positive emotion. We begin to realize that all negative emotions are fear-based and created by our ego or false self. Fear is the polar opposite of love and is an emotion that is self-created by our negative thoughts produced by our Ego. However, it can be used as a friendly reminder to stop thinking and become still and totally present here and now. Fear cannot survive in the present moment—the only moment there is. In fact, the Ego finds stillness quite indigestible because our mind is no longer operating to conjure up negativity. Stillness awakens us to become aware of our true 'higher selves' as Eternal Beings of Unconditional Love. Our awareness confirms that we're an integral part of the one life or 'consciousness.'

What is Consciousness?

Consciousness is a spiritual term used to describe how aware we are of our true higher selves. Awareness is another word that can help explain how we, as eternal beings, are inseparably connected to Source Energy or the One Life. God is another term frequently used, especially by many religions, although it is often misinterpreted and misunderstood as a separate being or entity. These are all different ways of attempting to portray our origin and true nature, which is actually ineffable. It can only be experienced for oneself in the present moment, the only moment there ever is. This 'Presence', a form of consciousness, is the infinite non-physical energy underlying everything in our finite, physical Universe, without which nothing would exist. It is also the source of pure unconditional love and greater intelligence, which is eternal.

Energy is constantly vibrating at certain frequencies, depending on various factors and conditions. In fact, our human emotions also influence and determine what frequency we as physical beings are vibrating at. This is an extremely powerful concept to grasp because it allows us to live consciously and be aware of how our feelings are affecting our energy levels and quality of life at any given moment. It has also been proven that positive emotions vibrate at much higher frequencies than negative emotions. World-renowned best-selling author Dr. David R. Hawkins published a book called *Power vs. Force,* and it explains how a

'Scale of Consciousness' he created uses Applied Kinesiology to test the vibrational frequency of different emotions. He was able to successfully prove how, on a logarithmic scale, high vibrations (+ve emotions) counterbalance low vibrations (-ve emotions) exponentially.

The Scale of Consciousness is based on a log scale of 1–1000 and depicts how an Expanded Consciousness, consisting of purely positive emotions, is far more powerful than a Contracted Consciousness, which includes all negative emotions. Because the scale of power advances logarithmically, higher levels of emotion far outweigh and counterbalance lower-level vibrations. He was able to calculate the critical consciousness level at 200. He determined that the emotion of Courage represents this 'tipping point' between manifesting a life of passion and meaning, rather than merely living a life of survival. Most humans live unconsciously in a survival mode because their emotions are generally negative and fear-based, falling below the critical level of 200, i.e., they are either bored, just getting by, or suffering more extensively.

For most of my life prior to becoming a coach, I suffered from extreme negative emotions, including guilt and shame. In fact, these two represent the lowest levels and most harmful forms of all emotions according to the Scale of Consciousness. I was constantly plagued by intense feelings of blame and humiliation, and my life view was both evil and miserable. My eventual acceptance and acknowledgment of my unhappiness are what transformed my life. Instead of merely surviving, I began enjoying life and started thriving. I finally had the courage to let go of my painful past, which was critical and instrumental toward the process of my empowerment. It was my turning point from living in a predominant state of fear to one of love.

Human consciousness is also expanding more rapidly now than ever before, so people are spiritually waking up and realizing that we don't face reality, but we create our own reality. The universal Law of Attraction is then able to work in our favor because we're living consciously and deliberately manifesting what we truly desire in life. Once our overall level of consciousness calibrates at over 200, true freedom can be enjoyed and experienced for the first time because we're no longer imprisoned in the negative mindset of our Ego—our false sense of self. Life starts working in our favor, rather than against us, when we have the courage to let go of our painful past.

The fact that we're all extensions of source energy in the physical world means there are no limits to what we can actually achieve—it's in our nature. A fundamental requirement for attracting great things depends on whether we are in alignment with source energy and our higher selves or with our egos (fictitious selves). It's important to have a desire or goal to work toward; however, it is completely meaningless if you're not allowing yourself to experience the goodness of that fulfillment now. The Universe doesn't care what thoughts or wants you may have, it only responds to what vibration you are emitting, i.e., the Law of Attraction will always prevail and manifest whatever you choose on a vibrational level. It's as simple as that. All that exists is universal well-being in all its abundance—which we are either allowing or resisting, i.e., we're letting that well-being in or we're keeping it out.

Practicing good thoughts will stop resistance to our own well-being. A flood of positive ideas and possibilities come our way once we're aligned with our true power. I personally practice basic mindfulness of what I'm thinking and feeling at any given moment. It's a technique that I've assimilated as part of my daily routine. Life constantly astounds me with synchronicities as though I were creating my own luck. I'm able to experience all of my desires, not through struggle, but through my ease of letting go of past pain. Social conditioning equates great outcomes with long hard work, which is untrue. Abundance is our birthright and all that's required is an inner belief that this is so. Life then becomes easier as well as more enjoyable. In fact, absolute freedom can only be appreciated when we're no longer ruled by our thoughts and our emotions. It's why my passion is teaching the holistic technique called E.F.T., which literally frees us from our negative emotions by tapping into our innate freedom.

Attracting Abundance with the Emotional Freedom Technique (E.F.T.)

Since our human emotions control our energy levels, it's vital that we learn how to control our emotions. In other words, freeing ourselves from negative emotions is imperative to allow our bodies' energy meridians to remain unblocked and free-flowing. The Emotional Freedom Technique (E.F.T.), also known as 'Tapping', is an emotional needle-free version of acupuncture called acupressure. It has become an increasingly popular holistic process used for this very purpose. It is based on new discoveries regarding the connection between our body's subtle energies, our emotions, and our health. E.F.T. has been reported successful in thousands of cases covering a huge range of emotional, health, and performance issues. It often works where nothing else does.

Negative beliefs and social conditioning (i.e., our thoughts) regarding anything will create negative emotions and block our body's energy meridians. Once this blocked energy has been freed via Tapping, the powerful Law of Attraction will begin to transform our life by responding to our predominantly positive emotions. Therefore, E.F.T. allows us to deliberately create our reality, rather than just face it. The incredible life-transforming results I've witnessed, including my own, is what inspired me to teach it to others and also choose the following affirmation for my coaching practice: "We don't face reality, we create our own reality." In fact, I started 'walking my talk' soon after my life began to turnaround, and it wasn't merely a coincidence, it was perfect timing. By grasping this concept and practicing E.F.T., I literally 'Tapped Into my own Well-Being' to manifest a life of abundance. Tapping Into Well-Being literally means accessing our natural state of wellness, which we're either allowing or disallowing into our lives. Nature epitomizes this fact by observing how it constantly thrives in its natural state of well-being—flowing abundantly and unrestricted.

E.F.T. is based on the same meridian points used in traditional acupuncture, an ancient practice used for over five-thousand years to treat physical and emotional ailments, but without the needles! Instead, tapping with our fingertips on certain pressure points is used to input kinetic energy onto specific meridians in our body while we think about a specific problem. Many people have difficulty comprehending why you first need to accept the negative issue before pursuing positivity with affirmations and meditation. However, a light must shine on the darkness in order to solve the mystery—a fear, a worry, a physical pain or illness, an unresolved problem, etc. Until we acknowledge and deal with the negative issue, it will never be fully resolved and will continue to rear its ugly head, regardless of how positive we are. E.F.T. is therefore not only a powerful healer but also an extraordinary teacher. Tapping on these meridian points while focusing on the past negative belief and associated emotion engages both the brain's limbic system and the body's energy system and encourages a sense of safety and resolution.

As the science of epigenetics is proving, when we change our internal environment (emotions, beliefs, etc.), we allow external changes in our physical life circumstances to emerge. It explains why our beliefs and thoughts, which affect our emotions, have such a significant impact on our physical environment. This includes our health and the amount of abundance we attract. We can only attract a life of true success, abundance, and prosperity if we sincerely believe and feel this is possible. It's for this reason that I offer a 'Tapping Into Well-Being' course focusing entirely on abundance. (http://www.gussouthey.com/programs). I teach people to literally tap into their natural state of well-being, specifically shifting and reprogramming old beliefs regarding abundance to start living a more joyful and prosperous life that is both desired and deserved.

Life is Extraordinary

Life is truly extraordinary, or it's rather ordinary, depending on our perspective. In other words, life is an opportunity to thrive, or it's a journey to merely survive. These represent two typical human beliefs. We should often ask ourselves this fundamental question: Do I want to thrive, or do I only want to survive?

Most people also think of life as something they have or is 'theirs.' We are both socially and collectively conditioned to fear, from a young age, and believe that our lives are vulnerable and affected by external events or other people. This belief or mindset denies the fact that our mind can be a wonderful tool and reliable servant, but it can also be an ignorant and dangerous master. We are completely identified with almost every negative thought, which creates a life of stress and anxiety. Consequently, our minds are heavily influenced and no longer serve us beneficially. We basically become servants of the external world. However, life is not something we have or can claim ownership of because it isn't a thing and it doesn't belong to us. WE ARE LIFE.

Once I realized this for myself, an inter-connectedness, love, and appreciation for everything arose within me. My new belief, or knowing, transformed my entire view of life as well as my personal experience of it. Instead of feeling threatened and needing to protect myself, a deep inner peace constantly reminds me that I'm always connected and inseparable from the one eternal Life/Source/Consciousness. I no longer need to do anything in my life to feel fulfilled because I'm already a beautiful expression of life itself! In other words, peace is not something I need to search for because it's essentially my true nature. That blissful state is accessible to me at any given moment. I frequently use the following affirmations for inspiration: "Life is not a struggle, it's a blessing," "Simply be yourself, no excessive doing is required," and "You can only be free in this world, if you are free of this world."

I love to help and guide others by quoting the inspiring phrase "We don't face reality, we create our own reality." It reminds me of how I transformed my own life. Initially, by 'facing reality,' I allowed myself to live life in my own hell. Once I reached an ultimate low point, I realized how nothing could be more insane than living in an illusory hell and being my own worst enemy. It awakened and inspired me to begin 'creating my own reality,' and I finally experienced heaven, our eternal home, for myself.

I am now living my divine life purpose by teaching others how they can do the same.

Gus Southey

Gus Southey is a certified 'Law of Attraction' Coach, Energy Healer and Author who uses energy healing to guide people toward a life of unrestricted and free-flowing abundance. Money can't buy you happiness. On the contrary, abundance will only flow into your life if you're already happy for no reason. In his blogs and articles, Gus explains how E.F.T. (Emotional Freedom Technique), also known as 'Tapping', frees you from all negativity to allow joy and abundance to flow freely into your life. This involves energetically removing negative emotions, social conditioning, and beliefs by literally tapping (with E.F.T.) into your natural state of well-being. What you need (and what Gus provides) are proven actions that work to attract bountiful abundance, and his coaching motto is, "We don't face reality, we create our own reality". He also provides expert advice on live webinars hosted by The Wellness Universe, the world's first online directory and resource center to support and promote well-being on a global scale.

Contact Information

Website: http://www.gussouthey.com/
how-to-stop-self-sabotage-and-why-we-do-it
Facebook: https://www.facebook.com/groups/IWYWG/
LinkedIn: https://www.linkedin.com/groups/10335211/

10X 'Mindset Shift'

My Journey to Becoming a Disruptive Entrepreneurial Spirit

Iain Acton

This chapter is about my personal 'mindset shift' from aspiring to be a game changer to becoming a disruptive entrepreneurial spirit. It is a story about my personal growth and refusing to be defined by a single label and persisting through my various struggles at each critical 'mindset shift' from artist to employee to entrepreneur.

A pattern emerges during each 'mindset shift': business as usual, awakening, venturing, capability building, theory to practice, and connecting the dots. The 10X 'mindset shift' is a journey of learning, doing, and reflecting, but most importantly, it is about attaining the confidence that 10X improvements are not just desirable but possible.

Disruptive at Heart

Why would anyone want to be disruptive? Surely this kind of thinking is just going to get you into trouble. Surely disruption is bad? At least from the perspective of those being disrupted, it is. But for the disruptor, it is a means to an end! The person doing the disruption is merely trying to change a situation he/ she is deeply dissatisfied with. This drive to change something can be positive or negative, and that really depends on the overarching goal and whether changing the status quo will create more value for people.

The disruptor is motivated because they are uncomfortable with something. What I see around me is people working a long time getting to their comfort zone, and then getting far too comfortable. Later, they are only concerned with staying in their comfort zone. This chapter is not for such people.

I was a bit different when I was growing up. Okay, I know you're thinking—I was the 'disruptive' kid, the one in the back flicking food at other kids. (I wasn't.)

When I was a kid, I excelled in seeing the world differently. I would break things to pieces and invent new stuff. It did not always work as I expected it to, but it was new! I found it exciting—creating new stuff. I had the ability to see and conceive things differently than most other people.

On the downside, I struggled to write fluently and put things down on paper. I remember feeling frustrated every time I wrote an assignment. I would have to write a bit, reorder it, chop it up, rewrite the bit I had just written, write a bit more, reorder it, rewrite it, and so on. I was slow at reading.

I remember in my early twenties, I finally went in for an assessment and the lovely lady said to me that my real problem was that I was thinking faster than I could interpret and write what I was thinking.

Quite simply, I did not have a great working memory, so I could not capture all my thoughts before they evaporated. And once they 'evaporated,' I had to re-condense them. For me, this process was hard work and meant that writing was not an attractive activity. I would avoid it as much as possible. Some of my teachers thought I was stupid, most knew I was not, but there was only one who saw my creative abilities.

I'd found my first mentor in my art teacher. He took me under his wing, championed me, and gave me the confidence to know that my talents of seeing the world differently could be nurtured and honed. He got my artwork published in the school magazine, and three of my paintings hung around the assembly hall. I became one of the three school head prefects (head prefects managed all the other prefects). This was all because I had someone who championed me.

Through my teens, my belief was that I would become an architect or a designer. I planned it all out and started studying A-Level Math, Physics, and Art. This was supposed to lay the foundation for my design career. But things never really went according to plan.

While I excelled in Art, even winning the school art prize, I ended up failing physics and did okay in Math; University did not feel right at this stage. I needed time to rethink my plan and decide what direction I should take. I left school and started working at a reprographic house (stage before printing). The first six months were good, but I soon became bored with the drudgery of repetitive work. I quickly realized I needed to get back into my art.

A Blank Canvas

That is when I decided to go to foundation art school and then on to university.

At this point, my journey to becoming an artist felt like a destiny rather than a career plan. I still had a career plan; it was just simpler and less prescriptive. I started to follow my instincts and became comfortable with only planning a few years ahead.

The artist is often misunderstood. If you can draw, you must be a good artist! In reality, the artist is on a much longer journey to understand what he or she wants to say about the world. And this generally starts by learning how to draw stuff.

I had a natural ability to draw accurately, but it took me quite some time to learn that drawing accurately was not actually important to being a successful artist. Many people can draw accurately, but in most cases, it is not a valid differentiator. It is only a stepping stone to success, not success itself.

Drawing builds skills such as observing, interpreting, and recording the world. My journey to becoming an artist was about establishing my unique way of interpreting the world. I had to understand what subject to interpret, how to interrogate the subject, and then how to communicate it to that meaningful other—the audience.

A blank canvas is something all artists need to get used to dealing with.

In 1996, I started my foundation art course at Blackpool and the Fylde College. I became very good at interpreting local architecture and seascapes. Here, I was focused on elevating the beauty beyond what you could see; I wanted to get to some deeper interpretation of what I could see or feel.

By the end of the year, I was confidently collaging my stories together. I used discarded wooden door panels and cupboard panels and used them as a frame for seascape paintings at sunset.

All of the five pieces were sold out! To top it off, in the same week, I got my acceptance letter to the BA Fine Art Painting at the renowned Chelsea College Of Art. I remember waking up the next day with a warm feeling that I was finally at the start of building my career.

Chelsea was amazing! But I quickly found out that as much as I loved making art, I did not fit into the art world. I found it shallow, what some might call plainly 'pretentious.' I found this difficult to engage with, but I had to give it my all.

My work had progressed from painting seascapes to creating mixed media installations based on optical reflections and refractions in the city. These installations would only be viable for an elite gallery owner.

I had started to consume so much of the pretentiousness around me that I was on verge of becoming what I was consuming. I realized that it was not what I wanted. I knew I needed to just stay focused on keeping my head down and get the results that would help me progress.

I got a 1st for my practical work. But I was most proud of my

2:1 for my written work. Basically, I discovered that a word processing and visual planning software could help me with my working memory issues.

Dealing with My Artistic Mindset

Once I'd left Chelsea and London to move to the Midlands, I longed to be back there. After all, I had spent the last four years of my life eating and sleeping art. I wanted to take advantage of what I had learned and achieved. But reality hit home. I needed to earn a living. I needed a job.

First, I worked as an antiques restorer, then a 3D-design technician, a printmaking lecturer, and got my professional diploma in teaching and learning in 2003. But these were fill-in jobs. Ironically, what was once my biggest weakness, my writing, actually got me my first real career job. This job also enabled me to enroll on the MA Product Design in September 2003.

Three years after finishing Chelsea, I thought I might need to make a few adjustments here and there, but I was entrenched in my artist mindset. You see, product design requires certain visual sensibilities, but in reality that is only a small part of product design execution.

I really had to start over again to understand 90% of the work. The hard bit was rewiring my whole thought process away from being an artist. It was hard—switching from my subjective, unique understanding of the world to look at it from the perspective of the user.

In hindsight, this seems obvious; but at the time, I did not know why I could never get my thinking straight. I was trying to be a product designer, but I was still thinking like an artist.

I could not let go of this dominant, artist mindset. It was getting in the way. I was fundamentally misunderstanding the key principle of great product design—you design for the needs of the end-user. I was wrapped up in my own artistic needs and self-expression.

My artist mindset put me in risk of aligning my product design work to the pretentiousness of the world of art.

Fortunately, I was not just doing an MA in Product Design. I had my day job as a design research assistant at Design Knowledge Network. Within six months of joining, I was promoted and things really clicked about nine months into my new role.

I was asked to take on a project with a medium-sized sofa manufacturing company that employed around 350 people. After a brief tour of the factory, my colleague and I met the Managing Director. He got straight to the point.

"Sales are flat, costs are rising. We are looking for ways to increase sales, and we need to reduce manufacturing costs by 5% over the next 24 months. What can you do?"

I took a deep breath and said, "Well, from what I have just seen you have built an impressive manufacturing setup, have a well-drilled staff with great team spirit."

The MD smiled, more a grin than a smile, and I continued

confidently, "We can determine the specific market trends affecting your business performance. Our goal will be to align your product and manufacturing capabilities to the right opportunity in the market."

I paused briefly and continued, "In fact, I did some research a few months back that highlighted several..."

I was confident and clear about what we did. I then started to highlight the product development opportunities, building some rapport with MD so he knew that I knew what I was talking about—which I did. The conversation progressed swiftly. I went back to the office and drew up a proposal defining a series of research interventions around consumer behavior, changing customer needs, and follow-up work to include design research and strategy definition. The proposal was signed off by the Managing Director, and I got to work.

At this point, in 2004, there were two versions of me. On the product design MA, I was still trying to be an artist. As a business and design researcher, I was talking the language of CEOs and MDs. I felt like a walking contradiction.

On the one hand, I was lost and struggling to understand my personal direction and creative contribution, while on the other hand I had built a professional confidence I never knew I had.

My emotional, creative brain was irritated and frustrated while my rational brain was happy being rational. I just had to work out how to bring the two together. Looking back, I now understand that the MA Product Design became the vehicle to manage and resolve my mindset shift.

After about three weeks of desk and customer research for the sofa company, several themes emerged. However, one thing stuck out above all the rest: smaller sofas. At this time in 2004, conventional sofas were large three-piece suites. However, broader consumer living trends were small flats and compact modern houses. One gentleman I interviewed started telling me about how he was downsizing from a three-bed semi-detached house to a two-bed, ground floor flat. The kids had moved on, and he wanted to be in a more convenient location with less travel.

That insight combined with other broader trend data from desk research was enough to convince the sofa company to create a whole new range of compact sofas. It was a huge success. The order books at the next three shows were full. It would create over £2.5million in new sales over two years.

Working with local business leaders across the Midlands was genuinely inspiring. I was just grateful I could bring something valuable to the table that helped them gain that competitive edge. Over the next few years, I discovered the different facets of how to make a business grow. Initially, we pitched out services as a 'marketing strategy' or 'marketing plan,' but these were just buzzwords. What we did was understand the gap or pain the business was experiencing. This was about tuning into the business executive team, understanding the market they were in, and most importantly, the immediate challenges on their doorstep.

There were three things I could offer:
1. Create new propositions through product market alignment
2. Build reputation and trust through better storytelling

3. Access new customers by tapping new or hidden channels

Tactically, there were many ways to position and execute these offers, but they offered a way to engage a business using simple language.

By late 2005, I realized that my MA Product Design was a vehicle for me to challenge my underlying mindset. I had to resolve a conflict between the artist mindset that I had spent twelve years honing and the new mindset I needed to move forward with my new career trajectory.

The MA helped me adapt to and understand a new language in a protected environment. But my artist mindset was a stubborn beast and required a constant challenge. In the back of my mind, I was constantly fighting to keep the artistic values and sensibilities I had established over the last twelve years subdued.

I was afraid of losing something I had spent so long developing. I had built an artistic self, an identity if you like, with a particular way of seeing and interpreting the world that had turned into a habit—a very real way of being and having a purpose in the world. I wasted a whole week once on my MA Project work. I had become paralyzed by this fear of losing my artistic self. I needed to offload everything.

I went to see Graham.

Graham was a dynamic, edgy designer. He worked for some of the leading consumer brands in the market. Ironically, both his personal design work and commercial work was inspired by art. He was just the tonic I needed to bring clarity to my dilemma.

I told him about my day job work with companies and then about my struggles with the personal MA projects. After an hour or so listening and questioning, he proposed a solution, "Don't do personal projects." In the real world, designers work for clients. He was basically saying base all your work around the client's needs, and do not allow your personal agenda to feature. I had been struggling for almost a year because I was treating my MA projects from the perspective of an artist. That frank and open conversation showed me a route forward.

I realigned my MA projects with my client work. And I never looked back! But what I really learned was I will never lose the core of my artist mindset, I could go back to it at will. It's almost like riding a bike. You could get rusty, but you wouldn't forget it.

So I was building a new mindset, different from my artist mindset. The two ways of thinking overlap and work together. For example, my ability to deal with a blank canvas is transferable to design projects with a lot of unknown variables or a high level of uncertainty.

Over the following nine years, some forty plus business projects later, I was directly involved with creating upward of 10 million pounds in new sales revenue and supported efficiency gains of several million pounds. But I had started to become comfortable—comfortable with my office seat and comfortable with my methods.

Being comfortable really is a contradiction. On the one hand, you crave comfort; it can help you perform more efficiently. But on the other hand, it stops big improvement gains.

Building My 10X Mindset

You are not going to achieve a breakthrough if you're content with being comfortable. The only time comfort is good is if there is no way to improve or gain significant improvements, but in my experience, this is rarely true. I knew I was at a transition point. I had been getting comfortable for a while. Then, around 2010, I become aware of a concept called 'disruptive innovation.'

Disruptive innovation is about innovating in a way that causes big sloth-like companies to die. This is what Netflix did to Blockbuster. A small upstart company or project is often the protagonist. It innovates by building a new business model for a niche market segment. It manages to go under the industry radar at first. However, once the upstart dominates that niche, it then dominates another niche, and then another, until eventually the whole industry is turned on its head. Disrupted.

Netflix created more value for less cost. Its business model was fundamentally different to Blockbuster's, even though the core product was essentially the same.

I realized that I wanted to create more value for less cost. I wanted to be a disruptive innovator. I got the key principles straight away. I wanted to help create 100 million pound opportunities with one upstart project rather than 10 million from 40 projects. But I was absolutely not in tune with this way of thinking.

This was the start of my 10X mindset shift.

Since I didn't know how to get there, I just continued reading the right books, educating myself, and surrounding myself with smart people.

"Align to the right market opportunity." This phrase was in most of my business research proposals from 2004; it was something I intuitively understood. When a company was stagnating in the market, its products and services tend to lack full alignment with the market. Some people say it's competitive threats that are at force, but from my perspective, copying the competition is not to be considered; differentiating from them is what should be the goal.

I was always focused on uncovering the right market opportunity so my clients shift their product back in line with the market trends and needs. It was not until 2012 that I really understood how to tackle the market alignment problem systematically.

The trend research I was doing was creating value, but it was not a systematic, repeatable process and was only focused on incremental innovations. I wanted to understand how to uncover bigger disruptive opportunities. I was going to need a better, more systematic approach.

Everything changed for me when I went to a workshop in 2010 called "Systematic Innovation – Trend DNA". This transformed what I knew about product development and creative problem solving. As I'd done quite a lot of brainstorming sessions, I thought I knew quite a bit about creativity. Well, I did know a bit, I just needed to know a lot more. One thing that left the biggest impression on me is how all systems evolve through a series of s-curves. Making a leap to the next s-curve required a discontinuous jump. Performing these jumps required lots of insight and great execution.

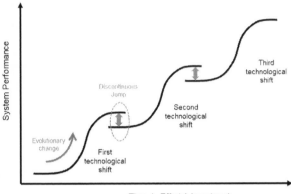

S-curves exaplain how systems evolve

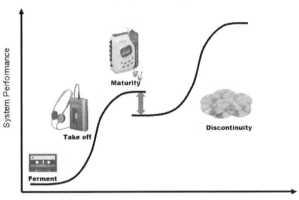

Example of an S-curve step-change in the music industry

At a high level, they grouped into technological, market, and strategy insights. This opened my eyes to a whole new systematic approach to creative problem-solving, and I met my Systematic Innovation mentor and soon-to-be business partner Professor Adrian Cole.

We worked together for around eighteen months on a few small projects using Systematic Innovation. Then we ran our first small and medium-sized (SME) business Systematic Innovation workshop for a group of six businesses. What was impressive about these ½ day workshops was that we got to know the limitations and characteristics of each business; we quickly recognized how we could help those that were ready for that help. Efficiency was key.

This workshop was a huge success, and we managed to take on two businesses as side projects, even as we were both working full time. My ambition about what I wanted to do next had started to become a reality already.

Now, I wanted to build capabilities to help companies or entrepreneurs figure out their next s-curve. Over the next 6 months, Adrian and I went about planning a new innovation consultancy business called Disruptive Lemonade.

In August 2012, I left my day job and Disruptive Lemonade was born. We officially started trading in October 2012.

Between 2010 and 2012, I spent months reading books on systematic innovation, disruptive innovation, and business model design. One notable read was the seminal book by Clayton Christensen *The Innovator's Dilemma*. I became fascinated by what might be considered by one person as counter-intuitive was totally logical and natural to another. I realized that it is all about what frames our intuition and judgment; it is our mindset that creates the frame. So a corporate mindset is very different from that of a disruptive entrepreneur. The good news is that both of these mindsets can be developed.

Let me go back to this phrase "Align to the right market

opportunity." There's a reason I keep bringing this up. There was a big gap in knowledge that I had to overcome if I was truly to understand markets and start to uncover 10X opportunities. *The Innovator's Dilemma* introduced me to the market concept 'Jobs-to-Be-Done'(JTBD), which is basically a theory of markets based on how customers define success.

This is subtle but truly transformative. Rather than describing the market as the product or who the customer is, it defines the market around the 'job' the customer is trying to get done.

Most people say we want to understand the customer, who are they, etc. While that might be true, the hook you hang everything off is the 'job' they are trying to get done. Your product or service only exists to help the customer get the job done. This is the foundational knowledge of my 10X mindset. It underpins everything.

Broadly speaking, there are three variables we need to understand to consider if a disruptive opportunity is viable: the market, the technology (the critical capability), and the strategy (how to position, package, and execute).

Now there is one thing I find really frustrating—when everyone jumps on the technology bandwagon and say they are building this or that disruptive technology. I speak to entrepreneurs, and they say we are building disruptive Artificial Intelligence (AI) tech or disruptive Internet of Things (IoT) tech.

So I ask them straight up—what is the acute underserved or overserved market need that this disruptive technology addresses? How have you validated it? Which niche market segment is in most pain? The answers are typically weak, not validated, or just blank.

Now the big problem with a technology-led 'disruptive mindset' is that the technology is at best only 1/3 of the picture. That means 2/3 is not about the tech. Technology has nothing to do with the actual market opportunity. The market does not care about your technology, and customers only care about the 'job' they are trying to get done.

Technology is an enabler of disruption rather than a determinant of its possibility. Disruption is a theory about markets rather than technology. This was the most important aspect of my 10X mindset I had to get right. Understanding how to systematically decode any market into the underlying 'jobs' and the varying segments with underserved and overserved needs are what enables a business to build a viable growth strategy. So aligning to the right market opportunity is the most fundamental activity of any type of innovation, but it is absolutely critical for uncovering disruptive 10X market opportunities.

Creating 10X mindsets

One of Disruptive Lemonade's early clients was a large automotive company. One of the big things we had to do with many of their teams was to develop the right mindset. One department we worked with was an engineering research team that was developing features for autonomous vehicles. It quickly became apparent that the engineers wanted to come up with better ideas for autonomous type features.

System problem solving was a natural place that the engineers gravitate to, but a broader approach to creativity was not always a key skill set of engineers. With Systematic Innovation, we could 'engineer creativity.' As you can imagine the term 'engineering creativity' went down well with engineers. It was during these projects that I started to understand a model for developing 10X mindsets.

It is based on the s-curve principle above and sees the mindset like any other system. One of the engineers, David, developed a 10X mindset by making the discontinuous jump from his engineering mindset as follows:

1. Business as usual
2. Awakening
3. Venturing and capability building
4. Theory to practice
5. Connecting the dots

David's challenge was to find breakthrough ideas and opportunities in the rapidly evolving automotive vehicles industry.

1. Business as usual

David is a deep-rooted technologist with a strong engineering background. He instinctively knows how things work. His role was about finding new technology capabilities using smart systems that make driving easier or more enjoyable. David was not always satisfied with the technology ideas he and his team selected. They really did not know which technology ideas would be most valuable and accepted by the market. Which ones would be most successful? Which ones would fail? Often they relied on personal judgment to select ideas.

His day-to-day engineering mindset was what I call the 'build a better mousetrap mindset.' David's s-curve analysis suggested his current mindset was reaching a performance limit. He had spent years optimizing his engineering mindset, but now he was at a stage where the law of diminishing returns applies—more effort and resources he spent on development equals less and less returns.

2. Awakening

We needed to help David make the jump into a new mindset s-curve. Like any discontinuous s-curve jump, you have a painful, uncomfortable period where you experience a drop in performance before you see improvements over 'business as usual.' His default engineering mindset needed a fundamental shift. He needed a big jolt followed by a structured programme of activity.

To begin the change required, David needed to formally acknowledge the mindset shift that could unlock his ability to create 10X more value. We helped David frame the context and nature of his challenge. As we broke the challenge down, he diagnosed himself. He told us what change was required.

The dimensions of his mindset (the way that solutions are formed) needed to broaden (less about engineering detail). His problem solving needed to go from micro to macro. He needed to expand his natural desire for systems knowledge to more fundamental knowledge about markets and business model patterns.

He began to understand that his new s-curve was not about optimizing engineering systems but about understanding and exploring the broader automotive market from the customer's perspective and how new business models could unlock more value. David needed to consider the fundamentals of why people buy and use cars and the broad spectrum of jobs that people use cars for in their daily life. While this might seem obvious to an outsider, it is not obvious when your task is to create and engineer a better car.

It is not too difficult to loosely hypothesize what new, disruptive business models might be possible in the automobile industry but to move from hypotheses to validation required more fundamental market-based questions to be asked that are far more challenging to answer. For example:

- What new market segments are likely to emerge for autonomous cars?
- What are the most important jobs for each segment?
- What customer jobs and related jobs are most unsatisfied?
- Which needs are underserved, overserved and adequately served for each customer segment?
- Which underserved segments or overserved segments should the company pursue?
- What market and product strategy will yield the best returns?

One of the common problems I identified while working with technology-driven entrepreneurs and corporate innovation teams is that the level and detail of market knowledge required to define opportunities is significantly underestimated. They don't know what they don't know and are not aware of what data collection is possible or required.

Let me be clear, markets are complex. There are literally hundreds of customer jobs and tens of thousands of needs that any industry is built on. They require specific approaches and structured, systematic data collection methods to uncover attractive 10X opportunities. Now, David does not need to be able to uncover these opportunities himself, he just needs to know that the customer job is the market, that they are definable in a very high level of detail, and they believe in the customer-driven approach.

In other words, he needs to be on board.

3. Venturing and capability building

David needed to make a big commitment to start his journey.

We worked with David and coached him in defining his personal objectives and helping him create a realistic plan. David ultimately was the one that had to do the work; he knew what would stretch himself out of his comfort zone. We helped him to go through his capability building development steps by supporting in many ways:

- Personal training plans
- Identifying a live project
- Coaching for a mindset shift
- Consulting projects

David needed to understand the theory before he could begin practicing effectively. A rigorous training programme combining market discovery, business model design, and creative problem-solving tools helped him to understand the fundamentals of a 10X mindset. In training, we use a combination of case-based practice with live mini-projects.

It is not just the tools that frame the mindset. An overall process is imperative. The process helps with selecting the right tools to use but most importantly learning that using tools poorly will yield poor results.

4. Theory to practice

Learning theory is not always easy, but once grasped it is easy to fall into theory fallacy where you think you know what to do. Going from theory to practice is rarely a smooth journey.

David needed to apply what he had learned to real projects. He was a rapid learner, which was good. However, he often slipped back into his old mindset and started leaning into his crutch of ideas rather than listening to the market. David also needed to build experience in both a safe environment and the real world so that his confidence and decision making became more refined. The coaching and the detailed market research consulting from Disruptive Lemonade was imperative to keep David's mindset shift on track.

5. Connecting the dots

As a coach, I helped David see the dots that were there. But David needed to join the dots himself to master his new mindset. He needed to understand the guiding frameworks and tools in enough detail to know how he wanted to put projects together, what he wanted to coordinate, and when to bring in consultancy to support execution. Over time, he developed three core project types based on market risk and business model maturity. This allowed him and his team to build a success blueprint for each project type.

Think 10X, not 10%

David's s-curve discontinuous jump was about moving from a 10% improvement mindset to 10X improvement mindset. His individual journey and resulting mindset is unique and will blend the best of his engineering mindset with the foundational principles of the 10X mindset. My journey since co-founding Disruptive Lemonade is continued mastery of uncovering 10X market opportunities and supporting entrepreneurs, innovation teams, and CEOs in building the right blueprint that helps them exploit the most attractive market opportunities. I look forward to continuing to help those wanting to get out of their comfort zone, get to the next s-curve, and start to change the world around them.

Iain Acton

Iain Acton is an entrepreneur, a coach, an author, a teacher, and an artist and has spent 15 years mastering systematic market research methods and a disruptive innovation mindset. He co-founded Disruptive Lemonade in 2012 and has since had the privilege of training, coaching, and consulting over a thousand marketers, engineers, managers, and directors from a diverse range of globally recognized brands such as Jaguar Land Rover, Rolls Royce, Dura Automotive, Just Eat, and disruptive startups such as Fintech social banking startup B-Social.

He travels globally on behalf of the University of Warwick to talk and teach 'Disruptive Innovation' theory and 'JTBD' theory into practice. Recently, he co-authored 'Entrepreneurship in Emerging and Developing Economies', where he addresses the entrepreneurial application of customer centricity using JTBD and highlights the trappings of product thinking and confirmation bias. He has learned about how to prepare properly to establish a 10X mindset and help his clients routinely set up the right attitudes, behaviors, and knowledge to be successful and how to focus on what is most important, pinpointing the most attractive value gaps in the market.

You can find out more about him from his 'Insights For Growth' blog where you can book a FREE webinar and learn how he helps his clients to grow and exploit a £100 million+ 10X mindset.

Contact Information

Twitter: @iainacton
LinkedIn: https://www.linkedin.com/in/iainacton/
Insights For Growth Blog: www.iainacton.com
Disruptive Lemonade: www.disruptivelemonade.com

FLOW

IGNACIO PEREZ

I hate writing books. In fact, this is the first time I have ever agreed to be part of one.

It's not for a lack of offers, but a mounting inner resistance. Every time I pick a pen and paper, I hear a familiar voice in my head. We have all heard it at one time or another. It paralyzes some, takes a beating out of others, and makes us question it all.

Sound familiar?

I'm talking about the voice that says you can't, you will not, you should, you must, what if, can I and will I. It's the voice that robs you of the satisfaction of trying. It's a voice that turns execution into a nightmare of self-instruction. It's the executioner of dreams and possibilities.

The reason why I agreed to write this chapter is to help you get out of your own way. I'm not saying this as a self-proclaimed 'guru' because many such do around the world, and I wouldn't like to steal the attention they so desperately seem to need.

My job in writing these words is to remind you of what you once knew was true. It is my intention to bring you back to that place in time when everything seemed effortless, when learning new skills required no conscious effort, and when life was a game and not a chore. I'm talking about a time when there was no judgment and you were one with that voice in your head.

Of course, you don't remember that time. Part of the dysfunction of the 'inner critic' voice is to have you forget that it existed. But, as we are going to see, life doesn't need to be this hard. There is a simpler way to living—one where we are more effective, successful, and enjoying of life.

If you are still reading this, it's most probably because there is something inside you that resonates with what I speak. It is the part of you that knows to strive for excellence and not surrender. It is the unlimited human potential we all share, and it is your greatest ally in living a life you would be proud of.

This chapter will show you the simple way 'out of your head.' It will also help you reach your top consistently and boost your performance. Finally, it will speak of the reasons why achievements elude many.

The Dysfunction

Why would a toddler ever want to walk on his feet? Doing so would mean leaving behind a stable four-prong position for an unstable, risky, and unknown method called walking. Yet, every day millions of toddlers take their first steps; to their observant parents and relatives, it amounts to nothing short of a miracle.

What could possibly go through the minds of these toddlers?

Nothing.

And that's why the miracle is possible.

Toddlers attempt the unknown out of observation of their surroundings. By many accounts, they haven't yet developed the voice in their heads that judges, analyzes and comments endlessly.

How far would you have gotten if every time you stood up as a toddler and fell down and you'd snapped at yourself? Imagine a toddler in an act of self-condemnation after a 'failed' attempt: "Dumb boy! Even Grandma can walk, what's wrong with you?"

It sounds ludicrous, and it is. As toddlers, we learned by doing. There was no interference from our minds, and we were completely absorbed in the doing. We could say we were 'in the zone', or as many psychologists call it the 'flow' state.

When we are in flow, time seems endless. We are present to nothing but the task we are occupying ourselves with. A tennis player is said to be in flow when he is so focused on the ball that he fails to notice the roaring crowds around him. To achieve such a state of concentration and flow, your mind needs to be calm like a still, clear pond. Any interference or thought breaks the flow and directs one's attention elsewhere. Where attention goes, energy flows, so it is impossible for the distracted kind to accomplish anything remarkable.

If it were possible to communicate with toddlers, they would seem dumbfounded at the concept of being in flow. For them, there is nothing but flow. Toddlers have yet to learn about the concept of right and wrong and therefore have no inner voice guiding their actions toward any right outcome.

Without the tension that arises from attachment to outcome, toddlers learn experientially. Toddlers stand up, fall down, and learn not by self-instruction but by deliberate experimentation. They perhaps think "When I grab the sofa, I'm safe! I don't fall. Let's stay here for a bit." The process is natural, enjoyable, and mentally effortless.

Compare this with how the majority of us learn or work throughout adulthood. Tennis players smash their rackets against the grass court in anger over missing easy shots, skateboarders brake their four-wheelers and toss them out in frustration, and football players grit their teeth in anger with heads hanging low after they miss a shot. Thoughts race their minds. It seems unavoidable to lose flow as we age.

Somewhere along the way, we lose our innocence. Experience is replaced by self-instruction. We lose trust in our natural abilities and resort to controlling them through self-instruction and judgment. We grow fearful of making mistakes and appearing incapable in the eyes of others. The inner voice manifests for the first time, and for some, it never leaves.

Is the inner voice necessary? Does it even serve a purpose?

Consider this: we use around 200 muscles in perfectly orchestrated unison to take any single step. Whilst taking that step, your nose is distinguishing over 50,000 different scents, and by the time you have finished reading this paragraph, your body will have replaced more than 60,000 cells around your body.

The most impressive aspect about this all is that it happens without your conscious interference. You simply don't have to think about any of it to have it happen!

Your body is capable of impossible tasks not even the most sophisticated artificial intelligence systems in the world can come close to replicate.

Yet, regardless, you downplay your abilities, you grunt at yourself when you mispronounce that word again during French lessons. Or you scold yourself for not turning parallel when skiing, even if you have told yourself to do so for the thousandth time. Why can't we obey simple instructions?

It seems the more you consciously try to do something, the results grow progressively bad. And this is true in all areas of life.

In the introduction to this chapter, we talked about how you need to 'get out of your own way'. That sentence contains the dysfunction most of us, save for the few enlightened ones, suffer. If you must get out of your way, then how many of 'you' are there?

Most of us so closely identify with the voice in our heads that we have never realized the distinction within. There is, of course, a true self and a false self within us. The false self, often called the ego, is the voice in your head we were talking about. It tells the true self, your physical body and nervous system, what to do.

Remarkably, the false self is under the illusion it can control the true self. It simply does not work to command yourself to serve a perfect volley and your body to execute the action perfectly. Once the false self demands an outcome from the true self, tension is introduced to the body. Miscalculation sets in, and the natural abilities your true self possesses fade into the background, overshadowed by the repetitive ruminations of the mind.

This is the dysfunction you must be aware of: Until now you have fallen under the trap of the false self. It tricked your true self into believing it could control any outcome and that it knew what's best. So long as the false self interferes with your natural abilities, you will never get to know the true extent of what is possible for you.

The fastest way to sustained peak performance is learning how to keep the false self, the inner voice, in your head quiet when you are performing so that it does not interfere.

Don't take my word for it; you will believe in it once you experience it yourself. For now, just know this approach is credited by the most successful and accomplished people, companies, and teams in the world.

Legendary coach Steve Kerr used this approach to take the Golden State Warriors to a record 73 victories in a single NBA season. MVP point guard Steph Curry practices in monastic silence, memorizing hundreds of plays by the feelings in his body. These professionals have learned how to dominate their minds (which is the false self) to minimize interference with their true self and enter a state of flow at their will.

Entering the blissful state of flow and effortless action can be a challenge. You cannot force it, for it would be another example of mental interference. It's the reason why extreme sports are so popular; they bring with them a portal into flow. When you are base jumping at 20,000 feet, skiing down a sixty-degree icy slope, or racing on the backs of a wild beast, there is little time for thought. Any lapse in concentration can turn fatal.

Both your false and true selves know there is real danger this time, and without effort or conscious trying, the inner voice recedes into total silence. You are present and focused at every second, giving your fullest attention to what you are doing. Whether you do things right or not, it doesn't matter. What matters is either you survive or you don't. There is little to worry about.

If you have ever been in a situation of no return, you will have been witness to the true extent of your capabilities. Possibly you are still wondering where those abilities arose from. Because people rarely find an answer, they depend on these extreme situations to return to that state of flow.

You don't need to risk your life to get back into flow. As a matter of fact, you don't need to learn anything new. Before the expectations of the world settled upon your conscience, you were in a state of constant flow. The only thing you need to do at this time is to unlearn the bad habits you have picked along the way that prevent you from experiencing this state.

Because these habits are deeply ingrained, it is futile to battle against them. We must learn how to let go and substitute them for empowering ones, only then do we stand a chance to enter flow at will.

To this end, I have put together a series of daily habits that, with practice and repetition, will get you performing at your very best by minimizing interference.

Daily Habit #1: **Inner Body Awareness**

To remove mental interference from your actions, you have to start by claiming back consciousness from your mind. A very effective way of doing this is to take your attention away from thinking and directing it into the body.

Try it now.

Close your eyes and breathe into your lower abdomen until you can feel the rising and lowering of your abdomen. Focus on the feelings in your body. Are your hands alive? Is there life in them? Don't think about this consciously but rather feel the sensations around your body. Direct your attention to your feet. Can you feel a tingling sensation? Perhaps warmth or coldness? Are you tensed or relaxed? Whatever you feel, just let it be. With your eyes still closed, scan your body from bottom to top and let the waves of consciousness flow over your entire body. Open your eyes.

How do you feel?

Practicing this simple exercise for 5–10 minutes a day will put you in touch with your 'inner body', which are the sensations of your body. With time, you will be able to feel your inner body with your eyes open whilst doing activities that were previously done unconsciously. You will not be distracted by thought.

Repetition is the key to mastery. Therefore, to ensure the false self is left without fuel to run on, you'll have to train your inner-body awareness every day. This is no different to boxers going to the gym and sparring or firefighters running surprise drills. You can start taking targeted practice with any mundane and repetitive tasks. You could do this while you are driving, doing the laundry, washing the dishes, or going out for a run.

Pick one activity and place your full attention to the feelings and sensations during that activity. If it is running, sense closely the soles of your feet at impact with the floor; if you chose washing the dishes, feel the temperature and texture of the water running through your hands. If you experience thoughts, worries, or even mind projections happening, simply return to the sensations. By doing this, you are shutting the doors to the false self and learning to trust your intuition.

With practice, you will achieve longer and longer periods of bliss, awareness, and flow. Time will appear eternal, and your creativity will sore. With little interference, you will get more done in less time and you will gather a greater sense of personal satisfaction from even the smallest of actions.

Now that you are training your mind not to interfere and using it rather than it using you, it is time to put your true self to action and channel your energy toward the consecution of your goals. This is done by training where you place your focus and is the subject of the next daily habit.

Daily Habit #2: **Attentional Training**

Since the late nineteenth century, psychologists and scientists of the mind have been challenged by the study of attention. Most of their efforts have been focused on measuring attention and focus, but little has been devoted to the question of whether attention can be trained and developed.

Nothing shapes our experience of the world more than where we focus our attention. Whether we focus on being able or not, life will conspire to make us right. William James, the father of modern psychology put it perfectly, "For the moment, what we attend to is reality." James also realized that all geniuses in their respective capacities were capable of sustained attention for long periods of time. Only by focusing our full attention to our work can we realize our flaws and correct them intuitively.

If you hire a running coach to improve your endurance, the coach might correctly observe you don't raise your knees high enough. The natural reaction would be to mentally hold thoughts of the sort of "Knees up!" or "Up, up, up!" in an attempt to force our bodies to comply. However, as we have seen throughout this chapter, this would only add interference and block our natural abilities to improve and develop.

At this point, most of us are at a loss. If you can't instruct yourself what to do, how can you ever improve? This is the point where we must learn to let go of the bad learning habits we have been accumulating throughout life and learn to return to the childlike innocence of experiential learning.

The first step is to observe your action without judgment. In the case of running with low knees, feel your knees as you run. There is no need to control anything. Once you are connected and clearly feel the sensations of your knees, explore the maximum height they reach as you run. Again, don't think about how high they go, just notice and don't try to control or push for any outcome

Rest your attention for as long as you wish on the elevation of your knees until you feel you are anchored with the movement. At this point, visualize your desired action. Simply envision what you want to happen, which in this case is to run raising your knees higher. Concentrate on the images and feelings of this new desired action.

There will come a time when you naturally feel confident in running in this new envisioned way. It's a feeling unlike that which comes by forcing us to do something—this time there is an effortless feeling to it. Once you are at this stage, simply let go. You will be amazed at the results.

Whatever you want to improve upon, whether it be work, sports or even relationships, start by placing your full attention to your current actions. After this, visualize your desired outcome and then simply let it happen. The simplicity of this approach cannot be underestimated, and the only way you will know its revolutionary power is if you try it for yourself.

As with everything in life, the more you practice, the more natural it will become and you will produce greater and more stunning outcomes. Never stop practicing.

Why You Should Listen To Me

I speak from experience.

Nobody taught me these truths. Of course, there were books

and great mentors along the way, but my tipping point came at a time of no return.

As a wonder kid, I had achieved what most dreamt of at an early age.

Perfect scores, awards, medals and championships filled my room. Parents spoke highly of me, and everyone envisioned great things for me. I was voted the most likely to succeed as well as the most likely to date a supermodel. Everything seemed easy, flowed naturally, and filled me with great satisfaction. I loved my life.

When the time came to pack my bags and head over to university, I did so to a foreign country. I had been accepted into the crown jewel of Aerospace Engineering institutions. In fact, it was the highest ranking university in the country on the subject. To add to its reputation, the design for the elliptical wing that gave the air superiority to the Spitfire to defeat the Nazis in the Battle of Britain was developed at the university by a professor of aeronautics. What do you do when you think you have reached the top? I don't know what others do, but I turned inward.

I sank. I doubted myself. With the incessant thinking that never stopped, life seemed too much to handle. Nothing made sense to me. It was haunting and hellish.

I saw my classmates graduate and move on with their lives at a time where my days were filled with psychologists, doctors, coaches, and any person who I thought could help me. The most macabre element of it all was not knowing what was going on. I only felt the symptoms of what was later diagnosed as a psychological pressure to perform.

For over three years, I battled in my head as I pushed through to complete my studies. It was a time of isolation, paralysis, and dread. I felt like a failure, having been left behind in finishing what others had accomplished with grace so many years ago. I frequently pictured myself in future precarious situations, without the ability to overcome them, and I had little hope for my future to be any different because my brain was literally fried from overuse. Even the simplest tasks such as reading became a gargantuan task of Hellenic proportions. The only thing I could focus on was doubting my own abilities. Dante's Inferno seemed a summer house compared with what went inside my head. At times, I fantasized about giving it all up.

I was so identified with my mind and so utterly ruled by my false self without respite that I often wondered about the meaning of it all. It seemed I was always protecting an image of myself that had little regard for the external reality it lived in.

Through more downs than ups, and with the invaluable support, guidance, and direction offered by family, friends, and professionals, I managed to complete my studies. One name stood out, Tsvetelina Dimitrova, who would become the love of my life.

Shortly after graduation, I met a performance coach who turned my life the right way up. He did so by bringing me back to the childlike innocence that had supported my early successes in life. This was accomplished by training me on quieting my inner voice as well as learning to trust myself again. Learning to let go was perhaps the greatest leap of faith I have had to take to this date, and I don't say this lightly, having run a half-marathon at a time I was overweight, asthmatic and severely undertrained.

How could I trust myself? Especially at a time I was so paralyzed and afraid of making mistakes I often would lay awake in a puddle of my own sweat. This hippie nonsense didn't make sense at all, but what did I have to lose? I might as well prove that this guy had built his entire professional career on a fallacy. Fuelled by my false self's survival instinct and desire to discredit, I took the plunge. I religiously followed the daily habits I have outlined in this chapter. And they worked.

It seems ages ago, yet the transformational nature of embodying these habits has stuck with me ever since. Everywhere I go, I carry with me a deep sense of gratitude toward the selfless beings who make their mission in life to guide others through their tempests. It seemed only right to give back. It had always been in the back of my mind. I had to help coaches reach the millions who seek their answers yet don't find them in a sea of confusion and commercial solutions.

It wasn't until much later that I met my partner Sai Blackbyrn. He shared the same passion I had for coaches. In the years that ensued, we built systems and platforms that have reached thousands and helped hundreds of coaches make a remarkable living through their passion. Every day, I give back to those who so readily subdue their interests for those of their clients. None of this would have been possible had I not allowed my true self to flourish and prosper.

I never dreamed of this life. In fact, I never thought I would make it alive for so long. I got to enjoy this life by trusting in my abilities, not the inner voice in my head. Does this mean I no longer doubt myself and I live in utter Zen? No, not at all. But I know that when it matters, I can perform at my best. I know I will never hold myself back anymore and that I can snap out of it in an instant and constantly offer the best version of myself. What's more important is that I get to enjoy every waking second as if I were a child again.

Rest assured, if an Olympic level, grade A over thinker such as I can tame the dark recesses of his mind, so can you. Believe me. Whatever it is you take out of this chapter, get out of your head and do the daily habits.

Notice how your life starts to flow with you rather than against you. Notice your sense of peace heighten. Welcome your own inner revolution, and when people ask you what 'switched', tell them. Share the gift.

And when this has happened, drop me a line. Share your story.

After all, it's the only thing that is left behind.

Ignacio Perez

Ignacio Perez is an Aerospace Engineer turned champion of coaches. He runs Coach Accelerator with Sai Blackbyrn, the first accelerator program to specialize in coaches and coaching businesses.

Throughout the years both have served hundreds of coaches fill their practices and achieve financial freedom through their passions as coaches.

He is an avid reader and mentor whose life has suffered from multiple ups and downs. He makes it a habit to show others how to trust their instinct and let it flow.

You can read more about his work on his Forbes column: https://www.forbes.com/sites/ignacioperez/

Contact Information

https://www.facebook.com/strategycoachperez
Ignacio@sai.coach
https://www.forbes.com/sites/ignacioperez/

LEADERSHIP IS A JOURNEY, NOT A DESTINATION

JUSTINE ROBBINS

T his is the story of my journey through one of the darkest periods in my life. A journey that taught me I had the tools and resources within me to overcome any adversity. However, to unlock them, I would need to look in the mirror and embrace everything I had rejected about myself. Embracing me led me to understand the value of being a heartfelt leader. It also taught me to connect with myself and others on an emotional and spiritual level and to lead with my heart, not just my head. Removing the cloak of denial, rejection, doubts, and fear enabled me to explore my reality through a different perspective. It allowed me to take responsibility and change my outcome. I finally discovered what it truly meant to embrace all of me while accepting and appreciating my flaws. I found joy and happiness within myself, rediscovered my strengths, and opened my heart to uncover the real meaning of being a leader. I realized that I had embodied and embraced all of myself and, in doing so, could contribute more to others.

Leadership is a journey, not a destination. It is a mindset and inner calling; it is something that inspires you to do more, to be more, and it captures your heart.

So, where did my story start? I was sitting on the floor in my room, surrounded by piles of bills, bank statements, letters, and records of financial transactions. I was trying to unravel the trajectory my life had taken. I wanted to know what was true because what I earlier believed to be true was not true anymore.

It was 2am in the morning, and I had been at it for hours trying to untangle the mess. All I wanted was to crawl away, hide in a hole, and never come out. I was wondering where to start and how to untangle a ball of string that seemed to have no ends. I was hoping to find the answer in the pile of papers. It was wishful thinking, but I was latching onto anything that offered a glimmer of hope.

I knew I had lost the lifestyle I had built for my family because I was in debt. I didn't know the magnitude of it. I didn't know how much I owed and to whom. I didn't know if I still had a house. I was terrified someone was going to knock on the door and evict me and the kids to the streets.

My sense of security and safety had been ripped away. It was gone in a heartbeat, and I was left raw and vulnerable. Everything I had worked hard for, everything '**we**' had worked so hard to create, was for nothing. The sacrifices we made to build our future was wasted.

How could this have happened to me? I had it all together.

Well, actually, I believed I had it all together. The illusion cracked.

I had prided myself on working hard and having everything under control. I was great at juggling multiple balls. I always had a lot going on, and I liked to be busy. I even joked that I may drop a ball every now and again, but I knew exactly where it was and would pick it up when the time was right—all without skipping a beat. I know that I had dropped these balls, and they shattered like glass. I was clearly not as composed and together as I believed.

I was broken. I was betrayed. I was lost, and I was hurting.

I felt heavy and couldn't move my body or lift my arms or even stand up. I couldn't get enough air in my lungs. There was a huge weight pushing on my chest that was stopping me from breathing, and I felt suffocated. It felt like I was in a huge, black void of empty nothingness all alone. My throat was raw, and it ached from gasping for breath. My head was pounding, my eyes were sore and red, and I felt like I had cried a river of salty tears. Physically, I was in pain; emotionally, I was in shock and was devastated. Yesterday I knew things, and everything was all right. Today, I couldn't make sense of anything. I felt completely lost, helpless, and alone.

Even today, after many years, I can still recall this vividly. I have a mixture of feelings for what I went through—compassion and sympathy for what I was going through; sorrow and sadness for the hopelessness I felt; and an outpouring of love and admiration for being resilient. Knowing that this breakdown was a pivotal point in my life changed how I saw myself and the world. It shaped my experiences and my becoming.

Today, with the benefit of time and perspective, I realize that people were dealing with their own feelings. Their words to me indicated their inner turmoils and thoughts. It was not entirely about me. Back then, however, I was sensitive and vulnerable.

I took it to heart and assumed it was judgment, criticism, and blame. It hurt. I didn't feel supported or understood. I retreated into myself and didn't share anything with my loved ones. It was just easier to pretend that everything was okay. What I actually experienced was shame. I felt ashamed because I had failed and disappointed many people. I was angry and cruel, and I directed all of the blame at myself.

I repeatedly questioned myself. How did I get here, and what happened? I wanted to know why did he hate me as much. There were no answers, just more questions.

My dad flew in and took charge of the situation. The presence of lawyers and accountants, who were there to set things in action, made it feel real. It was true. My mum also came to support me and the kids. I was grateful to them for being there and taking charge, but it also made me feel small and weak, like a six-year-old who had been foolish and had needed to be bailed out by an adult. I was a successful, professional woman, and now I was a failure. I needed daddy to save me. In one moment, I lost my sense of independence and identity. My self-belief that strong, capable women could achieve anything was replaced by a scared little girl who felt like a failure. I was no longer successful, and somebody else's action had become my undoing.

> **"I am not what happened to me, I
> am what I chose to become."**

"Carl Jung, Swiss psychologist founder of Analytic Psychology"

There were people who relied on me. At home, it was my two beautiful children; at work, I was leading a transformation project that impacted 250 people. 70 individuals who were displaced from my team needed support, guidance, and a leader who was on her game. They needed a champion who could give them a voice and be compassionate. They needed someone who could support them through their multitude of feelings—fear, loss, anger, betrayal, anticipation, and joy. They needed to find their way, and I was determined to be there for them. They needed me, and I wasn't going to let anyone else down.

Keep moving, take deep breaths, and just keep going. That's my motto.

So, I did what felt right, and I spent more time at work hiding from my problems. I was unable to face what I was feeling, so I focused on others. The universe has an amazing way of sending us opportunities to learn and grow—only if we are open to embracing them. Unfortunately, opportunities don't often appear as rainbows, sunshine, and happiness; they are usually disguised as thunderstorms, dragons, and tornados trying to rip your head off and destroy you. They say it doesn't rain, and then it pours. While I was going through my crisis, the company that I worked through was going through its own identity crises. My values were out of sync with the company, and I could no longer do my best work. In short, my time was up.

So, this is how it looked. I was separated, unemployed, and in debt. I had to put up my home for sale, sold my beloved car, and rented a unit that required relocating. I was also nursing two damaged and weak hips. My world had unraveled. I was a single mum who was dealing with a financial separation and custody battle—all while finding new schools for the kids and settling two young children into a new life. I was struggling. I could sense what others, who were in pain, were experiencing.

My intuition allowed me to be empathetic, compassionate, and loving. For others, I created a safe place—an environment for them to fall and bounce back. A space where they could overcome their challenges and find their way through. On the other hand, I couldn't create a similar safe place for myself. I couldn't be kind, compassionate, or empathetic. I couldn't love myself. I felt that if I allowed myself to cry, I would start crying and never stop. It was almost as if my heart would break open and a lifetime of hurt would flow out. So, I just kept going, kept putting one foot in front of the other, kept breathing, and kept moving.

The universe kept throwing me challenges. Two broken hips on crutches for nine months. Deep breath. I can do this. Marital Breakdown. Deep breath. I can do this. A lost home. Deep breath. I can do this. A lost car. Deep breath. I can do this. Redundancy. Deep breath. Keep breathing and keep moving. In the end, I had nothing left. I looked around, and I was alone. I couldn't keep pushing through. I had nothing left to give, and no one was coming to save me. I needed to retreat and heal. I had to grieve, mourn, hurt, and let go. I had to feel the pain that I was suppressing. I had to cry.

When I finally let it out, it came in waves. They gushing waves threatened to overwhelm me. I had to grieve the loss of everything—my lifestyle, family, career, home—but most of all, I had to grieve for the way I had treated myself. I had to accept that I had not allowed myself to be loved, supported, heard, nurtured, or cared for. I had rejected myself, and I had not allowed myself to receive. I could give but not receive. I had no soft place to fall simply because I hadn't allowed myself to fall or believed I was worth being caught. Somewhere, I believed that I did not deserve love or kindness and accepted rejection and emptiness. I didn't want to be this person anymore, and I finally let go. I released myself from the belief that I had to hold it together. I finally let my feelings take over, and it hurt. It was a lifetime of pain, which was all bottled up, that finally released. It really hurt. Over time, I realized that I could cry and it would stop. I could be kind, and I wouldn't fall apart. I could be vulnerable, and people would meet me with love. I decided to ask for help and support. I embraced my kids, held them tight, and healed from the inside out.

So, how do you heal after you have hit rock bottom?

You embrace everything you have rejected about yourself; you find kindness in your heart; and you learn to love and accept yourself. You show yourself how to be a leader from your heart.

Up until this point, I had always seen myself as a people leader, a champion of people—someone who saw the brilliance within others and helped them to unlock their potential, so they could reach their goals and help the company to reach theirs. And I was. But, I realized I had been holding back. I had been holding back the real me—the me that didn't always have it together, the flawed me—and was presenting to others the image that I thought I should be—the image of the person I thought they wanted and needed. I was being 90% myself, but it was the 10% that comprised my vulnerability, which I held back to protect myself, that contained the real beauty. I could see everyone else's brilliance, but I couldn't see my brilliance; instead, I hid what I saw as my flaws and presented what I thought was the best part of me. It wasn't till I embraced them and understood their true purpose that I saw that they were really my brilliance, they made me unique and real. And realizing this enabled me to embrace heartfelt leadership.

You can't truly believe in anyone else's greatness if you can't see and recognize your own.

Leadership involves embracing the whole person and helping people to achieve their goals and objectives. The art of leadership is not simple. It requires you to embrace all of you, to focus on who you are being and what is going on for you, so that you can step beyond you to be present for others. It's leadership from the inside out. It involves building capability in others so they can see and be aware of challenges. It involves enabling them to identify their specific role in any situation and to challenge their thinking, so they can move forward with the best strategy. It also involves providing different perspectives and creating a safe environment for risks and mistakes. A leader holds a compassionate mirror for people to learn and grow.

At this point, I was not the leader. I was the student and realized that I had only looked externally for answers. What I hadn't realized was that all the answers were within me. Of course, I had been told that numerous times, but I didn't believe it then. Now I believed it. I really believed it. I knew I had to explore my unconscious self as this was where the answers were hidden. I had to discover my way forward. I had to step up and become a heartfelt leader for myself. As a heartfelt leader, I would lead with my heart, with love, and with kindness. If I wanted to become the leader I aspired to be, I had to first lead myself. I had to go within and release everything I had suppressed to find the brilliance within myself.

John Maxwell, an American pastor who wrote extensively about leadership, says, "Leadership is less about what you **do** and more about who you are **being**"; he later mentions that "if you want to lead, you need to grow. The first person you should change is you." So that is it. Leadership starts with you

I was going to rebuild myself from the inside out.

I created a new environment for myself—one of love, acceptance, and creativity. It would embrace all of me, my feelings, thoughts, weaknesses, and flaws. I was whole. I was perfectly imperfect, and I had a lot to offer. What I had to offer was all of me. It was not just the good bits or simply the strong bits. It was the whole package. Leadership is my passion, and I was passionate about sharing it with the world. So, I reclaimed my life and found myself.

These are my key learnings I discovered about myself, which I subsequently applied to become a heartfelt leader:

1. **Embracing**

Heartfelt leadership is embracing everything about us and others that scares us and everything that is in conflict with what we believe—embracing all the things that we admire, value, believe, care for, and understand. It is questioning without judgment; it is combining the rational and emotional. When we attempt to question what drives us, we further question our thoughts. We are left wondering if they are originally ours or if they have been subconsciously superimposed by society. By challenging their origin and their impact, we can grow, expand, and evolve. We can choose how we respond and what we believe instead of accepting a traditional belief system that was handed down to us as children, which we somehow never upgraded. Most people accept their beliefs, stories, and values to be true; they give no further thought about its origin because it was intrinsically built into them.

I embrace the concept of "We don't know what we don't know." For me, this implies that we can remain curious, constantly evolve, and learn continuously. There is always something more to know, and we just don't know it all yet. We can learn and discard beliefs that no longer serve us. I embraced everything that I had rejected. I also managed to discover the reasons behind my rejection. **Fear.** I embraced it all and learned to appreciate their value. I embraced it all to release the power they held over me. I realized that they all were a part of me and had a purpose. They had been protecting me—keeping me safe. And by rejecting them, I was stuck. Now it was time to grow. In the end, I could move beyond the pain and hurt and appreciate myself. I discovered answers to questions I didn't know I had. I dug deeper and my values grew clearer. I built boundaries, and I knew what I wanted to achieve. Most importantly, I rebuilt my core until I was rock solid. With my newfound strength, I embraced vulnerability and finally understood that to be vulnerable is to demonstrate strength, confidence, and love. It is, in fact, the opposite of weaknesses. My biggest lesson was and remains accepting that I am enough and that I deserve all the kindness, forgiveness, investment, and time that I invest in others.

Previously, I had taught people I didn't need much and was self-sufficient. I sacrificed my desires for others, even when it wasn't for the greater good. I taught myself that I was not worthy. Now I needed to teach myself love, self-acceptance, and joy. I began slowly. I built fluid boundaries that would help me and support others. I identified what was not negotiable and stuck to it. I uncovered the feelings that I wanted to experience consistently and prioritized them. I raised my standards and expectations. Finally, I redefined success to win-win—win for me and win for others. I realized the one thing I really needed was to be a friend—a friend to me. We never treat ourselves with the same kindness and consideration we give to our friends. So, I took on the persona of a friend whenever I spoke to myself and self-reflected. I did it through the eyes of a friend, and it worked for me. I was kind, compassionate, and still kick arse honest when necessary.

In the end, I learned to accept the person I was and the leader that I was. I discovered that compassion, empathy, kindness, and nurturing suited me and brought out the best in me. Now I had the full package: a strong authentic inner core that guided me; leadership skills I had fostered and developed over many years; and the compassion, vulnerability, and empathy that I had just discovered and embraced inwardly and reflected outward. I could now truly embrace my individuality as an authentic heartfelt leader. Because I was authentically me.

2. Accepting

Acceptance comes when you really appreciate who you are. It strengthens when you realize that you are exactly the person you are meant to be. To accept that you are enough. You need to realize that you are imperfectly perfect—the same as everyone else. We are all imperfectly perfect. More importantly, you need to acknowledge that you have everything inside you. Everything you want to achieve and who you want to Be is already within you. You just need to accept it and Be. In my case, I dug deep and faced the uncomfortable truths and meanings I had created. I had to discover the person I was at my core. I had to accept that all my flaws and failures had brought me to exactly where I needed to be. Here. Now. It is not our successes and our strengths that teach us; it is those dark nights that reveal our true strengths. We grow through adversity.

Being a leader is being willing enough to get uncomfortable and push yourself to the edge of your comfort zone and beyond. We must accept that we all have our journeys to travel and that it takes compassion, resilience, and vulnerability to walk our own path; as leaders, we will hold the light for others so they can walk their path. You can't shine the light for others if you are in darkness. Shine a light into your heart, embrace and accept all that you are and reflect this out into the world—a connection from your heart to others.

3. Expressing Your Individuality

Leadership is a mindset, a commitment, and a conscious choice; it is something you believe and demonstrate in everything you do. It is not something you can demonstrate without inheriting the traits yourself. It is a part of you, not something you do. Be true to who you are and embrace your inner shine. We are all humans connecting with others, and we connect on a personal level—heart to heart, head to head, and person to person. We know when people are being authentically themselves, and we know when people are hiding behind a cloak or mask projecting a personality. Leadership is being vulnerable and being open in everything you do. As I said, it's being perfectly imperfect.

You can't lead others if there is no one following you. People follow leaders they trust. They want leaders who are unique and real. They want heartfelt leaders who connect through their hearts and actions and who genuinely care about others. Think of any great leader. What about this leader stands out for you? Is it a moment where they connected with you on a personal level? Or is it a connection where you felt cared? That is what great leaders do. Great leaders connect as an individual, not as a boss. They are unashamedly themselves and are open about their flaws without magnifying them. Their personality embraces their quirks, passions, and idiosyncrasies. They do not reject or reduce themselves. They do not try to be someone else. By being themselves, they open the door for the rest of us to be ourselves, to think, feel and express our uniqueness. They inspire us to be true to ourselves. They create an environment of acceptance, where we can thrive by taking risks, collaborating, creating, and engaging. We can bring our best selves to work. We can perform. We can inspire others to shine. Everyone wants to be seen, heard, validated, and accepted for who they are as an individual. Leaders demonstrate this and allow others to model how to be authentic and vulnerable in the face of criticism. They show them how to do it with grace and dignity.

Manage Your Story

You have heard my story. It's similar to many others that have been written where the protagonist overcomes a daunting challenge. For me, it was letting go of who I thought I was supposed to be. It was giving myself the kindness and compassion that I demonstrated to others. By doing this, I discarded many beliefs that kept me stuck. It taught me the importance of creating the right mindset, of the language we use, and the power of stories. I reframed my story from *I'm not good enough* and *I am a failure* to *if we change how we think about things, we can change anything*. These new beliefs are more empowering for me. And, if I am going to have a story, I might as well make its end a good one.

Everyone has a story. Most people carry their stories everywhere they go and unveil it when the situation arises. We give these stories meaning and with the meaning, we make them real. They expand from being just stories and gradually become our beliefs. We then make them part of our identity; through the retelling, we reinforce their meaning, and strengthen the emotion invested in them. Our emotional investment in the story gives it a new life, and we live the meaning. The meaning makes it real. It shapes our identity and soon enough we are defending it, justifying and protecting it—even if it is not real. At the end of the day, we fail to understand it is us who ascribed meaning to the situation in order to make sense of it. We are meaning making machines at the end of the day; we attach meaning to everything and consequently respond/react to the meaning, not the situation. Our interpretation is a result of our history, belief, and values. Thus, our meanings too are riddles with our experience.

People's stories limit them; they use them to justify their situation, relationships, and their whole lives. The stories, however, are told from a specific perspective—our perspective. It is not the truth; it is how you see the story in your memory. And we know what a tricky thing memory is. The stories change their shape and narrative every time we replay it. Our beliefs are convenient assumptions, created from the meanings we assign, to make sense of situations. Most of our beliefs were created when we were kids, and we have not updated them. They are not true.

If you want to change your reaction, create a different meaning.

I created a meaning that I reframe most things to: "People are doing the best they can and sometimes they make mistakes, we all do." I find that this belief of mine fits most situations. It is empowering and does not trigger any unhelpful emotions in me. Pause for a minute, and think what would change if you always had an empowering meaning. How would you frame it?

The meaning we attach to our stories influences how we see ourselves. By applying these meanings subconsciously, we create our own triggers. Have you ever experienced someone who has completely overreacted to a situation? Taking it completely out of context and making blanket statements. It just seems completely over the top, and you don't know where it has come from because it is very unlike them. In fact, the simplest explanation is this: they are reacting to an old situation and meaning that the new incident has triggered. It has everything to do with the meaning they have assigned, the meaning that isn't even true. Now, have you ever done this?

When we are emotionally triggered, we react rather than respond. We react with emotion and our fight or flight instinct is triggered. We react and don't differentiate between past incidents and the current situation. Our beliefs and stories serve as our triggers, and we merely react without thought. We react like our identity depends on it. Because it does.

How can you address this?

Identify your stories, your triggers, and your biases. Let go of your old sack of stories and meanings because they are no longer serving you. Be aware of your triggers, and moderate your response accordingly. Analyzing your stories will help you disassociate from its ascribed meaning. It will enable you to be present and become a leader for others. Reframe the meaning to empowering ones.

How can you identify if you are being triggered?

Ask yourself is what I believe true? How do I know this to be true? What am I reacting to? Is it the situation or is it an emotion? Is my reaction appropriate to the situation or am I reacting to something else? What else could it mean? What have I deleted from the situation?

Choices and Responsibility

You are here today because of your choices; where you end up tomorrow is also because of your choices. Sometimes the choices available come with consequences that we find unpalatable, and we end up saying that we didn't have a choice. Well, remember that you always have a choice because choosing to do nothing is also something you can do.

I created my situation because of the decisions I made and because of my priorities and the relationship I had with myself. I realized I had the power to be able to influence and change the situation because I could change my response. My choices kept me stuck; now, if I can change my choices, then I can change the situation and change the outcome.

Here are the steps I used to change my reality:

- Accepted the situation as it was, not how I wanted it to be
- Accepted some responsibility for the situation, however big or small
- Became aware of what was influencing my perspective of the situation

- Changed my perspective of the situation and changed its meaning
- Made a different choice

One of the lessons I struggled to grasp as a leader was accepting that there was only one person I could change and that was me. I could influence others, but I couldn't make anyone else change. They had to want to change. The piece I really struggled with was I could see the possibility in them, but they had to want it for themselves. It was not enough that I could see it, articulate it, and was willing to walk with them. They had to be willing to change and be willing to do the work. And a lot of people aren't willing to change. They are happy feeling sorry for themselves. When someone doesn't want the change for themselves but want the benefits, you need to let them go. After all, it's their journey and opportunity, not yours. It is also not your failure as a leader if they don't want to embrace their potential. It's like those 3D puzzles where an image comes out of the page at you. You can stare at the page and not see anything, but once you've seen it you can't not see it. It is so obvious after you have seen it. You try and explain how to see it to others and they just can't see it. They are not ready. You can't see it for them; they have to find their way.

I see people all the time struggle with taking responsibility for their life. One of the reasons is that responsibility, fault, and blame are often bundled together. When we feel like we are at fault, we are filled with negative emotions—of shame and fear. No one wants to feel bad. People give up or avoid responsibility altogether rather than face these emotions. However, there are a couple of steps that sit between responsibility and blame: outcomes and root cause analysis. But these critical steps often get lost in that process of blame. The desire to not be at fault and feel uncomfortable drives us to allocate blame quickly. I am right and you are wrong. In the end, the real problem has not surfaced at all. All we have done is assign blame and then gone back to the cycle of fire-fighting without solving the real problem. Remember that the problem is never the problem, it is only a symptom of the real problem.

The root cause or the real problem is either a people or a process issue—often both—and it always involves multiple people. Blame is negative and leads to deflection and justification, which leads you away from identifying and solving the real problem. You're not moving forward. You're just stuck and feel overwhelmed. So what can you do? Disentangle responsibility, blame, and fault. Look internally first before you allocate blame. Ask yourself how did I influence this situation? What could I have done better? What needs to change? How could I set people up for success next time? What can I do to fix it, so it doesn't happen again? People find responsibility challenging because blame generally accompanies it. Remove blame from the equation, and it's a lot more appealing. This is where leaders can make a difference. Heartfelt leaders understand that blame doesn't lift individuals or the company. It merely creates an environment of fear, stifles growth, and maintains the merry-go-round of fire-fighting.

Environments of Success

So, how can you create an environment of success? Terry Cole Whittaker once said, "What you think of me is none of my business." Begin with that. In my journey, I discovered many people had an opinion on what happened. They knew what was right, what was wrong, what I should do, and even how I should feel! Those who supported me the most, not necessarily the ones who cared the most, did so by me by allowing me to move forward and find my answers. They didn't lead with their opinions, they didn't overwhelm me with their feelings, and they didn't judge me or the situation; instead, they asked me questions and helped me to explore the right way forward for me.

They created an environment where they were present for me, they asked me what I needed, and they gave me space so that I could explore and discover other options. They challenged me gently when it was necessary. They did this lovingly, with encouragement, and gave me the confidence to continue. They used the art of questioning to help me to see different perspectives. They enabled me to find my answers; because they were my answers, I believed in and took ownership of them. We all have the answers within us, but we just don't have the language or experience to unlock them. It is difficult to hold a mirror for yourself and be objective. Sometimes, we need someone to hold the mirror for us and encourage us to look and understand what is reflected to us.

I noticed the impact on me when people told me their opinion. I just shut down. I didn't disagree or argue with them, it didn't seem worth it. I just agreed, nodded passively, and sat there bewildered about how they had made it about them. When someone leads with their opinion, they create a dynamic that plays out everywhere. It creates a proper division: either people agree or disagree. The opportunity to create, build, and explore is gone; the discussion is now limited to arguing about the opinion. It can shut people down. Debates often involve people talking at each other instead of talking to each other. The passionate believers feel the need to convince the other of their opinions. What we must remember is that, often, *opinions are simply judgments in disguise.*

I had a lot to say and share, but I didn't want to make it all about me when it wasn't. I was pretty sure that many of my opinions were flawed. I was going to be more thoughtful with who I shared my opinions. Most importantly, I wanted to understand what others were going through and what they were thinking.

Here are a few strategies I created that has worked well in different situations:

Lead with your opinion and follow it with an invitation to discuss: "I think I could be wrong, tell me how?" *This is great for an open debate and collaborative thinking.*

Ask everyone for their opinion. Debate, share your opinion explaining how and why you have reached it, and thank them for theirs. *This is a great way to come up with a single outcome, which allows for everyone's opinions to be heard.*

Ask others their opinion and question deeper to understand how they came to the decision. *This is great for building thinking skills and understanding.*

Ask yourself if sharing your opinion has any value to another person. If not, step back; if yes, go ahead and share. Then, ask a question that brings the conversation back to them. *This is great for balancing the space, listening, and challenging dominant perspectives.*

So, this is exactly what I did. I focused on getting other people to voice and share their opinions. I aimed to understand what they were thinking, feeling, and going through by asking questions.

I was not there to judge but to understand and discover their beliefs and meanings they had created. I was curious and open and realized my opinion was less important in most discussions than I originally assumed it to be. Helping others to articulate their opinions gave me gifts I hadn't realized was possible. I discovered that people's opinions are about them, their beliefs and their lives—not me. I stopped taking it personally, and avoided snap judgments and overreactions. The discussion expands when I ask more questions and restrict sharing my opinions. By doing this, I helped others achieve clarity, and I understood better. I did not expect to feel more heard by sharing less, but that is exactly what happened. Debates, open conflicts, and questions increase, but misunderstandings and hidden conflicts decrease. As a result, people feel heard and engaged.

So, what did I learn through my journey?

I can sum it up in two words: love and resilience.

I am not the same person who sat on the floor many years ago. I am stronger because I embraced vulnerability. I embraced my feelings and value my intuition more than my opinion or thoughts, which I now understand are mere moments in time. I admire and appreciate the silent challenges people are dealing with every day, while we remain unaware of the power of love and kindness. We need to creating an environment for them to explore and solve their own questions and challenges. Remember what the poet Maya Angelou said, "At the end of the day people won't remember what you said or did, they will remember how you made them feel."

As a leader, I strive to support the whole person and not just the version that turns up to work. I create heartfelt connections while appreciating that everyone has stories that influence how they think, act, and what they bring. I see challenges as opportunities to expand and grow, to teach and learn, and to gain a greater understanding of self. I am a better leader because of my journey. I now know who I am and who I am not; I love and accept all of me and thereby give all of me to others. I don't hold back. I build trust and connection. I stand confident in my core, and I forgive myself quickly and often. I nurture myself and celebrate all successes—small and large.

Leaders who connect with their heart understand that life is a journey of discovery. You can only connect and lead with your heart if you know who you are. John Maxwell says, "Leadership is a noun, it is an action, not a position." I would like to elaborate further. I think leadership is a journey, not a destination. It is a mindset, an inner calling. It is something that inspires you and captures your heart. It is a commitment to do more and to do better every day. To do this, you need to embrace the person you are. Embrace you because you are you.

You are first and foremost an individual with feelings, fears, and doubts. To be the best leader, you need to be the best version of you; to do that, you need to nurture yourself. Be kind, forgive yourself, hold the mirror as a friend, and be grateful that you have the privilege to influence lives. Invest in yourself as both the individual and the leader. Be open and curious, never stop growing or taking risks or having a go. One of the greatest gifts we can give ourselves is forgiveness. It allows you to release stuck emotions, so you can let go and move on. I practice it daily when the dog eats the cat food for perhaps the thousandth time.

Businesses are living systems made up of people—people

building connections with each other. Leaders are in the business of people. Invest in yourself and your leadership. If your people deserve it, so do you; as you invest in you, they will grow and expand and that will grow your business. And if you ever find yourself in a crisis where the universe sends you dragons, remember they are really opportunities in disguise. Pull out your sword, slay the dragon, and smile. **You've got this**.

Dust yourself off and have another Go. You are worth it.

Justine Robbins

Justine Robbins is a CEO, Growth Strategist, Business Consultant, Human Behavior Expert, Coach, Board Chairman, Author, and a passionate leader of people. Over the last 25 years, she has held senior executive roles across multiple disciplines in ASX 100 companies and supported business owners and leaders to grow their businesses. She is passionate about building leaders for the future, leaders who build leaders, and leaders who build companies. Justine draws on personal observations, in-depth business experience, human behavior expertise, and real-life application to assist leaders in achieving clarity so they can act with purpose. She is also passionate about locking people's potential and creating heartfelt leaders who lead from their heart and reflect out to the world. Overall, she combines results and connection through leadership. She currently lives in Melbourne with her children Mitchell and Grace.

Contact Information

She can be contacted at www.justinerobbins.com or justine@ justinerobbins.com. Alternatively, you can reach out to her on LinkedIn: www.linkedin.com/in/justinerobbinsaus.

DETERMINED TO HEAL

KALEY ZEITOUNI

I was on the bus by 7:00 am for my quarterly neurology appointment at one of the best multiple sclerosis (MS) centers in the world. After 20 years of living with MS, this was just another routine day.

I was Dr. David Magalashvili's (who everyone calls Dr. David for obvious reasons) first appointment of the day. He welcomed me with his usual warm smile, and we sat in silence for several minutes while he reviewed the scans of my most recent MRI on his computer, as we did at each appointment. The difference this time was that he kept stopping to turn and look at me with a wide grin. I started to wonder what this was about but sat and waited quietly. He finally turned his whole body away from the computer, faced me, and announced in his heavy Russian accent "YOU VON! Kaley, I can't believe I'm saying this but you beat this! You beat MS."

It took me a moment to compose myself, and I finally said to him, "I've been focused on healing myself for the last few years, and I really felt in my heart that I had healed. But to hear *you,* an MS specialist tell me this, *now* it feels like a real miracle." That day he changed my diagnosis of Relapsing Remitting MS, which I had for 20 years, to No Evidence of Disease Activity (NEDA), a category that is rarely used or even spoken about.

The miracles have only continued to flow since that day, but let's first go back to the beginning.

The Beginning

Twenty years ago, at the ripe age of twelve, I awoke one morning to my eyes rapidly moving right to left and the feeling of ants crawling all over my feet. The vision symptoms led to extreme nausea, so I kept my eyes closed at all times, even to eat. The sensation in my feet gradually took over my whole legs. Every day brought a new surprise symptom. It took three months to receive the diagnosis of multiple sclerosis (MS), during which my initial symptoms worsened and new ones appeared daily.

After what felt like the longest three months of my life, going from doctor to doctor, keeping my eyes closed the entire time to avoid extreme nausea, needing help to walk anywhere or do anything because of the sensation in my legs, I finally received a diagnosis. To be completely honest, it was a relief to hear a doctor confidently tell me that I had multiple sclerosis. I finally had an answer and a direction. As one can imagine, during this time, my parents and I had been imagining the worst, so at least a chronic illness seemed better than a fatal one.

A New Life

Everything about my life changed, and I really mean everything. The worst part, by far, was the treatment—daily injections. As a seventh grader, not wanting to miss out on school trips or sleepovers, meant I had to learn to give myself the injections, and my body was always covered in sore spots. Of course, the symptoms themselves also changed my life. Some days, I needed help showering; sometimes, I slept for three days straight. I got rid of clothes with buttons because the lack of fine motor skills on some days meant it could take fifteen minutes to get a shirt on. I needed all kinds of accommodations at school such as exemption from gym class, extended time for testing, and even a notetaker when my hands were too weak to write. I could spend days listing the practical adjustments that were necessary just to get through each day in my life.

Just as every negative in life has a positive counterpart, there were positive changes in my life as well. My family spent more time together, my parents stopped arguing all the time, and I focused less on my grades and more on making meaningful memories. Up until my diagnosis, I was extremely studious, shy, and I struggled to fit in. But suddenly the awareness that I could wake up the next day and not be able to see or walk was a powerful dose of perspective. It allowed me to let go of things that didn't matter and motivated me to make the most of each day. I have always felt extremely blessed to have had this profound perspective from such a young age.

Another incredible gift I received during my diagnosis was determination. This gift came in the prickly package of a neurologist who said to me, "You'll be in a wheelchair by the end of high school, and don't plan on going to college." It was both the best and worst thing I could have been told at the time. It terrified me, but also lit a fire under me. I was determined to prove him wrong. Mind over matter was not just some cliché for me. Maintaining a positive outlook was the key to ensuring his words would never come true. I have seen the difference in someone's physical health when they believed a negative prognosis like this instead of ignoring it.

There is always secret door number three of course, which is to utilize a grim prognosis as fuel for a journey to health and transformation. I am so grateful I chose that path.

In many ways, I think my tenacity was a simple fact of my age. As kids, we feel invincible. We fall off the swing and get right back on, even if we're gushing blood. I was also too young to understand the repercussions that this disease could have on my life, despite being warned several times by different people. This is one of the keys to living the life you want. **We become what we believe.** I had refused to believe that this was going to ruin my life; I had refused to believe the words of that doctor, and I had refused to absorb the fears and anxieties of those around me. On a practical level, of course, there would be limitations and consequences. However, since I did not allow my mind to focus on that aspect of the illness, neither did my body. **The good news is you don't have to be a kid who feels invincible to adopt this mentality. It is accessible to us at any age.**

The Ripple Effect

The changes I made in my life began to have a ripple effect on those around me. Friends and community members shared how my response to this experience was influencing them to live their lives differently. Because I started talking to God every day from the moment of my first symptoms, my faith at this point had become very strong. Nothing in my life was constant anymore, so God became my constant, my sense of stability. As a result, when I realized the impact that my life was having on others, I also realized that it was time to ask the question, "Why me?"

Of course, many people ask this question, but for me it was about actually answering it. **"Why me" is a question that I believe every person must ask when faced with a challenge.** It should not be asked with the sorrowful "poor me" tone but should be asked in an engaging, challenging tone. Ask yourself this: **Why am I being given this challenge, this experience, as opposed to my neighbor? And, how am I uniquely positioned to face it?** I felt that I was given MS for a reason, and that sharing my story and life could inspire others to live more meaningful and passionate lives.

When I was thirteen years old, I began sharing my story with audiences across the US and continued through most of high school and college. At fourteen, I started the nonprofit organization Youth Against MS (YAMS) Inc. to inspire today's youth to raise awareness and funds for MS research, realizing that they have the power to make a difference. We had a Board of Directors comprised of teenagers, and during our active years, we raised hundreds of thousands of dollars. It was a remarkable experience to have had as an adolescent. I learned so much and was blessed to have a community rally around me. Seeing our successes showed me that I truly could do *anything* I set my mind to, which became crucial for my healing journey later. I experienced, firsthand, the power of perseverance and the capacity of one person to make a difference in the world. It was an exhilarating childhood, and I wouldn't trade it for the world, even though the MS part wasn't exactly easy.

Not All Roses

In all of this, I struggled with many limitations, including managing treatment that was sometimes worse than the disease itself. One medication gave me full 24-hour flu symptoms once a week for four years. I have given myself injections on flights while traveling to speaking gigs, even during turbulence. There were times when my symptoms were so bad that I couldn't stand for more than five minutes at a time. For almost a year, I couldn't climb stairs or open a bag of chips. One day out of the blue, I woke up paralyzed and blind in one eye. Getting through the day was often a massive challenge; yet, I possessed this intense drive to make an impact and keep doing everything I was so passionate about. Looking back, I'm not sure how I did it all. I think that the blessing and curse of illness is that you want to do *everything*, to squeeze everything out of life that you possibly can. As a result, I was often not honoring my body or heeding its messages.

On the other hand, while growing up with a chronic illness certainly wasn't easy, in many ways it was all I knew. I didn't have much to compare to prior to my diagnosis so, in truth, being diagnosed so young was a blessing because I didn't have to face any major *losses*. I was too young to experience major changes in important relationships. When I missed 60 consecutive days of school, I had to catch up of course but there weren't severe consequences like the potential loss of a career or the inability to support a family. Instead, those parts of my life integrated organically with my illness. Just as we integrate various life experiences and aspects of our personality as we grow up, MS became part of me. As a result, things that might have been a challenge for someone else to adapt to, seamlessly became part of how I lived my life.

In a way, my approach to my diagnosis made it feel like the challenges were worth it. I was inspiring thousands of people and making a difference for others living with MS. My life had a sense of purpose from an early age, which is a truly exhilarating way to live. And I can't leave out the incredibly unique and fun experiences I had as a result of my public role in the MS community: I went to VIP Hollywood events, developed relationships with celebrities who were passionate about my mission, was in the news regularly, and was often the center of attention, whether at home, on my high school campus, or in the news. I experienced higher highs and lower lows than most people experience in a lifetime, so *mostly* it all felt worth it.

Desiring Health

I vividly remember looking at my first MRI scans when I was twelve. The doctor was only going to show them to my parents, so the three of them walked out of the room together. I promptly hopped off the bed and followed them around the corner. The scans were already up on the screen and as I looked at them, I could sense everyone's discomfort. I had already seen the images though and started asking questions. While looking at the images of scars on my brain my most pressing question was, "Can the scars heal? Can my brain repair?"

"No. It's impossible," the doctor coldly replied.

While my ears heard him, I refused to accept his harsh decree. What he said was simply impossible. How could the same human body that is built to perfection, that has the potential to create another human being, lack the ability to repair neurons?[35]

It was at that moment I had an innate awareness that my body likely had everything it needed to heal. I knew intuitively that I did not have to spend my life living with illness. But, at twelve, that intuitive message felt like barely a whisper. I didn't have the tools to know what to do with it. But on some level, the awareness of the capacity of my body and my experience of the power of the mind was always there.

Time to Heal

One day at age twenty-eight, I decided I did not want to live the rest of my life with illness. I was over it. So I set out to actually heal, not just gain some relief or reduce symptoms. I wanted to dive into the mind-body connection and do anything possible to heal. **I firmly believe that healing begins with the belief that it's possible.** Today, whenever a prospective client reaches out, my first questions are, "Do you believe you can live without illness?" and "Do you believe it's possible to heal?"

With faith, that healing was possible. I set out on my journey in two stages. In stage one, I examined the connection between mind, body, and soul. I assessed my beliefs around illness and explored how MS was serving me. In stage two, I set out to discover the root cause of my MS. Growing up, my parents and I spent thousands of dollars on alternative paths to healing,

---

[35] Since that day in 1998, many studies have been done showing that the brain can in fact repair itself, including myelin (fatty tissue that protects nerve cells, which is what is attacked and becomes scarred in MS). My second MRI scans already showed signs of repair, and my neurologist immediately sent them to MS centers globally that triggered many of these studies.

all while still following Western medicine as well. While most things provided some relief, I wanted to fully heal and stop spending thousands for a little relief. I knew I had to get to the source, even if it meant facing painful parts of myself.

Talking to My Body

The concept of reincarnation is part of many traditions, and as a Jew, I was already aware of what Judaism refers to as gilgulim, or 'soul cycles.' When I began my healing journey, I immersed myself in the topic of reincarnation in order to better understand the respective roles of body and soul in each lifetime. I was curious if this might lead to a deeper understanding of my illness and the path to healing. When we decide to reincarnate, we actually *choose* our bodies, which means we choose all the risks associated with a particular body. When I learned this, I had to face the question: Why did I choose a body with the potential for MS? And an even bigger question: Why would I have chosen a body that could experience illness rather than one with perfect health?

Our bodies and souls work as a team in each lifetime, and our bodies are actually here to help us stay on track. They are part of our life journey; in fact, they have a responsibility to help keep us moving toward our life's mission. The human body has an innate wisdom that it uses to give us a gentle nudge or, if necessary, a big push to completely change course. Furthermore, our souls, which also want to keep us on the path we planned for this lifetime and are always yearning for spiritual expansion, can communicate to us *through* the body.

For anyone living with illness, this not only sounds strange but is almost heretical. Trust me, I personally know how hard this is to hear. How can my physical suffering be the body's way of helping me? Like most people who are living with illness, I had a conflicted relationship with my body for years. I was frustrated when it failed me, grateful when it gave me relief, but overall I experienced disappointment and pain that my body limited me so much.

To turn to my body with this new knowledge that it was, in fact, trying to help, even if I didn't know how yet, was difficult to say the least. It was a pivotal moment in my healing though, and ultimately life changing.

Here is an example that practically anyone can relate to: You're working toward a deadline—maybe for an exam, project at work, or an upcoming event—with crazy hours and trying to just push through to cross the finish line. You feel overwhelmed and exhausted, but instead of taking a break, you keep pushing yourself until suddenly you wake up with a cold or flu. Think about an experience like this that you've had. When you called in sick that day, did you notice that sense of relief that you were finally getting a break?

Often, it is easier for us to get sick than to feel an emotion. It's also much more acceptable in society to refer to physical illness than an emotional challenge. As a result, we subconsciously opt for physical illness. And the body is remarkable at helping us. In fact, it actually feels *safer* for the nervous system to experience pain than to feel emotions. The body thinks it's protecting us. While it took me time to fully understand this concept, I *believed* it right away because I saw the immediate results with my own symptoms.

Using Emotional Freedom Technique (EFT), I was able to calm a symptom down enough to ask my body what it was trying to bring to my attention or what message it had for me. **We live in a society where we are not encouraged to face our feelings.** Furthermore, there simply isn't time. We go from one meeting to the next, popping painkillers because we don't have time to be sick or have a migraine.

But if I wanted to live a healthy life, I had to carve out time and make this a priority—both to deal with emotions in real time and to take the time to understand my body's messages. With time, I learned to hear the messages my body was trying to send me with each symptom. For example, the eye pain I was experiencing (one of my more severe MS symptoms that often felt like I was being stabbed with an ice pick from behind the eye) was my body's way of drawing my attention to something that hurt to see on an emotional level. It might have been a behavior within me or even others. **Our feelings must be acknowledged. They are important indicators and signposts, and they don't just disappear when we ignore them.** Sometimes simply by acknowledging that feeling, the pain would finally ease up. For example, say something like, "I feel sad when I *see* my parent/partner/self behave this way." By acknowledging my deeper feelings, my body no longer had to bring something to my attention through a physical, and often very painful, symptom.

Back to "Why Me"

As I got better at this, I learned to manage symptoms so well that they would disappear instantaneously. Around this time is when the second stage of my healing journey began, and I set out to discover if there was a root cause for my diagnosis. I had to come back to the initial question I asked shortly after my diagnosis: Why me? Why did my body develop MS as a solution in the first place? As an adult, I see how the daily symptoms were serving me or drawing my attention to something, but what was my body trying to solve at age twelve?

I don't have many memories from before I was diagnosed. I always attributed this to the feeling that my life only really began after my diagnosis because that's when life started to feel meaningful. Apparently, the lack of memories was also because I was protecting myself. I believe both reasons to be true and real parts of the new self that has emerged from this journey. Regardless of the reason, I had to access that time of my life if I was going to understand my illness and free myself from it.

I found different meditation tools that allowed me to revisit my childhood in order to explore what could have possibly triggered the onset of my MS. Of course, this is different for each person, but ultimately, our body thinks it is providing a solution, even if it isn't a good one and even when there are downsides. The body believes it is helping.

For days and weeks, I would meditate and get stuck at the same point. Finally, I broke through and memories from my childhood started flooding back to me. I bet you are thinking something terrible—perhaps abuse. Hardly. Not even close actually. I had a great childhood. But my family relationships were strained, as so many are. I came into the world as a healer, a fixer, with deep wisdom at a young age. I saw ways to help my family relationships and even expressed how to improve them. Unfortunately, as a child, I was voiceless to try and help. Who would listen to a seven-year-old child giving parenting advice? But this isn't about my parents, this is about my *perception* of the circumstances. As a result, I felt invisible and was carrying this deep drive to make things so much better. I did not remember these feelings and experiences until I started my healing journey. When the memories started coming back, everything made sense suddenly. I felt invisible as a child, so my body made everyone else invisible. I didn't feel heard, and suddenly I was the center of attention. All the things that my parents would argue about, big or small, didn't matter anymore; they and my brother were facing the very real fact of my illness, my limitations, and my needs in every moment. We came together as a family. And no surprise, I found my voice as a public speaker within months of being diagnosed.

I finally found the root cause of my diagnosis and understood how my body thought it was providing me with a solution. It was truly a transformative moment in my life. For the first time, I didn't feel betrayed by my body. Of course, there was a risk involved with my body utilizing MS as a solution in this way. It could have backfired and made matters worse. But whether or not what the body *thinks* it's providing as a solution works or not, I had to acknowledge that my body was trying to help. I finally understood why it did what it did. Being able to acknowledge this already made a substantial impact on my healing since I was no longer in conflict with my body. But was I ready to heal? Was I ready to live without MS and *let go* of all that entails, the good and the bad? Yes, that's right, there is good, too.

Unpacking Illness Identity

Even after understanding the soul, mind, and body connection and unpacking it, I discovered that I still had a block. Illness was part of my identity and I had to decide if I was willing to release that identity. Was I ready to let go of the ways in which MS had served me all these years? **Illness was my way of life. It's all I had ever known, and it had become part of my identity.** I have found that to be true in *everyone* with illness regardless of the timing of diagnosis, even if we don't necessarily realize it.

When something came up in my life, if I needed an extension on a paper or didn't feel well enough to go to work one day, I almost didn't even have to explain it. I had MS, and that was enough for both myself and others to understand. It probably didn't help that in high school I became known as the 'MS girl.' It was a title given lovingly since I was a public advocate for the cause, but the downside is I came to *own* that identity.

Before I knew if I was ready to let go of that identity, I had to first understand how MS was currently serving me separate from the original solution my body thought it was providing. I also had to get clear about where MS was tied to my identity. To understand this, I stopped calling it MS, which accomplished two very important things.

First, like I said earlier, **we become what we believe. Our cells and organs will align with whatever we tell them.** Removing MS from my lexicon and mindset allowed my cells to begin reorganizing and gave me the opportunity to start envisioning what life would be like without MS. As you can imagine, having been the 'poster child,' this was very difficult. I had to take a step back from the MS community that had in many ways become an extended family, in order to begin separating myself from being the 'MS girl.' Sure I still went to my neurology appointments, but I listened more than spoke and was mindful not to absorb any feedback specifically about MS. I had to create the space for the cells in my body to consider health as an option.

Secondly, removing MS from my vocabulary made me aware of every time I *would have* used MS as a crutch or an excuse but couldn't. That forced me to understand what feelings I was avoiding or where I was receiving something my friends and I came to fondly call 'MS Perks.'

MS Perks (n) — Anything that you or friends and family can utilize or receive that is a benefit [36], service, or experience that healthy people cannot access.

Some of my favorite examples include cutting the lines at Disneyland, booking concert tickets in the handicap section even though the arena was sold out, handicap parking, and the list goes on. But these are all the surface-level perks. I 'benefited' in much bigger ways. In high school, teachers never said anything to me if I had an overdue assignment. Everyone assumed it was because of MS. I always had the most justified excuse. Even when I entered the working world, I could always

---

[36]   Note that when I refer to the benefits of illness, these are not usually clear benefits. We are often not consciously aware that there are payoffs to being sick. For this reason, I will keep 'benefit' in quotes and to be sensitive to the fact that each benefit from illness comes at the often severe cost of health.

pull the MS card. I even pulled the MS card when I didn't feel like going to a friend's party but didn't want to hurt their feelings. Most of the time, it felt fair to receive these perks, given how much I was suffering. I always felt there was a balance. But if I wanted to live MS-free, then I had to learn to live without the perks.

The surface-level perks, like the handicap spot, were easier to let go of. But even that was a big adjustment. I felt strongly, however, that I'd rather be healthy than park front and center. We think that's obvious, and that anyone would prefer that, but if we have any chance of healing, we actually have to make the *active choice* of health over this seemingly small 'benefit.' The harder things to let go of were things like having MS as an excuse. It was an important awareness that forced me to examine my beliefs, fears, and blocks. For instance, I discovered my deep need for approval when I realized it was easier for me to be late on a deadline because of illness rather than say something like, "I haven't had time to finish the project" or even justly explain why something was delayed. Not having my MS excuse felt scary because I was going to be judged *based on me* without MS to protect me. When it came to my relationship, I had to learn to express my desire for love or affection rather than say, "I'm in pain, can you give me a massage?"

Without being able to say 'MS,' I had to explore what I actually felt or wanted deep down and then face the fear of asking for it as a valid need in and of itself. That vulnerability was *so scary!* With practice, not only did it get easier, but it was also freeing! It felt wonderful and powerful to say what I was truly feeling and to be honest about a limitation or a need. Even if I had to face consequences or didn't get what I wanted, I survived the experience of owning the feeling or need, and that was okay. I was learning that my feelings were safe and that it was okay to be vulnerable. My body was learning that I didn't need the MS excuse. I also had to actively replace as many of the 'benefits' of MS with healthy behaviors and lifestyle changes so that I was still attending to my needs.

Prior to this journey, I was not consciously aware that in any of these instances my illness was serving me in these ways. Of course I believed that if I pulled the MS card to get out of attending an event, it was because I was actually sick. After all, I *was* actually sick. But could I receive love and affection without having to be in pain or have any other number of symptoms? I did not know how to accept love if it wasn't under the guise of illness. It forced me to face questions such as "Am I inherently worthy of love?" If for no other reason, unpacking illness identity is worth it to address this one question.

If I wanted to really heal, I had to work through all of these parts of my identity and face these life-altering questions. Am I inherently lovable even if I don't have the sympathy card? Everyone always admired me because of everything I had overcome and how much I was accomplishing despite my illness. Would I still be appreciated and admired if I did all those things as a healthy person? What is my true worth based on? The list of questions goes on. More than most people can imagine. We don't think about these things. They seamlessly become part of our identity and are regularly reinforced. Illness was so deeply integrated into my identity that it was all I knew. It took over a year to parse all of this out.

Saying Goodbye to MS – With Gratitude

Living life without illness identity required a lot of practice. It was challenging because it was so new but also liberating. For example, canceling plans because I didn't *feel like* going out rather than because I was *sick* empowered me. I stopped using MS in my vocabulary, whether it was with my boss, family, or friends. I had to get comfortable recognizing my needs and owning them rather than using MS to obtain them. And I spent hours visualizing the rest of my life living illness free.

When I was ready to let go of my illness identity, I thanked my body immensely for the solution it provided for me at age twelve. I thanked it for the ongoing support throughout the years and even the symptoms, whether it was blindness or urinary incontinence (lack of bladder control). I thanked it for trying to help me and for providing me with solutions that I didn't previously acknowledge. I asked for forgiveness from my body for all the anger and frustration I expressed toward it. And most importantly, I told my body that I didn't need these solutions anymore and that I can take care of these needs for myself in other ways. Finally, I promised that I would continue attending to my future needs.

And, as simple as it sounds, that was it.

Living a Miracle

Being MS-free is a miracle beyond anything many people can fathom. I can travel without having to work around my treatment schedule. I don't have to keep a catheter and eye patch in my purse at all times 'just in case.' I don't procrastinate waking up because it might be yet another day of pain. I don't live the life of the average healthy person. I know what it means to be sick, so every single healthy day is exhilarating. It's miraculous to be in this body that has given me such a gift both in illness and in health.

Radical Responsibility

Being MS-free also requires radical responsibility. I know that at any moment my body has very clear ways of communicating with me that are far from pleasant. This means that if I want to remain healthy I have to process emotions *when* they come up; show up for relationships with integrity; honor my limitations just as every human can only work so many hours or needs a minimum number of hours of sleep; and so much more. I have to take care of this body, which has given me such a huge miracle. And doing that requires taking care of my mind and soul: regular meditation, regular inspiration, regular checking in, and regular reminders of how far I've come.

Sharing the Miracle

The greatest gift of all has been guiding others to experience relief from their illnesses. I am living proof that the body has everything it needs to heal, and with faith and determination, miracles are possible. I am amazed by the breakthroughs and symptom relief that my clients experience when they courageously face a fear or experience an emotion. We can invest all the time and money in the world on our health and healing, but until we are *ready* to heal, until we examine every aspect of how illness serves us and let go of illness identity, we won't get the full results we seek.

Making Miracles

In reflecting upon my three-plus decades on this earth, I am amazed by how much power each of us holds. **We are all a part of the Creator and therefore can create any reality we choose.** This does not mean you are to blame if you are sick. But it means that we have access to tools that can change our circumstances or at the very least, change the way we handle our circumstances. My diagnosis in many ways made me who I am. Early on, through my diagnosis, I discovered my ability to inspire others; I accessed newfound stores of courage and honed my skills as a public speaker.

The courage to live each day with illness is the same courage needed to open the healing channels. In many ways, once we've adapted to illness, it can feel easier to be sick than healthy. Not only does it become part of our identity, but the world around us supports its existence. Taking medication, even if it isn't very effective, is easier than facing our fears, our emotional scars, and sharing our deepest needs. But remember, you are already so brave for each day that you survive with symptoms, show up for yet another treatment, and continue to hope for healing. What if you channeled that courage into expressing your feelings, journaling, or crying? It sounds simplistic, but my experience tells me that it isn't. The strength and courage are already there. What if the energy you put into managing your illness you channeled into obtaining and creating the same 'benefits' while remaining healthy? Sometimes, we just need someone to support us through these steps, which is an honor I have each time someone decides to begin their healing journey with me. While I never guarantee full healing because everything is ultimately in God's hands, I get to watch miracles unfold as people experience relief from their symptoms. Every time it happens, I thank God and the human body. I also remember to thank myself for having the courage and determination to walk this path, to create a new identity, a new self, and a new life so that others can experience everyday miracles, too. Even if it's experiencing one day, even one hour, without pain, I know firsthand that is a life-changing gift.

Final Thoughts

What if diagnosis was about understanding the problem your body is trying to solve rather than claiming something is inherently wrong with the body? How would you approach your illness differently?

We all face different challenges. In every moment, we have a choice of how to manage each challenge. We can turn it into the greatest gift, or we can let it crush us. We can be the victim or the victor. My belief is that when we are faced with a challenge, the soul is signaling us that we're ready now to face that particular step in our journey. This approach develops resilience that not only allows one to overcome the challenge in front of them but also makes it seem more manageable.

May you be blessed to know that you are part of the Divine, to see the opportunities in your challenges, to have the strength to overcome and flourish on your path, and may you be blessed with abundant health.

Kaley Zeitouni

As a speaker and coach, Kaley Zeitouni combines her professional skills as a Marriage and Family Therapist with her personal experiences facing life's biggest challenges to empathically guide others through transformative healing journeys.

Kaley began her career at fourteen when she founded the nonprofit organization Youth Against multiple sclerosis (YAMS). As a natural born leader with an unwavering passion to make an impact, Kaley has inspired thousands across the globe as a motivational speaker sharing her experience of being diagnosed with MS at age twelve. After twenty years of living with the autoimmune disease, Kaley healed herself from MS and now coaches others with chronic illness to experience relief from symptoms, transform their health blueprint, and live healthy lives. During her healing journey, Kaley faced the sudden death of her fiancé. Through this transformative experience, she created a grief-coaching program to help others who have lost a spouse or partner to truly heal and restore a sense of wholeness in their lives. Today, Kaley lives in Jerusalem and continues to empower and inspire others to heal from within, whether from loss or illness.

Contact Information

Website: KaleyZ.com
E-mail: Hello@KaleyZ.com
Facebook: @KaleyZeitouni or fb.me/KaleyZeitouni
Instagram: kaleyzeitouniofficial

To the Broskies-
May you forever enjoy the
transformation and expansion of
your souls.

♡,
Kaley

TRANSFORM YOUR HEALTH, TRANSFORM YOUR LIFE

KIRSTEN WARD

"The first wealth is health."
Ralph Waldo Emerson

T he best day of my life was the day I got married; the worst day of my life was when my husband died eight weeks later.

As a 42-year-old, never-been-married woman, I had waited to find the perfect guy. Of course, Glenn was not really perfect, but he was perfect for me and we were perfect together. You know how you want to be with someone who lets you grow into a better person? Glenn did that for me, and I can only hope I did the same in return.

Glenn and I had a whirlwind, romantic relationship. And it happened at warp speed. I was engaged, married three months later, and widowed two months after that. My head still spins thinking about how I experienced in just five months—becoming a fiancée, wife, and widow—what other people experience in a lifetime. We had plans to have children, and he was building a business of four small personal training studios. We were elated to have found each other at this stage of our lives. This marriage was Glenn's second and my first. Everyone in my family could see how we complimented and adored each other.

We were shocked and unprepared for Glenn's untimely death. Yes, he had CLL (chronic lymphocytic leukemia), but he was being followed by a highly esteemed doctor in one of Boston's top hospitals. We were told that CLL is a long, slow, progressive disease. But the diagnosis was completely wrong; Glenn had an aggressive form of CLL that had gone undetected for three years. After our honeymoon, what we mistook for the common flu was actually pneumonia. Glenn collapsed, and I rushed him to the hospital where he was admitted to the ICU with sepsis. Twenty-four hours later, he went into cardiac arrest. I held him in my arms as he gasped his last breath.

After Glenn's death, I felt like my life was crumbling around me. I had my own demanding full-time job, his four personal training studios to manage, a mortgage beyond my finances, new roommates to help contain costs, and probate court proceedings to address the lack of a will. On top of dealing with the grief of losing Glenn, our dreams and future plans were destroyed. At forty-two, my hopes for having a child were gone. I felt robbed. *How could life be so unfair?*

I hated my life. I was sick with anger and rage. Every part of my existence was covered with gloom. Coworkers and supervisors were unsympathetic, and I was dealing with employee and manager challenges at the personal training studios, as well as franchisee issues. My home life was just as terrible—with roommate problems and boxes and closets filled with Glenn's personal belongings that I needed to sort through.

I woke up every morning not wanting to get out of bed. I didn't bother to shower or put on makeup. I went to work dressed only in black. It was how I felt—depressed and tired of living. I wanted to curl up under my covers, cry myself back to sleep, and die. Every cell in my body hurt. Whenever I took an airplane trip, I prayed the plane would crash. I thought about how I could end my life: *Maybe I should drive off a cliff? Or take some pills at night and just go to sleep?*

During this lowest point in my life, all of the self-care habits I had worked so hard to form in the past completely fell apart. I stopped exercising and eating well, and my old eating disorder resurfaced. Since the time I was very young, I'd felt a palpable pressure to be thin and I struggled with a food obsession throughout high school, college, and early adulthood. Pursuing a career in dance and working as a personal trainer exacerbated the problem. During those early years, my relationship with food, my body, and myself was completely out of alignment. My food fixation was like a volcano—at times erupting and at other times remaining dormant.

While it had been dormant for more than a decade, the fixation came back in full force after Glenn's death. I tried to numb myself with ice cream, chocolate, and sugary delicacies. The binge-and-purge cycle was very addictive. It became more frequent and felt like an old friend.

I was miserable for several years. I'd hear people complain about what felt to me like a trivial problem, and I would arrogantly reply, "Nobody in your life died today!" Unconsciously, my sole purpose was to make everyone around me unhappy. Slowly, I recognized that I was making my life more unbearable because of my perspective, my attitude, and my general hatred of everything and everyone.

I was 'holding onto Glenn,' not wanting to let him go. But no matter how hard I tried, he was slowly disappearing. First, the scent of him on my pillows faded, then the voicemails were gone; his clothes and belongings were packed off to donation centers; and then three of the personal training studios went bankrupt.

While Glenn's death was the most devastating experience of my life, it was also his greatest gift to me. His death and my subsequent eating disorder propelled me to transform my relationship with food and ultimately the relationship with myself.

I had gained unwanted weight, and my body hurt from lack of exercise. Despite my serious contemplation of suicide, I knew that was not really an option for me. I needed to have a conversation with myself. *How was I going to continue living my life: miserably or happily? Would Glenn really want me to be so sad and live the remainder of my life as a wretched widow?* As I grappled with the recurrence of my eating disorder, more questions arose and I questioned my relationship with food:

- *How do I truly transform my relationship with food?*
- *Why would I even want to modify my eating behavior?*
- *What if there was a way to live free from my food obsession?*
- *What if I could manage stressful situations with peace, acceptance, and clarity of mind?*

Prior to marrying Glenn, I had been trained and was working as a Certified Diabetes Educator (CDE®) and a health coach, and it became clear to me that now I wasn't doing what I advocated to my clients. I had to take a deep look inside.

It felt nearly impossible to change my eating habits. With other compulsions, such as smoking, you can choose to stop the behavior. But you can't stop eating! *How was I going to transform my relationship with food and with myself?* It was time for me to re-initiate my self-care habits and make living a healthy life a priority again.

Let me be clear, I didn't go from being grouchy one day to being happy the next. It was a process. I had good days and bad days. Slowly, there were more good days. I asked a friend to be my workout buddy, and I was very fortunate to have family and friends who were always around to help.

The experience of prematurely losing my husband taught me that even the worst of circumstances didn't need to send me down a permanently destructive path. Life is never going to be completely free of trauma, and one person's sense of trauma might differ from another's. People can be knocked down long and hard, but the question I needed to ask myself was: *How long am I going to be knocked off my feet before I choose to do something to get back up?*

Are You Putting Your Life at Risk with Unhealthy Eating Habits?

According to the National Association of Anorexia Nervosa and Associated Disorders, at least 30 million people of all ages and genders in the United States suffer from an eating disorder such as anorexia and/or bulimia.[37]

Included in the eating disorder paradigm are people with type 1 diabetes who are at risk for diabulimia, which is deliberate insulin underuse or omission for the purpose to control weight. About thirty-eight percent of women and sixteen percent of men with type 1 diabetes have disordered eating behaviors.[38] [39] [40]

Unconnected to eating disorders but related to overeating, obesity, and weight control is type 2 diabetes. As of 2015, 30.3 million Americans have diabetes. Another 84.1 million have pre-diabetes, a condition that if not treated often leads to type 2 diabetes within five years.[41] It is also commonly known among health-care providers that if one loses approximately 5–10 percent of their body weight, it can decrease their risk of developing diabetes by 58 percent.[42]

---

[37] "*Eating Disorder Statistics: National Association of Anorexia Nervosa and Associated Disorders.*" National Association of Anorexia Nervosa and Associated Disorders. https://anad.org/education-and-awareness/about-eating-disorders/eating-disorders-statistics/.

[38] Goebel-Fabbri, et al., '*Insulin restriction and associated morbidity and mortality in women with type 1 diabetes. Diabetes Care*', 31(3), 415-419.

[39] Hanlan, et al., '*Eating disorders and disordered eating in Type 1 diabetes: prevalence, screening, and treatment options*', 13(6), 909-916.

[40] Hudson, et al., '*The prevalence and correlates of eating disorders in the national comorbidity survey replication*', 61(3), 348–358.

[41] New CDC Report: More than 100 million Americans have diabetes and prediabetes. Center For Disease Control and Prevention (CDC). https://www.cdc.gov/media/releases/2017/p0718-diabetes-report.html.

[42] Johns Hopkins Medicine, Digestive Weight Loss Center, Diabetes: https://www.hopkinsmedicine.org/digestive_weight_loss_center/conditions/diabetes.html.

Diabetes brings a unique set of challenges that require people to make significant changes in their lives. A diabetes diagnosis and the daily complexities of managing the disease can make a person feel knocked down, frustrated, angry, hopeless, confused, and even traumatized. Yet, none of those feelings have to be permanent. I would not necessarily classify people with type 2 diabetes as having an eating disorder, but my experience is that most of my patients with type 2 diabetes have struggled with weight management and healthy food choices at some point in their lives. I've been able to help them restructure their lifestyles around healthy behaviors.

Tips to Transform Your Health

One of my goals as a health-care professional is to help anyone who is dealing with an eating disorder to transform their relationship to themselves with food. I understand! My own food challenges have enabled me to have patience and empathy for my clients who are overweight or struggling with diabetes.

If you aren't certain about any undiagnosed eating behaviors or if you constantly struggle with food intake and your weight, here are some powerful questions to ask yourself:

- Do I use food to numb my feelings?
- Have I made multiple attempts to change my eating patterns with no success?
- Do I feel guilty about overeating?
- Do I spend significant time thinking, concealing, planning, and recovering from my eating patterns?
- Do I worry that I've lost control over how much I eat?
- Would I say that food dominates my life?

If you've have answered 'yes' to two or more of these questions, you may be using food to self-soothe. Or, conversely, you may be denying yourself food as a form of punishment. You can use the following tips to help you make positive changes and meet the challenges that life may throw at you.

1. Be Honest with Yourself

I remember the self-deception and lies that permeated my life during my dark time, and I find them almost humorous now. Sometimes, I'd convince myself that I didn't have a problem because I nourished myself with healthy foods and only vomited the unhealthy, last thing I ate (ice cream, cookies, etc.). Other times, I convinced myself I had no obvious problem because I wasn't emaciated like the anorexic people shown on television. At the end of the day, I was dishonest with myself.

The first step to transform your health is to be honest with yourself. Think about your own patterns and recognize the lies that you may be telling yourself. Ask yourself these questions, and be brutally honest with your responses.

- What do I believe is true regarding my weight?
- What story do I tell myself about my health?
- What excuses and justifications do I make about eating healthfully?
- What objections, real and not real, do I make about physical activity?
- What do I consider to be my biggest challenge regarding my health, and what story do I tell myself about that challenge?

2. Look Deeper

If you want to transform your health, take a deeper look. The way you eat is merely the tip of the iceberg. Many people know that over ninety percent of an iceberg's mass is beneath the surface. If you want to be healthy in mind, body, and spirit, you need to explore the deeper waters of your life. You can begin by journaling, which will provide insights into the ideas and beliefs you hold about your health.

Source: www.bridgetinbeeld.nl

- What negative comments do you tell yourself about your weight and health?
- What messages do you give yourself? Do you think you are you a bad person? Are you lazy? What responsibility do you have regarding your health?

- What does 'healthy' mean to you?
- How would you rate your health today, and where do you want it to be in five, ten, and fifteen years?
- What do you consider your ideal health?
- How would you feel physically and emotionally if you were at your healthiest?
- What is the internal dialogue in your head? Do you hear an angel or a devil?
- What self-sabotaging messages do you say to yourself?

3. Create Healthy Habits

Food habits are developed at an early age, and many people are brought up in households with poor nutritional patterns. In such cases, people may miss opportunities to learn how to create good eating habits. You can start with these basics:

- Always sit down to eat a meal, that is, never eat standing up.
- Avoid 'screen time' when eating. This includes watching television, using your phone, tablet, computer, etc.
- Chew your food and eat slowly.
- If you're a fast eater, use chopsticks to slow the pace.
- Put your fork and knife down between each bite.
- If possible, take as much time to eat your food as it took to prepare.
- According to the U.S. Dietary Guidelines 2015-2020, eat a variety of foods, and in general, aim to eat 5 to 10 servings of vegetables and fruits each day.[43]

---

43 U.S. Department of Health and Human Services and U.S. Department of Agriculture. 2015 – 2020 Dietary Guidelines for Americans. https://health.gov/dietaryguidelines/2015/guidelines/.

- Eat at consistent times of the day and avoid skipping meals. Healthy times to eat generally range between: 6–8 AM for breakfast; 11 AM–2 PM for lunch; and 5–7 PM for dinner.

If you gravitate toward the kitchen to soothe yourself with food when you're stressed, bored, or emotional, be prepared by having ready a different behavior or a reminder to stop. Try one or more of the following strategies:

- Place a sticky note on the fridge as a reminder to drink a glass of water prior to eating a snack.
- Devote ten minutes to mindful breathing or meditation to determine if you're truly hungry.
- Journal your emotions prior to eating a snack or meal.
- Instead of self-soothing with food, find a positive behavior to quiet your emotions. Ask yourself, "What is the most loving thing I can do for myself right now?" It might mean a bath, a short stroll, or playtime with your children or pets. Kids and pets quickly put you in a good mood, and spending time with them is a wonderful way to get the endorphin kick that your brain wants. Put on your favorite motivational song, or watch a quick, funny video to change your mood.

You get the idea. The first step is to break the pattern of using food as a crutch. Find what works for you!

4. Set Yourself up for Success

Many people set themselves up for failure. No one can be successful with a meal, exercise, or lifestyle plan when self-sabotage undercuts the goal. How many of us have gone to the supermarket while hungry? Before you know it, you have chips, candy, and cookies in the grocery cart, and you're chomping on a candy bar as you walk through the aisles. This example is just one illustration of how the best intentions can be ruined by seemingly minor circumstances. Think about the ways to avoid such traps. This approach may take a bit of thought and planning, but your success will be worth it! Here are some tips I recommend:

- Plan meals for the week.
- Take lunch to work instead of eating out.
- Eat out less frequently.
- Grocery shop after having eaten a meal.
- Grocery shop with a food list.
- Have healthy snacks that are ready to grab in the fridge or cabinet.
- Avoid bringing home foods that are not on your meal plan.
- Share a restaurant meal with someone else.
- When eating out, ask for a take-out container and immediately set aside half of the meal to take home.
- Prior to going to a new restaurant, look at the menu online and choose your food ahead of time.
- Schedule fitness activities like you schedule your business meetings, doctor's appointments, dinner dates, etc.
- Put sneakers and gym clothes in the car or bring them to work so that you can go directly to the gym after work.
- Find a workout buddy.

5. Focus Your Mind

According to the National Science Foundation, the average person has approximately 60,000 thoughts per day; of those, eighty percent are negative and ninety-five percent of those are repetitive. Conscious and subconscious thoughts make a difference in our confidence and how we feel about ourselves. Start on the pathway to incorporate a healthy mindset by focusing on the positive aspects of your life.[44]

To get out of my despair, I started a gratitude journal. It helped me focus my mind in a different direction. At first, it was difficult to find anything that brought me joy. Then I realized my dog was an antidote to my gloom. He greeted me every day with love, jumping up and down, and licking my face. He helped focus my thoughts, for the first time, on something joyful. Take time to start a gratitude journal that may help you to focus on joy, too. Every day, write down three things you can be happy about. Here are a few ideas to get you started:

- I am grateful for my family.
- I am grateful for my friends.
- I am grateful for my excellent health.
- I am grateful for my dog.

To stay on course and remain committed to your goals, find an internal motivator that will serve as a key component of your plan. Early in my career as a diabetes educator, I taught a class on motivation. A young man in the class, who was recently diagnosed with diabetes, said he had just found his motivator.

---

[44] "The Average Person Has between 12,000 and 60,000 Thoughts per Day." Siobhan Kelleher Kukolic. https://siobhankukolic.com/the-average-person-has-between-12000-and-60000-thoughts-per-day/

It was his young daughter. His goal was to take care of himself so that he would be able to provide for her, see her graduate high school and college, and get married. He put photos of her everywhere—on his phone, in his wallet, and in his car. It was his way of staying focused and providing constant reminders of his goal throughout the day. Every day, multiple times a day, take time to clarify your purpose and re-commit to yourself, your body, and your health. Ask yourself these questions:

- Why is it important for me to improve my health?
- If you have diabetes: How will I feel when my blood glucose is under control?
- What are the external motivators to improve my health?
- What are the internal motivators to improve my health?
- What needs to change for me so that I have more of a commitment toward my goals?

6. Accept the Reality

If you have recently been diagnosed with diabetes, your first reaction may be to deny the diagnosis. This response is not uncommon, but the sooner you can embrace and accept the situation, the sooner you will be on the path to less suffering and better health.

When I worked at The Joslin Diabetes Center in Boston, I had a patient who was blind because of complications from many years of uncontrolled diabetes. He said he denied his diagnosis for years, did not take his medications as prescribed, did not modify his diet, and ignored his health. Today, poor health, blindness, and neuropathy are his constant companions. He regrets he did not take action sooner, and he now suffers from the reminders of how his neglect damaged his life

I remember a lesson on acceptance that a coach taught me as I grappled with my personal loss. She said that my suffering was completely optional. I looked at her with a puzzled expression. She explained that suffering is not accepting what is true. The truth was that my husband Glenn was gone. There was no bringing him back. That was the moment I realized there was no point in resisting the facts. It was time to pick myself up and stop my own personal suffering. Doing so didn't mean forgetting my loss or ignoring my grief, but it gave me a way to feel the emotions without being consumed by them. Acceptance allows a person to move forward.

Are there any situations in your life that you are choosing to ignore? Here are some questions to ponder:

- When do you NOT put your health first?
- How come you do not place health as a priority?
- What situation do you meet with resistance?
- How can you move from resistance to acceptance?

7. Look for a Different Perspective

People aren't surprised when I tell them that Glenn gave me many gifts during his lifetime. He was an amazing man with a gentle heart. But they are very surprised when I tell them that he gave me more gifts in his illness and death. I am a different person as a result of my loss. Granted, I would rather my husband be alive today; but during the preparation for the funeral, my clergyman asked me an important question, "If you had known that you were only going to have two months as husband and wife, would you still have married Glenn, knowing the profound sadness that was in your future?" The answer was an unwavering "**yes**." Glenn's death was the worst and the best thing that happened in my life.

This same kind of insight applies to my eating disorder history. It has given me the understanding and compassion for others who struggle with unhealthy eating behaviors and weight issues. Where can you look at a circumstance in your life that is both your nemesis and golden opportunity? Every challenge and every obstacle we face is truly a gift and a chance to look within and learn. Some positive, affirming questions can help to walk this path:

- What is the blessing in this circumstance?
- What is the lesson for me to learn?
- What gifts may come from this situation?

8. Embrace Self-Love

While there were times when my the eating disorder behaviors were absent, the reality was that thoughts about my body, my weight, and my personal self-worth were always destructive. An imbalance persisted in my life until I Iearned how to change my perspective. The true path to my transformation encompassed a triad of self-love encompassing mind, body, and spirit. Truly loving and accepting myself was a process. It can be that way for you, too. Here are a few tips to increase or improve your self-love:

- Ask yourself what will serve as your highest good?

- If you were your own best friend, what would you say to yourself?
- If love were a person, what would s/he say to you?
- Do 'mirror' work: Look in the mirror and say, "I love myself, I love myself, I love myself." Do this even if at first you do not believe it!
- Every day for a month, write down one thing that you love about yourself. Don't repeat anything! "I love that I am vivacious, intelligent, funny, quirky, happy, loving, forgiving, etc."
- There is a YouTube video that I love. In it, a little girl named Jessica embraces self-love perfectly. Start some daily affirmations like Jessica does. You can watch the video here: https://www.youtube.com/watch?v=qR3rK0kZFkg

My late husband Glenn made a huge impact on me while he was alive. His death then shaped and transformed me into who I am today. At some point during my self-discovery, I realized that if I were to continue living, I wanted my life to have meaning. If I could make a difference in people's lives, helping them to be healthy, happy and fulfilled—like Glenn helped me—then my life would be worthwhile. This vision has become my passion and my mission.

May your journey toward greater health and self-love be a gift in your life.

"So many people spend their health gaining wealth, and then have to spend their wealth to regain their health."

A. J. Reb Materi

Sources and References

"*Eating Disorder Statistics: National Association of Anorexia Nervosa and Associated Disorders.*" National Association of Anorexia Nervosa and Associated Disorders. Accessed March 12, (2019). https://anad.org/education-and-awareness/about-eating-disorders/eating-disorders-statistics/

Goebel-Fabbri, A. E., Fikkan, J., Franko, D. L., Pearson, K., Anderson, B. J., & Weinger, K. (2008). '*Insulin restriction and associated morbidity and mortality in women with type 1 diabetes. Diabetes Care*'.

Hanlan, M. E., Griffith, J., Patel, N., & Jaser, S. S. (2013). '*Eating disorders and disordered eating in Type 1 diabetes: prevalence, screening, and treatment options. Current Diabetes Reports*'.

Hudson, J. I., Hiripi, E., Pope, H. G., & Kessler, R. C. (2007). '*The prevalence and correlates of eating disorders in the national comorbidity survey replication. Biological Psychiatry*'.

Johns Hopkins Medicine, Digestive Weight Loss Center, Diabetes: https://www.hopkinsmedicine.org/digestive_weight_loss_center/conditions/diabetes.html

New CDC Report: More than 100 million Americans have diabetes and prediabetes. Center For Disease Control and Prevention (CDC). July 18, 2017: https://www.cdc.gov/media/releases/2017/p0718-diabetes-report.html

"*The Average Person Has between 12,000 and 60,000 Thoughts per Day.*" Siobhan Kelleher Kukolic. June 11, 2018. Accessed

March 12, 2019. https://siobhankukolic.com/the-average-person-has-between-12000-and-60000-thoughts-per-day/.

US Department of Health and Human Services and US Department of Agriculture. *2015 – 2020 Dietary Guidelines for Americans*. 8th Edition. (December 2015). Available at https://health.gov/dietaryguidelines/2015/guidelines/.

Kirsten Ward

Kirsten Ward, MS, RCEP, CDE®, is a bilingual English-Spanish Certified Diabetes Educator (CDE®), coach, and motivational speaker. As a child, Kirsten loved ballet and modern dance, but that love also triggered an obsession with food and weight. The pressure to excel and the need to be thin led to an endless cycle of struggle and negativity. Now free from this destructive pattern, Kirsten is dedicated to helping others overcome similar obstacles and learn to thrive.

Specializing in body dysmorphia and diabetes education, Kirsten supports and motivates her clients. With patience and empathy, she provides essential tools that teach her clients how to be resilient, vibrantly healthy, and happy.

Kirsten started her career as a CDE® at The Joslin Diabetes Center, a world-renowned diabetes education and treatment center. She later worked in a variety of industry positions related to diabetes treatment. Kirsten is one of only forty exercise professionals in the United States who specialize in diabetes education. She is a national and international keynote speaker who also trains other health-care providers who work with English- and Spanish-speaking clients.

Kirsten also works closely with internationally recognized transformational leader Marci Shimoff. As a certified life coach and happiness trainer, Kirsten's focus is teaching people the key principles from Shimoff's New York Times bestseller *Happy For No Reason: 7 Steps to Being Happy from the Inside Out.*

When she is not actively engaged in helping others positively transform their lives, Kirsten adores spending time with her family and friends, traveling, walking her dog, and dancing.

You can reach out to Kirsten to attend her FREE webinar and learn how to reverse insulin resistance to help prevent or manage diabetes. You will also receive a FREE copy of her handout titled "Sugars and Sweeteners: High, Medium and Low Glycemic Index Choices" when you email her at info@ saygoodbyetodiabetes.com.

Contact Information

Email: info@saygoodbyetodiabetes.com
Website: www.saygoodbyetodiabetes.com
Facebook: saygoodbyetodiabetes.com
LinkedIn: https://www.linkedin.com/ in/kirsten-ward-885014a/

DISCOVERING THE ENGAGEMENT QUOTIENT – A SOMATIC LEARNING JOURNEY

LISSA POHL

I t is an honor to share the story of my becoming a somatic engagement coach with you, dear reader. This chapter describes the determination, persistence, happenstance, and divine intervention that was required. It speaks to the challenges of a *calling* that often felt outside the realms of popular acceptance and easy money—both symptoms of being ahead of my time and frequent reminders of its mixed blessing. It reminds us of the necessity of self-reinvention and cultivating patience until the world catches up. This is for those of us who live and play with ideas that lie outside the norm and push the boundaries of convention.

Remembering the Body

"What brought you to this workshop today?" I ask a group of leaders who are standing before me and are grappling to learn the concepts of embodied leadership.

"A car", they say.
"What made the car get here?"
"Gas", they reply.

"What are you standing in right now?" I ask.
"Shoes."

After a while, they give up, and I offer a hint by patting down the front of my body and then give them the absurdly obvious answer, "You came here in your body". Once their eyes stop rolling, and before they can make their way to the exit, I half jokingly say that they have never paid so much to learn what they already know—that they have a body, and that their body is not only what brought them to the workshop but it is, in addition, the primary 'tool' for learning about becoming a dramatically more effective Being.

The fact that most people struggle to find this answer is indicative, not only of how disengaged we are from our own bodies, but also of how much we take them for granted. Yet, it's the body's innate somatic intelligence, "the place where sensation [perception], emotion, and cognitive interpretation of events all meet and interact to form one's moment-to-moment experience of life" (Blake, 2009) that allows us to do anything, including learning about leadership and engaging others. The fact that 90% of those I work with find this simple realization annoyingly absurd is precisely why I became a somatic engagement coach.

Connecting the Dots

My interest in developing a somatic, embodied approach to learning leadership competencies goes back to my early childhood in Boulder, Colorado. It was the time I discovered my delight in the art of dance. I was so enthused that my younger brother would rush over to me and tightly wrap me up in his arms to prevent me from dancing—thereby prevent any further embarrassment. I was known at school, at camp, and to my friends as a free spirit interpretive dancer—a flying rocket ship who rarely touched the ground. Rarely did I find a dance partner who could go where I went while dancing. I was literally *moved* by music and found that it could transport me into realms where imagination and movement became one. I did not care what others thought because the music and the movement were all I needed.

Though I was naturally athletic and rhythmically inclined, studying formal dance was never my pursuit; instead, I ice skated, rode horses, and sang. To be an exceptional dancer, I reasoned, one had to be flexible, and in my early years, my back had developed a slight curvature. This left me envying the elegance of others whose backs allowed them to stand up straight without effort. Later on, at age 16, I discovered the transformative power of Rolfing®—a form of myofascial-structural integration, or very deep massage, that results in improved balanced and aligned posture through both physical and emotional release. This type of therapy was a bit too 'out there' for my parents, so I waited until after high school to wait tables in Flagstaff, Arizona to earn enough to pay for the ten required sessions.

Through Rolfing®, I was able to see and feel the connections between mind, body, emotions, and spirit. Each session began and ended with a before and after picture of my body. I found this type of feedback to be very powerful, giving me a new sense of pride as I grew an entire inch in height and saw my posture improve dramatically over the four months it took to complete the ten sessions. By manipulating matter (in this case my body), I realized how it is possible to shift and release both physical and emotional patterns and traumas stuck in the myofascial tissues of the body. This realization that the potential for change is deeply rooted in the body planted the seed of my interest and gave rise to later pursuits in the mind–body connection.

After high school, I set off for college to be a marine biologist and took myself to the Pacific Northwest and the amazingly beautiful city of Bellingham, Washington. After a couple years doing the hard sciences, which I loved, I figured out that life as a marine biologist looked more like bobbing up and down on the cold, rough Alaskan seas counting stinky dead salmon on a fishing boat inhabited by sex-obsessed fishermen from Japan rather than dancing with dolphins in the warm, sandy lagoons of Hawaii.

After turning away from marine biology I followed my boyfriend inland, across the mountains, to Spokane and switched my academic focus to sign-language interpreting for the deaf and deaf-blind. Why the about face in disciplines? My boyfriend had a deaf nephew, and when I interacted with him I found it frustrating that we could not communicate. This two-year-old boy was just starting to learn language and here I was unable to understand the simplest things—that he wanted milk to drink or he loved red cars. I found that learning sign language felt very comfortable, and I naturally revelled in using my hands to communicate, so why not learn an embodied language that would help to bridge the divide?

Spokane Community College offered a program in sign language, and I soon realized that I could get my AS Degree through this new-found passion. After graduation, I was accepted into the Interpreter Training Program in Seattle where

I spent a year experiencing our capacity to communicate in nonverbal ways by using American Sign Language (ASL), a spatial, nonlinear language that most deaf Americans use to communicate. Once again, I was confronting the important role that physicality plays in communication. Learning ASL did more than allow me to communicate or 'talk' to deaf and deaf/blind individuals; it challenged me to use and effectively integrate all the physical senses and develop my ability to focus awareness outwardly while remaining fully aware of what I was doing with my body. Learning this spatial language assisted me in developing an acute perceptual awareness and empathy.

After my passion of combining dance and sign language to interpret songs for the deaf was squelched by the strict dictate of the director of the ASL interpreting program, I decided to complete my undergraduate degree at Western Washington University. By this time I had met my future husband who was studying music there and so back up to Bellingham and the hard sciences I went to delve more deeply into the body's structural, biological, and organic processes via a degree in Nutrition. This discipline deepened my understanding and love for the sciences and the phenomenal nature of the body. I was unaware at the time just how much this experience would provide an essential background for my approach to studying human potential development later on.

After completing my BS degree and getting married, I applied my knowledge of nutrition to serving as a diet consultant, wellness coach, and natural foods educator for Puget Consumer's Coop (PCC) in Seattle. What I came to understand, in no uncertain terms, was that optimal health has many ingredients: a healthy natural environment, balanced nutrition, adequate exercise, and emotional well-being. Even though I felt that I could assist others with many of these, I saw that being able to address one's emotional well-being was difficult and that sometimes the relationship between food and unhealthy behaviors was complex and generally resistant to change. I also noticed that my clients could take the purest and most expensive vitamins, eat organic foods, and live in the healthiest environments, and their vitality would still suffer. After much frustration, I came to realize that optimal health and happiness were an 'inside job.' The question remained "how does one access this optimal state of being?" Fortunately, I didn't have to wait too long before I stumbled into a coaching methodology that would assist me in finding, and seeing, the answers to this question.

Camera, Lights, Action – Seeing The Full Spectrum

In 1996, I experienced the Sage Learning Method, an innovative and transforming coaching technique originally developed by learning theorist Martin Sage of Austin, Texas. At a workshop called "What To Do With The Rest Of Your Life," I had the opportunity to watch individuals, including myself, visually transform over the course of three days. The workshop began with everyone getting their faces filmed on a video camera and then continued with two full days of intensive somatic feedback, experiential learning, and coaching. It ended with getting re-filmed and comparing the before and after pictures. I literally watched 30 people walk into the workshop looking one way and walk out looking very different—most looking 10–15 years younger, healthier, and more vital.

What was happening here? How is it possible that one's looks could change so dramatically over such a short period of time?

What role did the workshop environment play in effecting these changes? Was it the nature of the somatic feedback coaching technique that allowed people to shift such that their cells appeared to come along for the ride?

During those three days, I experienced a dimensional shift in the way I perceived and moved through the world. Colors were brighter, and my children were extra clear, sharp, and connected to me. It was as if I had had cataract surgery of the Spirit. I seemed to be flying feet first through the streets of Seattle instead of walking! I was fascinated, to say the least. This was not some sort of shamanic drug-induced phenomenon but a profound shift in my own perceptual abilities.

Later that year, I attended Martin's three-day *Self Actualization* workshop that took all of this to another level and dimension. Martin, as it turns out, had mastered his energy to such an extent that he was able to manifest physical sensations in others (i.e., heating someone's side up when standing near them or making them feel as if they were floating above the ground). After the workshop, Martin came up and gave me a hug and very intentionally held the part of my back where I have a curvature. That night when I got home, I experienced a physical downloading of energy out of my back and through my arms that lasted about 45 minutes. I was literally energetically pinned down to my bed. After it stopped, I could stand up straight without trying! This raised more questions for me as to what was going on in this type of coaching. No deep tissue manipulation had occurred, so how was it that I was more aligned in my body than I had been before?

So intrigued was I that in 1997 I decided to get some coaching with Cathy Hawk of Clarity International®, a graduate of Martin Sage's coach training program. At that time Cathy lived north of where I lived in Seattle. She had further developed and systematized this unique coaching process into what is now called the Lights On Learning™ method. After dragging all of my girlfriends, my husband, and kids to various Lights On Learning™ workshops, I decided to go through Cathy's year-long coach training program. My own transformation was striking. The photos below were taken during a workshop called Powerful Partnering where, for the first time in our marriage, my husband and I got to explore and get feedback on what we could do together to live a 'Lights On' life. These photos were taken two hours apart. See figure 1.

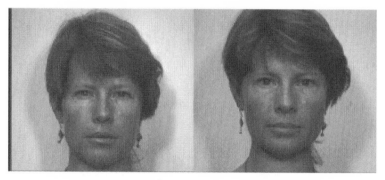

Figure 1 – Before and after LOL photos

I completed the Clarity Coach certification, but I was less interested in being a life coach than I was in seeing how this powerful coaching method could be taken to organizations and leaders. I was committed to bringing it to the world and to find a way to keep leaders' lights on! After all, if the great leaders of the world are going 'Lights Out,' how would we ever find our way forward as human beings to make it a better place for everyone?

It has been over 20 years since I became a Clarity International®
coach, and I continue to work on bringing this powerful method
to leaders and organizations. Though it seldom feels like it, my
professional journey has proven beyond the shadow of a doubt
that patience <u>is more than</u> a virtue—it is absolutely mandatory.

Dirty Laundry

I started SHift, my coaching business, in 1998, and my Seattle
clients were enjoying great results. The referrals were starting
to come in through the door. The next year we moved our
family to Lexington, Kentucky so that my husband could join
forces with his brother in their own architecture firm and enjoy
greater proximity to his side of the family. Seattle had become
crowded, and traffic jams were the norm. Our family of four
was outgrowing our small, mission style stucco house, and real
estate had become insanely expensive with the explosion of the
dot com industry. Even if we sold our house for three times
what we paid, we could not afford to move to a larger one in a
comparable area. So, off we went to Kentucky.

For years before we actually moved, I had been very reluctant
about even considering Kentucky as a place to live. It ranked
near the bottom in the US for educational attainment and was
known for having the highest rates for obesity and poverty.
It was in the bible belt, a place cloaked in southern tradition
and values, and where, contrary to what they taught us in our
history classes, the civil war was still alive and well just under
the surface of the heavy clay soil.

However, truth be told, I was reluctant mostly because I was a
child of the progressive West. I had grown up in the sixties and

seventies in Boulder where one could study and practice any alternative healing or spiritual modality. Boulder was the home of Ida Rolf, marathon runner Frank Shorter, Celestial Seasonings Tea, and where the Buddhist leaders of the world descended to teach at The Naropa Institute. Seattle was similarly spirited. A place where the mountains kiss the sea, the great outdoors called you out to play, and a pioneering and entrepreneurial energy permeated the art-filled streets. What in heaven's name would I do with myself in Lexington? How would I make a living?

Yet, I had finally found what I really wanted to do with the rest of my life and after having become a certified Lights On coach I arrived in Lexington excited and ready to start my own coaching business. SHift was bound to be a success because it leveraged my talents and incorporated my interests in connecting the dots between the mind, body, emotions, and spirit. Then, reality set in.

It turned out that in Lexington, the word coaching was more synonymous with baseball or other children's sports than in life or leadership coaching. I set out to meet everyone in town who could give me support and assist me in creating the networks it would take to build my business. I also needed to find others to lend a much-needed ear to listen to my professional and entrepreneurial woes. There were a couple of pioneers in town doing life and executive coaching and they commiserated with me, but since coaching was such a new concept, it was slim pickings for finding clients locally. Additionally, having young elementary school kids who were also adjusting to the culture change, I could not see myself traveling very far to do this work.

There was something else that made it very challenging to do this work in Lexington. It evaded me for quite some time, but one day when I was driving down the road, the reason why my words and enthusiasm were seemingly falling on deaf ears became plainly clear. It was the simple fact that what I had to offer was so far ahead of its time that it was a huge leap for most people to make, or even to understand. A quote by Mark Twain sums it up nicely. He allegedly said, "When the end of the world comes I want to be in Kentucky because everything happens 20 years later there." And indeed, Lexington was seemingly 30 years behind Seattle in the adoption of coaching. On top of that, the Lights On Leadership™ (LOL) coaching technique was probably 10–15 years ahead of the times, even in progressive places like Seattle or Boulder. If I added up how far ahead of the times LOL was in Seattle (15 years) with how far behind Lexington was (30 years), I came up with it being 45 years ahead of its time. I was only 40 years old when I came to Lexington, which meant I wasn't even born yet. I found myself in a time warp. This work was not even a blip on the radar screen of human potential development. It was the right fit for me but an epic failure for the market I found myself in.

I chalked this revelation up as another one of God's cosmic jokes. It made me laugh out loud. It also brought me some comfort and relief because it meant that I did not have to continue to bang my head against the wall, continue to push boulders up nonexistent hills, and perhaps most importantly, allow me to stop judging myself, others, and the place I lived.

Have you ever had to face an epic defeat and start all over from scratch? Or had your professional heart and dreams broken? Here I was, starting my new life in Lexington, and I had just found my true calling, my life's passion, the thing that got me up in the morning with a feeling of purpose, and now I was muted by the circumstances I found myself in. After struggling for years to build a business utilizing this innovative and transformational learning technique, and spending many thousands of dollars, I had to give it up. Lights On became a 'lights out' proposition and my nemesis. A nemesis in the sense that it made no rational or financial sense to pursue it and yet, deep down, I knew it was my calling and it would come back and nag at me, taunting and daring my Spirit to bring it into the world. I found myself cursing the day I ever laid my eyes on it. As a result, I would soon find myself in a heap of dirty laundry in my basement, crying and bewildered as to what I was going to do.

Phoenix Rising – Waiting for the World to Catch Up

During this very trying and depressing time, I told my husband that I thought I would be better off living in India because "at least in India I would know that I am not speaking the same language". Here, in Lexington, I was using the same language but continually missing the mark. So what do you do when you find yourself in a foreign land where you don't speak the language and you really need to earn an income to assist your architecture entrepreneur husband and maintain your own self-worth?

You do five things. First, you revert to what you know and are skilled at. For me that was painting interiors, fixing walls, and becoming the wallpaper peeling princess of Lexington. I started my own little business called Painting Pizazz, which allowed me to make some inroads into the community and the neighborhood, along with a very small income. I garnered respect from the paint supply experts, and it kept me away from the dirty laundry.

Second, you call an astrologer to find out how long Jupiter is going to be in retrograde or is that Mercury? Only to find out that your sign Scorpio, is ruled by Pluto the destroyer, and your chart has more Pluto in it than he has ever seen before. "What does that mean for me?" I asked. He said that I had better get used to creating things and then watching them change, mutate, or get destroyed. Basically, he said that I needed to become the phoenix who spontaneously combusts and then rises from the ashes. It meant that I had better get used to waking up and dying on a regular, in my case, daily basis. Even though this horoscope reading was fairly accurate in reflecting what I was experiencing in my life at that time, I am not one to wholeheartedly place my spiritual well-being and future actions in astrology or any type of divination. However, there was an intriguing synchronicity that came from my session with the astrologer, and honestly, it was a bit chilling. What I found out, after I did some research on Pluto and his destructive tendencies, was that the symbol for Pluto (see Figure 2) is exactly how I have been initialing my name, Lissa Pohl, for the past 18 years. Oh dear... I was Pluto!

Figure 2 – Symbol of Pluto and my initials

Third, you get yourself involved in creative and out-of-the-box initiatives and events that allow you to find your tribe, stay intellectually engaged, and keep yourself amused with your lights on. I joined the inaugural Idea Festival planning committee. The Idea Festival was Lexington's attempt to attract innovative shakers and movers and their startup companies to set up shop here. I was instrumental, pun intended, in bringing the world's largest harp to downtown Lexington for the festival. The Earth Harp, invented by William Close, is a unique musical installation that turns any architectural or natural space into a stringed instrument. In Lexington's case, we made a harp out of a nine-story parking garage and adjacent park. The public would then come up and play the building with a very large bow.

Fourth, you get a local and seasoned corporate consultant to take you under his wings by spontaneously bursting into tears the second you see his amazingly creative and playful training space called the Innovation Station. This fine gentleman did not quite know what to do with me, but he recognized that I was without a tribe and so he invited me to assist him with marketing the University of Dayton, Ohio's executive leadership development programming in Kentucky. I was able to attend many of the programs for executives in Dayton and found that doing corporate organizational leadership development still resonated with me. My new-found colleague and mentor recognized my talent for facilitating the soft skills of leadership and team development, and he kept me busy honing my skills as well as laughing and learning until the next big transformation took place. To him, I will be eternally grateful.

Fifth, you continue to educate yourself in the field you are interested in working in. I will delve into this a bit later in this chapter.

A Horse of a Different Color – Equine Assisted Learning

I started riding ponies and horses when I was five. I did some showing, training, breeding, and foaling, and generally hanging out with them until I sold my last horse to go off to college. So it was likely that one of my children would also have the horse gene. Before we left Seattle, I leased a horse and taught my oldest daughter, then eight years old, how to ride. Shortly after we arrived in Lexington, she and her sister started riding lessons. She kept lobbying for a horse of her own, and so when she was 12 we bought one together. It had been 22 years since I had engaged with them, and I was ready to get back in the saddle as well. Mirkos was a tall, dark, and handsome Chilean thoroughbred. He was at a racing farm where I was taking the girls to learn more about horses. He had slightly injured one of his tendons while breezing at Churchill Downs racetrack, so the owners decided to retire him at the young age of five. To this day, nineteen years later, I consider it a privilege to have such an amazingly kind spirit and teacher in my life.

At the turn of the millennium, the field of Equine Assisted Learning (EAL) was just starting to develop. EAL is a facilitated experiential learning modality wherein people work with horses using ground activities and relational problem solving to be more effective at leading, developing high-performance teams, or to understand how to somatically engage another being.

Why horses? Horses are sense-*able* beings that can assist us in developing our ability to communicate somatically. Being animals of prey, horses have a completely different perspective and instinctual orientation that determines their behavior toward their environment. For instance, with eyes on the sides of the head, a horse employs a 360-degree awareness of spatial relationships, allowing them to perceive and immediately react to things that enter their environment. They sleep no more than two to four hours per day. This hyper-vigilance is what keeps the horse safe in a predatory world. Horses communicate almost exclusively through body language and because they are social, herd animals, they are ever in search of a hierarchy and clear leadership. Therefore, developing a successful leadership role with a horse requires us to 'show up' as a leader. It requires that we develop an understanding of and a proficiency with body language as opposed to our habitual reliance on words as the primary mode of communication.

At a very simplistic and instinctual level, the horse's present-moment awareness results in its ability to quickly process information and feedback from the environment to take action that ensures its own safety and that of the herd. The intention behind EAL is to give humans an experience that allows them to better understand how to leverage sensory information from stimuli in the environment and to act on it in the present moment—much like a horse does. Insights people have with the horses usually have direct parallels at work or in their personal lives. When skillfully facilitated, an EAL program can give us direct feedback about organizational system pressure, communication breakdowns, and inauthentic intentions because the horses directly reflect the moment in which they show up. On the other hand, and just as plainly, congruency of thought, feeling, and action; a clear vision and intention; patience; and connection are mirrored back to the two-legged participants by the four-legged teachers. When this happens, it is called 'join up' (Roberts, 2002). Join up is the moment when the horse decides to put its trust in you and willingly follows you anywhere you go without a halter or rope attached (see Figure 3). You and the horse are somatically engaged, and knowing what engagement feels like in our body gets us one step closer in being able to increase it in the workplace.

Figure 3 – Join Up with horses

Transforming Feedback

Feedback, according to Pennsylvania State University professors and organizational researchers Rothwell and Kazanas (1998), has been seen as "the single most significant <u>non-instructional</u> solution to human performance problems." It is so important that "any approach that can improve the clarity and timeliness of feedback was perceived by trainers in one study to be among the most significant approaches to solving human performance problems" (1998). If this is so, then why wouldn't a leadership development professional or a leader in the trenches want to make feedback an instructional solution to the challenges we face—including engagement?

After playing around with EAL for a few years, I was able to see very direct connections between the type of feedback the horses gave my clients and the type of feedback I used as a Lights On Leadership™ coach.

First, both methods reveal and make conscious the somatic nature of the relationship by heightening one's perceptual awareness through utilizing present moment body-based feedback—the first between horse and human and the latter human to human. Second, both utilize non-judgmental and objective forms of feedback that people tend to assimilate more readily. Horses do this by moving their heads away or completely disengaging by walking away from people who are trying to get them to do something in a predatory way. Horses do not care if you are the queen of England or the Sheik of Dubai. They just want to know if you are someone who they can trust, are safe to follow, and have what it takes to lead them. Lights On coaching utilizes before and after digital images of one's face, which is a very objective form of feedback, and much like a horse, the camera does not lie.

Feedback in a LOL session is in the form of simple, objective statements about what is actually happening in the body of the person getting coached. Transforming feedback is not judgment or an interpretation of what is being seen nor is it story or advice. It's the process of noticing when balance and vitality enter the system of another person in response to standard coaching questions. It is much like how a horse watches us to determine when our words, body, emotions, and actions align. A skilled somatic coach can see when another person's system moves toward balance, integrity, and congruency.

Examples of transforming 'lights on' feedback include:

- "The right side of the mouth turns down when you talk about your work."
- "Your left eye is brighter, larger and clearer than the right eye when you talk about your new job opportunity."
- "Your nose turns to the left, and the right ear is lower than the left ear."
- "The left side of the face is narrower than the right side."

I have found that one's engagement is directly proportionate to the quality of the feedback they are getting. That is, it depends on how it is delivered and the intentions behind the feedback. It is the very subtle and mostly unconscious "micromessages" (Young, 2007) we send that impacts one's level of engagement. It is clear that criticism, or unwelcome advice, can have the effect of shutting the recipient down or cause a *lights out* reaction. You can only imagine my delight when I came across neuroscience research conducted by emotional intelligence expert Richard Boyatzis and Associates at Case Western Reserve University (2010). Their research confirmed what I had been seeing happening with my clients during a Lights On Learning™ coaching session. Their research identified subtle changes in the brain patterns of students who undergo MRIs while exposed to a video of themselves responding to questions that generate positive emotional attractors versus those that generate negative emotional attractors. This research represents a huge leap forward in identifying the types of feedback that produce more expansive/engaged [a *lights on* response] or contractive/disengaged thinking and behavior patterns [a *lights out* response]. Fortunately, one does not need an MRI machine to determine how best to engage others. All we need to know is that the body shows us what is going on in the brain.

Even though there are strong links between these ways of getting feedback, LOL can be a rather intimidating experience if you have never been asked to look at yourself in such an objective and somatic way. On the other hand, getting feedback from the horse is much easier.

Confirming Ideas and Grounding the Work

Once I saw how working with horses prepares people to receive somatic feedback, I began to think about how working with them could lead my clients to the LOL work, and that perhaps I should be more deliberate in connecting the two methods. The horses would open their eyes and minds to the importance of leveraging their own somatic intelligence to lead and engage others. The LOL method would then give them the skills to be able to do this in real time at work, only without horses.

However, in 2006, developing and leveraging somatic intelligence in the workplace was a 'far out' concept. There were few people doing corporate work with horses and even fewer doing the LOL work with executives and organizations. In essence, I needed to find a way to ground my ideas and to explain what was happening while coaching and working with the horses to various contemporary leadership development theories. At age 44, I enrolled myself in graduate school and spent the next two years working part-time, mothering full-time, and spending most of my evenings at local coffee shops working on my Master of Arts Degree in Transformational Leadership Development.

Writing my thesis *Embodying Leadership: An Integrated Approach* (2006) proved to be a profoundly transforming experience. I can honestly say that it is the best thing I have ever done personally and professionally. It allowed me to formulate my own ideas about somatic leadership and to find my voice—both verbal and written—while at the same time creating a solid theoretical foundation from which I could build my programming. It gave me the confidence to be a pioneer in the emerging field of somatic intelligence. It has given me the courage and grounded knowledge to present at international conferences on leadership development and connected me to a much bigger world in which to do this work, including going to the Middle East to do EAL work with leaders in the Qatar Foundation. It has given me a place at the table with others who have similar passions about advancing human potential on the planet. Most of all, it has allowed me to befriend the Lights On Learning™ Method again and understand the connection it has with Equine Assisted Learning, thus allowing me to identify the corporate leadership niche it best supports, which is in assisting leaders in tackling the challenge of disengaged workers.

One Way Ticket To Here

Pursuing my degree was, in part, my attempt to introduce the innovative Lights On Learning Method™ and EAL to others interested in transformational and integral leadership and legitimize their use as leadership development methods. Getting my Master's degree allowed me to explore theories of renowned researchers in this field and to find a way to connect to what I was seeing happening with my clients doing both EAL and LOL. All the jobs outside of Lexington in the leadership development field required a Master's Degree, and so getting it was a one-way ticket to get our family out of Lexington. It's amazing how focused and motivated one can become when your soul feels trapped.

In 2006, right as I was finishing my degree, cosmic joke number two happened. I was starting my job search and planning my exit strategy when I was referred to the third largest Applebee's Restaurant franchiser in the US. Where was this business based? You guessed it, in downtown Lexington. The CEO was an adventuresome entrepreneur and thought that leadership with horses sounded interesting. So, he came out to my barn and I put him in the round pen with a couple of horses. He immediately saw the power of EAL to teach people leadership and asked me if I could do this with his managers. "Absolutely!" was my reply. As my mom would say, "Never look a gift horse in the mouth." Next thing I know I was gainfully employed doing exactly what I had just been studying in theory. I had the privilege of creating the *Hands-On Leadership* program. This three-day leadership program for store managers incorporated a half day with the horses along with other customer service modules that assisted them in working more effectively with their staff and customers.

Even though this 22-month stint as the corporate "horse whisperer" closely resembled being in one very long episode of the then-popular TV sitcom "The Office", it confirmed my hypothesis that both EAL and LOL could be adapted to a corporate setting and provided me with a much needed corporate experience. It also meant that we did not have to relocate once again. You can probably hear and feel my husband's huge sigh of relief!

By 2008, casual dining had had its heyday; with the recession looming ahead, leadership development for managers was no longer a priority. Instead, creating operational training to figure out how we could sell more cold beer to our dwindling customer base became the focus of our department. The writing was on the wall, and I began to search for my next opportunity. All the networking I did in the years I was struggling to build my own business now paid off. I was in the right place at the right time to make the leap out of the corporate world into academia. The Department of Community & Leadership Development at the University of Kentucky hired me to be the Assistant Director of the Center for Leadership Development. The Director was interested in being one of the first in the nation to create an Equine Guided Leadership Education program. After seven years of attempting this, the internal support we needed from the College of Agriculture, where our department was located, never materialized. Yet, in the eleven years I have been with the university, I have had many great opportunities. Getting certified as an Equine Experiential Education Association (E3A) Advanced Corporate Practitioner in 2012 led to me to conducting pioneering research in *The Effectiveness of Equine Guided Leadership Education to Teach Emotional Intelligence to Expert Nurses: A Pilot Study* (2014). Later I became a Master Trainer for E3A and have had the privilege of presenting at international conferences and mentoring several students who are equally intrigued with these notions of somatic leadership and EAL.

Seeing How To Serve – Engaging the Disengaged

There is a huge cost for not leveraging all of our senses to consciously engage others. In the US alone, it is estimated that disengagement at work costs between $450 and $550 billion each year in lost productivity (Blacksmith & Harter, 2011). This is more than the national defense budget! Research finds that 71% of employees in the US and 87% worldwide are not engaged at work (Mann, Harter, 2017).

"Leaders are the stewards of organizational energy—in companies, organizations and even in families. They inspire or demoralize others first by how effectively they manage their own energy and next by how well they mobilize, focus, invest, and renew the collective energy of those they lead" (Loehr, Schwartz, 2003). If leaders have a direct effect on the engagement of their followers, then they are also directly connected to the productivity and efficiency ratings those workers produce. Dealing with apathy, or active disengagement, is a huge leadership challenge. Possibly one of the most difficult because it is a symptom of the great disconnect that most people have to their innermost dreams and their highest potentials. Therefore, there is a need for methods that can better equip leaders to be able to get to the heart of purpose and meaning and create inspired and engaged followers.

Most leaders seem to understand the importance of supporting intellectual pursuit (IQ) in their teams. In addition, impressive research on the value of developing emotional intelligence (EQ) concludes that it too can lead to higher profits, productivity, and professional satisfaction (Goldman, Boyatzis, McKee, 2002). So if IQ + EQ = Engagement (EnQ), why are we still leaving trillions of dollars on the table each year? When it comes to engagement at work, what part of the equation is missing?

Perhaps, just like the clients I mentioned at the start of this chapter, the missing component of the engagement equation is closer than we might realize. As we have seen, clues to our passion and purpose can be found by simply observing the information that is exchanged between two living beings, whether it be horses or humans. The realm of the human experience that includes using all of our senses, our physical intelligence (PQ) supports and *enables* the other three realms: the intellectual (IQ), the emotional (EQ), and the spiritual (SQ). Ignoring it is more than an oversight. It is a profound missed opportunity for developing human competency and effectively tackling the question of worker engagement. The statistics mentioned above make it well worth the time and effort for each one of us to take a closer look, literally and figuratively, at ways in which we can leverage this forgotten intelligence to embody leadership and rewrite the engagement equation so that IQ + EQ + PQ = Engagement (EnQ).

I suspect that one reason PQ is so often overlooked is that as humans have evolved, the primal role of the body (safety, food, and shelter) has increasingly been usurped by intellectual, emotional, and spiritual pursuits. These days, the body's vast intelligence has been reduced to a vehicle of convenience transporting those other pursuits around. The result is not unlike having a car firing on just three cylinders instead of four. You can get around with three firing, however, the ride is not as smooth and it takes more time and effort to get where you are going. Being able to access and utilize all of our senses and perceptual abilities as leaders, i.e., firing on all four cylinders, makes the experience more efficient and pleasurable. What if the physical realm of experience were to, once again, take a front seat with the intellect and emotional intelligence and, therefore, a much larger role in how we educate, communicate, and evolve? What sort of dynamic might unfold? To me, this is where life gets exciting!

Living an Engaged Life

I like what Alan Combs, author of *The Radiance of Being: Understanding the Grand Integral Vision: Living the Integral Life* wrote on this topic. He said, "One thing of value learned along the way is that spontaneous, natural, intelligence shines effortlessly, like the morning light bursting through an open window, when the mind is made clean and clear of the incrustations that life deposits upon it" (2002). In my case, the incrustations appeared in the form of self-doubt, judgments of others, and the difficulties and loneliness of being a pioneer in the emerging field of somatic leadership and engagement.

Had you told me in my 20s that I would become an expert in the field of Equine Assisted Learning and doing somatic engagement work with leaders all over the world, I would never have believed you. Looking back at my own journey, I see how each experience, challenge, and transformation that has occurred along the way makes perfect sense. They came to me when I was ready for it—not just because I thought I deserved it. It has taught me that even when we find ourselves in a place that is neither emotionally or physically conducive to letting our light shine, we have to find that inner cord that weaves together all the clues about who we are and what we are passionate about and hang on to it for dear life. At the same time, we need to weave it into a safety net that not only saves ourselves but offers support to others, who are on their own journeys to gain perspective, and the courage to explore and manifest their own potential.

References (As cited)

Blacksmith, N., Harter, J. (2011). "Majority of American workers not engaged in their jobs". *Gallup Well Being*. www. gallup.com. Retrieved March 7, 2012, from http://www.gallup. com/poll/150383/majority-american-workers-not-engaged-jobs. aspx

Blake, A., (2017). Developing Somatic Intelligence: Leadership and the Neurobiology of Embodied Learning. *Embright*. org. Retrieved 6-7-17, from http://embright.org/wp-content/ uploads/2013/03/Developing-Somatic-Intelligence-NLJ10x.pdf

Boyatzis, R., Jack, A., Cesaro, R., Khawaja, M., Passarelli, A. (2010). *Coaching with compassion: An fMRI study of coaching to the positive or negative emotional attractor.* Presented at the Academy of Management Annual Conference, Montreal, August, 2010

Combs, A. (2002). *The radiance of being: understanding the grand integral vision: Living the integral life.* St. Paul, Minn., Paragon House.

Goldman, D., Boyatzis, R., McKee, A., (2002). Primal leadership: Learning to lead with emotional intelligence. Boston, MA., *Harvard Business School Press.*

Loehr, J., & Schwartz, T. (2003). *The power of full engagement: managing energy, not time, is the key to high performance and personal renewal.* New York, NY: Free Press

Mann, A, Harter, J. (2017). The Worldwide Employee Engagement Crisis. www.gallup.com. Retrieved May 24, 2017, from http://www.gallup.com/businessjournal/188033/worldwide-employee-engagement-crisis.aspx

Pohl, E. (2006). *Embodying leadership: An integrated approach.* Unpublished thesis as partial completion of a Master of Arts Degree at the Union Institute & University, Cincinnati, OH Contact author for copies of document.

Pohl, E., Dyk, P., Cheung, R. (2013). *The effectiveness of equine guided leadership education to increase the emotional intelligence in expert nurses: A pilot study.* Academia.edu, from https://www.academia.edu/16578558/The_Effectiveness_of_Equine_Guided_Leadership_Education_to_Develop_Emotional_Intelligence_in_Expert_Nurses_A_Pilot_Research_Study

Roberts, M. (2001). *Horse sense for people: Using gentle wisdom of the join-up technique to enrich our relationships at home and at work.* New York, NY: Viking.

Rothwell, W., Kazanas (1998). *Mastering the instructional design process.* San Francisco: Jossey-Bass.

Sridevi, M., Markos, S. (2010). Employee engagement: The key to improving performance. *International Journal of Business Management.*

Young, S. (2007). *Micromessaging: Why great leadership is beyond words.* New York, NY: McGraw-Hill.

Lissa Pohl

Is turnover creating a brain and talent drain in your organization? If you are a leader in search of practical techniques for creating vitality, passion, trust and connection with your teams then you will be interested to discover the Engagement Quotient (EnQ). Developing versatile, resilient, and engaged teams, as it turns out, is as close as your physical body. Lissa Pohl, Chief Vitality Sleuth at The Engagement Quotient (EnQ), is a global expert in somatic intelligence and engagement. Her unique work embraces a number of innovative learning modalities including Equine Assisted Learning (EAL), Lights On Leadership™, and The Leadership Circle 360 Profile to provide C-Suite leaders the heightened perceptual awareness and feedback they need to understand how to engagingly inspire and develop their people to become leaders in their own right.

Lissa holds a Master's degree in Transformational Leadership Development and is a Master Trainer for the Equine Experiential Education Association (E3A), an international non-profit organization that certifies people to facilitate Equine Assisted Learning for corporate clients. At the University of Kentucky, she conducted pioneering research into The Effectiveness of Equine Guided Leadership Education to increase Emotional

Intelligence in healthcare professionals and has presented on these subjects at leadership conferences worldwide. Her clients include the Qatar Foundation, HEC Paris Executive MBA and Development, Johnson & Johnson, University of Kentucky Healthcare, and Applebee's.

Visit www.EnQcoaching.com for more information on how you can increase engagement in the workplace by becoming a Somatically Intelligent Leader. Get FREE access to papers on why somatic engagement coaching and collaborating with horses is so effective at increasing your company's Engagement Quotient (EnQ).

Contact Information

email address: lissa@enqcoaching.com
Website: www.enqcoaching.com
Facebook: www.facebook.com/enqcoaching
LinkedIn: https://www.linkedin.com/in/lissa-pohl-126a042/

6 Simple Rules for Defying the Odds

MARK MUDFORD

"We can't guarantee his ability to talk again, or even how well he might communicate with the outside world…"

"We have no idea how this event has affected his memory…"

"… we can't even guarantee his survival through the surgery…"

I can only imagine how truly terrifying these words must have sounded to my (now) wife. This is because I can't remember them being spoken. Neither can I recall the first two weeks I spent in the high-care ward of my neurosurgical unit. But for her, it must have been devastating. In a way, I feel lucky my memories only become clear later into the ordeal—when we knew I could still talk, think, and even recall memories. The full extent of the impact (including walking unaided or other permanent neurological effects) would not be confirmed for months. In time and against all the odds, I was fortunate enough to regain all of my original self; but for those first few months following surgery, no one could tell me what my future held.

To complicate matters, it would also be months before I was medically cleared to return to work. By the time I was able to start thinking again about my business, I had no business. My clients had all moved on. My inbox was empty. Suddenly there was no income, nor any way to quickly resurrect an income. Now THAT realization was truly frightening.

I thought about the journey that had led me to that moment. Previously, I had supported and served business owners and industry leaders as an external business consultant. However, over time, I had become less aligned with the traditional consultancy model in which I was expected to deliver a specific solution based on my (and not the client's) expertise. I had noted as we moved from initial exploratory meetings to the full consultancy intervention, my clients reported a better sense of engagement at the earlier meetings. In fact, they often spoke to me about having heightened perceptions and stronger intuition as a result of those initial discussions alone, which often proved to translate into a long-term boost in business acumen. In contrast, the *momentum* gained during the actual consultation that followed these meetings often suffered a substantial drop once I had moved on.

This was initially puzzling to me, especially given the significant positive effects clients reported that appeared to be the direct result of our initial conversations. During these conversations, I realized that I was seeking to understand the client's situation, often asking questions that raised their own *awareness*, and clarified their own *responsibility*, in relation to the challenges they felt they were facing. This is something that I have, over time, come to know as a coaching conversation. However, I did not recognize it at the time.

Determined to find out more, my journey back then had led me away from needing to be the 'expert' to, instead, further cultivate my skill sets of observation and communication.

It was at this stage I realized that I had actually begun to adopt a coaching approach. This piqued my interest even further, as I had previously consumed the books from the pioneers of the field. In earlier days I had absorbed everything I could from leaders such as Zig Ziglar, Norman Vincent Peale, and Dennis Waitley before discovering trailblazers such as Tony Robbins and Stephen Covey. Realizing this historical link to my earliest business passions gave me the courage to move my approach from that of a consultant to that of a business coach. In doing so, I also set out to research everything I could find on the coaching industry. This reforged both my experience and my abilities alike, allowing me to deliver solutions of maximum value to the client.

It was then my unforeseen tragedy had struck. Following a painful and unrelenting headache, my fiancée had rushed me to Emergency at our local hospital. After the attending doctor waded through the list of usual culprits, he concluded that a migraine was the issue and instructed my fiancée to take me home. However, she followed her intuition and declined. Three times he requested. Three times she refused. And saved my life. This was despite the fact that the doctor was far more highly trained and qualified than she to make medical decisions. Later, she explained that she had stood her ground because in all our years together, she had never seen me in that much discomfort or had seen physical pain ever bring me to tears. In desperation, the doctor sought out his superior to bolster support for my discharge. To his dismay, the registrar instead advised him I was too old to be experiencing my first migraine and should actually be sent for a scan.

After the scan, the doctor returned with a different demeanor and begged my fiancée's forgiveness. The scans had revealed a massive bleed in the brain. To his credit, he then worked tirelessly to find me a bed in a specialist neurosurgical ward. As if inspired by the defiant courage of my fiancée, he persisted, cajoled, persuaded, and influenced until he managed to get through to the specialist he was seeking. Immediately, I was bundled into an ambulance and rushed to a hospital two hours away.

As I have said, I have no memory of this part of my story. It holds no strong emotion for me. In fact, no specific emotion about that night has ever returned. But when talking about it with my wife, the apprehension and pain are still apparent in her despite the years that have passed. It sometimes feels that, in the absence of my memory of those first few weeks, those who loved me took on that burden of fear instead. To this day, I remain merely the observer who reflects on how lucky I really am.

My fear, however, did find me as soon as I arrived home: to a future that was no longer certain; to health that was not yet assured; and to a business that no longer existed. What could I do? Where to begin?

I realized this was exactly the situation many of my previous clients had found themselves in. I decided to put my own wisdom into practice.

The first step was to understand what those initial conversations with clients had contained, which had so powerfully impacted them. It was my attempt to connect with the knowledge I already possessed to resurrect my business and complete the metamorphosis into a coaching service. I realized that my previous success had been a journey over time; along the way, some really important clues had been revealed to me. If I could just distill those nuggets of truth and use them to find a path through the fear and anxiety that now gripped me, I was sure I would be able to recreate success.

In time, this reflection would clarify the six rules that now underscore my coaching approach:

Rule #1 Let Purpose Be Your Context
Rule #2 Everyone Is Unique…and Usually a Little Bit Right
Rule #3 Wisdom Is the Result of Experience, Not Age
Rule #4 Analogy Gives Clarity without Preconception
Rule #5 EVERYTHING Is Connected
Rule #6 Success Is Not A Solo Journey – Build a Tribe

Everything in this chapter is experiential. However, everything here is also backed up by scientific research. If you would like to explore further and learn about my passion for research, please visit the references listed in the footnotes.

Rule #1: Let Purpose Be Your Context

Background

> *"I am here for a purpose and that purpose is to grow into a mountain, not to shrink to a grain of sand."*

Og Mandino

My time in the Australian Army best illustrates this idea. Military leaders are often thought of as just using 'one way' to lead (and that was certainly my own belief before taking my oath). However, I was soon exposed to varied leadership styles and skill sets. One senior officer, in particular, stands out. This man was an army chaplain who had previously served as an infantry officer before turning to his new calling. As Padre, he usually acted as our spiritual adviser and counselor—building in us a sense of trust in him and a sense of sanctuary away from the operating environment. Occasionally he would be more directive, when more urgent circumstances required a natural leader whom we could follow. Because of his ability to be sensitive to the context in which he was leading, officers and soldiers loved him. Despite the fact that we were, at times, undergoing challenging personal and professional growth, we were always inspired by his presence.

I recall one conversation with him—where we were discussing my development—when I had asked him for his favored approach in leading troops. He replied that his preferred style was simply the one that best fits the moment. Rather than being able to answer specifically, we touched on scenarios that would support more than one 'right' leadership style. It was here I first understood that a change in purpose could easily result in a change in the selection of strategy, even when everything else remained the same.

Beyond just an understanding of the theory, this officer always *demonstrated* that leadership was contextual. This changed all my preconceived notions. It was a contrast to what I had expected, but a valuable lesson to be able to understand. In the decades that followed, this truth has never left me.

My primary purpose today is, ultimately, to be of service to others. That underpins everything I do—from the way I am available for my family and friends to the clients I choose to partner with. Some of my clients are high-performing individuals who are seeking to improve their already impressive results—a coaching context I enjoy working in. But my deepest passion is to help other business owners and leaders overcome circumstances that have had a massive negative impact on them. Such a passion does not preclude me from coaching those who have not experienced such challenges, however, my familiarity in the context of trauma gives me a certain unique connection with professionals who have experienced similar events.

<u>The Research behind My Story:</u>

There are many perspectives regarding how best to define purpose. Some encourage the distillation of purpose based on an evaluation of self (such as 'follow your bliss'[45]). Others suggest a more practical method to address the possible shortcomings that can result from this type of approach[46] and suggest that one can *develop* rather than *discover*[47] their purpose. As we will explore later in Rule #2, *comfort in ambiguity* is also an important ability for today's leader. Ambiguity also appears important in defining the purpose, as it appears that either bliss 'following' or purpose 'developing' can be the appropriate process, under different conditions. This fact is further supported by the uniqueness of an individual (which is also further explored in the next rule).

Purpose assists in 3 specific parts of our journey:

I. In Advance

By embodying our purpose prior to taking action, we greatly

---

[45] Henderson, '"Follow Your Bliss": A Process for Career Happiness', 305.
[46] Berkelaar, 'Bait and Switch or Double-Edged Sword? The (sometimes) Failed Promises of Calling', 157-178.
[47] Davies, *The Happiness Industry. How the Government and Big Business Sold Us Well-Being.*

improve our ability to select and develop the correct solution for that context. By extension, the specifics of a detailed purpose is better than a generalized one. Clear and specific purpose removes unnecessary distractions as we develop a strategy. They may enable better engagement with our creativity to identify options that would otherwise remain hidden in plain sight. Imagine the possibilities today for the (once) phone industry leader, Nokia, had it not 'lost sight of its purpose'[48] to allow Apple's present-day domination.

II. During Execution

A clear purpose also allows for solid decisions to be made, even under extreme circumstances. Consider the words commonly attributed to Viktor Frankl: "Life is never made unbearable by circumstances, but only by lack of meaning and purpose." Seasoned business people know that, despite even the most meticulous planning, there is always a chance of the unforeseen impacting both planning and execution. In these circumstances, they will rely heavily on their creativity and clarity of vision. These, in turn, are heavily dependent on a sense of psychological safety[49] that a clear purpose can help provide.

III. Upon Review

Purpose may also assist as we reflect on past outcomes. It will help place frustrations or apparent failures in a more appropriate light. For example, as we reflect on setbacks we may have encountered across our journey, the context of our purpose balances them against the overall outcome we have achieved

---

[48]   Chevreux, et al. 'The Best Companies Know How to Balance Strategy and Purpose', 26.

[49]   https://markmudford.com.au/psychological-safety-and-the-team/

(and they may start to feel more like costs paid in the name of success). In particular, processes that also utilize abstraction through analogy or metaphor (which will be expanded upon in Rule #4) can also help regulate emotional responses that would otherwise distort the true value of any outcome we have achieved. This allows us to fully engage the most advanced part of the human brain, which, among current understandings of the brain's mechanisms[50] is often considered to be the 'seat' of creativity.

Therefore, a correctly-defined purpose can potentially provide advantages throughout all three phases of any activity. It allows us to be: (i) clear on what needs to be done while developing a strategy; (ii) able to effectively evaluate unexpected changes, or even significant setbacks, as they appear during execution of that strategy; and (iii) ultimately able to better weigh benefits and issues as we reflect on our results.

In practice, I always keep purpose at the forefront of my mind. It clarifies context for any decisions that I am required to make. Honouring purpose can identify the one obvious action to take, or it can clarify the most valuable action in the case of what appears to be multiple 'right' choices.

Rule #2: Everyone Is Unique…and Usually a Little Bit Right

Background

"Everyone is a genius. But if you judge a fish by its ability to climb a tree, it will live its whole life believing that it is stupid"

Anonymous proverb

---

[50]   Heilman, 'Possible Brain Mechanisms of Creativity', 285-296.

I think I began to understand the value of this rule largely through reflection. In more recent years, I am grateful to have received instruction in powerful approaches such as Conversational Intelligence® (C-IQ) with the late Judith E. Glaser. Through the C-IQ paradigm, I have come to recognize that by seeking to understand another's perspective, I was choosing to 'stand under' their reality. But, back at the time I had started using it, this had just seemed like the sensible thing to do.

After my initial time with the army, I worked within the security industry while attending university. I was lucky enough to hold some interesting roles including instruction in the disciplines of Defensive Tactics and Firearms. During that time, I also worked the door of a nightclub with Greg, a professional with many years' experience. Greg was always slow to anger, yet startlingly fast to physically intervene when it was necessary. One night, three men were rejected at the door for being too intoxicated. Greg quietly opened the rope and asked them to leave. They had begun the usual barrage of insults that quickly escalated when Greg didn't react. At the height of their verbal aggression, screaming "You're nothing but a...", Greg just looked over and said, "Yeah, I've been known to be" before stepping back to his spot on the door. The three men froze in their outrage. I could see them frantically trying to think through what had happened. But there was nothing left for them to say. They had hurled all the abuse they could, hoping for an escalation. Instead, all they got was agreement. I gently prompted them to move along, and they wandered off without further comment—still looking confused at what had transpired.

Greg and I had previously discussed our approach. We had agreed that we didn't see our job as needing to demean or control. The incident discussed above was just business as usual.

It wasn't a challenge we had to meet or a trial in which we had to prove ourselves. Fights came often enough without us needing to instigate them. It was likely there was some reason for the mindset they had presented (other than alcohol). In fact, when one of the men returned the following night to apologize, he explained that the group had been drinking all day following the funeral of one of the men's fathers. Greg's professionalism and complete lack of ego at that moment had been the perfect reaction. That memory has stayed with me all these years, and I have never forgotten that there is always another side to every story.

Of course, it was also important that we had first honored the previous rule. In our discussions, we already knew our purpose (Rule #1), which was to ensure the best night for our patrons and staff. We agreed that this meant having a conversation with everyone who came to the door so we might use our intuition to either allow entry to those who met our expectations, or respectfully turn away those who were unable to respond appropriately. In the nights that followed, our decisions were, for the most part, well made. By remembering everyone was unique, and treating them as such, our decisions were clear and fair. This generated the best outcome for the club and our patrons alike.

The Research behind My Story:

There are actually two aspects to the idea of uniqueness. They are the views that *everyone is unique* and that *everyone is a little bit right.*

Everyone Is Unique

There are numerous reasons as to why we are all quite unique. For many years I had been aware of (and acted upon) my knowledge of this at the spiritual and psychological level. In more recent years, the biological reasons were also revealed.

It has been documented that our DNA partly consists of 'unchangeable' *template* genes (such as eye color). Based just on this unchangeable component, we find there are trillions of combinations possible. This is many times more combinations than all the humans *who have ever lived* on Earth. This nearly *guarantees* genetic uniqueness for everyone alive today[51]. It is also well documented that genes will mutate. In fact, some studies estimate that every human being holds between 30 and 60 mutated genes[52]. When including these mutations, the number of possible combinations of unique gene sets increase. So even when we take into account only the genes that produce differing *traits*[53] (as much of human DNA appears to have no function that we are able to ascertain at this stage), we are still dealing with such a large combination that strongly favors genetic uniqueness.

Gene *regulation* adds another layer of complexity. The study of Epigenetics, and approaches such as C-IQ, also considers this function. In layman's terms, *transcription* occurs via signals from both the environment we live in and from other cells in the body. Specific genes can be turned on and off by transcription. If we add this function to the complex combination of all possible genetic

---

[51] https://markmudford.com.au/unique-genes/

[52] Ibid.

[53] Tennessen, et al. 'Evolution and Functional Impact of Rare Coding Variation from Deep Sequencing of Human Exomes', 64-69.

combinations, our genetic makeup can evolve even further.

This makes environment a key influence in ensuring our uniqueness[54] – from the womb[55], to the world we live in[56], and even the internal environment we create within ourselves[57]. Indeed, people with biologically similar gene patterns (parents, siblings) might still react in different ways to the same stimulus. In this way, our uniqueness can be considered ever-evolving.

Our perceptions also play a role. We can all have a different perception of the same event within the body. Consider the nearly identical states in the body when we experience either excitement or anxiety. Our perception (or how we choose to interpret this biological reaction) creates yet another potential difference. Our biology responds, and we perceive its meaning (as either excitement or anxiety). Thus, our own cognition can further influence our uniqueness in any situation.

Everyone Is a Little Bit Right...

It is also important to recognize that, in any situation, everyone can be a little bit right. This is why, in particular, having *comfort in ambiguity* is a must for today's leaders and successful business people. But realizing that opposing views might both contain grains of truth isn't a new concept. Hobbes and Locke argued

---

[54] Glaser, *Conversational Intelligence: How Great Leaders Build Trust and Get Extraordinary Results*, 82.

[55] Teh, et al. 'The Effect of Genotype and In Utero Environment on Interindividual Variation in Neonate DNA Methylomes', 1064-1074.

[56] Canady, 'Increased screen time promotes depressive symptoms in teens', 3-5.

[57] Echouffo-Tcheugui, et al., 'Circulating Cortisol and Cognitive and Structural Brain Measures: The Framingham Heart Study', e1961-e1970.

about it in the 17th Century. Older texts, including ancient religious writings, can seem either inconsistent in their views, or even appear to contradict themselves[58].

However, the hostility and partisanship that dominate the news cycles, political debates, and even our discussions in general today also create risks for anyone attempting to develop and implement a solution. I am often bemused by the hostility that is over-represented in the media. It seems the norm to no longer have colleagues or peers. They have been replaced by opponents. This ignores one very basic fact: all of us have unique views within our shared understandings. When we forget the fact that everyone is a little bit right, we become vulnerable to things such as confirmation bias.

In practice, I always honor the uniqueness of an individual. I first look for the parts of someone's perspective that I agree with before considering to comment on the things that I don't.

Rule #3: Wisdom Is the Result of Experience, Not Age

Background

"Any fool can know. The point is to understand."

Albert Einstein

As I progressed along my working journey, I was given some extraordinary opportunities within my workplaces to make a positive difference. One that I feel humbled to have been involved with was a high-profile corporate project that was really impacting my organization at the time. After being fortunate

---

[58] https://markmudford.com.au/ambiguity-a-history/

enough to have seen some good results on smaller projects, I was handed an issue that had, to that point, defied any attempt at resolution. The organization was struggling with customer orders being 'stuck' during the provisioning process and were unable to resolve it. This was affecting tens of thousands of orders. Rather than just defining a technical solution that looked good on paper, I physically went and worked with the team who had been dealing with this issue. By first clarifying the problem with them, and then engaging them all for the suggestions that resulted in preventing more orders from entering the 'stuck' phase, we finally had a clear path to co-create a strategy to attend to those stuck orders that remained.

As with previous examples, this rule also required all of the earlier ones to be honored. In this case, our purpose (Rule #1) was to deliver the best customer experience. This ensured that our decisions and actions were always in context. Given the team I was now working with had been across the issue from the start, they really were uniquely qualified (Rule #2) to deliver the solution. When difficulties arose, or multiple solutions were produced, we were uniquely placed as a team to get the best outcome by combining their experience at the operational level with my strategic view of our corporate capabilities. At team discussions, we knew that any disconnect we encountered usually meant both sides would probably be a little bit right. By committing to always speak openly and honestly, and finding the common thread, we could develop the most powerful solution in the shortest possible time.

The customer team had also developed informal processes that had become unwritten shortcuts as they attempted resolution of orders. We were also able to capture this and ensure that the *entire* wisdom of the customer team was drawn upon—ensuring anything they contributed was always as valuable to the development of the solution as the corporate imperative that I represented. In honoring all of these rules, the employees dealing with the difficult issues felt supported and engaged, and the customers they were dealing with also felt the care and attention they were owed. In the end, the team took each order and walked it through to completion. In the space of a month, orders in the tens of thousands (some of which had been outstanding for up to 24 months) were reduced by 75%. Corporate was extremely happy, and accolades, recognition, and rewards flowed to the hardworking team as a tribute.

The Research behind My Story:

'With Age Comes Wisdom' is certainly a myth. I have met some very senior business people who are extremely naive and make foolish decisions, and some relatively young people who drip with insight, despite being barely out of their teens. It appears that overcoming adversity is the catalyst that results in wisdom[59]. Research that stretches across interdisciplinary fields backs this up[60]. In addition to this, there is evidence that wiser people pursue activities that are more meaningful, which in turn enhances mental health[61].

In fact, when faced with the most extreme of circumstances, one of the most valuable things any survivor can be grateful for is the experience they now have in coming through that challenge. Of course, they have to get through it first to gain the full value

---

[59] https://markmudford.com.au/with-adversity-comes-wisdom/

[60] Bachmann, et al. 'Practical Wisdom: Management's No Longer Forgotten Virtue', 47-165.

[61] Webster, et al. 'Wisdom and Mental Health Across the Lifespan', 209-218.

of the experience, but simply knowing this will occur can also turn a paralyzing situation into a more positive opportunity. This can assist in gathering energy to pass more quickly through the difficulties. In times of my greatest adversities, I have always found it helpful to remember the words (perhaps incorrectly) attributed to Winston Churchill, "When going through Hell, keep going."

Rule #4: Analogy Gives Clarity without Preconception

Background

"A journey of a thousand miles starts beneath one's feet."

Lao Tzu

I have always been a fan of analogy. From my earliest days of reading the masters of business and entrepreneurship, I understood its potential. In addition, I have found analogy and metaphor to be extremely powerful in enhancing understanding when dealing with other cultures. After finishing up in corporate, I worked throughout South East Asia, helping some of the poorest populations develop their business skills and acumen. Often, our conversations suffered educational, language, and/ or cultural differences. This could create an impasse. At those times I would introduce a narrative or an analogy to assist people in developing their solution. Why? Because I have found that facts are subjective, at least as far as interpretation at the personal level is concerned. But analogy was often the tool that overcame these limitations by highlighting the process rather than the specific details.

When I was working in a region that was strongly Christian (over 92% of the population), I can recall referring to the parable of the Talents[62] from the Bible. This was in an attempt to get the local vendors to start thinking about the value of putting their money to work, especially those who already had very little and were naturally afraid to risk their last available funds for business. I remember one particularly devout businesswoman who was re-opening her small store. She was struggling with the realization that she would need to invest her precious coins in fittings, stock, and operational expenses in order to take that step. After discussing her concerns, we talked about that parable, and in particular of the man who simply hid the money that his master gave him, where it did not grow. I was buoyed to see a knowing smile light up her face; then she laughingly told me that she would not (as she put it) 'bury her gold' by not spending her money to allow the business to succeed.

We had, of course, already explored the earlier rules. She had already clarified her purpose (Rule #1). In this case, it was survival for her family and the only way to reliably provide food for her children. She also realized that, as a local with previous business experience, she was uniquely qualified (Rule #2) to build the store up. She recognized that she had valuable wisdom due to her previous failures with the shop (Rule #3). She now understood that these things, combined with the skills of those who were supporting her in this courageous move, held the key to her success. This memory remained an important one for me as I faced my own litany of dilemmas after my time in the

---

[62] *Matthew 25:14-30.* A master leaves on a long journey, entrusting gold to three servants. When he returns, he asks his servants to account for their decisions regarding their gold. Two have put it to use and are rewarded. One has buried it and squandered any opportunity for it to grow. This servant is punished.

hospital. How could I let my fear stop me from re-launching my business, when this amazing woman had been prepared to (again) risk everything she had, for hers?

The Research behind My Story:

In the West, Aesop had his fables and Socrates (according to Plato) had his teachings. In the East, Confucius had his sayings, while Lao Tzu had his parables. All the major religious teachings contain similar instruments. In fact, the narrative form has been a powerful instrument throughout the history of writing. Even the earliest surviving works of literature, *The Epic of Gilgamesh*, shows our preference for narrative. Of course, this does not consider even older cultures who have practiced oral tradition for millennia.

However, an analogy must not be too prescriptive or it will lose the power to relate to a situation. An overly prescriptive approach will give no room for the analogy to be 'real' to the listener. Consider when we see someone mimicking another— do we concentrate on the message they are conveying, or will we be distracted by the prescriptive approach itself? Abstraction can be less distracting and therefore a more effective process than adopting the literal. This also highlights the importance of the delivery, particularly at the broader level. For example, consider the positive impacts at the interorganizational level if a leader uses charisma to deliver an analogy in a positive way. Yet that same message might be perceived as negative if it is delivered narcissistically[63].

Science has also indicated that analogy engages a different part

---

[63] Gupta & Misangyi, 'Follow the leader (or not): The influence of peer CEOs' characteristics on interorganizational imitation', 1437-1472.

of the brain to normal thought[64]. This means we can access more of the brain in the analogical process. In addition, it allows us to view an otherwise emotional situation in a way that does not appear (or feel) threatening. Without a negative emotional response, we have access to the higher functions of the brain that are responsible for our greatest abilities—including creativity, wisdom, and insight. This can assist in 'downregulating' the negative effects and 'upregulating' the positive effects of our neurochemicals[65]. Either of these reactions will enhance the executive function of the brain.

In addition, the selection of the analogy is also important. There are many difficulties in transferring what we currently know into new contexts[66]. This can be due to either the complexity[67] and/or the uniqueness of the learning. It is also suggested that, in order to put the analogy to full use, the listener must first have mastery of the prerequisite skill set(s)[68] that underpin it (in the same way that using the analogy of a surgeon performing an operation might only be of value to other surgeons). Therefore, it is important that any analogy to be utilized is very familiar to both the coach and the client, or it will not deliver the benefit of higher executive functions.

---

[64] Gilead, et al. 'From mind to matter: neural correlates of abstract and concrete mindsets', 638-645.

[65] Glaser, *Conversational Intelligence: How Great Leaders Build Trust and Get Extraordinary Results*, 82-83.

[66] Day & Goldstone, 'The Import of Knowledge Export: Connecting Findings and Theories of Transfer of Learning', 153-176.

[67] Nokes-Malach & Mestre, 'Toward a Model of Transfer as Sense-Making', 184-207.

[68] Vogelaar & Resing, 'Changes over time and transfer of analogy-problem solving of gifted and non-gifted children in a dynamic testing setting', 898-914.

Finally, there is also value in understanding the metaphors or analogies being used. Examining someone's speech will highlight indicators of thought process, preferences and bias. Approaches such as Clean Language and Symbolic Modeling[69] show just how powerfully embedded such things can be in all of us.

In practice, all of this suggests that it is best to select an analogy with which my clients are extremely familiar. It is also essential to select one that they already have skills in (as we are seeking to engage the part of our mind within which our intuition and creativity reside, not wasting resource in activating our learning centers). Finally, as we are using an analogy to avoid responding emotionally to the situation, we must be careful to choose one that the client can relate to in a positive manner. This will allow us the full benefits of *upregulated* positive neurochemicals in our bodies—capturing the benefits of our biology.

Rule #5: EVERYTHING Is Connected

Background

> *"Invisible threads are the strongest ties."*

Friedrich Nietzsche

The bleed that resulted in my hospitalization seemed to come out of the blue, at least initially. However, it was the direct result of an earlier injury. A number of years ago, I had been diagnosed with Post Traumatic Stress Disorder (PTSD). At the time I was diagnosed, I recall feeling overwhelmed with emotions when I

---

[69] Campbell, *Mining Your Client's Metaphors: A How-To Workbook on Clean Language and Symbolic Modeling*, 2.

was told the news: a combination of fear (based on the limited knowledge I had about the condition), a sweeping sense of relief (that I had not been going crazy and there was a reason for my struggle), and lots of other emotions—all crowding into my body.

While undertaking Cognitive Behaviour Therapy (CBT), I also set out to discover as much as I could about the condition. In the process I came across research that indicated that this type of injury was also held physically in the body. However, for some reason, I chose to only work on the cognitive side, as if everything could be resolved just by addressing my manner of thinking.

The situation that resulted was incongruency between mind and body. This was not dissimilar to a driver in control of a vehicle that had its accelerator stuck to the floor. My mind was the driver, and the CBT I undertook allowed me to gain better control of my abilities to drive, and even make better driving decisions. But the vehicle, my body, remained with its engine revving at maximum. Ultimately, it did not matter how much I improved my ability to drive (to anticipate situations, note reactions, or engage other options) because with the accelerator stuck fully open, only misuse of gears and overuse of brakes remained available. Of course, driven this way for so many years, the vehicle had to wear out. Eventually, my body paid that price.

As with other examples, aligning with previous rules was also necessary to move forward. Following my hospitalization, my purpose (Rule #1) was the most basic of all—to survive. The uniqueness of the situation (Rule #2) was underscored by being generally the youngest in the neurosurgery ward. However, my awareness of the mind-body link suggested that if I HAD acted more wisely (Rule #3), I would have avoided my current situation. Finally, my recovery proved to be a journey (Rule #4) with the destination being a return to who I was before the bleed.

The Research behind My Story:

All around us, there are examples of connection. Science has only started to make inroads into ancient knowledge on this subject. For example, Meditation and stillness—in its modern interpretation of Mindfulness[70]— are once again recognized as an important, indeed a vital, addition to any employee's activities. And even at the smallest conceivable level, what scientists call the quantum realm, it seems we are connected in ways that we cannot yet fully comprehend[71].

There is an obvious risk in believing that all things are directly connected. If we overextend the concept that everyone is a little bit right (Rule #3) it is as bad as ignoring it completely. Then we will be in danger of confirmation bias, in which we cherry-pick as valuable only those things that directly support our views, minimizing or even ignoring things that challenge them. For this reason, it's always important to seek disconfirmation of our perceptions—to validate that we have not stumbled into this sort of cognitive bias. As Voltaire famously stated, "Illusion is the first of all pleasure."

We should also consider the effect of the environment (both external and our own internal thinking). Beyond what has already been discussed in Rule #2, it is possible to encounter

---

[70] Khoury, et al. 'Embodied Mindfulness', 1160-1171.

[71] https://markmudford.com.au/quantum-connection/

risks such as 'groupthink'[72], in which an individual may support an option that is harmful to themselves just to align with the group. This also raises the possibility of breaching psychological safety[73], as examined by Project Aristotle[74], in which psychological safety was considered a critical component for making any group effective in their actions.

Other important connections that seem true include the benefits that seemingly unrelated areas provide each other. These stretch from the more obvious examples such as exercise appearing to allow stressed individuals to perform at the performance levels of stress-free colleagues (in mice, at least)[75], or less obvious links such as how remaining sedentary may negatively impact our personality (once thought to be very difficult to change)[76], and even to the effects our environment appears to have—not just to our moods and emotions, but now even on our long-term cognitive functions[77].

In addition, while the process of learning teaches us to connect with the cognitive abilities of the mind, it largely ignores the

[72] Glaser, *Conversational Intelligence: How Great Leaders Build Trust and Get Extraordinary Results*, 171.

[73] https://markmudford.com.au/psychological-safety-and-the-team/

[74] Anderson, 'The Future Of HR: Part 2: Organizational structure'.

[75] Miller, et al. 'Running Exercise Mitigates the Negative Consequences of Chronic Stress on Dorsal Hippocampal Long-term Potentiation in Male Mice', 28-38.

[76] Stephan, et al. 'Physical Activity and Personality Development over Twenty Years: Evidence from Three Longitudinal Samples', 173-179.

[77] Dadvand, et al. 'The Association between Lifelong Greenspace Exposure and 3-Dimensional Brain Magnetic Resonance Imaging in Barcelona Schoolchildren', 1-8.

'emotional-engagement'[78] system that is hardwired into all of us. Porges' Polyvagal Theory[79] has been instrumental in shining a light on some of these factors. As a result of recognizing the mind-body connection, research is currently exploring other aspects essential to recovery. These include alternative treatments—utilizing links to eye movement, body movement, and even physical expression[80]. There may also be differences in our own responses based on the way we perceive the injury. For example, we might either passively accept PTSD as a *disorder*, including all the negative connotations this then leads us to. Or we might choose to instead unpack and repack memories and feelings associated with the injury to instead access them as an opportunity for *growth[81]*.

Finally, we must also consider connection on the rules themselves. Individually, the rules may form a part of the solution for any client. In reality, they honor the fact that they, themselves, are connected. In this way, no one rule can exist without the others, and each will enhance the other. They operate as a continuous improvement loop, each raising the others to new levels.

In practice, all of this means we need to honor the connections we intuitively know about—not just the connections that appear obvious. This includes all of the rules, where advantages though

---

78   Van der Kolk, *The Body Keeps the Score: Brain, Mind, and Body in the Healing of Trauma*, 88.

79   Porges, 'Orienting in a Defensive World: Mammalian Modifications of our Evolutionary Heritage. A Polyvagal Theory', 301-318. See also 'The Polyvagal Perspective', 116-143, by the same author

80   Van der Kolk, *The Body Keeps the Score: Brain, Mind, and Body in the Healing of Trauma*.

81   Joseph, *What Doesn't Kill Us: The New Psychology of Posttraumatic Growth*.

actioning one will lead to advantages when implementing others.

Because of these connections, and my own personal struggle, I love to coach those who have 'stayed in the fight' for longer than they should have. I am passionate about coaching those who have ended up with this type of injury. They have already demonstrated discipline and courage under harrowing circumstances to have ended up with such an injury. However, it's still vital that survivors remain aware of the less-obvious connections (in particular, the mind-physical connection that I ignored). Regardless of this, my observations of my client's achievements to date support the likelihood that success is their most likely outcome from any structured program that connects the rules to their wisdom and resilience.

Rule #6: Success Is Not A Solo Journey–Build a Tribe

Background

> *"If I have seen further it is by standing*
> *on the shoulders of Giants."*

Isaac Newton

I have always believed that success is a team sport. When I partner with clients, we join each other's teams. This is why I named my business "Mark Mudford *& Associates*." Because no one succeeds in a vacuum. In the context of Tribe, it is the quality of people, and their diversity of views, that make for the healthiest environments and most powerful solutions.

I am a member of the International Coaching Federation (ICF), an organization that works tirelessly to ensure the standards in our industry continue to improve. The ICF also provides me the opportunity to connect with an incredible group of fellow coaches who are undertaking their own journey—some who have overcome challenges I may soon face and some who may benefit from my own perspectives and experience. I also have the .coach team, who support me in managing my business approach with the technical and strategic aspects of my online presence. The group also provides me another opportunity to be a part of a cohort with other successful and influential business professionals. Added to this is the wonderful community from Judith E. Glaser's C-IQ, who have continued to support and guide my seemingly insatiable appetite for research in the intersections between business, social sciences, neuroscience, and epigenetics.

Apart from this, I also have an amazing family. My incredible wife, Arlyn, who teaches me something new about the wonder of gentleness and respect every day. I also have those who I call my Personal 'Board of Directors'–a few key people with very unique perspectives and skills who help me fine tune my own skill sets (and yes, even coaches need a coach!) or test my thoughts and perception to co-create with me the incredible content and insights I later share with others.

Of course, the previous rules are always present for Tribe: (Rule #1) by understanding and embodying our own true purpose–which for me is to serve; (Rule #2) through applying our unique skill sets while being respectful of the fact that every client (and every other member of the Tribe) will always be a little bit right–which for me means to energize the uniqueness of all, yet also seek out our common understandings; (Rule #3) via accessing the collective wisdom of the Tribe, which clients have found particularly powerful during co-creation conversations; (Rule #4) to be dedicated to continuing our individual and collective *journey* together, sharing our experiences along the way; and (Rule #5) never losing sight of the fact that everything is connected (even in ways that science is only now learning to measure).

In many ways, this final rule also delivers the power of Tribe to all the other rules. It amplifies them, allowing them to multiply benefits that could not be achieved alone. Through Tribe alone, we have morphed the business from consultancy into a successful business coaching service. Our success has been overwhelming, and I am humbled every day by the amazing impacts and responses we achieve.

The Research behind My Story:

As explored when discussing Rule #2, the study of Epigenetics looks at how the environment changes every person in a very individual way. As a result, every person is unique in ability, thought, and behavior. As individuals, we are also in a constant state of flux as we release the potential of the group and then begin anew to further develop one other. These facts on their own highlight the value of Tribe.

Interconnection at the biological level, also touched on throughout the Rules, is further supported by the C-IQ theory of the multiple brains[82], now updated to 6 by the inclusion of the gut. Both my experience with PTSD and the C-IQ approach support the concept that nothing may occur in isolation. This also suggests that, because we are already social

---

[82]   Glaser, *Conversational Intelligence: How Great Leaders Build Trust and Get Extraordinary Results*, 82-83.

creatures operating within a social structure, we are also not designed to succeed in isolation.

The benefits of socialization are heavily at play here. We know that socialization has many positive physical effects such as improving physical health[83] or even overcoming injuries such as PTSD[84]. It has been linked to improving the enjoyment of experiences[85]. Even business success in overseas markets can be strengthened by this rule[86]. It is important to remember that the individual gifts of every member, including gratefulness, can be enhanced this way. The resulting advantages at the individual level then further benefit the Tribe.

In practice, this means that the Tribe brings together the skills of the individual to a benefit greater than the sum. This is then amplified further by the associated benefits that we humans, as tribal creatures, then provide through things such as encouragement, guidance, and sacrifice.

Conclusion

I did not write this chapter as a self-appointed expert. We are all unique. We all have greatness within us. My purpose is to serve,

---

[83] Cohut, *Socialization: How does it benefit mental and physical health?* Available at: https://www.medicalnewstoday.com/articles/321019.php

[84] Rodriguez, et al. 'The Effect of a Service Dog on Salivary Cortisol Awakening Response in a Military Population with Posttraumatic Stress Disorder (PTSD)', 202-210.

[85] Caprariello & Reis, 'To do, to have, or to share? Valuing experiences over material possessions depends on the involvement of others', 199-215.

[86] Gould, et al. 'Opportunities and opportunism with high-status B2B partners in emerging economies', 684-694.

and it is my humble hope that this chapter may give someone a gem of insight on their next step or a glimmer of light in the darkness.

These six rules are connected and promise to deliver their own benefits, multiplied again by the benefits of Tribe. They have allowed me to keep balance in a world that felt somehow more chaotic after my discharge from the hospital. In fact, they are so valuable that they form the basis of every coaching conversation I now have. Others have also reported experiences similar to mine in clarity of direction and resilience in the face of our often-ambiguous world. Clients tell me these rules are at the root of many of their successes. Anyone who has embodied these rules has already begun that journey to success. A journey that will deliver them true alignment with their values and beliefs.

Let's finish as we started—with the six rules.

Rule #1: Let Purpose Be Your Context: Find your true purpose, connect with it, and then allow it to drive your business to new heights.

Rule #2: Everyone Is Unique…and Usually a Little Bit Right: Recognize and celebrate your contribution to the world. Realize that your staff and customers bring a uniqueness that deserves to be honored. Embodying this knowledge will harness your business.

Rule #3: Wisdom Is the Result of Experience, Not Age: Revel in your experiences, and realize that the knowledge you have gained from your 'failures' or 'catastrophes' is actually your greatest asset. Once this is clear, be prepared to use those learnings to unleash your success!

Rule #4: Analogy Gives Clarity without Preconception:
Remember that an analogy will be more powerful than a
prescriptive solution. So, first, find the right analogy and then
use it to improve your situation in business and life... and the
lives of everyone around you.

Rule #5: EVERYTHING is Connected: Realize the power
of small improvements, and understand its impact on your
business and your life. Create a positive environment where
you can best support your staff and serve your customers.

Rule #6: Success Is Not A Solo Journey–Build a Tribe: This
is the golden rule. It simply states that you cannot succeed in
isolation. Build your team with those you trust. Build it with
those who have the skills and experience that you lack, or the
support that you require. And get ready to see your business
explode!

References

Anderson, B (2017), 'The Future of HR: Part 2: Organizational Structure', *HR Strategy and Planning Excellence Essentials* (Aurora), HR.COM.

Berkelaar, BL & Buzzanell, PM (2015), 'Bait and Switch or Double-edged Sword? The (sometimes) Failed Promises of Calling', *Human Relations*, vol. 68, no. 1.

Bachmann, C, Habisch, A & Dierksmeier, C (2018), 'Practical Wisdom: Management's No Longer Forgotten Virtue', *Journal of Business Ethics*, vol. 153, no. 1.

Campbell, G (2013), *Mining Your Client's Metaphors: A How-To Workbook on Clean Language and Symbolic Modeling*, vol. 1.

Canady, VA (2018), 'Increased Screen Time promotes Depressive symptoms in Teens', *Mental Health Weekly*, vol. 28, no. 23.

Caprariello, PA & Reis, HT (2013), 'To do, to Have, or to Share? Valuing Experiences over Material Possessions depends on the involvement of Others', *Journal of Personality and Social Psychology*, vol. 104, no. 2.

Chevreux, L, Lopez, J & Mesnard, X (2018), 'The Best Companies Know How to Balance Strategy and Purpose', *Accountancy SA*.

Cohut, M. (2018). 'Socialization: How does it benefit mental and physical health?'. [online] *Medical News Today*. Available at: https://www.medicalnewstoday.com/articles/321019.php

Dadvand, P, Pujol, J, Macià, D, Martínez-Vilavella, G, Blanco-Hinojo, L, Mortamais, M, Alvarez-Pedrerol, M, Fenoll, R, Esnaola, M, Dalmau-Bueno, A, López-Vicente, M, Basagaña, X, Jerrett, M, Nieuwenhuijsen, MJ & Sunyer, J (2018), 'The Association between Lifelong Greenspace Exposure and 3-Dimensional Brain Magnetic Resonance Imaging in Barcelona Schoolchildren', *Environmental Health Perspectives*, vol. 126, no. 2.

Davies, W (2016), The *Happiness Industry. How the Government and Big Business Sold Us Well-Being,* Verso, UK: London

Day, SB & Goldstone, RL (2012), 'The Import of Knowledge Export: Connecting Findings and Theories of Transfer of Learning', *Educational Psychologist*, vol. 47, no. 3.

Echouffo-Tcheugui, JBM, PhD; Conner, Sarah C. MPH; Himali, Jayandra J. PhD; Maillard, Pauline PhD; DeCarli, Charles S. MD; Beiser, Alexa S. PhD; Vasan, Ramachandran S. MD; Seshadri, Sudha MD (2018), 'Circulating Cortisol and Cognitive and Structural Brain Measures: The Framingham Heart Study', *Neurology*, vol. 91(21).

Gilead, M, Liberman, N & Maril, A (2014), 'From Mind to Matter: Neural Correlates of abstract and concrete Mindsets', *Social Cognitive and Affective Neuroscience*, vol. 9, no. 5.

Glaser, JE (2014), *Conversational Intelligence: How Great Leaders Build Trust and Get Extraordinary Results*, ed. 1 Books24x, Brookline, MA: Bibliomotion.

Gould, AN, Liu, AH & Yu, Y (2016), 'Opportunities and Opportunism with High-status B2B Partners in emerging Economies', *Journal of Business & Industrial Marketing*, vol. 31, no. 5.

Gupta, A & Misangyi, VF (2018), 'Follow the leader (or not): The influence of peer CEOs' characteristics on interorganizational imitation', *Strategic Management Journal*, vol. 39, no. 5.

Heilman, KM (2016), 'Possible Brain Mechanisms of Creativity', *Archives of Clinical Neuropsychology*, vol. 31, no. 4.

Henderson, SJ (2000), '"Follow Your Bliss": A Process for Career Happiness', *Journal of Counseling and Development*, vol.78, no. 3.

Joseph, S (2011), *What Doesn't Kill Us: The New Psychology of Posttraumatic Growth*, ed. b ProQuest issuing, New York: Basic Books.

Khoury, B, Knäuper, B, Pagnini, F, Trent, N, Chiesa, A & Carrière, K (2017), 'Embodied Mindfulness', *Mindfulness*, vol. 8, no. 5.

Miller, RM, Marriott, D, Trotter, J, Hammond, T, Lyman, D, Call, T, Walker, B, Christensen, N, Haynie, D, Badura, Z, Homan, M & Edwards, JG (2018), 'Running Exercise Mitigates the Negative Consequences of Chronic Stress on Dorsal Hippocampal Long-Term Potentiation in Male Mice', *Neurobiology of Learning and Memory*, vol. 149.

Nokes-Malach, T & Mestre, J (2013), 'Toward a Model of Transfer as Sense-Making', *Educational Psychologist*, vol. 48, no. 3.

Porges, SW (1995), 'Orienting in a Defensive World: Mammalian Modifications of our Evolutionary Heritage. A Polyvagal Theory', *Psychophysiology*, vol. 32, no. 4.

--- (2007), 'The Polyvagal Perspective', *Biological Psychology*, vol. 74, no. 2.

Rodriguez, KE, Bryce, CI, Granger, DA & O'Haire, ME (2018), 'The Effect of a Service Dog on Salivary Cortisol Awakening Response in a Military Population with Posttraumatic Stress Disorder (PTSD)', *Psychoneuroendocrinology*, vol. 98.

Stephan, Y, Sutin, AR, Luchetti, M, Bosselut, G & Terracciano, A (2018), 'Physical activity and Personality Development over Twenty Years: Evidence from Three Longitudinal Samples', *Journal of Research in Personality*, vol. 73.

Teh, AL, Pan, H, Chen, L, Ong, M-L, Dogra, S, Wong, J, MacIsaac, JL, Mah, SM, McEwen, LM, Saw, S-M, Godfrey, KM, Chong, Y-S, Kwek, K, Kwoh, C-K, Soh, S-E, Chong, MFF, Barton, S, Karnani, N, Cheong, CY, Buschdorf, JP, Stünkel, W, Kobor, MS, Meaney, MJ, Gluckman, PD & Holbrook, JD (2014), 'The Effect of Genotype and In Utero Environment on Interindividual Variation in Neonate DNA Methylomes', *Genome Research*, vol. 24, no. 7.

Tennessen, JA, Bigham, AW, O'Connor, TD, Fu, W, Kenny, EE, Gravel, S, McGee, S, Do, R, Liu, X, Jun, G, Kang, HM,

Jordan, D, Leal, SM, Gabriel, S, Rieder, MJ, Abecasis, G, Altshuler, D, Nickerson, DA, Boerwinkle, E, Sunyaev, S, Bustamante, CD, Bamshad, MJ & Akey, JM (2012), 'Evolution and Functional Impact of Rare Coding Variation from Deep Sequencing of Human Exomes', Science, vol. 337, no. 6090

Van der Kolk, B (2015), *The Body Keeps the Score: Brain, Mind, and Body in the Healing of Trauma*, New York, New York: Penguin Books.

Vogelaar, B & Resing, WCM (2018), 'Changes over Time and Transfer of Analogy-Problem Solving of Gifted and Non-Gifted Children in a Dynamic Testing Setting', *Educational Psychology*, vol. 38, no. 7.

Webster, JD, Westerhof, GJ & Bohlmeijer, ET (2014), 'Wisdom and Mental Health Across the Lifespan', *Journals of Gerontology Series B: Psychological Sciences and Social Sciences*, vol. 69, no. 2.

Mark Mudford

After a very successful career in corporate life, Mark had taken all his learnings and experience to build up his own successful business. Overcoming various challenges, he was able to pursue two of his deepest passions – to make a difference in people's lives and provide for others. Then one day, he woke up in a hospital. Missing all memory from the preceding weeks, it would be many months before he could return to his business. By that time, he HAD no business. Everything he had built up, over such a long time, was now gone – seemingly, in an instant.

By that stage, Mark's career had spanned many years. From years in the military and then security industry, followed by nearly a decade in senior positions in corporate before moving into the not-for-profit sector—all before finally moving into business for himself. Throughout his career, his development had also been enabled by a strong scholarly focus that saw him the recipient of multiple awards for Undergraduate, Honors, and Masters levels degrees as well as significant recognition in more practical/technical courses.

After tragedy struck, he decided to tap more completely into his own experience and knowledge base. He also realized that his expertise had previously been assisting business professionals in difficult circumstances, which was now exactly where he found himself. With the thought of 'physician, heal thy self' echoing in his mind, he set out to action his own wisdom. And he began to truly experience the amazing power of growth from adversity.

Today, he coaches around this exact process, supported by the latest research in the sciences and the areas of business leadership and entrepreneurship.

The best part? Every one of his clients is able to make the breakthroughs that uniquely apply to them.

Contact Information:

Website: www.markmudford.com.au
LinkedIn: https://www.linkedin.com/in/markmudford/

FINDING LOVE AGAIN

MICHAEL GOLOWYN

Setting the Scene

In September 2015, I was in Bali and attending to business when I went to log in my daily call with my long-term partner Jackie. The previous evening, we'd had an argument and I was looking forward to smoothing things over and coming back home to South Africa. As soon as the call connected, something felt wrong. The usual relaxed and happy mood of our calls was not there. Instead, it was replaced by a tightness. I could not understand what it was at first, then it immediately hit me. I knew what was coming before it happened. She blurted out "It's over, I can't do this anymore, I'm leaving." Just a cold, matter-of-fact statement.

Four years prior, I moved to South Africa from my birthplace Perth in Australia to be with Jackie and make a home together. I stayed with Jackie, her five-year-old daughter, three dogs, and four cats. We had become acquaintances over the years on my previous visits to South Africa as a traveling surfer. It wasn't until years later though, when we really started speaking to each other, that our connection deepened and I chose to make a radical move and switch countries. It was a typical relationship with its ups and downs, but all of us got along very well and I felt like there was nothing that we could not face together. I believed we were in it for the long haul. So when Jackie ended it, with no warning, I was shocked. The rug was pulled out from beneath my feet. In an instant, I went from being a stable family man to a foreigner in a strange land and was feeling alone and unwanted—a tourist with his heart ripped open, used, and cast aside like trash.

This was not my first episode of enduring the pain of a long-term relationship ending. It was one of many. By now, however, I had already been studying and applying the work of Dr. John Demartini, a human behavioral specialist, for close to a decade. Being very familiar with applying Dr. Demartini's work as it was, I hadn't really used the knowledge in a highly emotional grief test case on myself. Now was an opportunity. I wanted to put my money where my mouth was. It was an interesting thing to be able to analyze and observe my mind as it was going through this major upheaval. I am a scientist by training and have an innate interest in knowing how things work. I wanted to know how grief worked in the mind and if it could be transcended. What follows is the story of the situation I found myself in, how I overcame it, and met the woman of my dreams within an hour of completing the process.

Background

The fact that before I was even eight years old, my mother leaving the family had propelled me onto a trajectory into adulthood full of painful relationship breakups was not lost on me. I knew that somehow and somewhere this abandonment thing was affecting my life, but I had no clue what to do about it.

My mother was (and still is) a sweet, caring woman who loved us very much. But an extremely volatile domestic situation forced her to take refuge in Sydney, way out on the other side of the country. Since our father was deemed to be the best equipped, financially speaking, with stable employment to provide a home, my brother and I remained with him in Perth. At the time, I don't recall too much sadness at mum leaving. I remember climbing onto the back seat of the family car and putting on the seat belt so we could all drive mum to the airport that day. I do remember lying in bed at night, trying to fall asleep, without the tenderness I was used to. The touch, the affection, the attention, and time my mother gave us each night, tucking us into bed, and reading us a bedtime story were now absent. There was no one anymore. My dad did his best, but he needed to work, and he provided babysitters for us when we weren't at school. I knew he loved us, but the physical touch and affection just was not there. It wasn't the same.

I wouldn't say that I was feeling abandoned, hurt, or left behind in any way. As a seven-year-old, you are just trying to make sense of the world. We don't question the authority of our parents that young, and with my Dad having a lot on his plate, facing a divorce, working to make ends meet, I tried to help in the only way I could. I kept quiet, stayed out of trouble, and did what was expected of me. I buried my emotions, pushing them deep inside me. It was only until much later, when it started to express itself in my adult relationships, that I felt something was not quite right.

The experience of my mum leaving me as a child repeatedly resurfaced through my teens, my twenties, and even into my thirties as a series of abandonment scenarios that I couldn't make sense of. Surely 'finding love' was not supposed to be this hard? Each of my intimate relationships ended painfully and abruptly, and the same patterns kept repeating themselves. I sought therapy over the years to attempt to alleviate the pain and find some answers. I even took up yoga and meditation for several years as a means to return inward to the self, hoping it would somehow cure me of this affliction. There is a good deal of merit in traditional therapy, yoga, and meditation to move on from painful experiences, and it did help ground me and form healthy habits, if nothing else. But after many years of seeking, I still wasn't closer to finding answers that plagued my failed relationships.

Answers

It was a cold wintery day in August 2006 when I found myself in surfing paradise at Jeffreys Bay, South Africa. I was sitting out in the surf, on my board, looking around at what surfers call absolute, world-class waves. For a lifelong surfer like me, it was heaven. Smooth, groomed, and salt-water freight trains steamed down the point, offering us some of the longest and most exhilarating rides of our lives. Heaven as it was, it was also one of the most depressing and darkest moments of my life.

Two weeks before this, I had just caught my lover red-handed with another man. I was 30 years old at the time, based out of Abu Dhabi, and working offshore in the oil fields of the Persian Gulf as a Hydrographic Surveyor. During my time 'on land,' I met and 'fell in love' with Teresa. We would spend all our free time together when I was back onshore; we would discuss the future and make plans. I trusted her implicitly, so one night when she said she couldn't come out and had to look after her son, I believed her.

A colleague, Brad, and I ended up going to a local hotel for a few drinks at the rooftop bar, where Brad was first to go into the elevator. He came right back out and pointed his thumb at the elevator, blurting "Teresa is in there!" "Bullshit!" I replied.

I thought he was having me on, so I walked into the elevator and couldn't quite believe what I saw. There Teresa was, with a ridiculously guilty look spread across her face. It immediately dawned on me what was taking place, and so I looked around the elevator and wondered which one of the half-dozen men present she was supposed to be with. I didn't wait around to find out. I had to get outside for some fresh air and collect my thoughts. I walked back to my room and spent the night in a kind of daze, not quite believing what was happening. Over the following days, Teresa blocked my calls and attempts to contact her, but I managed to get some answers from her friends. It turned out she had been two-timing me and for quite some time as well. After a week of attempting to contact her to get the full story, she ended up choosing the other guy. I was left feeling like an empty shell tossed into the gutter. Actually, it was worse.

I didn't understand it at the time, but a study by Fisher et al. (2010) investigating the effects of grief and heartbreak on the brain using Functional Magnetic Resonance Imaging (fMRI), found increased neural activity in the areas of the brain associated with craving and addiction when subjects were shown a photograph of their ex-partner. An even earlier study (Breiter et al. 1997) reported that the same regions of the brain (nucleus accumbens) are activated during cocaine administration, and activity in this region is positively correlated with a craving for cocaine. It is no wonder that romantic rejection causes such a profound sense of loss and negative effect. It's the same as experiencing withdrawal from a powerful narcotic substance, which can induce clinical depression; in extreme cases, it can even lead to suicide and/or homicide. This described my state precisely.

The next couple of weeks were excruciating. I couldn't speak to anyone about what I was going through. I was in a strange foreign country, and I couldn't perform or focus on my job. It was seriously affecting my career and life, and it started to take its toll on my physical and mental health. I had to get out of there. I immediately turned to something that I had always been passionate about in the past – world-class surfing, travel, old friends, and quiet solitude. So, I booked a ticket to an old stomping ground that brought back fond memories, Jeffreys Bay, South Africa.

I can distinctly remember sitting in the surf that August, looking at the shoreline thinking "I'm in one of the most amazing parts of the world, surfing some of the best waves of my life with some amazing friends, and yet, here I am, feeling miserable, absolutely crushed." Suffering from essentially a mixture grief and depression, I remember clearly thinking "If a relationship and a person can make you feel such happiness, then how is it that they can also make you feel such sadness?" I didn't realize at the time but that one question put me on a decade-long quest to find answers. And boy did I get some answers! Enter Dr. John Demartini.

Two weeks after the trip to Jeffrey Bay, I was back in Australia and an old ex I had not seen for 12 years contacted me. In fact, Cassy was the first woman to break my heart, my 'first love.' Was this a coincidence? After a brief catch up, I explained my situation to her. She gave me a knowing look, went to her bookshelf, and handed me a copy of Dr. Demartini's book '*The Breakthrough Experience*' (2002). In it, Demartini explained that there is no such thing as happiness without sadness, pleasure without pain, or gain without loss. He went on to develop his arguments in rational, step-by-step logic and backed it up with real cases with clients, modern scientific theory, and esoteric knowledge. To a technically trained scientist with an interest in metaphysics, John was speaking my language.

Several years later, I finally managed to attend his seminar scheduled in Melbourne. That seminar was a strange experience. On the one hand, I was blown away by John's principles and logic, weaving mathematics and physics into his theories of the mind and 'source'. On the other hand, I felt let down by the practical exercise, and I wasn't able to achieve the fabled 'breakthrough' I had read so much about. Despite this setback, I was convinced his work had merit and booked into more advanced workshops and training. I'm glad I persevered. It was during the follow-on training that the breakthroughs started to arrive thick and fast and in such a synchronized torrent that it left me utterly certain of the power and value of this work. So began a decade-long period of researching, studying, and applying the principles, based in universal law, that underpin all of nature, existence, and human behavior.

A Mother's Love

Jackie mentioning that she was leaving me was a shock, but at that moment, I still had the capacity to begin to ask myself some balancing questions.

"As Jackie is pulling away from me, rejecting me, who is coming toward me, accepting me, wanting me in that same moment, to the same degree?" Immediately, the images of several women friends and acquaintances flashed into my mind.

"Are they moving toward me and accepting me as much as Jackie is rejecting me?" "Yes" was the response.

I was certain. They were women who had shown interest in me, but I wasn't available at the time. I suddenly felt the presence of their energy moving toward me. It wasn't actually them, but the part of my psyche that had split off certain information and stored that other half of 'reality'. I was utilizing part of a technique developed by Dr. Demartini, one he taught in his books and seminars. This step is designed to see the hidden intelligent order of the universe in our lives. It's about becoming absolutely present with the moment you are working on and observing your perception of what is transpiring. In a field of conscious awareness, our perceptions are always conserved between our conscious and subconscious minds. For instance, when we perceive someone pulling away from us, in that same moment, someone or multiple people are coming toward us (metaphorically or physically) and into our lives, wanting us to the same degree the other person is rejecting us. This brief exercise took the edge off the shock and emotions that started to bubble up when Jackie left me. I was able to see the balance taking place in my psyche and in my life at that moment. It was enough for me to relax with a clear mind and fall into a deep sleep that night.

> *"All human beings receive a balance of traits*
> *outward from others or inward from themselves to*
> *maintain equilibrium (Demartini 2007)."*

As a Hydrographic Surveyor, we use Global Positioning Systems and sonar technology to accurately map portions of the sea floor and ensure accuracy during the installation of subsea structures and pipelines. Sailing on the sea during the day, all the information we require to navigate safely is visible to our own eyes in all directions. I liken this to our conscious mind – things we are consciously aware of. But as soon as we want to explore the subsea environment, everything suddenly becomes a mystery. Things are dark and remain hidden from our immediate vision. We do not know what lies beneath the surface, how deep the water goes, and what the terrain is like. I liken the sub-sea environment to the subconscious or unconscious part of our mind, with its well-kept secrets, which is magnitudes more deep and powerful than our conscious mind. Communicating to the depths of the ocean is done by interrogating deployed subsea sonar beacons on specific frequencies. The beacons then respond on reply frequencies signaling their exact location. This is similar to asking our subconscious mind specific questions in order to dig out the hidden answer. The subconscious cannot refuse to answer if the question is specific enough and if it is asked in the right frequency. So we need to tune in and be very specific about what it is that is triggering our emotions.

The morning after the call with Jackie, even though I conducted some minor experiments with my mind, I was still upset about losing her and my family. I resolved to sit down, utilize my knowledge and training, and began probing my subconscious with specific, targeted questions. When we are overcome with emotions, our mind is filled with all sorts of thoughts and feelings, which invariably end up taking us over if they are not addressed. We lose control of ourselves and our lives. I didn't want to let that happen, like all the times before. So I tasked myself that morning to work on and transcend the biggest charge I had at the time, which was being angry! "What was it I was so pissed off about?" I asked myself silently. "Weakness!" the answer came. I was angry at Jackie for being 'Weak!' and not standing up for us, fighting, and seeing it through together as a couple and as a family. I saw her act as one of giving up, and doing it in a cowardly way, via the internet while I was still away on the other side of the world.

I was making some progress that morning, quietly sitting outside my bungalow, but I still had plenty of anger bubbling up until I came to the part where I had to identify in what aspects Jackie was equally the opposite. You see, human beings in their entirety are actually whole beings of light. That is, we each encompass the whole spectrum of human attributes that exist under the sun, and each human trait has its equal and opposite attribute, which we express in our own unique way. Therefore, according to this principle, labeling someone as 'weak' or 'cowardly' also means that they must embody the opposite trait of equal magnitude in some way or form. So I asked myself the question "Where is Jackie strong and brave?" but I felt my emotions blocking access to the deeper recesses of my mind. I asked again. Nothing. I asked one more time, this time slightly altering the language (frequency) "How is Jackie *courageous*?"

The answer leapt out of my unconscious and hit me before I could verbalize it aloud. Her making the decision to leave a secure home was one of the bravest things a single, financially dependent mother could do! At that moment, I realized she was both weak and strong, simultaneously, in leaving me. The two complementary opposite perceptions of the same act collided together in my psyche like two oppositely charged subatomic particles colliding together in a physics laboratory, annihilating one another to birth gamma light photons in the mind. This is true love. This was the goal of this work: to bring the opposite perception out from where it is buried in our unconscious mind, so it can be united with our conscious thoughts and give birth to light. his is what enlightenment is—a gaining of a complete quanta of wisdom and of completing the whole of that energy's frequency.

> "*Between extreme particles is a centre point of light. Between extreme emotions is the center point of love (Demartini 2002).*"

This was only the beginning. On holding that experience in my mind, my resentment toward Jackie was immediately replaced by a love for her that I couldn't describe. Then, it felt as though the floor further dropped out from under me as I immediately broke down in tears. I got up from my chair, tried to move inside the bungalow, and barely made it to the bed inside, where I curled up and let out big heaving sobs, releasing decades of pent-up hurt and anger. The inner demons I had been holding onto since childhood were being expelled from my nose and mouth in a tumult of breath, snot, saliva, tears, and the kind of heaving sobs that took me all the way back to my young childhood. Jackie was my mother. I saw at that moment how brave my mother was, how much courage it must have taken for her to leave. She left with nothing. How hard it must have been for her to feel like she had no choice but to leave. My resentment and anger melted away, allowing a tremendous love for my mother to rush in and take its place. As I lay there sobbing, I wanted to hold my mother and tell her how much I loved her and how I admired her courage to do what she did. I felt her immense love for me, being there when I needed her and felt her stoic motherly strength. What a feeling it is for a boy to feel a mother's love for the first time!

This was a large, missing piece of my childhood restored to its rightful place, and being an adult diving headlong into middle age, it wasn't too late for me yet. Love had been residing within my heart all this time. I wore a mask covering it my whole life with my string of broken relationships, all of them helping me chip away at that hard encrusted shell I wore like a protective shield for so long, attempting to reveal what was ultimately always there. It took me almost 35 years to crack that and thanks to Jackie, the mask began to crumble.

Even though my mother wasn't there for me for much of my childhood, she was the one consistent thread in my adulthood, the one person who was always there without question when I was going through all my previous relationship breakdowns. She never abandoned me when I needed her support the most. I would come to her home, and she would cook for me, let me rest, and sleep. When I spoke, she would listen. I felt like I was home. I felt loved, I felt like I belonged, and I felt wanted. All the things I was fighting to receive from the outside world, from fleeting lovers, came naturally to me once I hit rock bottom. I had been resisting it all my life, scouring the planet for that elusive love, and once I was tired of searching, tired of being beaten up by the world, she was there, ready to take me in.

Uncovering this new love and respect for my mother that I had been holding back all these years, simultaneously awakened the same courage and strength in me. I faced an obstacle, an emotional mountain to overcome, but now I had an inner poise and knowing, an inner strength that reassured me I was now in control. It told me that this wasn't a problem but an opportunity to grow, calling me to a higher level. At this moment, I became the embodiment of my mother's strength, courage, love, and wisdom. A new-found love and respect for myself emerged, like a phoenix rising from the ashes. My love for my mother and for myself was intertwined, and this was the key to further unlocking the tangled web of emotional pain that lay before me.

"Being deeply loved by someone gives you strength,
while loving someone deeply gives you courage."

Lao Tzu

Loss is an Illusion

On the way home to South Africa, sitting on planes and waiting around in airports, I made use of the idle time I had. Based on a technique Dr. Demartini had developed for rapidly transcending the grief from the death of a loved one, I adapted it to losing someone as a result of a breakup. Several years ago, I recalled taking a pro-bono client through the death of her son. Her son was a commercial squid fisherman working off the coast of South Africa. When the vessel returned to port, the mother received news that her son was 'lost at sea' and presumed dead—never to be seen again. The crew, skipper, and fishing company did not shed light about the incident, and they covered it up. Not having the resources to pursue an investigation, the mother gave in to quiet despair, never knowing the fate of her son. So it was not surprising that three years later, she was still suffering grief. Within 3 hours of focussed work, my client went from mourning over the loss of her son to an immense feeling of grace and love for her son for passing. His 'presence' was felt by both of us in the room, and we were both moved to tears and she could finally let him go and appreciate her life now. His essence was never missing; it has been in her life ever since, sprinkled now amongst the loved ones surrounding her. It was a beautiful transition from mourning to love.

I approached the breakup with Jackie in the same way. I needed to break down the grief into its composite parts and work with each one in turn. I began listing out all the aspects of Jackie I was now beginning to miss or mourn the loss of. We only miss the aspects of a person that which we are infatuated with, never missing things we resent in them. Infatuation isn't love, but an attachment, an addiction, an imbalance. I wrote things I started to miss about her. Things like her 'being there for me', 'support of family', 'intelligent conversations', 'physical intimacy', 'companionship', 'good cooking', 'witty sense of humor' and I kept going until I could not think of anything else. There were eight or nine different aspects in all. The total sum of these aspects combined to form everything we feel when we lose someone close to us.

The next part was based on the first law of thermodynamics in physics, namely the conservation of energy within a closed system. The conservation of energy is one of the most fundamental laws of physics. It governs all known natural phenomena, and no violation of the law has so far been observed (Capra 2010). Chardin (1959) in his posthumously published work 'The Phenomenon of Man' coined the term 'Nooesphere' to describe an enclosed region around man that encompasses the Earth as a field of thoughts curved around upon themselves, forming a single closed system where each element sees, feels, desires, and suffers for itself. This is also our 'sphere of awareness and intention' that Demartini (2013) describes in his work. Everything we are aware of in our life, that we have an influence on, has a finite psychical boundary. This thought field or Nooesphere also behaves like a radio station, where we can tune in and manifest anything as long as the resources are also within this field.

Another important component to understand is that thoughts, impressions, perceptions, emotions, matter, and things 'that matter' are all energy. Most of us are aware of Einstein's equivalence principle from his famous equation:

$$E=mC^2$$

Where E = Energy, m = Mass, and C = Speed of light

Here, the significant point is that energy and mass are interchangeable, but ultimately **nothing is lost, it just changes in form**. Our thoughts and impressions behave in a wave-like fashion but are also simply energy forms. Our perceptions of the world around us is no different: all matter, situations, people, and thoughts are conserved within our Nooesphere.

By constantly associating a lot of pain and negativity with their past relationships, single people who say they want to be in a relationship often unconsciously block (protect) themselves from meeting their soulmate. Instead, the components that make up their soulmate is fragmented out into the people already surrounding them. No one takes the time to notice that they are already surrounded by their ideal partner. By resolving the hurt from their past relationships and appreciating the various currently dispersed forms their soulmate takes in their life, the special person they are looking for will then appear.

I recall working on the aspect that I missed the most about in Jackie. It was her 'being there for me'. I asked myself "Who has come into my life to an equal degree after Jackie left and is 'there for me' now?"

"My Mum, Dad, and my friends actually came back into my

life" I answered, and it was true. My parents suddenly contacted and supported me, and friends I had not heard from in a long time suddenly got in touch and wanted to connect with me. I listed all the multiple forms of people who began expressing this trait of 'being there for me', including inward from myself, until I felt it matched what Jackie embodied. Then, I recalled all the negative aspects of the trait of 'being there for me' when I was with Jackie in the relationship. There were many more than I realized. As I worked through this, my infatuation for Jackie 'being there for me' started to wear off, until I felt it was balanced. I began to feel relieved that Jackie was out of my life!

"Where there is grief there is hidden relief."

Dr. John Demartini

Next, I began to list out all the positive qualities expressed by my parents and friends 'being there for me' until I could be totally grateful for them in my life at that moment. When I was finished, I no longer missed Jackie 'being there for me.' There was no emotion when I thought about that trait in her. In fact, I was becoming grateful to her for leaving. I proceeded down the list of things I missed about being in a relationship with Jackie and worked through them in the same way, asking the same questions. Each time, new and different people or opportunities surfaced in my life—ones I hadn't taken the time to notice before. I also took on a lot of the roles I normally reserved to Jackie myself, which started to fill me with a sense of strength and empowerment.

A recent study published in the *Journal of Experimental Psychology* (Langeslag and Sanchez 2018) has shown that the best way to combat the grief of heartbreak was to give a negative appraisal of the relationship. The academics agreed that in the long-term, it was an effective coping strategy; however taken as a whole, the technique falls short and the resulting relief is short-lived. First, we require a substitute to replace the old form we were addicted to; we need to work through the infatuation to the old form by associating negatives with it and then uncovering positives of the newly emerged forms. Done properly, this completely dissolves the perception of loss and releases the trapped emotional energy, which is now available.

By the time I finished three hours later, I was in a state of grace. I closed my eyes and Jackie's face emerged in my mind's eye. It was clear as day. I felt her presence there. I could say "Thank you for leaving, goodbye, I love you." I was in tears. I moved to a quiet corner of Johannesburg airport to have my moment of grace without strange looks from members of the public. These weren't tears of mourning, unrequited love, loss or sadness. They were tears of relief and gratitude.

> *"The masses live in the illusion of gain and loss but the master lives in a world of transformation"*

Dr. John Demartini

Final Act

Once I arrived in South Africa, I still had a lease on the house for another few months, so I stayed there. Sleeping in separate rooms, Jackie and I became roommates for the next two weeks. We essentially had separate lives but shared the living space. I spent a lot of time with friends and going inward at that time and generally tried to stay out of her way. I did notice I was not completely at peace, and was still harboring some resentment toward her, which was contributing to the unpleasant environment.

The morning she would leave finally arrived. She packed the remnants of her belongings, the cats, dogs, and her daughter into the family vehicle. It was a brisk and frosty goodbye and not because of the cool dawn air. Then they were gone, fence gate closing behind them as they drove off. It was then I collapsed on the driveway and just cried. Despite doing my best to combat the grief up to that point, it was all simply too much. Walking back into that big, beautiful house overlooking the ocean just felt empty. A space usually filled with laughter, joy, the life of animals, and a family was simply a void. An empty shell. I still had some work to do.

Thankfully it wasn't long before I was required back in Australia for an offshore job. This helped me stay busy. A week into my stint offshore, I signed up to a South African online dating website just to see if there was anything in South Africa that might interest me in staying on there instead of returning to Australia. At this point, I didn't really have anything to go back to. Having taken a shower and laying in my bunk after my shift, I signed up. Before being able to view other members, I was asked to write a profile and submit photos of myself. Not planning on using this service to meet anyone, I sped through the sign-up, filling out one-word answers for my profile and uploaded a selfie laying in my bunk, looking like a wet dog, hair everywhere. I didn't care.

It was kind of depressing going through the available women. However, I pushed my apprehensions aside and began messaging a few members to pass the time, including an attractive blonde named 'Karen'. The next day I made a bit more effort and added some details to my profile with more photos. I kept this up for another day or so, but my heart just was not in it. There was something preventing me from engaging, and it wasn't fair on the women on the dating site to string them along if I wasn't interested. I wondered to myself "What is it? I thought I cleared the grief from losing my life partner." Then I recalled the residual anger I felt while Jackie was in the house. Even though I let a lot go of her in my life, I still had various unresolved feelings. I steeled myself to finish this no matter what.

Over the next two days, during gaps in my shift work offshore, I worked on neutralizing my remaining infatuation and resentment toward Jackie by utilizing my knowledge and training under John Demartini. By the time I completed the process, I had a similar experience to the first time I finished the process. Instead of loving and being grateful to her for leaving, this time around, I felt true love for her, just as she is. I loved her as a person, as my teacher, and as a fellow soulmate sharing a journey. There was no more anger or attachment to the parts of her I used to admire. In its place emerged an immense lightness—an immense love—and I sensed her presence all around me, the sage in her gazing into my heart knowingly. Tears streamed down my face as I finally learnt and understood why she was in my life. It was a divine moment. A moment that signaled that I could now close that door.

Later that afternoon, I went and checked my emails. As I was scrolling through, there was a notification from the dating website saying I had received a message. I was actually about to close my account as I did not see a use for it anymore. I achieved my goal, saw what was out there, and had decided I didn't want to meet someone this way. In fact, I didn't want to meet anyone, period. I was content and absolutely satisfied to live a life of freedom as a single man again. I was looking forward to the next chapter in my life, and it was a blank canvas, with the focus on me.

Checking the latest notification I received, it was from a woman named 'Karen' and she was replying to a message I sent her earlier. I looked at the time the email arrived in my inbox. It was eerily close to the time I had completed the process on Jackie not an hour earlier. As I opened the email and followed the link, it took me to Karen's photo with a message next to it. I was immediately drawn to her stunning blonde hair and blue eyes that made me recall what I have thought my dream partner would appear like. I was intrigued, so I read the message and it suggested we continue the conversation on WhatsApp.

I was at work, halfway around the world in the middle of the ocean, living on a boat. Hardly a place to be meeting the love of my life, but there I was. Every sentence and question that was shared between us in that first five minutes confirmed this wasn't just any woman. This was a beautiful, intelligent, financially independent mother, and business owner who was open to the same spiritual ideas as me. She was from an Afrikaans background, which is something I had always admired since my first visit all the way back in 2000. On that first trip overseas to South Africa, as a wide-eyed 22-year old surfer, I stayed with an acquaintance who was a South African girl, living in Port Elizabeth. In the short space of time she hosted me in Port Elizabeth, her eyes, the wonderful accent and nurturing values had me stating with conviction "One day, I'm going to marry an Afrikaans girl!" I never forgot that.

I couldn't ignore the gifts of synchronicities being presented to me, and we continued to chat well into the night, forming a connection that simply never happened in all my years of dating and meeting women. This wasn't a blind infatuation but felt like two jigsaw puzzle pieces fitting seamlessly together. Karen was equally surprised to find I checked out against all the qualities on a list she made several weeks previously, when describing her ideal mate. And now, Karen takes up the story:

Karen's Story

Karen:

In the middle of a three-month-long subscription to an online dating site, something I have never done before, I stopped and decided to write down exactly what I wanted, which was in a letter format to God.

> *"Dear God, I know you are in control of my life. I know you have the perfect person for me, so here is what I want: Attractive physically, emotionally, intellectually, & spiritually. Funny, makes me laugh, and thinks I am funny; Loves to dance, travel, adventurous; A foreigner who works away offshore (yes, really!); Lots of energy; Successful & Balanced; Lots of good friends; Solid family values; Love animals; Love Children, especially my son; Financially secure; Must adore me and compliment me, think I am the most beautiful woman alive; Healthy & Fit; Good Lover – loves to cuddle and touch; 40 years old or younger; He must spoil me with gifts, love, compliments, attention & time."*

I had my usual high standards and honestly didn't believe there was someone out who could meet them.

About two weeks later, I decided to go online and see what messages I have. Every day they send you a few suitable candidates, this morning they sent me this one guy, 'Michael', who had sent me a short message. One look and I thought – "Oh God no, he took what looked like a selfie in the shower of himself, who does that!?" And he lives 700 km away from where I live in Cape Town – this site is getting desperate. I just closed my device and went to work. The next morning, I went online again, only to see the dating site emailed me his profile again. A loud voice in my head screamed at me saying "GIVE THIS GUY A CHANCE!!" I did and clicked the link. This time, however, I noticed he uploaded more photos of himself and I read through his comprehensive profile. I realized this guy sounds quite interesting, so I replied to his message and we connected. We moved over to WhatsApp later that day and could not stop texting each other for the entire day. In the first 48 hours, we formed a deep connection, a stream of coincidences and synchronicities appearing between our two lives; it was too uncanny to ignore. There was also an instant sexual attraction I felt for him even though we were only texting with the occasional phone call. Because he was overseas, living offshore in Australia, we could not meet for 6 weeks until he returned to South Africa. This gave us the time to get to know each other and really connect on a deeper level.

Michael invited me to Saint Francis Bay, South Africa, for ten days over Christmas. was extremely nervous the week before our meeting. I wrote in my journal that I hope with all my heart and soul that this is the guy I asked for, as I have waited long enough for him. My biggest fear was that he wouldn't find me attractive and that he wasn't over his previous relationship, as it was still a bit too soon after they separated. I needn't have worried. The ten days together was amazing and leaving him again was very hard! It felt like somebody ripped my heart out after we said our goodbyes at the airport – I couldn't stop crying for the entire day. It was a mixture of tears of sadness but also an overwhelming feeling of gratitude to have met him and the time we shared together. However, I had no idea how he felt about me and if I was ever going to see him again. I definitely knew I was in love with him at that point and hoped he felt the same about me.

Three years have passed. It has been a unique challenge since we live very different lives and we are more apart physically than we are together, but it works. Enjoying the good times. Learning and growing from the challenges. I love my sexy Aussie, even though he drives me crazy sometimes. I believe we are traveling soulmates and that we are here to help each other grow, evolve, inspire & motivate each other to live our true potential & purpose in this lifetime.

Epilogue

Three years later, whenever I think about the chances of finding someone like Karen, and her finding me, it still astonishes me. In hindsight, I can now clearly see the steps followed that directly resulted in:

- Getting over an ex-partner so quickly
- Attracting, someone who exactly resembles the description of my ideal mate within hours

Three main steps apply to working with whoever is suffering loss and heartbreak:

1. Transcend the grief of what we think we miss in our lives by understanding that nothing is missing, there is only transformation
2. Transcend any remaining resentments toward our past lovers
3. Transcend any remaining infatuations toward our past lovers

If someone wants to attract their ideal mate, it is powerful to declare the qualities we desire in a partner either before or after the process, so it sets the intention, but it's also important to relinquish attachment to them. Once the trapped emotional energies we hold onto with grief, resentments, and infatuations are released, it is now available for creation. In this case, manifesting our ideal mate. It happens right when we do not want it. I love life's paradoxes.

"It takes no effort to experience heartbreak, but it takes understanding to experience love." Michael Golowyn

References

Capra, F. (2010). *The Tao of Physics. An Exploration of the Parallels between Modern Physics and Eastern Mysticism. Fifth Edition.* Shambala Publications Inc., Boston.

Chardin, P. T. (1959). *The Phenomenon of Man.* Harper & Brothers, New York.

Demartini, J. F. (2002). *The Breakthrough Experience. A Revolutionary Approach to Personal Transformation.* Hay House, United States.

Demartini, J. F. (2007). *The Heart of Love. How to Go Beyond Fantasy to Find True Relationship Fulfilment.* Hay House, United States.

Demartini, J. F. (2013). *The Values Factor. The Secret to Creating an Inspired and Fulfilling Life.* Hay House, United States.

Fisher, H.E., Brown, L. L., Aron, A., Strong, G. and Mashek, D. (2010). *Reward, Addiction, and Emotion Regulation Systems Associated with Rejection in Love.* The Journal of Neurophysiology.

Langeslag, S. J. E., Sanchez, M. E. (2018). *Down-regulation of love feelings after a romantic break-up: Self-report and electrophysiological data.* Journal of Experimental Psychology.

Michael Golowyn

Michael Golowyn is an Australian relationship coach and Demartini Method® Facilitator[87]. Plagued by 20 years of failed relationships, suffering endless cycles of abandonment and rejection, Michael uncovered unique solutions to rapidly transform his grief to live an inspired life. Combined with his career experience as a Hydrographic Surveyor working in the offshore oil and gas industry, a field he has worked in for the past 15 years, Michael uniquely merges his two fields of expertise to help his clients transcend the grief from their failed relationships and use it as an opportunity to transform their lives.

Contact Information:

Email: michael@mgolowyn.com
Website: www.mgolowyn.com

---

[87] The Demartini Method® Dr. John F. Demartini© 2005. Property of the Demartini Institute. www.DrDemartini.com

SUCCESS TO SIGNIFICANCE: REFLECTIONS ON LEAVING A LEGACY

NIKKI SINCLAIR

There are certain realities in life that one cannot comprehend without first-hand experience. It took a sudden, unexpected event for me to fully understand just how fragile and unpredictable life can be. Since then, I've also realized that life is not so much about what you achieve personally but more importantly the influence you have on other people's lives. It's about the significant difference you make on your journey in this world and the relationships you build along the way. That is the legacy that you will leave behind.

The Event That Changed My Life in an Instant

He was lying on the floor, next to his training bike, when I walked into the room. Myles was always up for a practical joke. He was obviously 'dramatically looking for some sympathy' after his tough session, as our 22-year-old son, Ian, and I had 'deserted him' and opted for a leisurely Sunday evening walk with the dogs instead. Then, I noticed his eyes half-open, still, and when I spoke to him, there was no laughter, which I would have normally anticipated. Twenty-nine years of marriage brings with it a certain knowledge about your partner, but this wasn't something familiar. The next hour and a half played out like a horror movie.

I called for Ian and knelt down next to Myles, desperately trying to feel his pulse. Nothing. We started CPR immediately, simultaneously fumbling with our phones to dial the emergency numbers. It was a neighbor who first arrived to help, thankfully taking over compressions from a then exhausted Ian. After about twenty-five minutes, the paramedics arrived and took over for another hour, trying everything to get some response. No words can describe the shock when I realized that they had stopped trying to resuscitate him. They looked at each other and then at me, heads shaking imperceptibly. I had left the room earlier for a few minutes to feed the dogs, throw a sweater and toothbrush in a bag, and call our parents to meet us at the hospital. However, as I looked at the man I had loved for the past 35 years, it dawned on me that we were not going to the ER. I knew my world would never be the same, ever again.

Myles was declared dead at 8:44 pm on Sunday 16th December, 2018, aged 58. The autopsy later revealed that a ruptured duodenal ulcer had caused his sudden and untimely death. I'm told it was quick and painless. It was also, apparently, extremely rare—especially for a non-smoker, restrained drinker, and someone who seldom took any medication. He was always super fit and lived a healthy lifestyle. There was no apparent reason for him to die so abruptly; however, there is a deep assurance in knowing that he has left a lasting legacy.

As news of his death spread, hundreds of tributes, messages, and phone calls came in from all over the world, with stories about how Myles had impacted people's lives. I was astounded by the response and have since then wondered what it was that moved so many people to share their experience? What made people fly from the other side of the world, interrupt their family holiday or drive for hours, just to attend his memorial service? I've had some time to reflect on the life of a man who impacted thousands of lives—not by his many achievements, but by living intentionally, with conviction and passion and caring for people and the world he lived in. I hope his story will inspire you to take action, live purposefully, and leave your own lasting legacy.

Humble Beginnings

Growing up in a middle-class neighborhood, as a much loved but only child who lost his father even before he had a chance to meet him, Myles's memories of junior school were the long, boring holidays spent with his only aunt while his devoted mother worked. He was a shy child going into an all-boys high school and preferred to keep a low profile to stay out of trouble. Years passed by, and he went largely unnoticed until a teacher recognized a glimmer of talent and called him out in the corridor, "Sinclair! I'll see you at rugby practice tomorrow afternoon." Myles discovered a passion for the sport and was always grateful for that one schoolmaster who showed enough interest in him to get him onto the sports field.

Setting up for Success

Myles had dreams of being successful and had his heart set on becoming a Chartered Accountant—admittedly more for the perceived promise of financial reward than the love of working with numbers. He got a job, worked during the day, and studied at night to pay his way through university. He qualified, eventually (we lost count of exactly how many years it took him), and learned valuable lessons from his failures and perseverance. He had achieved a lot during his tertiary education, but if he was here, he'd tell you that his biggest accomplishment was stealing my heart and finding his lifelong soulmate. The truth is that he asked me to marry him before we even met, but that's a story for another time. We dated for five years while we were both studying and eventually tied the knot on a joyful day in January 1990.

After ten years of blissful marriage, we had three wonderful children, our first home, a tortoise (it came with the house), and a fledgling business that Myles had started in order to escape the confines of the corporate world. We lived on my junior teacher's salary while he built his first company, and even though there were times when we couldn't put petrol in the car to go the extra mile, we were extremely happy. He was a loving husband and a doting father. I genuinely felt blessed to have him around. Reading through one of his old journals yesterday, I came across a 'list' he had written in May 2000. At that time, our boys were aged 3 and 5, and I was pregnant with our daughter, Kirsty. I want to share that list since it reminded me of the importance of not only having goals and dreams but also of writing them down—something he had taught me and many others.

"10 things I want to do"

1. Inspire my children to be all they can be—to reach for the stars.
2. Fall in love with Nikki again and again and again.
3. Remain super fit until I go to glory.
4. Travel through Africa.

5. Hear my children preach.
6. Help, inspire, and partner with Nikki to impact the lives of others.
7. Own a home with a view of the mountains or the sea.
8. Hike the Himalayan foothills.
9. Learn to fly a helicopter.
10. Live in the USA.

The first seven goals he had achieved, except I must question the 'falling in love again' part—we never really fell out of love. Our love grew in depth and maturity over the years. I am so grateful we were able to set an example for our children to take into their own marriages one day. Myles's premature departure was a vivid reminder of how short life is and a challenge to us all to live each day to the full.

Daddy's Home

Myles often put family before work and other commitments. He would intentionally come home before 'jungle hour', even though he knew that he would probably be thrust with a crying baby or nagging toddler. The boys learned quickly that his presence at 5:30 pm was the source of calm and a game of ball and they would run to the door to give him a hug, shouting, "Yaay, Daddy's home!" And, I would escape to the kitchen thinking, "YAAAY, Daddy's home!"

Through the years, he supported and inspired our three children, and no matter how busy he was, he made time for them. I'm grateful that he *did* get the opportunity to hear them give talks and sermons, and it touched my heart that each one of them wanted to speak at his memorial service. They said it far better than I ever could. I have included excerpts at the end of this chapter from their tributes given in front of hundreds of friends, family, and colleagues in the chapel on the morning of 21st December. Their words are a testimony of the influence a father can have on his children. They *are* all reaching for the stars, and Myles's legacy will certainly continue through them and the significant impact they are making on the lives of others. Kyle, a final year medical student, will be part of the leadership team heading up the medical corp of the 10 000-strong '1Nation1Day' mission trip to Peru in July. Ian and Kirsty have also been involved in mission trips during their holidays and often help at various orphanages. They have learned the value of giving and acting with empathy from their father, and are already expanding his legacy.

Excellence, Purpose, and Influence

Many of the tributes we received were from Myles's friends and teammates from years ago. It was probably during his twenties that he began to learn the value of pursuing excellence in every area of his life and his commitment to underwater hockey (his favorite sport at university), earned him Springbok colors. Myles not only played for South Africa for many years but found purpose by encouraging others as a coach and manager and mentored many junior teams. He generously gave his time and shared his knowledge, skill, and experience. He had a quiet yet dynamic way of influencing others, not because of his leadership skills, but because of how he lived his life and cared about other people. Today, his legacy lives on through many international sportsmen (and women) proudly representing our country as a result of the time he dedicated to them.

There were many more stories from his colleagues and other

people he came into contact with during his lifetime. He was a good listener, especially when he perceived someone to be in need or distress. Many life-changing conversations took place in the most unexpected places and often at an inconvenient time. Anyone who knew him well was aware that his passion for coffee (and sometimes his intolerance of bad coffee) opened the door for many heart-to-heart discussions. To my annoyance, this would often delay us and any plans we had, but after receiving an SMS from a lady we met on one of these occasions, I realize how significant a few well-used minutes can be. We were driving down to the Eastern Cape for a family holiday when we stopped for a 'quick' cup of coffee. Myles had already eyed the authentic Italian coffee machine, which drew us in to sit down for coffee. After one sip, he turned up his nose and walked over to the woman behind the counter to inquire about the brand of coffee bean they had used. One of his favorite sayings was, "Life is too short to drink bad coffee." Over an hour and many tears later, we had heard Ansie's story of having to take over the business after recently losing her husband. In true 'Myles form', he wouldn't leave before giving her a crash barrister course to ensure that she satisfied all future customers. He took her details and kept in touch with her for the coming months, guiding her on business issues and encouraging her. This small gesture of empathy is one of the many examples of what he did for people and how it impacted their lives. Ansie was inspired to send a message when she learned of his death— even though 15 years had passed.

Action Speaks Louder Than Words

We all have the freedom to choose how we respond to the needs of those around us, but how many of us take action to change the things that are important? Myles made a decision to give his best to the causes he was passionate about and believed so deeply in, and there were plenty of them. In our 30s, we became aware of the stresses of many of our friends and colleagues. We realized that the root cause of most of these issues—relationship problems, depression, and discontentment with work was the mismanagement of money. Instead of ignoring the pain of those around us, Myles sourced an international 10-week personal finance course and started small groups to teach basic financial principles. Over the years, we have facilitated finance courses that have made a significant impact on how couples manage their money and have taught leaders in numerous churches to teach and share the content with others. His passion for coffee resulted in starting a coffee importing and roasting company with two friends. 'Bean There' coffee company creates employment and uplifts coffee farmers and communities in Africa and is thriving today.

Significantly More

By the time he turned 40, Myles was enjoying the fruits of his business and reaping the rewards of the time invested in his family. While prayer fed his soul, books nourished his mind. He had a perpetual craving for knowledge and always aspired to be a better person. Although we were thriving and enjoying life, Myles got to a point where he realized that 'success' was not all it promised to be. He became increasingly uneasy with the destruction of the world's natural resources due to man's negligence and greed and felt a pressing responsibility to do something about it. He believed that any significant change depended on taking action. He served on the board of A Rocha, a Christian Conservation Organisation, for many years. Myles was a man of integrity and what he 'preached' to others, he lived at home (sometimes to the exasperation of his children!). He gave talks on conservation, wrote articles for magazines, contributed financially, and presented a white paper at the Christian Economic Forum (CEF) when it was held in South Africa in 2016.

In his message notifying the community of Myles's passing, Chuck Bently, Executive Director CEF and CEO Crown Financial Ministries wrote:

"… I hope his (Myles) life will inspire you to be a better steward of the natural beauty and resources that surround each of us. Here are some final thoughts from his 2016 White Paper at CEF."

"My hope is that the Christian church will view conservation and care of creation as God does. It is estimated that there are 2.2 billion Christians on the planet. What if just 10% (220 million of those classified as Christian) actively conserved water, electricity, food, and other resources as a way of life? What would be the effect if those 220 million stopped driving their cars one day a month or one day a week? What if the church began to manage and conserve as suggested in the Bible? This really is the best way to fulfill Proverbs 13:22, 'A good man leaves an inheritance for his children's children'."

You can access Myles's white paper here
***

Next to his bedside was the last book Myles had been reading *The Leader Who Had No Title* by Robin Sharma. I picked it up recently and something on page 34 jumped out at me: "The 10 human regrets." The first regret had been underlined by Myles:

"1. You reach your last day with the brilliant song that your life was meant to sing still silent within you."

Although he had every intention of living beyond 100 years and many plans and goals, I know he had already sung many of the songs within him. We never know when we will reach our last day, but Myles was living a life of significance and had few regrets.

Gratitude Parts the Clouds

Writing this chapter has been emotionally difficult for me, but it has also been one of the best things I've done. As friends and colleagues have come to drop a meal, have coffee, or share a hug, I've realized that there isn't a single person who is not dealing with his or her own challenges. While some have allowed their suffering to let them grow and draw their family or loved ones closer, others have been left to pick up the shattered pieces. I want to take you back to some of the more defining moments in our lives—the diagnosis of Ian's Tourette's syndrome at the age of five, the tragic loss of three close friends in as many years, my older brother and only sister emigrating, my sister-in-law's struggle with a bipolar disorder, my younger brother's diagnosis of stage 4 lymphoma, and the news that we would lose our main source of income overnight (when our children were in private schooling and university). Each of them brought its own heartache and hardships, but even with associated words such as 'incurable', 'tragic', 'distance', 'mental illness', 'life-threatening disease', and 'liquidation', we realized that although we couldn't change the situation, we could control our response. As Tim Hansel so aptly says, "At any moment in life we have the option to choose an attitude of gratitude, a posture of grace, a commitment to joy." Beside my bed, I have a 'gratitude diary,' and it has helped me focus on the good in every situation, especially when I've had a bad day. My aim is to write one thousand 'gifts' or things I am grateful for (an idea from I book I was given some years ago). My last entry was on 15th December, the day before Myles died. While I've been negligent to add to the list recently, I realize that there are many things I *am* thankful for. Being grateful is one way to let the sun shine through even the darkest of clouds. Tonight, I will write that I'm grateful for my three children; for the special people who arrived on that fateful night to help, cry and pray with us; for the support, love, and kindness from our friends; for years of happy memories; and for health and food on the table, every day. I'm grateful for the lessons I've learned and for the gift of work and for amazing clients. I'm grateful that even in the tough times, we can laugh, and when we are in the deepest valley, we can only look up. I am also extremely grateful that Myles was wise and had his 'house in order.' Even though his death has left a huge hole in our hearts, he provided for our future financially—what a wonderful gift to leave.

Leaving a Legacy

As you pursue your life's journey, what legacy will you leave? Our legacy goes beyond us and tells of our lives and the effect we have had on others during our lifetime. Myles's story will live on, not through his many awards and achievements—those have been taken from the frames and stored in a box—but through the lives of the many people he influenced during his short life, and through his children, who will take valuable lessons learned from their beloved dad and pass them on to their own children.

How will reading this book change your life? Will you leave the world a better place than you found it? I hope you will be inspired, as I have been, to make the changes you know are needed in your life. After seeing the significant and life-changing impact Myles had on his coaching clients, I have decided that I need to find my own coach to get me to the next level and help navigate a life that will impact others. I have big dreams and goals, and I know I will need guidance through coaching and accountability to reach them. What will you do today that will lead you in the direction you want to go? Before you close this book, join me in writing down a list, or at least one audacious goal, and maybe one day you will find that list, look back, and realize how, by deciding to live a life of significance, you will have left an eternal legacy.

Tributes that were given at Myles's Memorial by his children:
Kyle (23)

What does one say in a 5-minute memorial service address about the person who has been the most influential and instrumental figure in their lives? How does one begin to summarise 23 of the best years of fathering in a few pages? Is it possible for me to stand here and paint a picture with my words that adequately portray the brilliance that was Myles Sinclair? These are all questions that I would have asked my dad when preparing for a talk like this, and, in fact, this is probably the first time my closest and oldest friends will be hearing something important that comes from me without first being filtered through him. He was my real-life 'Siri', although I like to think of my use of this service as reasonable and moderate in comparison to how many times a day Ian would call him for advice or his input and wisdom.

I'll start by telling you all a bit about the Myles that I came to know and love during his spectacular innings as my earthly father. Growing up, I honestly believed that he was a flawless man and the perfect father. He never missed a sports fixture or school production, he played soccer or garden cricket with Ian and me every day after work, and he always believed in us more than we knew how to believe in ourselves. He was intentional and ever-present, and my mother and he created a home environment that was nurturing and filled with love and life, where we grew to be the tightly-knit family that we are today.

A dear friend of my dad's told me yesterday that anyone in this chapel today who'd ever met Myles could stand up and give a series of extraordinary accounts of how he'd impacted or influenced them. Central to who my dad was was his ability to change someone's life through a series of simple conversations. He'd never miss an opportunity to connect with, challenge and encourage someone in a moment he thought might benefit them.

All the best elements of my Dad's character—his tender and unconditional love for us, his surety as a fearless yet servant-hearted leader, his heart for the downcast and marginalized, and his desire to pour himself out to build up the people around him mirror the persona of Jesus during his life on Earth. It would be wrong of me to attribute any of the best parts of who my dad was to personal development and self-determination. My father was the extraordinary man that he was because he abided in Jesus daily and gave himself in the service of the Lord.

During my life, my dad gave me many beautiful memories. Having never had a father of his own to inherit hobbies and passions from, he made sure that he shared plenty with each of his children. Together he and I discovered fishing, motorbike riding, and 4x4ing. He nurtured and grew my love for many of his favorite things such as coffee, reading, whiskey, and the art of thinking, to name but a few. These are all treasures that I'll hold onto for the remainder of my time on Earth. But, the most significant thing that my dad gave me was his example in the way he valued his walk with the Lord, above anything else in his life. When I first began my own authentic journey with God, a few years ago, after I'd rejected the concept of lifeless organized religion, my relationship with my dad significantly changed. He started to explain to me how he, like my earthly father, would inevitably fail and let me down from time to time, but that in our heavenly father we will find perfect love and lack no good thing. He helped me turn to Jesus and scripture first in my time of need, instead of turning to him and invited me to walk alongside him in our journey to God with all of our heart. He taught me how to 'love our neighbors as we love ourselves.' It was this shift in our relationship where my mentor also invited me to become his friend, as his brother in Christ that framed the last five years of our relationship—where we would both walk through the deepest and darkest of valleys we'd had to face in our lives. My valley came in the form of a diagnosis of severe uncontrolled hypertension that has the potential to put a full stop to my own story at any given moment. My dad sat with me through every piece of bad news and unfavorable test results and processed the concepts of life and death as they pertain to those of us with an eternal perspective. Those were hard years for both of us, but we concluded that it is of utmost importance to continually live with the knowledge that we are but sojourners to this world and that our true home and hope is in Heaven.

Together we strove to let this knowledge help us live in a manner worthy of the calling to which we had been called, to fight the good fight, to finish the race, and to keep the faith. We spoke of how difficult death is to those left behind, but that there are more reasons to celebrate than to mourn. Myles is finally home where suffering is no more, and we will join him with Jesus when our time comes. Between now and then, life is never going to be the same and there won't be a single day that we won't miss him dearly. But in our time of grief, we have already been overwhelmed by the transcendent peace of God. Jesus has been with us in every moment since that fateful Sunday night, and it has been in our weakness that we have most powerfully experienced His strength. It has been the loss of the only mentor I've ever needed, my best friend, and the rock of our family, but I have felt the surpassing Love of God more intensely at the moment than any other point in my life.

Ian (22)

What an extraordinary man, my dad. My comfort in times of need, he was a wise soul with years of wisdom beyond his life. My parents used to get a bit annoyed with how often I used to call both of them. Twice, sometimes three times daily just to hear their voice. I often asked for wisdom and counsel from my dad as he always knew what to do in situations where I didn't. And at the end of each call I used to make sure I said, "I love you" not because I thought they forgot, but because not knowing when their time would end, I wanted them to know each day just how much I loved them.

My dad is going to be missed by so many people for countless reasons. I know he would have wanted us to celebrate his life today.

In the last couple of days before my dad died, we had some very memorable times. I remember playing a board game, *Settlers of Catan*, which my dad hated even though he won. We had dinner with our family friends, held a home-church in the lounge, saw many people at the local craft market in our town, and he watched me perform magic... for three hours. It was my dad who got me into magic and taught me the art of performance. And every time I perform a trick, I will remember him.

Out of all the amazing times and memories I had in the last few days before he died, the one I will remember the most was his response to a beggar. My dad loved God, and he loved people. This one day, my mom, dad, and I were sitting at a coffee shop down the road when a beggar walked up to us and asked for money. My mom told him that we would buy him some food but what shook me the most was my dad's response. He sat, quietly and peacefully back in his chair, his face full of compassion. He greeted the beggar by name, and said, "Patrick, we will get you some food shortly, we are just going to finish our conversation, as it is important."

Two things about his response will always amaze me. Firstly, our conversation was about loving people. I was actually being lectured on being overly protective and treating my sister's boyfriend with less tolerance than he deserved. My dad always knew what was important and valuable, such as that conversation. The second was that he knew Patrick by name. I asked my dad if he had ever met him before or if he knew him. He didn't. And when I asked him how he knew the beggar's name, he said in a peaceful voice, "I'm just listening." I wonder how many of us are listening?

I want to strive to be like my dad. I want to listen as well as he did. I want to be a father like he was, a husband like he was, a friend like he was, and a mentor like he was. To end, I just want to read a short letter I wrote to my dad for his birthday in October.

Dear Dad,

Time is passing quickly, in the blink of an eye. I realize that it was only a few years ago I used to shout from the bottom of the stairs, "Daaaadd, let's Gooooo!" as we were late for school. And many more years ago, we used to have 'Beatie ups' where Kyle and I tried to pin you down on the bed and beat you up—never expecting to win but always having such fun trying.

As time passes, I find myself reminiscing over the many memories—good and bad. The many arguments and punishments formed and shaped the well-mannered, presentable, and respectable man I realize I have become (guess I'm still learning to be humble). Never did I ever comprehend that all the discipline (and the fear of 'Mr. Disi' that I only realized recently stood for Mr. Discipline) would have such a positive effect on me.

As you grow older, so do I, and I'm beginning to understand the wisdom behind my upbringing. I understand the thought, care, and consideration behind each action that was all underlined by love. It was a deep and unconditional love that has blanketed around my life, and I cannot begin to describe how grateful I am.

I sometimes wonder what life would have been like without two amazingly loving parents, and I find it difficult to comprehend because you are all I have known. But when I see my friends' parents, their fathers and their lifestyle—I truly realize the blessing you have been in my life.

When I think about you, all the valuable lessons I've learned and continue to learn, I thank God for you and all that you mean to me. You continually act in excellence, hoping that your children will follow your lead.

Dad, you have acted in excellence in so many ways and forms, and believe me, I have caught you in the act many a time and I continually strive to be like my role model. I strive to be as wise as you, as loving, as strong and courageous, and as dependable, and I strive to act in excellence every day because you have shown me how to do so.

So, thank you. I love you so much and cannot thank you enough. I remember you today on your birthday and the role you have played in my life. As time passes by, I remember with pure joy who you are and the loving father you have been. I feel inspired to be more like you. Happy Birthday, Dad! I drink a toast to the next 40 years where you can watch the men and daughter, that you have raised, grow up into powerful leaders, loving believers, and inspirational people.

Lots and lots of love, Ian

I read this letter with tears streaming down my face, filled with gratitude that Ian took the time to let his dad know, while he was alive, how much he meant to him. Maybe there is someone in your life who needs to know how much you love and appreciate them?

Kirsty (18)

In any little girl's ideal fairy tale, she marries her knight in shining armor and is treated like a princess. My knight in shining armor and my first love was, and is, my dad. My parents started a diary for each of us when we were born to store memories of our younger years. I have spent the last three days reading some of the letters my dad wrote to me, and, I'm sorry mom, as I already knew... I stole Dad's heart, and he, mine.

My Dad's goal was to live long beyond 100. I don't know if it is a coincidence or not but for the last couple of months, I have been thinking and having conversations about death with him, a few times. I am only 18, and many of you may think that death is a concept too deep for my understanding at this age. My dad raised me to know that my most valuable asset is my faith in God. Because of my faith, death does not scare me, and it did not scare my father. It was a conversation we shared more than once.

One day, recently, my Dad challenged me to write his eulogy. The idea was that when either of our time came, he would know what I wanted to say, and he would help me say it well. He said that it would be an eulogy for him, so he had every right to see or know all the nice things I would like to share about him. Why wait until someone is dead to let them know what we think of them. Of course, I would never have thought it would come so soon. You never do. My Dad was the editor of almost everything I wrote—somehow making me love improving what I already thought was great. I was grateful to have a professional editor that didn't charge! I battled writing the eulogy and spoke about it with one of my best friends a few times. It challenged me, but there was something about it, and through conversations, I felt the need to at least try writing it.

It is incredibly difficult to find the words to describe someone as loved as my dad. How could I cover my lifetime of memories and favorites? He always used to say, "You're gonna miss me when I'm gone," and he irritated me every time he said it, but he was right, as usual.

There is so much I'm going to miss about you Dad, and I know there are so many people who feel the same way. All these things, although sorely missed, I know are temporary. When I join you in heaven, we will carry on our traditions and our weird ways—our 'daddy-daughter dinner dates,' our 'tickle fights,' and, I think it's fair to say, I took the win when it came to giving the biggest frights. I'll miss comparing notes on sermons that contradict or challenge my thoughts and ideas. I'll miss you teaching me worship songs in sign language. I guess now I will just have to take mom's approach and make up the signs I don't know.

Trying to write this eulogy was hard, and the more I thought about it, I realized that even though it is good, it will never be good enough. I guess that was why he wanted to do it with me—to help put my thoughts into words so I would be happy with what I wrote. Although I regret never giving him a draft, these challenges made me realize how much more my dad means to me, and that it can't ever be put into words. I'm glad my dad knew I loved him, and he knew I adored him without me having to tell him. This is not that draft, but I hope it's okay for an attempt, without your help, Papa.

The first letter from my dad in my baby diary reads: "My prayer for you is that you will grow into the woman God intends you to be, that you will have a wonderful relationship with Him, and that you will lead the people of your time closer to God."

It really is so difficult to express or explain the relationship my father and I shared. To some of you, he was a father, a mentor, and a friend, but to me, he was all those things, my homework editor, and much more. He pushed me further than I wanted to go and made me think deeper than I was comfortable with, but his were always the first arms to comfort me. They were a reminder that I am capable, whenever the smallest fear or doubt entered my mind.

My Dad never stopped learning and never stopped teaching. A lifetime would not be enough to learn everything that he had to teach me. One of my biggest fears is that I have not learned enough from him. However, I know God thinks that everything he has taught me is sufficient for me to carry on and become the woman he wanted to raise.

The night my Dad died, I was in Mozambique, celebrating the end of my high school with friends. For many years, our family would spend our December holiday scuba diving in

Mozambique, often referring to the idyllic beaches as 'paradise.' I said goodbye to him on Friday night because I was leaving very early Saturday morning. He told me that he will join me in paradise the week after (we were going to the same area with our family and friends for Christmas). The suddenness of this event tells me that God had already prepared Dad's real paradise.

I had spent the last 30 minutes outside under the stars, speaking to my friends. It is always under a full night's sky that I realize how small we are and how great God is. Before getting to bed, I went to send a goodnight message to my boyfriend in the only spot with any Internet signal. I then saw a message from my cousin and her parents sending their condolences and Kyle's missed calls from an hour ago. I knew this wasn't a joke. I dialed my brother and with the first few words, I knew this was going to be the most difficult thing I would ever have to experience. But thinking back to that moment, somewhere I also knew that it was going to be okay. Soon, almost everyone was awake and praying with me. That night time passed so quickly, and yet it was so slow at the same time. There hasn't been one moment in which I haven't asked why. I don't understand why, but I knew and felt the strangest peace that he is home and it was needed to be.

My Dad was always concerned about being a great father because he never had a father himself, to compare to. I don't think anyone could do a job better than him. He has left enough people he mentored for me to learn from and he has taught me so much already. I know I will see so much of you in Ian and Kyle, Dad, I already do. They are definitely your sons and carry your legacy. I'm also grateful I can still learn from the woman who raised you herself. Gran, you could not have had a better son or raised a better Dad for the three of us. Thank you.

Daddy, I will never find another first love, and I will battle to find a man that even comes close to the person you were. As a little girl, I was disappointed when I was told I couldn't marry my Dad. Some fairy tales don't come true, but I have been able to watch my parents live their fairy tale for the last 18 years, and they have definitely set the standard high. I have never seen a power couple like the two of you, and I understand how easy it was for you both to fall in love and stay in love. I wish to find the husband my dad has been for my mom and strive to be the wife my mom has been to my dad. When that day comes, I know you will be walking me down the aisle from up there. You married the strongest woman I know, and I promise I will try to look after her as well as you did. This is not the ending to my fairy tale, but until then, Papa, I will miss you in everything I do, cherish every memory and thought that passes, and love the way you taught and loved. Until we meet again, I love you, Daddy… I love you to the moon and back.

Nikki Sinclair

Do you desire to make a difference in the world or leave something worthwhile to your family and others when you depart?

Nikki is a business owner, mother of three, and was the devoted wife of Myles before his sudden and shocking death a week before Christmas. Following a flood of messages and tributes honoring the impact Myles had on thousands of lives, Nikki asks some deep questions about the meaning of life and what it takes to leave a legacy.

Sharing snippets from Myles's intentional life, Nikki wishes to inspire you to make the changes you already know you need to make. Be it spending more time with your family, listening to the problems of a friend, or helping a stranger in need, we are all putting off something for tomorrow, thinking we have enough time. But, do you want to live a mediocre life and die with deep regrets or a magnificent life and leave an eternal legacy? You can make that choice today by taking action and living for what matters the most.

Myles's story will reveal that awards, achievements, and what we consider 'success' in our 24/7 lives on the treadmill of productivity are not contributors to leaving a legacy. Leaving a legacy is about a few simple acts and a little selfless time.

Contact Information

Telephone: +27 83 369 4748
E-mail: nikkis@wol.co.za
Website: marriagemeander.co.za
Facebook: Marriage Meander
Instagram: marriagemeander

Surrender: The Key to the Door of Life

PAUL HUNTING

At no time in my life did I ever seek 'the Holy Grail' nor sought to 'transform my life'. All I've ever wanted is to be is happy. The gut-rending paradox is that while being happy is a simple choice and the most natural state of being human, it's also the most challenging goal for us to achieve in this harsh world. My journey to health, wealth, and happiness—the true 'holy trinity'—only really began when I realised that **it's not so much we need to transform our life but surrender to the life we originally had.**

First, My Back Story

My parents survived World War 2, leaving me to survive the peace. I think their job was easier.

'Coincidentally,' for the first year of my life, they were part of a yogic community called Shanti Sadan. Shanti, of course, is Sanskrit for 'peace!'

I just Googled it as I write. It seems even though seventy years have passed, it's still going strong!

> **"Shanti Sadan** is a Centre of Traditional Non-Duality. The non-dual teachings are about our true Self, and about the reality within and around us."

How about that! This is exactly what my coaching work is about! It must have been absorbed into my unconscious mind.

My first given name was Vikram, and since names and purpose seem to be connected, I decided I might as well Google this too.

> "The most common understanding of the **name Vikram** is 'valorous'—one who is wise, brave, and strong as well as victorious."

Not a bad start to my life so far. In hindsight, my destiny was pretty clear from day one.

However, things went downhill fast from there. After a while, for some reason unknown to me, my life took a very different turn: my parents left Shanti Sadan, changed my name to 'Paul', split up with each other, and sentenced me to a life of hard labor in the Church of England school system. The meaning of my new name, Paul, is 'small.'

The meaning of 'Church of England' to me was sin, guilt, shame, unworthiness, dogma, rules, and cruel punishment for making simple human errors.

Learning to Shut Up and Shut Down

My early memories flutter by like butterflies, and I think it's easier to remember the bad ones. One of the pretty young teachers at my primary school was Mrs. Newall. I really adored her, but when I ran to her one day, arms wide open, dying to give her a hug, full of the innocence and joy of a 5-year-old, she pushed me away as if I were a dirty rag. Crusty old Mrs. Tomlinson with the thick brown stockings and pince-nez glasses told me that I didn't love my mother. Why would anyone tell a child that? I'd never felt pain like it before. It was so desperately untrue, and I was devastated. I'd heard the term 'hurt feelings,' and now I knew how it felt.

I did, however, end up getting my revenge. She was 'testing' the class (of 6- year-olds!) with general knowledge questions, one of which was: what do you call a female elephant? Great question for a class of young, inner city kids—if you deliberately wanted to destroy their self-esteem. Of course, no one knew the answer! No hands waved eagerly in the air to be picked and praised. Then mine crept slowly but surely up. Defiantly, I looked her right in the eye and said… 'cow!'

In a flash of intuition, I'd connected some random dots. Having heard of a 'bull elephant' from boys' adventure stories, I wondered if that might possibly mean 'male elephant,' if so, then the female might be a 'cow elephant.' O boy, how can you be so right and be so wrong? She sent me to the headmaster for a beating!

And that's kind of how my school life went. I was a bright, cheeky little rascal (and still am) whose spirit—my true self, was not allowed to shine.

My secondary school was even worse. They called me 'Hunting,' and I hated my name because all the kids would chant the rhyme, 'Cry baby bunting, your mother's gone a-hunting.' The bullying was institutionalised in the Church of England school system. The 'masters,' as they were laughingly called, modeled physical and emotional cruelty in equal measure. This was accepted because it was 'normal.' This was just how it was—deal with it. So, I dealt with it. And I died inside.

I built an angry, brazen veneer and used my wit to get laughs and approval; with my sharp tongue and facetious attitude, I cut people to shreds to get attention. This is where I learned one of my greatest defence mechanisms—being funny. I wasn't Robin Williams, but underneath my wit, I was an innocent child terrified to be who I really was, just in case I got punished or worse—rejected and consigned to the scrap heap.

Success in school and university wasn't hard, I was good at stuff. I could run fast and swim fast, so they made me captain of sports, but the prize that I really coveted, I never got. I was a maverick who spoke his truth, so they would not make me a prefect. They would not give me the authority that I craved. That hurt, so I converted to atheism. It gave me great pleasure to 'flip the finger' to the god-squad.

Although a rebel in school, I was still an idealist in the bedroom: cripplingly shy and desperate for a 'relationship,' but not the sort all my friends were bragging about. At seventeen, a late start, I fell good and hard for wild, sixteen-year-old beauty Pat Ferguson. She said all the right things and touched me in all the places that drove me insane with fire, love, lust, and passion. Gallons of testosterone were coming out of my ears. She wanted me as much as I wanted her, but when we were alone and naked on her tiny bunk with her parents downstairs watching TV, it didn't work. Like assembling an Ikea bed, I had no idea how A could possibly slot into B.

I loved her a lot and I was really excited, but I had no way of expressing it all physically. I figured that it'll be okay the next time. Next time, I'll have more time, and next time, it will be easier. But there was no next time. She simply broke it off with me.

Over the next ten years, I did nothing but ruthlessly prove over and over that I was not impotent. I was not a failure. I was not gay. I deliberately transformed myself into a callous, unfeeling sex-machine who would never, ever be hurt like that again. I was trying to transform myself into being like the others. Being different meant that there was something wrong with me. I was the misfit, and I was the odd one out. No one tells us about the true self, the soul, let alone how to communicate with it. We just get brainwashed with all the religious mumbo-jumbo. For a while, I even wanted that to be true, but because of this, my true self just starved to death inside me.

When forced to deny the truth of who we are, we have no reference point and no choice but to find our sense of identity and security in 'belonging' to our tribe, race, color, religion, peer group, nation, gang—anything that promises to take away the pain of nothingness and the misery of spiritual amnesia because we want to forget who we really are and settle for the make-believe personalities we create.

I died again and again every day I could not be with Pat.

I gave up on myself and failed my Advanced-level exams, despite having done extraordinarily well at Ordinary-level— in all subjects except English Literature. Shakespeare? Total mystery. Even more of a mystery given my current uncanny attunement with the deeper mysticism of the Bard!

The fear, the terror, of not getting to go to university and having to find a job was the only motivation I had to keep going. I took an extra year to re-sit my exams; as thoughts of university loomed, all I knew was that I wanted to study psychology. I wanted to understand myself. Although, it was not cool to admit it back then, I wanted to help people understand themselves, too.

The Last Straw

Fast forward to what I had intended to be my last day on earth. Now 28, with a career in advertising under my belt, and money for all the cars and velvet suits I could buy (yes, this was the 70s), plus I'd also notched up an ex-wife by leaving the woman I actually loved for a glamourous older woman. Why? Because, by now, I had turned myself into an insatiable sex-addict; but even the skinny, over-sexed Australian model was not enough, and the guilt and disgust I felt about who I was and how I hurt people got too much to bear. I was already on tranquilizers and antidepressants, so it was easy enough to take a big enough overdose to kill a jackass. So much for all the symbols of success and happiness. Everything that was supposed to make you happy didn't work for me, so I was now certain there must be something very wrong with me. What's the point of going on with this charade, this joke, this fiasco called life?

Like Hamlet, if we lose touch with our true self, the only choice left is to suffer or to die. He banished his soul, Ophelia, to a nunnery. What does Vikram, who is wise, brave, and strong as well as victorious do at this point? Is it more courageous to look death in the eye and say "lay on, Macduff?" Or is it nobler "to suffer the slings and arrows of outrageous fortune" to endure "the heartache and the thousand natural shocks that flesh is heir to?"

I had attained 'normalcy.' I now fitted in. I was one of the lads. I could brag about my sexploits, drink thirteen pints of beer in an evening, scarf down a vindaloo, and throw up in the gutter like the best of them. I was successful. I belonged to my species, but was I happy now?

Hunting the Grail – Refusing the Call

As we grope our way through life like those three blind mice looking for just the right cheese to satisfy that empty gnawing hunger forever, the subliminal scent of that cheese is also drawing us. Even when we don't realize it, cannot express it in words, the Grail, our destiny, or whatever you call the ultimate purpose in life is hunting us as much as we are hunting the Grail. All we have to do is be open and trust. Did I say **all**?

Six months after my attempted suicide, I was flying off to New Zealand. It's all so hazy now, but I had been discovered and resurrected by my then new girlfriend. My new strategy for happiness became to seek independence. I badly needed to be free from my mother's stranglehold on my umbilicus. An idyllic new life in Auckland, New Zealand called to me: sun, sea, fame, and fortune. I couldn't get any further away from what I saw as the source of my pain.

Unfortunately, I took all my baggage with me. Change is not transformation. I may have changed the wallpaper but not the lightbulb. The same desperate drama was playing in my head——just projected onto a different cast of characters, except for one thing: a horse. On a whim, one lazy Sunday afternoon, I'd bought myself a horse, as one does. George was his name.

Looking back, I can feel the tug on the fishing line as the Grail began to reel me in. One fine day, driving into the countryside to ride George, out of character, I picked up a hitchhiker. He told me about an event he was going to up north—a music and healing festival called 'Nambassa'. He tried to persuade me to come along (i.e., drive him all the way), but this was the last place on earth I would ever be found.

In the spirit of the true hero I had refused the first call to adventure, but something had been stirred inside me. After all, I wasn't here to shut the door to my past but open it to my future.

In the mythological 'hero's journey' when we refuse the call to leave our 'ordinary world,' things get a whole lot worse. A year later, when my dream life in the sun was predictably unraveling, I was as mysteriously drawn to Nambassa as Ferdinand was drawn by haunting music to Miranda in Shakespeare's "**The Tempest**." Was Nambassa a bit of a risk? Was it all a bit weird? Yes. Was my inner door open? Maybe just a little ajar.

It was there that I first saw and heard **Swami Satchidananda**, an Indian guru, address the multitude.

Even from a great distance amongst the heaving throng, I, the fiercely committed atheist, was struck by the spiritual light emanating from those eyes. The next day I attended a 'healing circle' and surrendered to the call inside. The inner door was flung open, and a day later I left Nambassa floating two feet above ground on the bliss of a pure, spiritual, and inexplicable cloud of unconditional love.

This, I knew, was not caused by drugs, alcohol, or hormones. It had an intensity, purity, and depth qualitatively unlike even the most spectacular orgasm—a full body orgasm that didn't stop after three seconds. For the first time ever, without knowing what on earth it was, I had unleashed the real deal: the real me. Was this really my true self inside? Is this it?

Two days later, I was back down to earth, but now I was on a true quest: how do I have this blissful, meaningful state of being on tap, by choice, all the time?

Nothing else mattered. Nothing. Nothing at all.

Satchidananda Again!

Fast forward six months. I was back in London for my birthday. I got wind of a conference happening in Wembley—the World Symposium on Humanity. It sounded like just what I was looking for. A short tube ride later, I was staring in disbelief at the program schedule in the lobby. Guess who was giving a talk in fifteen minutes?

After the talk, while queuing up to speak to 'the guru', I got chatting to someone else. A brilliant young woman called Arianna Huffington, who handed me a brochure about a personal development seminar she was sponsoring in London in a few months' time. Insight was its name. I read it, and I knew right then and there that this was what I was being called to do.

"I can't possibly stay here for three months," I squealed and added, "I have a job and a horse to get back to." "O yes you can," Arianna said sagely, as Satchidananda in his white robes and long beard disappeared out the door—never to be seen by me again. His role in my life was done—until his name came back into my life forty years later, in the most surprising way.

The Transformational Journey

I like seeing how easy it is to transform the word 'impossible' to 'I'm possible'. No way could my 'mind' see how I could afford to let go my fabulous job in NZ, pay for three months in London, pay for the Insight Seminar, and for my fare back. No way. Impossible. All the copywriting agencies in town said that there was no chance of freelance work. It just didn't happen. Until it did! I was opening the door (no pun intended) on my way out of an employment agent's office when the phone rang. He called me back, "Can you do a week's freelance writing starting now?" What I was paid in that one week was more than enough to finance everything.

The Insight Seminar was beyond amazing. I had now found the key to the door of life.

The 'miracles' of Insight were just beginning, and so too was my new life—or was it the old, original life re-membered?

With this new awareness, my work was also beginning first

inner, then outer. In order to maintain that orgasmic stream of bliss in my every living moment, I had to keep ridding myself of the lies, fears, traumas, and betrayals with which I had so expertly crafted my false self. Insight gave me the tools and keys for doing this. It also gave me the vision of possibility. I now knew that this is the work I had always wanted to do—everything that was excluded from my so-called psychology degree. It was everything that I needed to liberate my soul from the tyranny of religion and the false promises of the marketing and advertising world that addicts us to rational lies, fast food, and slow death.

Facilitator Training – Not for the Poor in Spirit!

Unbeknownst to me, the director of training for Insight was a devious, grail-seeking genius called Terry Tillman. Well aware of the mythical keys of the 'hero's journey,' his approach to training facilitators was to make it seem pretty much 'impossible' for us to succeed—if we were not living the spiritual principles at a high level. So where I was expecting support, encouragement, information, instruction, tips, and acknowledgment, I was seeing none! Or at least none that showed up in the way I expected it to. In order to see the unconditional love and support that was there, and benefit from it, I had to make the most terrifying journey of them all: I had to surrender the (false) sense of security and control lent by my false self and trust the inner wisdom and guidance from my soul.

For fifteen years, I grunted and sweated my way from seminar to seminar, from workshop to workshop. Until, in a Los Angeles training room, I finally gave up my quest. I stood up and without realising it consciously, I surrendered. I gave upward to the higher part of me. I confessed to Terry that I was unable to fulfill the requirements of the training, and I was dismally not ready for this work.

And the door of life opened wider than it had ever done before!

"Congratulations, Paul," he said, "this is the first time I've seen in you the true quality needed to do this work."

He wouldn't even tell me what this elusive quality was. I had been putting so much energy into trying to be a facilitator, trying to convince them I was good enough, and trying to hide my fears, doubts, and failings that I was losing touch with myself—my honesty and humility that allowed the true me, the soul, the inner master to come forward and simply be. In 'giving up,' I was actually 'giving upward'—surrendering to the higher self, the true me, and there I was, trembling with naked truth and innocence.

This is what I now realize Shakespeare means through the

voice of Hamlet when he invites us "To be, or not to be, that is the question." That is the fundamental existential choice we all have.

To Be or Not to Be?

To be or not to be—a facilitator? Not to be. Not, that is, in the form that I was hoping for. But at its essence level—yes, absolutely. In my coaching, I can now honestly say "I am facilitating insight" as a statement of present moment reality.

In tandem with my inscrutable facilitator training, I was pushing my boundaries as an executive coach to senior executives and CEOs in the very business I had cut my teeth on after graduating from university: advertising.

The closest I'd got to the horse-assisted transformation work, which would end up being the cornerstone of my life, was the pony-tail sticking out the back of my head. Executive coaching as a term was not yet being used, but what I lacked in experience, I made up for in chutzpah and confidence.

I would call up CEOs, brazenly talk my way into a meeting, and enrol them in my £5K, one-to-one coaching program. It was easy. I was rolling in clients, and, most importantly, I was using my raw wits and intuition to really make a big positive difference. It was great. My main contribution was to empower my clients to utilize their own intuitive wisdom and guidance. I encouraged my 'inner master' not to give me answers but questions. If I could come up with great questions and hold a space for my clients to find their own truth, I'd be cooking with gas.

Then, the 1990 recession hit. Not only were training budgets slashed, but also advertising budgets. It was a double whammy. Overnight, I was out of business, out of cash flow, and into the dangerous white waters of major debt. Even scarier, I was having what you you'd call a 'nervous breakdown.' It was an extremely over-sensitive state of being that made me feel like my skin had been peeled off, leaving me crying at nothing, raw and utterly vulnerable— but not in a good way.

Abandoning ship, my girlfriend and I set sail in our life-raft for the countryside—very close, as it happens, to where I live now, a beautiful fourteenth-century Cotswold town. Chipping Campden was its name.

An Epiphany – or My kingdom for a Horse?

I badly needed to do some riding, and I found just the place a short drive from our new house in Campden. I was always a bit of a mongrel as a rider: brazenly fearless but not exactly well-endowed with natural talent. But I must have shown promise because one day Anne, the owner of the riding school, put me on Spud. Spud was a dapple grey, 5-year-old, 17hh, 2" Irish sport horse. This translates to: very young, very big, very powerful, and very playful. He was also very friendly and affectionate in the stable. I was in love. Spud turned out to be way above my pay grade. As soon as I felt him move under me, I knew I was in big trouble.

As we set off along the tracks to the grass arena, keeping him at a walk was not an option. He soon realised that he was totally in charge of the situation. My first attempt to check him with the reins was met with a disdainful flick of his head that plucked me out of the saddle like a daisy and spread-eagled me across his ample neck. Ahead of us was a busy little road. Let's jump over the hedge and play with 'them thar cars,' he was thinking as I sat helplessly on his massive back. I was toast.

As I looked around for a softish piece of ground for an emergency exit, I heard my inner voice say "he needs leadership, and he needs direction, not control." Yes, I knew about leadership all right. I was a leadership coach, wasn't I? In fact, around the time that I was setting up my coaching business, I had taken Terry Tillman's notorious, three-month intensive experiential seminar, sparsely dubbed 'Leadership'. He'd designed the entire experience around the core principles of the mythological Arthurian Grail quest. It was 'Leadership' that inspired and galvanized me more than all my other trainings to let go of my past comfort zones and security blankets, to truly trust my own inner teachings, and take the massive inner risks it took to conquer the Everest of the advertising world. Right now, however, I was paralyzed with fear. Not so much the fear of death or serious injury, but a deeper existential fear: fear of having no control and fear of being totally alone up there on this frolicking beast who was taking great pleasure playing with me—this flopsy rag doll 'jouncing' on his back.

It's all a bit of a blur now, but I do remember making a clear decision to live, and to focus on just the very next step I wanted Spud to take. Again, I surrendered and the door opened. I visualized a circle of light on the ground. I observed my breathing and brought it into a rhythm. I imagined a column of white light from the heavens passing through my head and Spud's body into the earth. I listened inwardly and let my intuition guide my hands, my legs, and my body position.

Within minutes, everything had transformed. Spud was totally in tune with me and I with him. The bliss was gushing out of my every cell. I was getting higher and higher on pure 100% proof spirit. I was out of my head on it. Delirious—in a delicious way. And Spud, softly on the bit, head, and neck in a perfect crest was going exactly where I directed him to in the most beautiful collected walk, trot, canter—whatever I wanted. Anne was agog. All I remember her saying during the entire experience was, "You could go round Badminton like that." My dream, my vision, then was to compete at the world-famous, international, 3-day horse trials at Badminton, England. Here I was doing exactly that at the *experience* level—not just the *symbolic* level!

To me, to suddenly be able to ride like this was a miracle. I was in paradise. I was so transported into the ***Now*** that I totally lost all sense of time. So when Anne at last begged me to stop before I wore this giant horse into the ground, it seemed like only seconds had passed.

We sat in silence over lunch in the pub, until I asked her if perhaps we could do some experimental work with horses and groups of people. Would she be game to put on a workshop together? She certainly was, and 'Ride For Your Life' was born. Our first seat-of-the-pants workshop with twelve people pushed me into areas of self-exploration I would never have undertaken had I known in advance what it would have dragged out of me. But it worked! It worked amazingly well. Half the group were unsuspecting riders who'd never done any personal development work, and the other half were non-riders who had. It was a wild, crazy, and totally irresponsible thing to attempt, but it was terrific. Not only had I discovered an awesomely effective catalyst for profound learning and growth, I'd got myself a marketing differentiator that was truly unique. Who else in the world would be mad enough to defy all the modern conventions about working with horses and harness what all the great riders and leaders throughout history (e.g., Alexander the Great and Bucephalus) knew about how horses bring out the truth in us—the truth about our egos and limitations and the truth about our souls and infinite possibility?

A life-threatening experience evolved into a life-transforming one. That first crazy idea grew rapidly into a global phenomenon of bringing horses into boardrooms across the world. My purpose has always been "to bring joy by sharing the things I love." If I could find a safe, non-life-threatening way to bring the transcendent joy of soul self-awareness to my clients through communicating with horses in their own world, I would be fulfilling all my dreams and goals in one fell swoop.

Why Talk to a Guru, When You Can Whisper to a Horse?

For the first five years of 'Ride For Your Life', I would travel the UK giving my 3-day workshops mainly to riders. Then the 'horse whispering' brigade from the United States began to invade our shores, and suddenly I could see how much more powerful and safe it would be to work with the horses on the ground rather than mounted. A huge learning curve loomed before me, but the challenge of building a true leadership relationship with horses when they had a free choice to follow you as they would a fellow herd member, or not, was thrilling on a whole new, far deeper level.

Ironically, I discovered that I had a far more natural talent for horse whispering than for riding. My partner Geri (now my wife) and I bought this wonderful property in the district of Stratford Upon Avon (Shakespeare country) where we could keep our own horses and create a natural environment for them that liberated both us and them from the rigid confines of the orthodox horse world.

I am a maverick. I've always been a misfit, and now I revel in it being a strength. Me and 'orthodox' do not rub along well together. I don't worship the opinions of the opinionated at the altar of opinion. Why believe anything that may not be true? Belief is not necessary (except as a hypothesis to be validated, by my experience). If it's not true, why would you want to believe it. If it is true, why believe it, it's true!

When I sat down to write a book about my new approach to leadership through horse whispering, I found myself deciding between three possible titles. Interesting how this strange mythological term 'The Holy Grail' seemed to be stalking me like a (hopefully benign) predator after my blood:

1.   Canter the Banter
2.   The Holy Grail of leadership and how horses help us find it
3.   Why talk to a guru, when you can whisper to a horse?

My book coach voted for 'Canter the Banter'—it was short and snappy in a sort of 'best-seller' kind of way and alluded to an advanced, equine form of 'walk the talk.' To do this work with integrity and congruence, one has to become half-horse and half-human—a kind of Pegasus creature.

Of course, the 'Holy Grail' was probably the most powerful, enduring *metaphor* of man's fulfillment of his ultimate purpose in our vocabulary. It was right on track with the power of this work. But, back then, that's all I saw it as—a metaphor and a symbol of that ultimate prize—and not the reality of it.

Somehow, the rhetorical question, "Why talk to a guru, when you can whisper to a horse?" might be a tad long-winded, but, with a wry grin on its face, it captures the very essence of what you get when you come here: the clear, direct, honest, and unambiguous feedback a guru gives—awareness of when you are and when you are not being true to yourself.

Like a true guru, horses do not care about *symbols* of power, authority, leadership, or love—only the *reality*. They can sense, on an energetic level, when you're being inauthentic, playing games, when you are driven by deep existential fear, motivated by insecurity, self-doubt, arrogance, or need for approval, etc. And, they will immediately resist your attempts at leadership and gently but subtly assume leadership over you.

My job is simply to enable you to acknowledge the dynamics of that core, limiting issue, take 'leadership' over what is driving you inside, discover the truth of who you really are, and risk bringing this to the forefront of your life. As with a true guru, when you make this breakthrough by 'whispering to a horse,' you then enter into a spiral of increasing trust, respect, understanding, and engagement that literally makes what was absolutely impossible for you thrillingly possible!

So the 'guru' got my vote. My approach to writing is to find the questions to ask myself that will hopefully reveal the deepest answers to life's most thorny issues. "What *is* life's most thorny problem?" I asked myself. And I said, "Spiritual amnesia! We've forgotten who we really are and why we're here." "How did this happen?" I enquired inside. "The so-called 'priesthood' twist and distort the symbols and metaphors in the Bible to feed predigested baby food to the masses. Processed lies emptied of all spiritual nourishment. False promises that addict us to a life of guilt and misery." it replied. "O dear," I thought, "I'd better do some research."

And that's when, to my amazement, I discovered another latent talent: seeing the deeper subtext in biblical metaphors, symbols, and poetry.

Into what new shark-infested waters was I now being led? Biblical symbology? Man the lifeboats!

The Truth Forbidden
In Shakespeare's Verse Is Hidden

Editor's note: The following section is designed to give you a taste of the profound message to humanity hidden symbolically in Shakespeare's works. Consequentially, it delves very deep, very fast, into some very difficult, controversial areas of scripture and theology. Please be aware that it is intended to inform, not offend. If you have strong views that may be upset by this, we suggest that you simply skip this section. If you want a more detailed explanation, look for the free download link in the end.

While the ultimate truth is unchanging, our ability to understand it is evolving. When you understand the symbols, Shakespeare's canon blows a hole in the wall separating religious dogma from true spiritual awareness.

Over the past twenty years, as I've evolved in my understanding of and certainty with delivering my work with the horses, so has the 'brand name and logo' I use to promote it. 'Ride For Your Life' became 'horsejoy: authentic leadership' that has now grown into **PAUL HUNTING: Happiness Unbridled.** Since writing this piece, I'm wondering about changing it to Vikram: something or other!

In other words, I now have four symbols all denoting the same experience: your finding the source of deep, lasting happiness within you. What does it matter what I, you, or anyone else calls it—it's always aimed at the same reality and the same experience!

In this picture, the reality is a bunch of lines on a piece of paper.

Our minds, however, create perceptions from those lines, and find familiar symbols for those perceptions. Some see a rabbit. Others a duck. Others both. What do you see?

Imagine it was forbidden to talk about ducks. If you even said the word 'duck,' you and your family would be tortured, disemboweled, and burnt alive. What do you see now? Even if you did see a 'duck,' you would not admit it. You'd do everything in your power to become totally blind to the awareness of ducks. Yes?

Well, that's what has happened over thousands of years to the ultimate truth of the human condition: who we are, where we come from, where we go after death, and why we're here on earth. Unless you're a nihilist, there must be an answer, an ultimate truth, yes? Do you know with absolute certainty what that answer is?

Over the course of many thousands of years, there has evolved dozens, possibly hundreds of different 'logos', symbols for the very same source of unbridled happiness within us all.

My mother was Jewish, and I was educated to be a Christian. So my language and familiarity is with the Judaeo-Christian Bible. As was Shakespeare's in a way.

I've told you my 'victim story' of how I was beguiled by the symbols of happiness (relationships, sex, money, degree, job, car, food, etc) and became suicidal with pain, misery and despair when these symbols failed my expectations. That's the price we pay for putting symbols first in life. They do not deliver. They cannot. Symbols will not give you any more satisfaction than eating a menu will give you the experience of the delicious meal it promises.

To be happy, and remain happy, we have to focus our attention on the true source of the experience of happiness—and we can also enjoy the symbol if we still want it.

A few years ago I asked an 'artsy friend' to create this collage of some of the dozens of symbols that represent, say, 'Happiness Unbridled' found in the Bible, Shakespeare, and certain ancient mystical writings.

I find it fascinating how he intuitively put such major emphasis on two well-known symbols that are not generally considered to be interchangeable: 'The Holy Grail' and 'The Tree Of Life.'

What Is the Question?

Remember that I was saying I consider it more important that, as a coach, we ask our intuition to give us great questions, so clients can find their own great answers? So when I was asking myself "what and where really is the Holy Grail?" the inner answer I got was "wrong question!" The right question turns out to be along the lines of: what thing of priceless value have we **lost** that finding it again would give our life deep, abiding, purpose, joy, and fulfillment?

Traditionally, the Grail was said to be the cup that Jesus used at the last supper in which Joseph of Arimathea gathered the blood of Christ after the crucifixion. In receiving the blood, the cup was transformed into a fabulous bejewelled chalice of priceless value. Recently, it's said to be the womb of the Magdalene and the bloodline of Jesus. Dan Brown has millions looking for it in Rosslyn Chapel, Scotland. Can finding a holy relic make us happy? Can any material symbol?

One thing's pretty certain. In our Judaeo-Christian culture,

the Grail has something to do with the symbolism of the Christian ritual of the Eucharist.

Shakespeare's Lost Grail

What I am about to say cannot be proven in a way that will satisfy the rational demands of the mind, but if you do allow yourself to be open, and attune to it with your heart, it has the power to transform your life as it did mine.

My experience with Shakespeare tells me that the underlying theme, hidden in the subtext of all his plays, is the allegory of how 'Adam and Eve' lost the joy of the soul and how Jesus the Christ got it back for the whole of mankind. The forbidden secret heresy is that this Christ action has little to do with orthodox Christian dogma! And the spiritual promise of freedom and joy is available to all regardless of race, creed, color, or sexual preference.

Final Answer

There is one key verse at each end of the Bible that supports the thesis that something of great value to us all has been cut off – and subsequently reconnected:

In the beginning, in Genesis, it says we lost access to the 'tree of life'. At the very end, in Revelation, it says Jesus the Christ restored the access to the 'tree of life'. In a nutshell, that's what the entire Bible is about. Everything in between these two passages is commentary on these two key events. Commentary the Jews did not believe and the Christians misunderstood (or deliberately distorted).

> Genesis 3:24
> *So he drove out the man; and he placed at the east of* the garden *of* Eden Cherubims, and a flaming sword which turned every way, to keep the way *of **the tree of life**.*

> Revelation 22:14
> *Blessed are they that do his commandments, that they may have right to **the tree of life**, and may enter in through the gates into the city.*

Therefore it follows, like the night the day, that if we can find out what 'the tree of life' really means beneath the shroud of superstition, myth, and ritual, it will provide the final answer to the ancient mystery of the 'Grail', and the reality of the pearl of great price.

Are you ready for this revelation?

The Readiness Is All – Hamlet

Almost every enduring culture has stories and myths about the search for what we often call in ours 'the Holy Grail'. An element of this heretical myth, involves King Arthur's sword, Excalibur, symbol of the Sword of Truth. Excalibur was buried, stuck, in a stone waiting for the rightful king to show up: only he would be able to pull it out. Thus, the symbolism says if we can 'pull Excalibur from the stone' we have demonstrated an openness to rule our own inner kingdom in Truth. Today, this means we're ready to cut through the thousands of years of misinformation, to the reality, the actual experience. The metaphor of 'being stuck' signifies how we are 'stuck' in the confusion of so many seemingly different symbols that all in fact relate to the one fundamental Truth.

This idea is deeply buried and unorthodox now. (Hence my attraction to it.) Imagine what they'd have done to Shakespeare in post-reformation England if his views had been spotted in the plays. Not only would he have been burnt to a crisp, but also all his works.

Beginning with the witches' cauldron, *Macbeth* is a banquet of deliciously heretical, subversive, mystical teachings. Here's just a taste. If it whets your appetite for more juicy details <u>email me here and I'll send you my book Shakespeare's Revelation as my gift.</u>

Shakespeare is wise enough not to reference the Grail directly, but the cauldron is what he uses as an overriding symbol of the Grail chalice. And it's not the chalice that matters anyway - but the ingredients!

These are just a taste of the ingredients in *Macbeth* that tell the forbidden story:

Included in the witches cauldron are:
- ***an adder's fork*** (serpent's venom) and
- ***the liver of blaspheming Jew*** (Jesus Christ – tried and executed for blasphemy by Pontius Pilate)

Macbeth and Lady Macbeth fall from grace when tempted by the ultimate glory of becoming king and queen. Lady Macbeth (Eve) falls first, prays to Satan, and emotionally blackmails Macbeth (Adam) to murder the king and steal the crown. She fears her husband is too 'full of the milk of human kindness' (original innocence) to commit the deed.

Shortly before Macbeth slaughters the king, his friend Banquo (whose sons are prophesied to be kings) gives Macbeth (the traitor) a diamond (precious jewel of the Grail) from the king he is about betray to give to Lady Macbeth.

At the last supper, Jesus gives Judas (the traitor) a sop of bread dipped in the wine from the cup (Grail chalice).

Notice how closely Shakespeare's words match those in the Bible!

Jesus says to Judas (traitor):

> *That thou doest, do quickly.*

Macbeth says to himself (traitor), in a direct paraphrase:

> *If t'were done when 'tis done, then t'were well i't*
> *were done quickly.*

Macbeth laments the dire consequences of his betrayal (cutting off the tree of life):

> *The spring, the head, **the fountain of** your blood is*
> *stopped; the very source of it is stopped. The source from*
> *which your **royal blood** comes has been stopped.*

Royal Blood!

And with this poignant phrase, Shakespeare confirms he really is pointing to the Grail. '**Royal blood**' in old French, becomes '**san-graal**', the very root of the term Holy Grail, as delineated by Leigh, Baigent, and Lincoln in *Holy Blood: Holy Grail*, and by Dan Brown in the blockbuster *The Da Vinci Code*.

Macbeth's speech also relates biblically to Revelation and to what Jesus himself says he restores:

> *And he said unto me, It is done. I am Alpha and*
> *Omega, the beginning and the end. I will give*
> *unto him that is athirst of **the fountain of** the*
> *water of life freely.*

Macbeth confirms he's talking about the ingredients of the Grail chalice (that are poison to Satan):

> *This even-handed justice Commends the*
> *ingredients of our poisoned chalice To our own*
> *lips.*

Soon after the murder of the king, Macbeth realizes he has 'ironically' murdered **his own** soul:

> mine eternal jewel (that diamond, the Grail) I
> have given to the common enemy of man' (Satan)
> a fruitless crown put on my head (crown of thorns).

What is not yet clear is the precise meaning of the symbols of: eternal jewel and the sop of bread dipped in wine. For this we need first to look in the gospel, then back to Shakespeare for supporting evidence.

> And as they were eating, Jesus took bread, and blessed, and brake it; and he gave to the disciples, and said, 'Take, eat; this is my body.' And he took a cup, and gave thanks, and gave to them, saying, 'Drink ye all of it; for this is my blood of the covenant, which is poured out for many unto remission of sins.'

As with the entire biblical text, take any of it literally and we're eating menus again. To get the nourishment, we must cut through to the deep original truth, the bottom line of what it is really hidden and thus what is really meant.

The hidden truth in the Eucharist

In John's gospel it implies that 'the Word made flesh' is a symbol for 'The Body of Christ'.

My research confirms that 'the Word' is in turn a symbol for the sacred 'Name of God'. 'The Word', (Sound and Name of God) according to John, is the original sound vibration out of which, 'came all things': the sound of the creation. Science calls it the 'big bang'. But this is not just random noise, there is higher intelligence at play here.

This is a line linking just some of the key symbols concealing-and-revealing the deeper significance of the Eucharist: the ingredients in the cup:

> Bread = Body of Christ = Word made flesh = Name of God = sound vibration of creation = Tree of Life = Waters of Life = Wind from Heaven = Holy Grail = Bread = Staff of life = Body…and round and round…

> Wine = Blood of Christ = Spirit of God = Light of God = Waters of life = Wine…

When Jesus dipped the bread into the wine, he was symbolising the reuniting of the Sound of God with the Light of God. From the beginning, when 'Adam and Eve' fell, the sound of God was cut off from our consciousness. With the loss of this sweet, haunting song of the soul, we lost awareness of our true self, the God within. The mind (with its false concepts) supplanted the soul as the center of consciousness. We forgot who we really are, and why we're really here. We now define ourselves, not as the divinity that we are, but as the roles we play in our lives, the colour of our skin, our sexual preferences, the football team we support, and…etc., etc.

One of my many favourites, possibly Shakespeare's most explicit description of this tragic loss of the sound and awareness of the soul - and how to reawaken it - is in *The Merchant of Venice*:

Lorenzo serenades Jessica thus:

> *Such harmony is in immortal souls.*
> *But when this muddy vesture of decay*
> *Doth grossly close it in*
> *We cannot hear it*
> *Come, ho, and wake Diana with a hymn*
> *And with sweetest touches, pierce your mistress' ear*
> *And draw her home with music.*

In many spiritual practices, one chants the sacred name of God to awaken the awareness of the soul and thus literally eat from the tree of life, and drink from the waters of life. In my personal experience the impact of doing this is very, very real.

If you want to live with meaning purpose, fulfilment and happiness unbridled, you have that choice: to be or not to be. If you choose 'to be', then, for guidance on how to re-connect to your true self you can either talk to a guru - or you can always come here and whisper to a horse.

For the past few years, Terry Tillman, erstwhile director of training for Insight Seminars Worldwide, has been writing a book called 'The Call'. Not only has he just done me the great honour of asking to include this chapter, but we've also been 'called' to a new partnership taking our work on the Grail to 'God knows where'!

The tree of life (The Holy Grail) lives in the garden of our soul. The pathway to it is now open, albeit covered over by the weeds of time and the thorns of the dilemma of 'good and evil'. But it's here, now, and so worth cutting a swathe to: the very source of our nourishment, fulfilment, and the guilt-free holy trinity: health, wealth, and happiness.

Don't refuse *your* call to action
Click and ask for a free copy of:

Shakespeare's Revelation

Why talk to a guru, when you can whisper to a horse?

Or book a call to discuss any aspect of this controversial material

Paul Hunting

Paul has a passion for the lost wisdom of the ancient mystics and sages. He has the rare gift of understanding complex systems of symbologies and secret codes and bringing them down to earth so you can use them to transform your life today. Over 20 years ago, he had a vision of how to combine horse-whispering with authentic leadership development. He is the pioneer of 'bringing horses into the boardroom' to transform business cultures and the lives of their leaders.

He lives a simple, abundant, and earthy life in a tiny village near Stratford-upon-Avon devoted to his wife, 5 horses, 1 cat, and 12 chickens. He rides and swims most days, unless he's up all night writing about Shakespeare and the Holy Grail.

He has recently been honored to become a business partner with Terry Tillman, his erstwhile mentor and trainer, best-selling author, and founding member of the world renowned Transformational Leadership Council.

paul@paulhunting.com
www.paulhunting.com

A Vision Aligned

ROB WHERRETT

I t was just one of those kitchen sink moments, except it turned out to be a major shift in perspective. I was visiting home and chatting with my mother while we washed the dishes when the topic of beliefs came up. I don't remember how we got to the discussion, and it probably doesn't matter. But I do remember vividly what happened next. We were talking about values and ethics and what they meant. At one point, she referred to how she thought I should respond to something by saying *"It's your beliefs."* On the contrary, I immediately thought, *"No they aren't—at the very least I need to figure out what my beliefs really are."* I didn't say anything to her at that time because there's no point in upsetting your mother, is there? However, she had made a powerful statement about how other people perceive the world. The important question was—did it match my own view? It was a clarion call to consider what I'd never really thought about.

It got me thinking hard about what I truly believed in and what had simply been imposed upon me as a set of givens—things that largely pass unchallenged. I've got a bachelor's degree in Life Sciences along with Philosophy and, owing to that, I tend to take a more objective view of things. Generally what we are told is based on someone's opinion. However, fact and opinion aren't the same things at all; the present situation was a matter of what I believed to be the fact and not someone else's opinion. That all this might later lead to some serious arguments with my spouse wasn't apparent at the time but it was definitely the beginning of a major shift in my own thought process. It was also to lead to some truly life-changing events—not just for me but also for a whole bunch of folks—the impact of which spread around the world.

So I started by thinking about what I **actually** believed in and **not** what I was told to **believe**. It was pretty obvious that my rational view was out of alignment with the people around me. However, I didn't really do anything about it. Instead, I kept revisiting my thoughts until I was pretty sure of my position. For one thing, I didn't want to upset friends and family, particularly the latter and needed my own time to work out how to move ahead.

Starting Points

I'd met my wife through a mutual friend, and we got along really well from the beginning. She'd had an abusive first marriage, so there was a more laid-back approach to our relationship, which was refreshing and fun. I thought that we had quite a lot in common. We liked going on walks in the countryside, shared the same taste in music, and pursued the same interests. She also knew someone I had known and greatly admired, some 15 years previously, while I was studying at the University of St. Andrews in Scotland.

Her two daughters from the previous marriage seemed to approve. When we started dating, the girls were already teenagers. The elder daughter was studying Physics at the

University of Liverpool and by the time we got married, the younger daughter had also left home for college. So, things progressed and we settled down, moving South with my new job in marketing with a large financial services business.

As with most people in a relationship, there were assumptions and ideas on what the future would be like. Even though my wife was 10 years older than I am, we'd talked and agreed on having a child of our own. It all seemed to be working out.

However, with time, things did go sour. You can't describe it as nasty as we did have a lot of fun in the marriage but, imperceptibly, lines were being drawn. They surfaced in a variety of ways. Initially, there was a resistance on her part to engage with my friends and most of my extended family. I had a large family with many uncles, aunts, and dozens of cousins. She wouldn't even want to be involved with my parents, brother, and sister. My friends from university, work, and other places were spread all over the country. She never wanted to visit any of them and almost always found an excuse to get out of the way, if they came to see me.

At first, I assumed that she would take time to adjust to my family and friends. Her first husband was a musician in the Band of the Royal Air Force and had been violent and controlling. I felt sure that she would relax and open up with time and some TLC. The assumption that I could change a person who had no desire to change anything about herself was a huge mistake on my part. But how would I have known better? As humans, we enter into relationships believing that both sides are striving for the same outcome. The truth, however, is often very different.

Over time, she wanted to do everything her way. Very early on in the marriage, the idea of more children was dismissed. I was left alone to deal with my disappointment. The answer, ironically, also came from my mother who told me to deal with it as if it were a medical impossibility and suggested I find other ways of reaching fulfillment. That is what sparked the idea of using personal philosophy as a way of passing on something to the world.

After this, I found that my wife would never do things for complete strangers. On the other hand, I've always been open to new people and more than happy to lend them a helping hand, when the situation arises. But my wife only wanted to focus on her immediate family. Even a single joint visit in a year to my parents was begrudged, while it was an open house for her own relatives, often for weeks at a stretch. I didn't mind the visitors too much but it did mean that we were viewed as a guest house en-route for them traveling to and from mainland Europe.

She would even decide what we would do in our spare time and where we would go. I got thoroughly fed up of being dragged around the shops every Saturday and had to put my foot down to limit the shopping expeditions in favor of something more varied and interesting. Overall, it was an extremely controlling life.

At that time, we were living in Dorset on the South Coast of England. It was a lovely little town with friendly people, except it wasn't what she wanted. It didn't matter to her that it was where I worked and was making very good money. Money which was enough to pay for all the nice things in life, including trips abroad, theatre in London, and nice places to eat and buy clothes.

Defusing a Bombshell

When the person you live your life with is obsessed with their job, it can be trying. When that job involves taking care of terminally-ill cancer patients, it is bound to get stressful at times. So long as she was happy, I didn't object.

However, shortly after her 50th birthday, she was also diagnosed with breast cancer. Her family, understandably, went into panic mode and behaved as if she only had a few weeks to live. My own view (based largely on intuition) was that this wasn't something that would just go away but probably continue for about 10 years. In the end, I was proved absolutely right. To begin with, there was a rapid response from the family doctor and the oncologist, which involved an aggressive treatment with surgery. Unfortunately, nobody, including the healthcare professionals, could tell me what she needed in terms of support. I was left to follow my own instincts and got no guidance from the patient as well on what she wanted. As a result of all this, no matter what I tried to do, it was generally deemed to be the wrong thing.

Finding My Feet

However, this isn't about failure. What I want to show is how coming to terms with my own values and vision paved the way for good things to happen. Remember that conversation I had with my mother? Instead of trying to do what everyone else around me was doing (panic and worry), I set about doing what I thought was right. I had told myself that even if it didn't work, the intention had been the right one and that was all that mattered. After all, you can't spend your entire time trying to second-guess what someone else wants if they won't even tell you, despite you asking repeatedly.

I was beginning to follow my own vision, and indeed, good things began to happen. I started teaching occasionally at a business school. You might wonder what this has to do with anything up until now. Well, one of the things I started was some workshops on how to break out from personal boundaries. It began over dinner with a few business school colleagues, when I misunderstood what one of them had said. In response, I posed a crazy question that triggered the idea for the session that evolved.

The concept was to challenge the participants with a series of impossible statements. They would then have to work out what was going on by themselves. We called the session "*Nietzsche is my mother-in-law; and the relationship to system dynamics.*" Students were intrigued and turned up in droves. The session was a huge success. Several students said that it was the most powerful thing they had ever experienced. For example, Carsten, who is now a consultant in Cologne, has still stayed in touch with me because the session made such an impression on him.

What the exercise did was help people experience how it felt when the boundaries of what they thought possible were shifted outward radically. It was done without them knowing in advance that this was what was about to happen. This last bit was important because it was the dawning realization that was the most powerful part of this exercise. It showed them that things they initially thought were impossible were actually achievable. This creative approach came about because I was prepared to do what everyone else wasn't. I was helping people align their vision with my own—anything is possible, so long as they believe in it. However, the real key here is that one needs to be open to accepting that the outcome might be delivered in a rather different way than what was first envisaged.

The benefit of all this was double-edged. I got a real reward from running the sessions, especially when the students aligned with my vision. Meanwhile, the participants (most of them at least) went away with their heads spinning in a positive way. Admittedly, there were a few who didn't get it at all, but the worst they could come up with was that they had spent 90 minutes being confused.

Meanwhile, on the domestic front, things plodded along. By that time, I was freelancing and could be based just about anywhere, so long as there was an airport and a good train connection within reach. So, we had a discussion about where we might move to. The immediate demand was to move back to her family in Scotland. However, I refused because I knew if that happened, they would never be out of our house and I would be smothered. Further, it didn't make sense to me to be a complete hostage to someone else's illness; there had to be a balance of priorities. It took a great amount of persuasion to reach a compromise and we bought a lovely house in the countryside in the north of England, near to the town where we first met.

My parents were about an hour's drive from there. Her family was three hours up the road. She also had her old friends in the area, including some colleagues she had trained with. It was a good location in a National Park, with a large garden and views over the hills. My vision of us being in a great place and doing good things was beginning to materialize. By this time, we were 7 years on from her first diagnosis of cancer and had gone through a recurrence at the 5-year-point that was treated with radiotherapy. So, while the future was uncertain, at least there had been the opportunity to have some quality time.

Cue Unplanned Events

To compound the domestic situation, my business took a massive hit following the terrorist attacks of 9/11, and I was left to work out what I was going to do in a very different economic environment. The entire time, I was thinking about my values and wondering how I could align things. This allowed me to look at change with a coherent view. Further, the house move had allowed me to connect with new clients and put into practice some of the approaches that I could see were important to make things work.

I applied this to my personal life as well. Things at home had become unbearable. How do you cope with restructuring a business as well as trying to keep stress away from someone who by then was terminally ill? Especially when the work that paid the bills was constantly taking me to far ends of the country.

I knew I couldn't satisfy everybody, no matter how much I wanted to. And whilst terminal illness is horrible, my wife's family were there to support her. So we split up, and I focused on the pressing problem of rescuing a business and my career which at that moment was in pieces. My wife died a few months later from a secondary brain tumor.

One of the things I did when I met someone else was to spend time from the outset in aligning our values. This involved agreeing on ways to overcome the inevitable minor differences we knew would arise. It isn't something that many people actually do when starting a new relationship and over time it gets difficult to bring up the topic. So, what we did was a real game-changer. Since then, I've spoken to many people facing problems in their relationships, and it is also something that comes up in coaching sessions with clients. My advice to them is to always build a framework that can act as a reference point for dealing with issues.

In our case, we had a whole list of things we *wished* for. We called it the **Wish List** and mentioning it became shorthand for defusing any friction. It included hoping that one day *"we would learn how to take a goldfish for a walk."* Actually, that has been a useful metaphor for how we might approach things we had never imagined having to deal with.

Over the ensuing years, we have shared our lives with many people from different cultures. Some have remained friends, while others have moved on. But the one thing that knits everything together is the desire to be open to new people and ideas and to be there to help when things get tough. Sharing philosophy is as fulfilling as having kids, maybe as much as I had hoped for. I see personal development in others. They, in turn, take those ideas and weave them into their own lives and communities.

Making a Difference

By looking at things differently, I also started to challenge how clients were approaching major change. What became apparent were two things. In the first place, people were doing what they were told and not what they believed in. As a result, many organizations were tackling the wrong problems because people weren't personally invested in them. Work had become 'just a job'.

Secondly, people were under a lot of stress if their values were not aligned with those of their organization. I remember talking to a marketing manager who just wanted to do his job in marketing. What he couldn't see was that unless he helped out by joining a major turn-around program to rescue the business, he would not have a job at all. He couldn't emphasize enough that he had been hired as a marketer and not a change manager. I gently talked him through the likely outcome of his actions. It was a case of helping him align his long-term objectives with those of his company. If he helped them to survive, he would be welcome and probably move up the marketing hierarchy when things were back on track. The alternative was joining the dole queue.

Then there was a senior Corporate Finance manager at a global bank who simply wanted to veto spending on any organizational change that didn't meet her department's view of the world. That view, as it turned out, was solely focused on doing things to drive up the share price. Unfortunately for her, the CEO had issued guidelines about how the whole bank should be run, which included focusing on both the staff and customers as well as the share price. It was a wake-up call when I pointed out to her that she was writing the obituary of her career in the bank.

To begin with, I asked her how she thought the CEO would react if I told him that she was blocking his corporate strategy.

The response was sad but also quite comical. In her opinion, she was doing the right thing in accordance with the departmental brief but something that the CEO possibly might not like, if he knew. On the other hand, she was sure that he wouldn't find out. So I simply asked her if she was willing to take the risk. I told her that I might just inform him about her activities. When she realized that I wasn't joking, the look on her face was priceless. She changed her attitude on the spot. Her own survival and career objectives had swung sharply into line with that of the bank.

The result of these kinds of interventions was pretty big, as things started to move forward rather than getting stuck. In addition, I was finding that people and organizations were intrigued by my approach. Apparently, there was something about my way of doing things that was philosophically different from other people. It was becoming a recurrent theme—people assuming that somehow I could steer them through their life crises or out of business disasters.

Changing Lives

We've all seen or heard of people whose problems make our own seem insignificant. Most people contribute to charity and do other similar things but for the majority of them, that's as far as it goes.

That doesn't sit well with me. If someone needs help, I feel I should do something about it. It doesn't matter that the person involved isn't family or even from my own culture. I've actually dug deep and helped people from all across the world.

Take Chris, who is originally from China. He was studying for a Masters in International Business at a university here in the United Kingdom. We met via the Internet and he asked me if I knew how he could get a permit to stay in the country after he had graduated. As it turned out, I had spent some time as a consultant at the United Kingdom Immigration Department, so I did know quite a lot about the subject. However, just passing on information is easy; making it work is a different ball-game altogether. So, I took him along to an Innovation workshop that I was running and asked the students to come up with a plan to build a business for him. This was nearly 20 years ago.

We set up a company together and applied for a Work Permit on his behalf. A few years later, once he was able to apply for permanent residence, he set up his own company. He now has a British passport and lives with his partner and their twin children (Annie and Leon) in a large house on the edge of Newcastle. As a result of his work over the years, he has generated wealth and employment for dozens of people in the city. Yet, those employees have no idea about my involvement and how that gave them jobs.

There was another aspect of my involvement with Chris. My wife didn't want me doing business with a Chinese guy because she had lived in Singapore for three years when her first husband was posted there with the RAF. As a result, she had met quite a lot of Chinese people and didn't like them—deeming them untrustworthy. To be honest, my own experience is quite the opposite.

Sometimes, it isn't even about a direct impact. For a number of years, I had been a panel adviser for the UK government, and one day I was asked to give my input on a new country-wide pension scheme. Most business owners didn't want the proposed approach because of the costs involved. They would rather individual employees make their own arrangements. However, my values told me that working people needed protection from this attitude and also from their own inertia. There is always something else you can do with your money other than saving it for retirement. So, I suggested that the new scheme be made compulsory. It was a watershed moment—especially when I found out that nobody else had suggested it. When the legislation was passed and the new workplace pension scheme came into existence, it forced many working people into a situation where they were going to get an additional pension for the first time. At the time of writing, the numbers exceed 10 million people and are continuing to rise.

Do they know who suggested it? Of course, they don't. They probably don't even care. However, the satisfaction that comes from knowing that for the next working generation or possibly even longer, millions of people in the United Kingdom are going to be better off in retirement, as a result of my efforts, is priceless.

Crossing Continents

What I find is that keeping true to my personal vision translates around the world. It isn't simply doing what works within my own area or country. The boundaries disappear in my view of the planet. In fact, I'm more likely to reach out to those who don't have any state or institutional support to fall back upon.

This comes about in many ways, like personally helping Isifu, a young Ghanaian who lived near Accra. He was suffering from Sickle Cell disease but was trying to further his education and had already part-qualified as a Microsoft Certified Systems Engineer. However, he had been forced to give up due to lack of support.

Ultimately, with my help, he reached a point where he managed to graduate from a college in Germany (where he now lives) and could make headway into the world. Recently, we were having a conversation when he pointed out that without me he probably wouldn't even be alive. His parents had separated, and his mother was struggling with a small holding somewhere near Timbuktu, Mali. Meanwhile, his father, who was still in Ghana, had done little, if anything, over the years to support him. He was focused on his new life with a second wife and their children. However, I am happy to say that today, Isifu is in a place to provide some support to his mother and siblings, for many years to come.

In an unrelated event, I went to work in Malawi for a few months, as part of an international aid project to improve the entrepreneurial activity in the economy. At that time, Malawi was the fourth poorest country in the world. Unlike the NGOs, who liked treating the locals as recipients of Western handouts, I engaged directly with the people and got them thinking about how they could take control of what they were doing. As a result of this, I had a major argument with a guy from the United Kingdom called Peter, who didn't think that Malawians were capable of technical innovation.

Andrew Nkoloma probably disagreed. He was a bright, 20-

something, local university graduate who was very interested in renewable energy. After a short session together, we jointly came up with a way of solving some of the power generation problems in a country with plentiful water (Lake Malawi is the fourth largest lake in the world by volume) and abundant sunshine but poor infrastructure. The solution was based on generating hydrogen as a portable and storable energy source for use in fuel cells. Nkoloma then took the proposal to the World Bank to fund a feasibility study. Who knows what that may lead to?

Besides solving problems, there was also an enjoyable side to engaging with the people. Mathews Jafali, who ran the restaurant at the lodge where I was staying in Blantyre, loved to talk and share experiences. He was also in his 20s and understood that the prevailing worldview might not necessarily be the right one. Also, I was glad that I could help him see past the hype. We had several discussions about how to approach the problems in life, especially when resources are limited. He was keen to learn about good ways of doing things and very interested in my philosophy. As a result, he got me an invitation to his cousin's wedding so that I could experience the real Malawi culture. Being the only white guy among over a thousand Africans at a village wedding, it was an honor and a privilege. That they even admired my dance moves at the party was a bonus! Apparently, my dancing was the talk of the village for several days. On the other hand, what I took away from it was an abundant understanding of a very different way of life with its problems, challenges, and joys.

Drawing Conclusions

Over the years, what I have learned from all these various

events is that transforming my life didn't necessarily mean getting wealthy. Sure, I've earned good money but I've also come in contact with a vast array of people and cultures. Most importantly, I've seen firsthand how following a vision can deliver in the longer run.

People I have known for decades believe that my life is infinitely more interesting than their own. Of course, this could also stem from the fact that we as human beings assume the grass is always greener on the other side. On the other hand, I've impacted the lives of millions of people all across the world— and honestly how many folks can say that about themselves?

Sticking to a vision and understanding how it fits with my core values has been the most important lesson for me in this journey. Not only has it put my personal life in perspective but it has also improved the quality of my living. Thanks to my mother for making me question those values years ago.

As I started receiving positive feedback on my journey, I shifted my stance to getting more things aligned. If they don't align, I don't do them. I truly believe that it is better to focus on what really matters and leave the other things to fall away. Of course, that's not always popular with others but I don't want to be popular just for the sake of popularity. Instead, it matters that I can say, "*I made a difference.*"

Being true to your values and knowing why is critical. However, before you can be true to them, you have to understand what those values actually are. It cannot be some stuff you saw plastered on a slogan or a bumper-sticker. It ought to be about what you really believe in and what you don't. If you do that, you will find your personal life coming into balance.

Of course, your relationships might also change. Those around you who share your vision and mutual goals will become closer. Those who don't will drift apart. Be prepared to let them go but do it without bitterness. If all people had exactly the same values as yours, the world would be unrecognizable. So, you should respect their choices but you don't have to agree with them.

Above all, transforming and transformational experience is just that—EXPERIENCE. So, go sample experience and test it against what you believe in and where you want to be. If it matches, great; if it doesn't, then use your two feet and go somewhere else.

On different occasions, my own two feet have taken me to the remote islands of the Scottish Hebrides across Europe (including Norway, France, Germany, Ireland, and Switzerland) to the USA, and also to the other side of the world (Hong Kong and Singapore). I've also had people from India and Spain working for me and have worked for French, German and Australian corporations at different times. Along the way, I've always tried to relate things to what I value and my learnings over the years.

This approach has not only challenged me but also kept me going, pushing my boundaries further. It seems people like me that way.

Rob Wherrett

Rob Wherrett is an executive leadership coach and management consultant known for his great sense of humor and understanding. Some say it's his 'secret weapon'. He knows that transforming lives and businesses can be a huge challenge. He strives to bring out the best in people he works with and helps them deliver great results.

His books[89] are based on solid practical experience and an impressive track record of delivering critical change for people and organizations. Today, he specializes in guiding small and medium businesses through transformational change by helping people align with their values. He inspires and leads people by using creative techniques and innovative approaches that break down barriers and relieve stress. This is hardly surprising given his great experience in leading creativity and innovation workshops with management students from across the world. He is globally

---

[89] The Compleat Biz: The business model for the 21st Century, Reroq Publishing, St.Helier (2009) ISBN 978-0956130501; and 101 Executive Uses for a Square Camel: and other lightbulb moments in problem-solving, Reroq Publishing, Glasgow (2018) ISBN 978-0956130525.

renowned for challenging personal boundaries in people and opening up new possibilities for them. It is a very powerful combination to make things happen.

Currently, he resides in Scotland but he has lived and worked in many places while serving clients worldwide. They range from blue-chip multinationals to micro-businesses, and it never ceases to amaze them how he can make the complex so very simple.

Contact Information

Website: https://robwherrett.com
Facebook: @RobWherrettCoaching
Twitter: @wykkr
LinkedIn: https://www.linkedin.com/in/robwherrett/

INNER POWER AND DEMONS

SAI BLACKBYRN

"Success isn't always about greatness. It's about consistency.
Consistent hard work leads to success. Greatness will come."
Dwayne Johnson

Yes, I did begin my story by quoting 'The Rock', why do you ask? I quote him because consistency is at the heart of my story—story of how I gained control of my life by gaining control of my health. Be consistent with your work, your life, and any reasonable diet you can follow.

At no point in this story do I advocate that health is only limited to weight loss; however, for me personally, it has been a big indicator of my health.

My story starts from when I was a teenager—a time when we believe how we look is how we are perceived—but the seeds were sown much earlier.

Let me set the scene for you. Imagine you are a young impressionable child, and every conversation that takes place at your home, or when your family congregates, is centered around weight.

"How's your diet going?"
"Which diet are you on?"

"You look beautiful! It seems like the diet is working!"

Not that I fault them for saying this since almost everyone in my family has a history of obesity and diabetes, but every discussion revolved around weight! These conversations were very pervasive, and in hindsight, they clearly affected the way that I viewed the world. The impact of this kind of atmosphere first hit once I turned thirteen—right when the idea of sex and dating started to become very apparent to me. I felt very inadequate about my body image, and even though these conversations weren't aimed at me, they reinforced my feelings of inadequacy.

Of course, I assumed that being attractive to the opposite sex came with being attractive physically. So I would compare myself to other people and ask myself, "What can I do?" And the answer that came to me was obvious: "I should just diet!"

I did my research, and the one I ended up doing was the Atkins Diet, a severe version of it. So, in the Atkins Diet, you are supposed to start with 20 grams of carbohydrates a day. The diet recommends that you then build it up to 100–150 grams over the course of the next two to three months; I did not do that. I thought I would keep it capped at the minimum value and see my results that way. I also restricted my calorie intake to under 1500 calories per day.

Now, as anybody can tell you, eating that restricted a diet as a growing teenager is dangerous. On top of all this, I was running a quarter marathons a day, so sure, I lost weight like crazy. The problem was that I didn't realize the effect all this was having on my psyche. I didn't realize that my obsession with being fit and being thin was turning into anorexia. I didn't recognize it because I had nothing to compare it with. In my mind, I was just working hard unlike other people.

Anorexia and Body Dysmorphia in a Teenage Body

Age 13

Over time, as I continued to control my diet and be obsessed with the way I looked, my body image started to warp. I would understand much later that I had slowly started to lose my grip on what I actually looked like. I would constantly think that I was bigger and fatter than I was. I would pinch folds of skin in different places and think to myself repeatedly how this was something I needed to work on next. At that time, as horrible as it was, I was not aware of any of this. I was just trying to be, as they would say, 'fit.'

As bad as things were, teenage hormones made them worse. As any teenager can tell you, teenage hormones are a bitch. But try coupling those hormones with a severely restrictive diet, telling yourself you are ugly all day, and have punishing exercise routines, and you have a recipe for disaster. So, as I chiseled myself to what I believed was my dream body, I was depressed. Suicidally depressed. My mind would constantly yell at me that I wasn't good enough and that I should kill myself.

At the peak of this suicidal phase, I just could not get a grip, no matter how hard I tried. So here I was, building the body I wanted. I was also, in the process, destroying my emotional health completely. I would randomly start crying for no apparent reason. No matter what people around me said to me, I was obsessed, and I would remain obsessed until I made a serious attempt on my life.

I finally decided to to listen to my brain and make a move toward ending my life. One day, as I sat in my school in the countryside of England, I wrote my suicide note. The school had a river next to it, and I decided that I was simply going to drown myself.

I left the letter out for discovery and went down there. As I was taking my clothes off, getting ready to enter the water, I realized there was something I had left out of my calculations. I hadn't realized the one thing that would stop me from drowning: the water was cold.

I hadn't realized that it was the start of autumn, and the water was just too inconveniently cold for drowning oneself. I, for one, never had a good tolerance for cold to begin with. So here I was, just standing there, trying to get in. **A starved kid with low cold tolerance does not make for a good drowning candidate in a cold river, apparently.**

I spent the next half an hour just to get waist deep into the water. By this time, people had found the letter, and a bunch of them had now come out to try and stop me. They saw me, dragged me out, and got a nurse to interview me.

They couldn't understand what made me want to kill myself, but they did understand that I had lost a dangerous amount of weight in the last 5–6 months, so I was sent to the hospital. What I was never told, and what most people do not understand, is that a ketogenic diet is toxic. Your body goes into the catabolic stage, and a keto diet relies on this in order to break the fat molecules. But what people do not know is that ketones, the molecules produced in the process, are toxic. The age that I was doing the diet and the severity at which I was doing it all played a big role in how much poison had accumulated in my body.

As soon as I reached the hospital, I was told that with my levels, I was lucky to be alive at all. Had I taken another four or five days to come down, I would have been in a coma and my organs would have started to shut down.

Now, you have to understand that none of this seemingly affected me. All I could see, even in the hospital bed, was how gross and fat I was and how unappealing I looked.

That's what body dysmorphia does. It robs you of all perspective.

They diagnosed me with anorexia, which was something I had no idea about then. But when they described it, it sounded exactly like me.

Suicidal tendencies? Check!
Crazy obsession with losing weight? Check!
Not recognizing any pre-set goals? Check!

They told me I had two options. Either I could start eating, or they would put me in a recovery home. The recovery home sounded like the most depressing thing in the world to me. It would be a home full of anorexics, which in my head meant that I would be the only guy in a home full of suicidal young girls because anorexia was thought to be a woman's disease. So I couldn't think of a worse thing at all, except for eating.

The doctors told me that I had to eat or they would feed me

through a tube. I wasn't going to destroy all of my 'progress' by eating unrestricted food, so they put a tube in my stomach. That's how I was fed for a day. After a day of this, I realized that they weren't going to just let me go until I showed them that I could eat.

That broke something in me. It clicked in my head that since I wasn't going to be allowed to control my health, my body, or my fitness, I wasn't going to care anymore. I remember that moment clearly because at that moment I sat down and ate a big bowl of curry, which is the epitome of what you are not allowed to have in any diet.

No photographs have been added here because they could be triggering.

Indulgence, Self-harm, Rock Bottom

Age 14–16

Over the next two years, this loss of control over my body autonomy, as important as it was, made me harm myself. I had realized that I would no longer be allowed to mould my body as I wished, so I might as well do whatever I wanted.

As a recovering anorexic, I had only one thing to do: eat responsibly. Instead, I just started to eat. Whatever I wanted to and whenever I wanted to, I would just eat. I was also drinking hard liquor at this point, about 750ml per day. It got so bad that I was smoking about three packs of cigarettes each day and taking copious amounts of drugs. I had also gone from 45kg to about 110kg in two years because, in my head, I had no restraints if I wasn't going to be allowed to diet. I went from being hospitalized for being anorexic to being clinically obese. During this period, there were several incidents where I passed out from all the drug and alcohol abuse and woke up in a hospital. It got so bad that even my drug buddies thought I was too extreme, and they wouldn't join me anymore.

So I just started to abuse the drugs and alcohol alone because what was I going to do if not destroy myself?

My family had no idea what was happening, and they had no idea how to help. About this time, the bullying started as well, and I was back to square one with the suicidal thoughts. One day I sent a message to my family stating "I just want to die" and turned off my phone. My parents called the headmaster and head teacher, and I was taken out of the boarding school. Within a week, I stopped living at boarding school. I was going to travel every day, and my diet had marginally improved because I was now living at home. My drug use came down, but I was still smoking and drinking like there was no tomorrow.

The blackouts become routine, but my rock bottom was a blackout that threatened to liquify my brain. I was miraculously brought back to life, and I decided that as bad as things were, as horribly as I treated myself, it could all get better if only I could just get healthy once more. I just wanted to see myself healthy once before my drugs and everything else killed me. I wanted to see it while I was lucid. This was a turning point. I quit the alcohol, the drugs, and the smoking that very day. I could not quit eating because that way I would end up in the hospital again. There, in that moment of self-realization, started my true recovery journey.

Recovery and New Obsessions

Age 16–19

My mother knew of Wanny Winslow, a nutritionist and naturopath. She had helped a cancer patient get better through natural means, and I started to see her every other week. She set my diet with a heavy reliance on brown rice, veggies, seaweed, and fish, and I followed it diligently. I was asked to have low salt and no seasoning, and I followed it obsessively. In two years, I resembled Brad Pitt à la Fight Club after discovering healthy ways of exercising.

As good as I looked through, I was most happy about getting my brain back. I was whole, and I felt good about myself again. The volatility and the suicidal tendencies were gone, and I was truly happy. I realized for the first time how big a role our physical health and hormonal balance play into shaping what goes on in our minds.

The Present

It's been decades since that Brad Pitt moment, but I'm still me. I've retained my health and wellbeing. Over time, I phased out Wanny's diet into something a little more flexible, where I was allowed an occasional drink. I would mostly eat what I wanted to eat, but the lifestyle had totally changed now. The desire to have a lifestyle where I was healthy, where my mind was sharp, where I felt great, where I looked great, and where I had energy was so much greater than the desire to go down the yo-yo route.

The core difference between fad diets and sustained health is what you stick to. When I look at my friends and family members who have tried different things, I know for a fact that I am only healthy because of healthy choices I make every day. I realize now that physical and mental transformation happens with consistency. I got back everything I wanted through consistency and sticking to something day in, day out. With time, this daily routine became a lifestyle, and with it came the ability to manage a healthy lifestyle.

I have a baby now, and yes, I packed a few sympathy pounds with my amazing wife, but I'm still healthy, and I'm still me. I have learned to be healthy through life, not against it.

The family still discusses weight and diets like gospel, but I can see a few friends and cousins have escaped it. I can tell which ones will retain it and which ones won't, as sad as it is, because I can see who is consistent.

Just choose something healthy that you can do, and stick to it. None of the fad diets matter, none of it, truly. Just stick to something healthy, and I promise it will give results.

As a person who used to hold no value in myself and what I represent, I can tell you that's a poisonous way to live. I used to be jealous, insanely jealous, of my good-looking friends, and that does something very insidious to you. You aren't able to enjoy the world around you as it is, and you convince yourself that you can only enjoy it once you are 'pretty.'

I can assure you that feeling is not dependent on your looks. Even now, I have friends who are insanely good looking, and my teenage self would have wanted to kill things in jealousy. Now, I am confident enough even with my sympathy weight that I can hold my ground with my self-esteem. Be you, be better, but be you.

Sai Blackbyrn

Sai Blackbyrn is an entrepreneur, a coach, a mentor, a father, a husband, and a CEO. He started working toward his vision right out of high school, and his charm and natural understanding of human behavior allowed him to build Western Australia's biggest dating coaching company. As a young entrepreneur facing immigration problems, he's learned how to set up a foolproof online business that can be sustained from anywhere, no matter what. Sai has failed over and over till he mastered the recipe for success in the field of coaching, and he can help you build your business. You can reach out to him for a coveted seat in his FREE webinar and learn how he helps his clients scale up fast to a six-figure income. He helps clients set up a foolproof operation where the clients come to them – all ready for the process to start. Sai believes in fighting relentlessly for things he's invested in, so why not get him fighting for you and your growth?

Contact Information

Email: sai@sai.coach
Facebook: https://www.facebook.com/sai.blackbyrn

THE ART OF LETTING GO

SAMPO MANNINEN

This is a workaholic's spiritual journey to letting go of the burden of the past. Becoming aware of the pre-programming we all have in our minds is an important part of recovery and ability to let go of the thoughts that do not serve us anymore. For me, it also opened the realm of consciousness and the understanding that there is more to this world than just what we see with our eyes.

Born Workaholic

Born to a workaholic farming family in Finland, Scandinavia, I was raised according to Lutheran, habit-Christian rules, where work plays a significant role. In that semi-religious way of life, my family went to church only on the most important Christian dates, such as Christmas and other occasions. Other than that, there was no real devotion to Christianity or to any other religion for that matter. So, all that was left was a devotion to work. You just have to work a lot. That's how you raise a workaholic, and I am a living example of it.

For me, life has been full of ups and downs, successes, and intermediate hiccups, yet it has always pushed me toward my very own purpose in life. Sometimes it has been a soft touch of a feather, gently steering my path; another day it has been a boxing glove filled with a horseshoe commanding me to wake up. In all of these fifty-three years, one thing has become clear: Life tends to steer you in direction of your soul's purpose, no matter how much you struggle against it. Trust me, I have tried both ways.

Coming back to my upbringing, my mom turned an orphan during World War II. It was unsurprising that she still has strong emotional traumas related to war and its disasters. The shortage of everything was present every day for many years, even after the war was over. My dad's family also experienced the hard times of war. War is always a disaster for everyone, even for the survivors. After the bloody days, the only cure to their pains was to work and fight to achieve material well-being. That's exactly how they saw it. The measure of happiness was "If you have food on your table and work to do, everything must be fine and you must be happy." That preamble served as my pre-schooling to happiness and work ethics. I took it quite seriously and ended up graduating from that school. My two sisters and my brother ended up passing the same course, too.

Surprisingly, I, a farmer boy, ended up becoming a communications entrepreneur. I worked at TV stations, produced corporate films and events, and invested all my time in working. This weird combination of farming background and a career in communications turned out to be an interesting combination as it led me to some great working opportunities. I have done everything from rescuing a calf with my arm in a cow's womb to negotiating for hundreds of millions of dollars in the world's biggest banks on Wall Street. A friend of mine said, however, that the latter is pretty much the same as the first one, only that you are stretching into the other hole. I sort of agree.

To this date, I have worked in more than 60 countries on many kinds of projects with many kinds of people, mostly with global corporations and their communication departments but also with ordinary people in all walks of life. It has taught me a lot. Combining this with marriage and two kids makes it a lifelong lesson that I can barely begin to describe.

Recession. Big Time.

At the beginning of the '90s, there was a massive recession in Finland. Thousands of businesses went down, and established banks went out of business. It was a disaster for the country, not to mention its people who lost everything, and I was among those who almost lost everything. At 25, I had had my business running for some years and had been investing heavily in it, unfortunately with loaned money. I had about a million in debt when the interest rates skyrocketed to almost 20%. With disappearing business opportunities, it was practically impossible for me to pay my debts to the bank. I had to have all my assets set as a guarantee to the debtors, including my house and properties. I made it through the worst only because of my parents' intermediate help. It felt like I was hanging on a loose rope with my toes touching the ground every now and then.

After a couple of years, things started to brighten up a bit. There was more work to be done again. For me, it was also a more positive period as I met my future wife Minna. We fell in love pretty much immediately and had lots of fun together. I still had my dues, so I continued my workaholic lifestyle; when the business life speeded up, I got hooked up in working even more to pay off my debts. My wife-to-be Minna was also working a lot on her studies, so we were both occupied. Probably we both considered it the norm. At least I did—so much so that I had the flame burning on both ends of the candle.

You may guess what happens to a workaholic when there is too much work available? A burnout. When I had mine, I was not even aware of it. I sat in the editing studio, watching multiple computer and video screens like a cow on drugs. With a fuzzy brain and groggy eyes, I found it difficult to get started. My speculations over my less-than-mediocre performance resulted in me working more—in order to fill the gap. That was the only cure that I knew of at that time. Since I did not understand that I was actually in a state of burnout, I did not reach for help either. Surrounded by a family of workaholics, nobody noticed anything weird as I tried to work a lot. Several months went by with no major change in the situation, and suddenly I was awarded an entrepreneurship award for Successful Young Entrepreneur. I got rewarded for working more! What more could a workaholic ask for? Slowly, the effects of burnout started to fade away, and I regained a healthier state of mind. Nevertheless, I must admit that I do not remember much of the '90s.

Married. To What?

In 1996, I got married and had two wonderful children. It was an important time for embracing responsibility for the new members of the family. I still remember that feeling when driving back from the hospital when my daughter Nina, first, and later my son Lauri was born. I felt responsible for them, and I was grateful for this responsibility. The sad part was that my limited understanding knew only one way to prove it: Work.

I almost ruined my marriage in the beginning. There was a dream project at hand at work, and I had to travel for several weeks to create a big event for a long-time client. Completely soaked in the work, I trusted my wife would take care of things at home. She did, but she also exhausted herself. We both exhausted ourselves, just on different fronts. There just was too much on the table. Luckily, things settled a bit after that project, but a repetition already loomed in the horizon.

I was used to running the show at work, and that was often the case at home, too. When I was at home, I did more than my share of things and enjoyed it. I was used to doing things. We had a lot of good times: we traveled and did fun stuff together. After some years, another project required some travel, and this time my wife could not take it anymore without collapsing. A wake-up call number two for me. This time I started shaving off my time on work. Things seemed to return to a more normal pace. At first, cutting out a lot of work but then slowly, gradually taking it back again. Not to a degree it was before but to some extent anyway. Did I learn anything? Yes, I did but my inherited values of working were still too strong—way too strong.

Even though the working trips were now much shorter, I was still flying over 200,000 kilometers in six months when I started thinking about the purpose of it all. I had opportunities to meet and work with people in very different circumstances, and I am truly grateful for that. On the other hand, it made me question myself and the core operating principles of the world in general.

When a person working practically as a slave on a Dubai construction site can welcome me with his heart fully open and smiling, why is it so difficult for us westerners with all our possessions to do the same? Is it just that he does not know anything better? Or is it that I do not know better?

That was something that pushed me off the cliff to think about this more deeply. Even my trusted partner, Jari, in our company was surprised to see the change process in me. Thankfully, he understood, and I remain eternally grateful.

I somehow understood that I was repeating certain patterns, and I seemed to have the same answers to various questions. The answers tended to have the word 'work' included in them. I started questioning myself. Why was working so important to me? Why did I have difficulty with situations related to money and responsibilities? Why did I always put matters related to working for my customers first and my own life second? The last question formed the core of it all. My ultimate question was just Why did I ignore myself and my close ones? It took a long time for me to get on the track of the reality behind these scenes and processes. And, what I was to figure out was astonishing.

Waking Up

In 2006, I was handed some 'Indian spiritual guidance' in New Delhi in a form of a book handed forcefully by a bookseller on the street. The book was written by Holger Kersten and was titled *Jesus Lived in India*. The bookseller insisted that I read it by asserting that it had been written for me! A good salesperson, indeed. I ended up buying the book and read it on my way back to Finland. That was a start for questioning the old belief systems and questioning a lot of other things that I had considered to be the truth. It was also a start of reading a lot more.

Soon after that, I got another wake-up call in a form of an energetic and spiritual experience while editing a corporate film at the office. It was a late evening, and I was alone at the office when I felt tired of the work and closed my eyes for a moment and took a deep breath. Suddenly a huge vibrational kind of electrical force went through my body, and I thought that someone had come into the room and the breeze was due to that. That was not the case. I closed my eyes again, and off I went again. It was a bit spooky, and I didn't understand what was going on. Anyway, that experience was so powerful that it led me to do some research and I ended up reading about energy healing, spiritual awakenings, and some new-age stuff. I had heard my wife discussing Reiki healing with our next-door neighbor, but it never seemed to be my cup of tea. That's what I thought, but it did not prevent me from signing up for a Reiki course.

As a 'businessman', I didn't have the courage to tell anyone—not even my wife—that I had really signed up for a Reiki course. There it was: I, the man in the family, had gone loopy! There was no way I could tell anyone. So, for my wife, it was just another business course I was going to attend.

In that Reiki course, there was no spiritual awakening for me nor was there any levitation or any other spooky stuff you may have heard of people experiencing on their spiritual journeys. What there was, however, was an experience of something light, something other-worldly. It was something that I could not explain with my typical Scandinavian male-logic. I got proof of the energetic, mystical, and spiritual realm that existed somewhere around and within—proof that there's more out there there. That's how I would call it. That was the beginning of my journey.

Spiritual Journey?

I started reading more and more of my secret subject and took up meditation. I took part in various new courses and finally had the courage to tell my wife about the depth of my journeys. I still remember her face when we discussed my various energetic experiences over a cup of coffee. She was thinking that I had lost it. After finding my meditation practices to be difficult, I looked for help from the people renowned for their meditation skills. Dr. Deepak Chopra was one of them. Finally, after various courses and dozens of books, I ended up studying meditation at the Chopra Center University for Wellbeing to become a meditation teacher. Meditation had become part of me. I never thought I would become a meditation teacher but now that I had the personal experience of the benefits of the practice, I thought that "What the heck! I just might help others as well."

What I did was kind of coming out of the spiritual closet, and if you've read my story so far, you would understand that it was not a religious process for me. It was a spiritual process, and there is a big difference there. I believe that the world does not need any religion; what I think it needs is faith and love. Anyway, I decided to set up a local event on the subject and advertised the same in the front page of a local newspaper. It said "Meditation evening with Sampo," and it had my picture on it as well. It did not take too long for the phone to start ringing and people asking "Is everything ok with you?", "What have you been taking?", and "Have you become a monk or something?" I was kind of excited to see how the event would turn out.

I was happy to notice that about 30 people joined me in the event and that was quite a nice number considering the size of the town I lived in. I was also happy to see that some of the earlier curious callers joined me. They hadn't come to check if I was wearing a monk's robe or not; they were actually interested in the subject and wanted to hear me talk about stress and meditation. The event was a success, and I felt strangely good about my new take while knowing that it might cause some hassle in the business later on. In the end, even that turned out to be a positive hassle. I had just made some presuppositions based on my old belief systems that were actually not true.

I have been meditating every day since 2007. No matter how early I have to get up the morning, I make sure I have a moment for meditating before starting the engine. I want to do it.

Understanding Stress

So, something significant was dawning on me. I was finally beginning to understand that there is a reason for everything and that I have a say in that process. I had been carrying an excess load on my back. Well, that was both literally and metaphorically true. This resulted in stress. Very few people can say that they have never had any stress. At least I do not know of anyone who would attest to this. I did not feel any stress during my rush years—at least I was not aware of it. Maybe I was just so numb that the messages just didn't come through the filters. Also, back in the '90s when I 'tested' burnout, I was completely unaware of the things that were going on. When I was younger and immortal, I did not notice the bodily messages and symptoms of stress—quick heartbeats, high blood pressure, unusual hormonal activity—because I was an able man who was in a good shape. There were other bodily changes, too. My bloody leaflets were sticky and my digestion system malfunctioned, but I simply could not connect the dots. It just happens, and you don't necessarily know a thing about it. At least I didn't. Later on, I understood that I had been holding on to something that did not serve me anymore.

Inherited Burden

When I first read about the researches undertaken by Atlanta University[90] and New York's Mount Sinai Hospital[91], I could not believe it. The research pointed out that traumas are carried on for generations down the line just by the means of cell chemistry. The chemicals in our cells carry on the traumas even though we don't have the faintest idea of the original cause, and this is passed on for generations. Even though the traces start to faint after the fourth generation, they still exist. And we are not talking about the other ways of inheriting the traumas yet.

Considering all the inherited ailments that our family shares, it seems obvious that there is a connection between them and the past. Considering the several wars our beautiful country and our ancestors have been forced into in the last century alone, it is certain that there are old traumas in our cells. To top it off, I did unintentionally create some more with my blind devotion to work, which in hindsight was related to a sense of security. I really did not have a clear understanding of what had been going on in the lives of my parents and my grandparents. Now,

---

[90]   https://www.nature.com/news/
       fearful-memories-haunt-mouse-descendants-1.14272
[91]   https://www.biologicalpsychiatryjournal.com/article/
       S0006-3223(15)00652-6/abstract

many years later I have learnt some of it, but the true reality is still hidden from the cameras and my consciousness. Only my body knows it, and it eventually becomes the interpreter of my mental and spiritual life.

By working too many hours, ignoring my health, and ignoring everything else, I gave the hidden mental baggage an opportunity to turn into physical ailments in my body. It comes in so many different ways that you really have to know where to look to be able to notice it. The signals are sometimes so faint that the normal daily noise surpasses them with ease. For me, not noticing them in time meant a couple of surgeries.

O' My Mind

My dear teacher, also the co-founder of the Chopra Center, Dr. David Simon once made a bold claim that 95% of all our bodily ailments have to do with our minds and they are actually derived from the mind. For me, with very limited understanding of all this at that time, that was an outrageous statement. I was triggered to study the subject more because of this. I would like to tip my thankful hat to David for providing an impetus.

After studying MetaHealth, I have understood that there is a direct link among emotions, the brain, and bodily tissues and organs. That has been a huge revelation for me. MetaHealth is a completely new line of research that studies connections between emotions and organs and tissues, and it has already proven its importance in understanding traumas and why they play such an important role in our well-being. Today, there is a good bunch of doctors and health professionals around the world studying this more and actively use their understanding to help their patients. I really wish that it becomes a new paradigm for treating patients. Actually, I hope that it clearly surpasses the drug distribution business that seems to be our new global religion.

For me, all this was a call for a dance. I wanted to know more, so I dived into spiritual well-being studies in many forms: different energy healing techniques, Spiritual Coach studies, Life Coach Studies, Team Coach Studies, and Neuro Linguistic Programming (NLP), among many others, became a natural way to look at things. I believe that life is like an old wooden wheel, and we are at the center (the hub) of it. We need to be able to look at the hub from all different angles to be able to see both the light and the shadow. Similarly, we also need to be seen from different angles. Only then we will become strong enough to take on whatever life throws at us. The wheel is only strong when it has all the spokes in place. Only then the wheel will carry the load on a rocky road.

My Beliefs

I was once asked if I knew the answer to what percentage of the total mind is the subconscious mind? I did not know the answer. Well, it is roughly 98%. The conscious mind occupies about 2% of the mind space. Is it true that 98% of the choices in my life are made on a subconscious autopilot? Pretty much. When I think of my typical day in life I wake up at a certain time, do certain routines, meditate, eat a certain type of breakfast, take certain turns in crossings, sit at the same location in a coffee shop, etc. If you see, these are pretty much the same choices day in and day out.

Where do all these choices come from? Where does my habit of excess working come from?

As I mentioned earlier, a lot of them are inherited from our parents, the society, schooling systems, working environments, religious institutions, and so on. Nevertheless, they are something that we have either inherited or learned, yet they form the foundation of our belief system. We often believe they are the natural and the only way to be and act. Eventually, we realize that they are just thoughts or ideas based on our values and beliefs. Just thoughts.

"My work is my life!"

"She doesn't love me anymore!"

"I am not good enough!"

"I cannot make it through my working day. There is no way I can come up with the money for my bills. I need to work more. I am scared."

These were statements from my mind. Were they true? Were they absolutely true and not only a result of my imagination? They were true to me, but they were also a result of my imagination.

For me, the capitalist worldview was a truth. Money was a truth. Doctor's prescriptions were a truth. Working a lot was a truth. Monogamy was a truth. Social ideals (a beautiful wife, a house in the suburbs, a Volvo station wagon, and a golden retriever) were a truth. But did the same truths apply to others? If you ask indigenous people or other people with a close connection to nature about the same, the results would definitely be different.

Money, or paper currency, is not worth much if there is no agreement on the interchangeability of it. The social ideals vary hugely on a cultural basis. So, if they are not the absolute truths, could it be that I could let go of some of my truths? When I finally started re-considering such truths, it became obvious that we all have truths of our own. Maybe there is an alternative way that could be applied. We really should consider letting go of many of our truths.

Why should I let go of thoughts, emotions, actions, and stuff? There is a simple answer to that. Holding decisively onto anything will eventually make us ill, either mentally or physically. Or both. It can also prevent us from receiving what life has in store for us. We have to clear some space for the new to appear. So, holding on to something is holding us back in many ways. The comfort of material possessions is an illusion; we cannot take any of it with us when we leave this life. It is about time we cut the chain of inherited traumas. We can do this by choosing consciously.

After the universe started to offer me some guidance toward my very own path, I've come to realize that either I volunteer to let go of things or the universe does it for me. Since I was a bit of a slow learner or just stubborn, it has partially done it for me. For example, I had to let go of a big chunk of my earthly possessions, including land. (Many tribes and indigenous cultures believe that we do not own the land, but it owns us.)

I have been close to bankruptcy, almost on the verge of a divorce many times, and experienced recession several times. I have had a severe burnout, lost dear friends, and had so many other things almost pulling me under or hanging me from my tie that I do know that they have been a bit more than just 'gentle guidance' to help me correct my course toward my true calling. And, that's exactly what I am doing now. I have been able to let go of so many thoughts and things that I don't even remember all of them. Once you are on your own track, there is no turning back. To be completely honest, I admit that there is still a lot more to let go. I also know that there will be sore points in my life, but they will not push me off anymore.

Death. The most important teacher.

I have been helping and coaching people for many years now. and the possibility to work with the terminally ill was a game changer for me. I had studied many religious traditions of the world, and I felt that none of them is the only truth. They all have love at the core, yet many of them have become just forms of controlling people. After having been taught about the concept of **life after death** in many courses and from many sources, after having read countless books about heaven and angels and consciousness in general, it only became a reality for me when I experienced the power of it. I want to share one of the most important experiences with you.

Some years ago, a friend of mine asked me if I could go and help a couple with their situation. The core of the situation was a deadly brain tumor in the head of the man in his forties and he had been given a couple of weeks of time on this planet and had already been advised to make the necessary earthly arrangements as soon as possible. So, I paid them a visit. I stepped into the house and saw a girl of about 2.5 years of age running around happily. Her mother apologized for her behavior and explained that her daughter was diagnosed with

ADHD—Attention Deficit Hyperactivity Disorder. I kneeled down in front of the girl and asked if she would give me a low-five clap on my hands. What happened then was miraculous. This girl put her hands on mine and held them there for a good while, looked at her hands, then looked at me in the eyes, and looked back at our hands again. This went on for a good minute or so, and her mother looked at me with a scared face. She asked, "What are you doing to her?" The girl then gave a short laugh in my direction and said "Hi" and ran away. That was a holy encounter where we both knew that we knew each other from some other dimension or domain. I answered her mother "Old friends just greeted each other." We had never seen each other before.

But the big thing was yet to come. The women of the house went for a walk leaving me and her husband alone for the session that was yet to be defined. I had absolutely no clue as to what I was supposed to do. I asked him if it was okay for him to have an energy channeling session, which he agreed to and mentioned as an aside that he had no faith in alternative stuff. However, he was in a situation that was unusual, and he agreed anyway. I prepared myself for the session by asking to be connected to the pure source of universal love—the thing I always do.

He was sitting on a chair and I started my session by standing behind him and laying my hands on his shoulders. After a while, I lifted my hands a bit up and felt enormous energy flowing through me. I lifted my hands a bit more and the power of the flow got stronger. I opened my eyes and saw the room becoming alive with colors changing and walls moving very gently. It was indeed an energy soup or a melange of things that I saw. At that moment I understood that I was playing my tiny part in a much, much bigger play. A play of something divine and my role was to keep my ego and the self outside the process. The 'I' had no role in it. The session lasted for about half an hour and after finishing, I asked the man about his experience and feelings. His reply was punctuated with several sighs. He said, "Phew, I cannot explain it. I cannot put it in words. What was it that just happened?" He got it exactly right. The words are a mediocre and limited way for describing something that is not meant to be expressed in words. These things are meant to be experienced. They are beyond this earthly, worldly world. Some months later, he passed away. Before he did, he experienced moments of normalcy where the disease had disappeared, but it re-emerged again. I thought that was it.

But it was not. The widow asked me to join her for visiting his body at the mortuary. Again, I was full of doubt and was wondering how could I help her on such a visit. The universe knew it better, though. I agreed to join her on the trip, and I went to pick her up for a ride to the mortuary. I was sitting in my car and was waiting for her to come down from her apartment. I sat there and meditated for a moment. When I looked at the blue summer sky with little puffy clouds, I witnessed something magical. The clouds started to form an image of the deceased man's smiling face and said, "Please tell her that everything is okay here, all is well, no need to worry." I was amazed and started looking for my mobile to take a photograph of that very unique experience. By the time I found it, the clouds had already moved on. My rational mind had wanted evidence of something holy. Clearly, that is not the way it works.

She arrived and sat down next to me. I told her what I had just witnessed and told her his greetings. With tears in our eyes, we started the ride toward the mortuary. It became a journey of very deep integration into the surrounding traffic and environment; it was also timeless. We were part of everything, and everything was part of us. For me, **a journey** is a trip that transforms the self. This was a Journey with a capital J indeed. After the funeral, she recovered from the sorrow in a matter of a couple of weeks and could help as a peer-helper for others in a similar situation. The Journey had become a Voyage, which I think is a Journey that you learn from and return to help other people to change as well—a voyage beyond the self. All this was a signature event for me. I really got the signature on everything I had been taught about life after death. The most beautiful signature signed by the universe itself. I was and am not afraid of death anymore.

My father passed away ten days ago. Everything I had learned about death in the earlier situations was a preparation for this important moment. I had asked the universe to allow me to be present when the time comes and it turned out to be so. Before and at the very moment of the Spirit leaving his body, I felt the presence of spiritual beings. While holding my father's hand, I felt reassured and at peace. Thank You, Universe. All is well.

Letting Go

We should die for something each and every day. Eventually, we will have to let go of everything. I really mean everything— even the stuff that we love the most. If we are ready to let go before we have to leave this realm of existence, it will create much more space for true enjoyment. When you are no longer attached to things, people, events, or the outcome of your actions, the activity becomes much easier. It becomes natural. There is no more drama in it. When something is natural, there is no resistance and all the energy is free to move in the best possible way. That is being free. That is the Art of Letting Go.

How do I let go, you may ask. There are many ways to do it. My manners and methods are the most obvious ones.

I started to meditate. Meditation was not a means of letting go at first. I started meditating hoping to relax. Now after thousands of meditation sessions and hours, it has become a part of me. It serves as that moment where I may lose the sense of time and place and just be. It is not something I have to do, but something I want to do. It helps me remember my true being every day. I also trust in intuition, and meditation is the portal for activating intuition. It is the hidden messenger that is always available for us. I have also had the pleasure of learning several tools and techniques that have helped me to let go of things that I was not even aware of.

These methods and techniques have been beneficial for me:

1. Go for a walk in the forest. Stop there to listen and breathe. Use all your senses and enjoy the natural healing that forests provide. This is something that Japanese doctors write as a prescription for stress and mental challenges, and it works, thanks to its natural meditative properties. We just need to make sure that the forests stay in good health and remain available for us in return.
2. A technique for understanding that breathing is not only about taking in air and oxygen but a process of exchanging energy. Just imagine each inhalation coming in through the top of your head and filling up your chest with light. Imagine each exhalation freeing yourself from any burden

and stuff that does not serve you anymore. Keep doing these and soon you will notice a beautiful exchange of energy vibrating in your body. Everything vibrates, and so do we.

3. A guided meditation on 'The Art of Letting Go' could also be helpful. Go to YouTube and type the same and my name in the search field and hit enter. Or even better, have it on your mobile on the Insight Timer app. This has helped millions of people around the world, and I continue to get positive, loving feedback for it.

4. A simple meditation of So-Hum. Sit comfortably and allow your hands to rest on your lap, preferably with your palms facing up. Close your eyes and breathe naturally with slow, deep breaths. With each inhalation, think of the word **So**; with each exhalation, think of the word **Hum**. Keep doing this for a couple of minutes, and you will notice a difference. This works even in a meeting if you have trouble focusing or find the energy of the setting upsetting.

Keep in mind that meditation is not something you do. It is something that you allow to happen. The less you try, the more you will receive; eventually when you do nothing, you will receive everything. Even though I still have the stuff to let go of, my life is now more aligned with my inner calling and purpose in life.

I intend to use the rest of my life for helping people to discover **The Art of Letting Go** while enjoying the ride. What is your intention?

Sampo Manninen

Sampo Manninen has combined more than 30 years of global communication business to a life of a father, a husband and a student of life. During the last 15 years, he has also dived deep into the world of spiritual growth. Besides being a CEO of his long-time business, he is also a Spiritual Coach, LCA Life Coach, Team Coach, Meditation Teacher and a specialist in many other walks of life, such as NLP. He is a wanted and engaging speaker in events, radio, TV shows, and other media. He is also an entertaining read with a deep insight into being both a spiritual and a physical being in the modern world. Thanks to his presence and experience in life, he has been able to help thousands of people to discover their true inner calling and to let go of the burden of the past.

Learn more about how you can find a deeper purpose in your own life by visiting www.sampomanninen.com.

Contact Information

Facebook: https://www.facebook.com/SampoCoac

The Bomb, the Mountain, and the Art of Walking

Sasha Raskin

I'm writing this while resting at a fourth of the way up the *grind* hike (its official name) at Vancouver, Canada. Twice higher than the 102-floor Empire State Building, engulfed inside a magnificent rainforest, this hike makes some individuals reach the borders of their physical and mental abilities. In this green lung of planet Earth, human lungs struggle for air, and their faces turn red. Meanwhile, the people who climb the mountain fall into a deep state of trance.

As I sit at the sides of the trail and rest, I'm watching some of them. Most people just keep on moving, perhaps afraid to stop. This story is about a bomb that went off in Israel, a few meters away from me, and is also about the nearly impossible climb of the great grind in Canada. But, most of all, this story is about humans as they walk the face of the Earth. In a symbolic and quite literal way, it also reflects what I am helping my clients with on a daily basis, whether they are individuals, couples, families, organizations, or counseling students. As a psychotherapist, coach, and counseling teacher, I help them achieve the things they did not think possible. I also aid them to reach places that are out of their comfort zones, to keep on walking even when it gets really tough to continue, and to create a lifestyle where they have time to have fun and take breaks. I would not be here today if I did not have mentors in my life who helped me do the same. There is no blood or bodies in my story, even though it involves a bomb in Israel. But there is plenty of hope and love for the human spirit that has infinite potential for growth and connection. In my work, I pass on what others have done for me. I help people continue walking forward, while they're climbing their mountains and overcoming their bombs.

If you go visit almost any coach's website, you'll probably find a lengthy explanation stating that coaching is not psychotherapy. However, the way I practice psychotherapy and the way I coach is not very different. In fact, I am not sure how much it matters if the person who is walking with you is a priest, a rabbi, an imam, a coach, a psychotherapist, a truly good friend, a family member, or your romantic partner. The important question to ask is in a sense a scientific one—does it work for you or not?

My office walls are covered with diplomas, but beyond the initial trust that these diplomas create, none of my clients really cares about them. They are only interested in one thing: Can I help them move forward toward the lives that they want for themselves? And even better, can I help them to pass that imaginary barrier to discover a life that is fulfilling beyond what they thought was possible and to help them believe that they deserve it?

I sit under a huge rainforest tree, completely awake. I feel the blood pulsating in my veins, the cold air, and the sweat of my forehead. A slight wind is touching my bare feet as I let them breathe and rest from the effort of climbing the endless stairs. There is nothing better than to feel fully awake and fully present, playing outside of one's comfort zone. However, this has not always been the case. In my teenage years, I suddenly realized that I am dreaming a dream—that I am operating in a pre-conditioned, pre-programmed way. As I grew up, I discovered the many ways in which I was living my life habitually, within the illusion of safety—buying the same groceries, ordering the same favorite dish at restaurants, and having the same type of romantic relationships. I felt comfortable, but as the Pink Floyd song goes, I really was comfortably numb.

Once I started noticing more and more, it was as if the illusion of freedom suddenly burst. What I perceived to be a clear choice was many times just a habit, influenced by my parents, school, and society. I based my choices in life on what was familiar and safe. My safety zone was a golden cage I chose for myself, and for the big part of the day, I was not even aware of it. I was trapped in constantly rehashing the past and planning the future, while the present moment was passing me by. I was drifting on autopilot. This was me, and many times it still is, but let's talk about you for a moment. What are you thinking about right now? How awake are you? Can you notice the next moment when you will lose focus and let your thoughts drift away? When will be the next time when you will automatically open your mailbox or Facebook just because it is one click away? And the big question, WHO'S THE ONE WHO IS REALLY IN CONTROL? And if for a moment, you entertain the idea that you are living your life partially asleep, then how do you WAKE UP?

The Bomb

Ten years ago, when I was on my way to a psychology undergrad class in Jerusalem, Israel, a bomb went off as I got out of the bus at the central bus station. It was very close and extremely loud. That foreign sound shattered the air and was both so sudden and overwhelmingly loud that I knew right away what it was.

The confusion on the faces of people around me as they struggle to climb the Grouse mountain reminds me of that time. They carry an expression of fear. Will I make it? Will I survive? After the bomb went off, I did make it, I did survive, and I kept walking for hours without stopping. That sudden burst of fear that made a lot of sense back then still keeps coming back to me, especially in moments of doubt. I have learned to recognize it very well—the tightness in my stomach and the lightheadedness as if the ground is disappearing beneath me. Where do these feelings come from? What is generating this texture of doubt and fear? When I am able to identify it for myself and with my clients, it is one big step through what stops us living a truly meaningful life.

Even though we rarely mention it, at the center of our lives is the most basic fear of death. The big question underneath this mask of trance is, "Do I have what it takes, will I safely get from point A to B?" I believe that this is the main reason as to why my clients come to see me when they're in a place where they keep on doing things that they don't want to be doing and keep postponing the things that really matter.

I am proud and excited to constantly see my clients achieve incredible results. For example, this one revolutionary company I coached created the first preventive wellness platform and set a goal to prevent 70% health problems by using technology. Within a few months, they launched their product, secured work relationships with leading hospitals, authors, and health experts in four continents, and launched their pilot program. During the first two months of our work together, the CEO struggled to even pronounce the word CEO out loud. It is scary to fully step into a leadership role and into personal power. He was scared to fail as he was scared to succeed. I felt waves of pride and excitement washing my body as I was watching him after a few months at the launch of his company's product, in front of three thousand people, introducing himself as a CEO—his voice firm and clear. A few minutes later he was sharing, with the same voice, a story of his own grief. Power and vulnerability. Inner power unfolds.

A different company I coached created an innovative healthcare platform that provides the technology and tools needed for organizations and founders, and providers to map out both personal and organizational networks and strengthen social connectedness for people. They were able to launch their product and secure funding. I helped them navigate the power struggles at the company, create clear boundaries, empower each other, and help each other feel seen. They were able to succeed even though a prominent person involved quit unexpectedly due to a family emergency right before the launch. He left with love and respect. At that session, everyone shed a tear. Something that could have broken a company made them stronger.

You do not have to be a CEO to grow as a leader. Some of my clients who do not manage companies or startups found their inner power in our leadership coaching. I've listed some examples here.

- A writer who spent 19 years on writing and rewriting his book finally published it two months after we started working together.
- A burnt-out programmer decided to quit his job after 10 years and is now one of the leaders at a successful new tech company.
- A coach who had a dream to build a center for women's empowerment recruited more than 50 new clients within two weeks.
- A retired Physics professor grew his part-time hobby into an essential part of a prominent thought-leader's book. He rebuilt a fulfilling life after a painful divorce.

Like many of my clients, for many years, I chased after what was not essential and focused on things that I didn't really care about. I started many companies: a food catering, marketing agency, a web design company, and a sound equipment company. While I achieved success, **I was focusing on all the wrong things.** My calling is to touch lives and help others fulfill their dreams. By letting go of the unnecessary, I decided to study and practice what I was most interested in.

Why is it that people many times do what they don't want to be doing (by postponing indefinitely) the dreams that they truly want to achieve? After six years of changing my majors in school, I finally decided to study what I really wanted to study—the human mind. I learned how people think and make decisions in my Bachelor of Arts program in Psychology. I learned how to help people to turn their lives around in my Master of Arts Counseling program. I learned how to help families and couples create the lives that they wanted as a certified marriage and family therapist. I make an impact in the field by training the next generation of therapists and coaches at my Ph.D. program in Counseling Education and Supervision and as a Counseling Teacher at Naropa University. I have coached hundreds of individuals, couples, families, and organizations to create the changes that they struggled to create on their own. And I do this with a severe ADHD and with English as my third language. So truly, if I can do it, anyone can.

And yes, surviving that bomb is also a part of my story. Ten years ago, when I heard the loud sound of the explosion and looked around, I knew it was a bomb that went off and I had just survived a terrorist attack. My instincts pushed me to start walking away. The same way they push me today to keep climbing the Grouse mountain, even though my body says no.

Unfortunately, living in Israel in my teenage years meant facing the possibility of dying in a terror attack daily. They were frequent occurrences, and people, tragically, somehow got used to them. When the bomb blew up, I did not know exactly where it had happened, but I did know that I needed to get away as fast as possible because there might be another bomb. My life did not pass in front of my eyes, as is often described in novels. The two only thoughts that I had were, "I need to get out of here right now" and "I need to make it to class." I started walking fast, but after a minute I stopped to look around and see if anyone needed my help. I did not see anybody on the ground. What I did see was another bus coming toward me, with some liquid dripping from it, and with both doors open, empty of people. Once again, my mind emptied of all thoughts except two: get out and get to my class.

I started walking again, very fast, while calling my mother, to tell her that everything is alright. We talked, and she asked me if I was okay. I said I was. She was sweet and supportive and did not question my weird idea of going to class after surviving an explosion. She knew what I knew; it was not about the destination. The class by itself did not matter as much as the act of walking.

I continued calling family members and friends as I walked, supported in my unusual journey by people that I loved and that I knew loved me. Their support was like the wind to my sails. My movement was fueled by their caring words. I posted on social media about what had happened and received love from all over the world. I felt connected, and I did not feel alone. I knew that I needed to continue moving forward, even though there was no real reason to do so. From what I know as a psychotherapist today, the fact that I was moving the body for hours after that traumatic experience and the fact that I was processing the information with people I trusted prevented me from developing PTSD. My movement allowed a trauma release in the same way that animals in the wild shake after they play dead to escape a predator. Needless to say, I was late for class. By five hours. It will take me approximately the same time to climb the mountain.

The Mountain

I'm resting now after walking uphill for three hours in what has been the steepest climb of my life. I'm almost at the top of the mountain, but now that I'm close to being done, I feel sad. The mental effort that it takes to climb one wooden step after another cannot be described easily. I am sure that for athletes it probably would not be as difficult. But, I am in pretty good shape, and it was extremely strenuous for me. And the majority of the people here are not athletes either. It is the surprise really that got me. For some reason, I thought that it would be easy. But as that song goes, *no one ever told you it's going to be easy...*

I was lured here by TripAdvisor's suggestion, and my initial plan was to take the train up the hill to enjoy the view. But when I arrived, after walking on the breathtaking Capilano hanging bridges, I couldn't get enough of the rainforests. After experiencing the magnificence of the gracious giant trees for the first time in my life at the Capilano park, I felt completely alive. The smell of rain and the incredible height of the trees touching the skies got me in a state of flow. I was completely awake from a long dream. The promise of what's to come can be a very powerful motivating force. So, in the heat of the moment, I decided that I will climb the mountain by foot instead. It was a spontaneous decision when I decided that I am going all the way to the top. I found the big red disclosure sign about the park taking no responsibility for any accidental injury or death to be somewhat amusing, but disturbing as well. However, it did not seem to stop the families that passed through. It didn't stop me either.

After fifteen minutes, I started to realize what I had gotten myself into. It was literally a non-stop climbing up journey. The stairs that were made from pieces of trees, spaced far apart, looked picturesque, but it did not make them any fewer stairs and any less arduous. And then at some point, when I was completely out of breath, I suddenly realized that the numbers I saw for the third time on a tree were not random. 3/40 meant that even after all that tremendous amount of effort, I still had 37/40 left to climb. And that's when the fear kicked in. Yep. That old familiar "Will I make it?" voice. That very familiar, very alive awakening to the fact that I exist and do want to continue to exist. At that point, I, of course, could have turned back and come down the mountain. But that would be a defeat. I felt the guilt, and I knew that it could direct me down the hill or be the fuel to push me up. I chose up. Just like that day, ten years ago, when I decided to keep walking for hours after the explosion, and even in that horrible moment, to stay in control.

A few hours later, at the moment, I am sitting under a tree that has the number 30/40 on it. I am left with only one-fourth of the climb. I am thinking of all the parallels between the climb and the hours I walked after the bomb went off, and how these experiences and similar ones like them shape my life. I am transformed not so much by what life brings, but by my ability to choose how to respond to them. I am shaped by the experiences that I choose to create for myself, and the way that I respond when obstacles arise.

I feel the emptiness that comes with approaching the top of the mountain and the end of the climb. It is such a mysterious feeling. Up until now, all that I could think about while moving my feet and catching my breath was how badly I wanted it to end. But, now that the end is near, I just want it to last. I am realizing how difficult it was at the beginning, but now that I see the end, even though I am more exhausted, it is so much easier. I see this many times with my clients. The most important thing is to start the journey. Once they start moving, the momentum carries them forward. They create a stack of successes that they can look back at, and that is all the proof they need to believe that they can do this.

The manner in which I see people look at each other while they climb the mountain stairs, encouraged by others, reminds me of my clients. Coaching them is so much easier when my clients know that they are supported by me and others in their lives. It is just so much simpler to keep on moving in life when you know that you're not doing this alone and that others are moving with you, too. This is why it is important to surround yourself with the right people. It is like the old saying that you are the average of the five people who you hang out with the most. I am not sure if I would continue climbing the mountain stairs if I was surrounded by people who were going down after giving up. Everyone around me continued walking up, no matter how tough it got.

I am noticing how much of this collaborative climbing is a game that people are playing together. There is a sense of competition, but it is a healthy one. It is a game that everyone will win, not on the account of someone else but by sharing a victory. And we're playing this game literally one step at a time. When I notice that the goals of my clients get overwhelming, it is usually a matter of remembering that they do not need to focus on all the steps at once. They just need to take one step at a time.

When I was working as a staff member at a substance abuse recovery facility, we would often remind the residents that they did not need to focus on finishing the entire three months of the program. All they needed to do was to finish that one day. And then do it again the following day. This little game of taking one step at a time that we play now is how nature works. It has worked this way since time immemorial. We're back to where we started as a species—far away from our phones, computers, and cars. We are back to the most basic way of living, taking the time out from our busy lives to remember. And what we discover together, once again, as we reach the top is that impossible things are always so much easier than what they seem to be.

The Coaching and the Therapy

So how do I help my psychotherapy and coaching clients to climb their mountains and overcome their bombs?

As a contemplative therapist in training, my home base is a humanistic and strengths-based approach, which is by itself a synthesis of many western and eastern approaches. From western psychology and psychotherapy, it draws from humanistic psychology, Freud's psychoanalytic theory, Jungian analytical theory, Rogerian person-centered therapy, and positive psychology. From the eastern traditions, contemplative psychotherapy draws from 2,400 years of contemplative practices, psychologies, and philosophies such as Buddhist psychology, meditation, and yoga.

While I find the empathic and person-centered contemplative approach to be incredibly helpful in creating a deep therapeutic bind with my clients, I believe it can go to much greater lengths when coupled with much more active marriage and family therapy modalities. Couples and family therapy is a huge umbrella for a myriad of theories and therapy modalities, some drawing from each other and some improving upon each other. They all, however, look at the world through a systemic point of view. As a certified marriage and family therapist, I am grateful to be able to use the many family therapy theories, assessments, and interventions I have been trained in, including but not limited to Bowenian family therapy, structural family therapy, strategic family therapy, emotionally focused couples and family therapy, narrative therapy, Gottam couples therapy and others.

The theories that I use complement each other by combining cognitive and emotional insight, taking action, and experiential relationship building. The contemplative approach allows the creation of a safe, supportive, and empathic environment. The clients learn to put into words their thoughts, emotions, and physical sensations and gain deep insights and integrate their experiences. In contemplative psychotherapy, the sharing and the clarity with a mindful and present therapist allows a sense of calmness of relief for the clients, and a renewed sense of trust in themselves and others. New ways of interactions, together with a deep emotional bond, can occur with the contemplative therapist, which can be applied to any other relationships in the clients' lives. Also, the strengths-based approach, together with the unconditional positive regard of contemplative psychotherapy, empower the clients to view themselves more positively, to believe in themselves and to feel encouraged to take more risks and step out of their comfort zone.

That being said, contemplative psychotherapy is a highly person-centered model, in which the session is mostly led by the client and the therapist is mainly providing empathic presence. The therapist is encouraged to let go of any agenda, not to give any advice, and not to be an obstacle between the client and healing. Even though research shows that the therapeutic relationship plays an immense role in how helpful the clients feel the therapy was, this kind of unstructured model cannot be very useful in helping the client to create change promptly. Also, the model is more suited toward working with individuals than working with couples or families. Merely listening to a couple in distress or just replaying the same family quarrel in the therapy office will not cut it. There needs to be experiential work to experience and practice new ways of interaction to reduce conflict and increase friendship. If the couple or the family would continue having the same fight, even though it is in front of a nodding compassionate therapist, it would be nothing more than a costly fight.

Contemplative psychotherapy is an incredibly powerful tool to create a safe container for therapy to happen. To adapt it for accelerated growth, and for working with couples and families, this is my call of action: the experiential elements and the systemic view that marriage and family therapy bring to the table.

One might ask, how does the contemplative view, which encourages letting go of agenda and a more passive role of a therapist, work with the more active modalities of family therapy. The answer is that the modalities I use from family therapy are by themselves strengths-based and very much humanistic in nature so that there is an overarching belief in human potential. The systemic view of focusing on the whole system, such as family and the society in large, is very much in correlation with the Buddhist view of interconnectedness that the contemplative psychology theory draws from. In both approaches, humans are connected much more than they think, and when one is affected, many more get affected as well. The systemic theory in family therapy and the Buddhist approach seek the true meaning and life's organizing force in our connection with others. Thich Nhat Hanh (1988) in one piece of advice summarizes how this interconnectedness should be nurtured, "If you wish to have children, please do something for the world you will bring them into."

When I lean more toward the contemplative psychotherapy style, very much affected by the Rogerian client-centered approach, I am not the one leading or prompting. At the same time, many of the interventions of family therapy that I use are very much the opposite, very direct, and very much leading the clients toward the goals they identified at the beginning of our work together. The thing is that I do not have to choose one approach or the other. Just like jazz, since I know the rules very well, I can drop the rules entirely and just enjoy being in the moment—completely present, improvising, and letting the interventions to choose themselves. There is tremendous freedom in not subscribing to the active role of a family therapist, or what looks to the outsider as the passive role of the contemplative psychotherapist. I can be both, depending on the client and the moment. Sometimes clients just want to vent and want to be heard. Sometimes, they very clearly want to create specific changes in their lives but do not know how. By combining contemplative psychotherapy with family therapy, I can be useful in doing both.

Combining the modalities mentioned above, however, is both an art and a skill. I need to be always attentive to the needs of the clients, determining when I need to be merely warm and attentive, and when my client is stuck in a loop—they are trapped in retelling the same story over and over again. Sometimes they enact the same old unhelpful behaviors with their partners or family members in the office. I step in, depending on the situation. There are times when I am more active-directive and probing, sometimes even challenging, deferring more toward the active styles of family therapy. For example, in couples therapy, especially starting with the fourth session, after I have gathered all the information I needed, and when I am practicing emotionally focused couples therapy, it is me who will many a time be doing most of the talking, rephrasing, and integrating their experiences, for the sake of both clients. In this way, they can both feel seen and heard by me, start to feel safe, and go deeper into exploring their feeling. I will gradually begin incorporating more emotional words so that we can move from just sharing content of the problems in the couple's relationship toward exploring the emotional impact that the negative cycle has on them, and by doing so, moving them toward a deep emotional bond. In doing so, I have a clear agenda: to facilitate the couple's work toward a secure attachment. Therefore, my personalized integrative theoretical model for conceptualization and working with individuals, couples, and families includes a cyclical flow between three components:

1. Assessment
2. Goal setting
3. Therapeutic work/Coaching

The thread that glues all these components together is the therapeutic/coaching relationship, which stems from the humanistic, person-centered, and holistic view that is the center of contemplative psychotherapy. None of this work would be possible if the therapist fails to create a sense of safety, warmth, compassion, and unconditional positive regard. If the therapist does succeed in that, gradually of course, then there is space for the therapeutic work to occur, and there is a buy-in on the client's end to experiment with sometimes a very new way of interacting and acting of the family therapy modalities.

In other words, being a contemplative psychotherapist gives me the ground to support my clients in an empathic way to experiment with new ways of being in the world—both in terms of more vulnerable sharing and taking further action in the world, in the office, and in their everyday lives. Thus, we use the therapeutic alliance for the sake of growth and healing. The paradox of change from Gestalt therapy then comes into play. If the client feels fully accepted, then there is a safe ground to experiment with change. The fear of failure is diminished as well as the fear of success. If the client knows and feels that no matter what they do in the world, they will be unconditionally accepted by me, they give themselves permission to play. Just like the child that developed a secure attachment with their parent in childhood feels comfortable as an adult to step outside of the comfort zone because they did so successfully many times in their childhood, in the same way, supported by the accepting therapeutic relationship, clients can step out of their comfort zone and let themselves grow.

The contemplative practices and psychologies that are incorporated in the contemplative psychotherapy model are tremendously supportive for my clients and me in the sometimes intensive and lengthy therapeutic work. Mindfulness plays a big part in helping me be calm and present, even amid the most challenging moments. For example, when a client shares a trauma or when an argument between a couple or family members get escalated, I remain grounded by doing mindfulness practices. I focus on my breath throughout the session and maintain a daily meditation practice; in doing so, I make sure that I am fully there for my clients to support them through the struggles, without them worrying about needing to take care of and safeguarding me from their problems. Additionally, almost all of my clients start a meditation practice from the moment we start working together. The tremendous benefits that a meditation practice brings are extensively supported by research. By helping my clients to create the habit of meditating daily, many times using accountability, we create another source of support, that is available for them for free, every day. Self-care is then expanded from one weekly therapy session to a daily practice that promotes relaxation and also prevents stress. In the longer term, meditation also brings powerful insights, and these can be further explored in therapy. After the meditation practice has been established, and many times in parallel, or instead, if the clients do not feel that meditation practice is something they want, we explore and practice mindfulness in the session. I may do a grounding exercise in the meeting if I see that the client's nervous system is overwhelmed. By doing this, I introduce a simple way to deal with emotions and also help the client to come back to a place where the therapy session can be useful.

My personal values and worldview have a lot to do with my model. The Buddhist idea in contemplative psychotherapy that everything is temporary and one does not need to take it personally is something I reflect on a lot during the sessions. In doing so, there can be a relief from the idea that things should always be perfect or that when things are not going the way my clients want, it is them against the world. The sense of constant struggle can be lifted; acceptance, with courage, to change things that my clients want to change can be accomplished.

I also believe in the tremendous power of family and romantic relationships. This has brought me to not just work with families and couples and learn as much as I can about the many family therapy modalities but also work from that model even when dealing with individuals. My assessment always includes getting as much information as I can about the people and family members in their lives, including the relationships among them. I keep referring to these people as sources of support, especially when my clients feel that they have to do everything themselves or when they are afraid to seek assistance from others. I believe that we are primarily social creatures and that our lives are tremendously enriched by a deep emotional connection to others. One of my goals in therapy is to create such a connection between myself and my clients and help and empower them to do so in their other relationships. I believe this to be an important goal; In the majority of the time that I spend in therapy with family and couples, we do experiential work, connecting with each other in a more profound and more vulnerable way.

However, it is important for me to remember that my particular model is not a perfect fit for everyone. Some clients might benefit much more from a very structured clear model, such as CBT, while some clients might just want to talk about their week. In such cases, goal setting in therapy might sound utterly alien to them. I completely understand that, and the Buddhist idea of non-attachment is definitely helpful in such a scenario.

That being said, I strive to make sure that I do the best on my end to fit the model to the needs of my clients. This from an ethical standpoint and also taking into account multicultural and diversity issues. For example, I am cautious with cultural appropriation. Even though Buddhist concepts are very close to my heart and are a central piece in contemplative psychotherapy, my office is not filled with statues of Buddha. Some clients might not feel comfortable with that, and I do not want to devalue cultural pieces of Buddhist countries where I did not grow up. Another critical point for me is to make sure that I listen to the needs of my clients. If they need to create a specific change in their life, I will not indulge in a lengthy contemplative psychotherapy process of emotional exploration.

For instance, let us assume Tonny, a thirty-year-old Buddhist male from India comes to see me because he has been unemployed for two years and is living with his parents. He experiences a lot of shame and guilt since he is entirely supported by his parents. Their savings are also running out, and they have implied that they can no longer support Tonny. My primary goal is to first create a safe and accepting container for Tonny to feel heard, seen, and validated—both for his struggle and his emotional experience. While the contemplative psychotherapy model implies non-agenda and letting the client lead the session, there is a dire need on my client's end and for his family for him to find a job; avoiding that would be doing them a disservice. I would ask him about his goals, and if he is open to it, I will work with him on finding a job. To do so, I would incorporate interventions and theory from family therapy. Using solutions focused brief therapy, I would look at what he really wants to achieve, how he can gradually get there, and what stops him. Using structural family therapy, I would identify power dynamics, alliances, and sub-groups that might be keeping him in that role in his family. Using strategic family therapy interventions, I would work with him individually or with his family toward the specific goal of individuation and finding a job, and if the family so desires, moving out to his own place. From positive psychology, I would look at what helped him overcome similar challenges in the past. Even though the session is taking place in the US, I would be careful not to try and impose the American individualistic view of leaving the house at the age of 18–24, since it might not be culturally appropriate. I would also be careful not to take an expert stance and share with him concepts from Buddhism since this is his own culture, but I definitely might refer to them.

My personal integrative counseling model also guides me as a counselor educator, beyond being a therapist. First of all, I emphasize continually to my students that there are many ways to practice therapy, and that different clients need different things. I encourage my students to develop their style. I also invite them to explore with me their own thoughts, emotions, and physical sensations to achieve a more profound insight into their processes as well as creating a deep, vulnerable relationship with me and each others. I emphasize self-care as well as the values of connection, empathy, secure attachment, and unconditional positive regard.

Many times throughout the week, I get filled with an almost overwhelming feeling of gratitude for all the clients who trust me to walk with them and for all the people in my own life who keep on walking with me, including the generations before me and the generations to come. And I am grateful to you dear reader, right now, for walking this path with me through these pages. We've arrived.

Sasha Raskin

Sasha Raskin, MA, is an author, a <u>life coach</u>, and a <u>psychotherapist</u> in Boulder, CO. He is working on a P.h.D in Counseling Education and Supervision and is an adjunct faculty at a counseling master's program at Naropa University. Sasha Raskin is the Founder and Executive Director of <u>Go New</u>, a global, ever-expanding not-for-profit platform for online transformational education and coaching. He's also a professional musician and a composer for theatre and movies.

Sasha has been in the mental health field for more than 10 years, worked with youth at risk, recovery, mental health hospitals, and coached individuals, couples, families, startups, and groups. He has created mindfulness stress reduction and music therapy programs within different organizations. Whether it's in person or via phone/video calls, Sasha uses cutting-edge, research-based techniques to help his clients around the world to thrive.

To learn more about what Sasha does or to schedule a FREE 20-minutes counseling/coaching phone consultation, please visit <u>https://www.truenextstep.com/free-consult</u>.

---

[92] Photo by <u>Sofia Drobinskaya</u>

Contact Details

Coaching Website: TrueNextStep.com
Counseling Website: HeartAndMeaning.com
Go New: Go-New.com
LinkedIn: Sasha Raskin

SERVICE BEFORE SELF

VENERANDO CORTEZ

In this chapter, I want to outline the idea of service before self, a strong attribute I possess. This has not only sharpened my intuition, but has also become an essential guidepost in the journey of my life. Sometimes, this idea can be perceived or misconstrued as lacking self-love or compassion by many. However, when one finds joy and buoyantly serves others keeping this very powerful idea in mind, it can unlock a deeper level of greatness and catapult into success. This has been a fantastic spiritual ingredient in my followership toolbox. As I rose up the ranks in my military career, it kept me resilient. More importantly, it has steadied my course in this ever-evolving entrepreneurial journey. Its importance to me is exactly why I want to talk about service before self. While this powerful human attribute can easily launch one into becoming a successful leader, it needs a few other ingredients. To properly achieve greatness, a combination of mentorship, proper guidance, and self-awareness is required.

"Everyone has a purpose in life and a unique talent to give to others. And when we blend this unique talent with service to others, we experience the ecstasy and exultation of own spirit, which is the ultimate goal of all goals."

Kallam Anji Reddy

There is a commanding force within this dominant trait, and a person who possesses this attribute may not even aware of it. You must have heard of the law 'Like attracts like', and that is exactly what is playing out here. When you execute this character consistently, you grow to embody it. Your vulnerability will be embraced within its strength. I speak of this confidently because I am experiencing this now. Many of my fitness clients, especially those who love to help others, are exhibiting similar behavior. Because they see me serve and help people at this level, it is bound into their potential. This, in turn, creates a positive domino effect. Something that will serve the greater good.

While I did mention that not many people are aware of this trait, I also think that its unawareness is not such a bad thing. Especially because not being aware of its power in the early stage can only increase its efficiency. Even in its early, unfound days, the trait attracts mentors and teachers simply because they will enjoy teaching you, and you will love learning under them. Teachers and mentors who care about you and assist you in improving your skills are exactly what the world needs. In turn, you are drawn to helping others. You are more inclined to serve others. This trait enables you to get the work done and you don't complain because you are enhancing your skills. Many young individuals who possess this 'service before self' attitude may not see their potential just yet or have no desire to lead but may become susceptible to others. Sometimes for the good and sometimes for the bad. This is where self-awareness becomes supercritical. But how does one cultivate self-awareness? Clearly, not everyone is born with it. This is where a mentor comes in. Mentorship can help you cultivate self-awareness. I was privy to this early in my career. The Air Force is built on a culture of mentor-mentee relationships, and we learnt early how life-altering mentorship can be. In other words, I was in an environment that aligned with my goals. This career choice of mine would help me further succeed in my career and life. 90% of my desires were fulfilled, and the 10% was the potential into which I could dig deep and explore. It was my ratio of improvement. It was my ratio of learning.

So, how does one cultivate this approach or trait?

If I had to narrow it down, I would pick three equally important and unique aspects.

Mind-set

"Patience, persistence, and perspiration make an unbeatable combination for success."

Napoleon Hill

Learning how to have the mind-set for success is crucial when you want a successful and blissful life. If you are like me, you might have many goals you want to achieve. Whatever these goals are, the key is to have a growth mind-set rather than a fixed one. Life is an effort-return phenomenon. People make efforts to gain actual returns. There is nothing more frustrating than putting in all your effort and witnessing a lack of results. At this point, your efforts are wasted. How can this be combated? Well, the truth is that the secret behind the efforts that went in vain is the person. It's what the individual did.

Human behavior is predominantly the outcome of an individual's mind-set. Mind-set affects the actions of a person and the consequences of effort. A negative or even a neutral mind-set can distort the actions and undermine the efforts. So, how does this negativity work? The answer is rather simple. Whenever a person possesses a negative mind-set, he radiates negativity. Negativity brings with it a host of other undesirable things: pessimism, despair, and disinterest. So when you're negative, it compels others to avoid, dislike, or even misinterpret your behaviors. Moreover, when a person is negative, he/she tends to see only the hurdles and subsequently magnify them. When someone sees just hurdles or magnifies hurdles wrongly, they are bound to experience stress in all its might. When a person is severely under stress, they cannot be sensible or creative. Do you see the loop? A negative mindset undermines rationality, creativity, dynamism, and productivity and does not help you thrive. On the other hand, a positive mind-set allows someone to deal with challenges with rationality, creativity, dynamism, and resourcefulness. What sounds less stressful among the two?

Going back to what I said previously, maintaining a 'service before self' mind-set in your life is perhaps the best thing you can do. You will be surprised how many great opportunities will knock on your door. With that, you can make changes to yourself and your life. Become a change agent, and don't be afraid of change. Maybe it is just me or it's this trait I cherish, but when you're successful, in your career or personal life, and travel the world, you will start observing people. Your success will put you in a position where you learn by interacting with people. Their interactions enhance you. Slowly and steadily, you will recognize those who contain this trait. They somehow seem to stand out in the crowd. Their attitudes and choices are more pleasant. And, you're naturally gravitated to talk to such people.

So imagine this. You're traveling the world. You are OUT there. Start by observing people especially those in the customer-service positions such as the security agents, Uber drivers, clerks, administrative officers, and the barista at the Starbucks you just visited, and the person manning the counter at the dry cleaners. You will soon notice, after paying attention, that people who run their business tend to have different attitudes than those are employed by them. Now, does that matter? Not really. What matters is whether the person doing a job, any job, is happy about it. If you're working as a security officer, what matters the most is you consider it the best job for you. You embody that spirit. Even if you are hoping to land a better job elsewhere, give it your best at the current job. The idea is to be thankful for what you have and continue to pursue what you intend to pursue. Remember, the mind-set matters. When you combine this attitude while taking action concurrently, you will achieve your goal.

Opportunity

"Success is where preparation and opportunity meet."

Bobby Unser

So, we've covered the mind-set. Let's talk about something that is rarely spoken about opportunities. Successful people are observant. Often, it reminds them about how it was for them. There would have been occasions where many who saw your potential helped you or connected you with the leaders in the field you worked. In the same way, there were many instances in my career where many leaders offered to help. They wanted to see me grow, and they wanted to challenge me in order for me to grow. However, I just didn't land up with this trait without hard work. It started with my career in the Air Force. Among many other values, service before self is something that the Air Force instils in you. When I joined the military, I wasn't as aware as I am now. I didn't pay attention to many things that were happening around me. I simply wanted to join the military and serve the country, and I did just that. Boy, am I glad I did! I'm typing this chapter now when I'm a month short of retiring after serving my country for twenty glorious years.

There were, of course, unpleasant experiences in my careers. But, I don't regret any of them. It is due to these and the interactions I had that I am who I am now a resilient and mindful individual. I was deployed. I underwent episodes of Post-Traumatic Stress Disorder, more commonly referred to as PTSD. But these were my experiences. They enriched me. They continue to shape my beliefs. At the time when I was suffering from PTSD episodes, I sought psychological and psychiatric help. I needed something to boost myself. I actively started reading about any potential interventions that would help me. That is how I found meditation. Over the years, I've come to realize that meditation hugely complements this 'service before self' trait. You see, even at my lowest, I grabbed opportunities to improve myself.

When I was in high school, people often suggested a position or a job for me in places they worked. This was when I was working at McDonald's and KFC. I never really thought about that or even realized its significance recently. Why would people want to offer me a job when I already had a job? They never did tell me the reason behind this, but I knew there was something behind it.

It continued to happen at different instances in my life. When I worked at the law enforcement officer, my first assignment was to start checking the identity of people when they entered the Air Force Base. This was not glamorous, but I loved doing this job. I knew that by volunteering to take this position, it helped my co-workers to get the other posts where they didn't have to deal with this element because with this position you had to be outdoor checking ID all night. My co-workers and I were happy. I also volunteered during my time off and always made it a point to help others in the most domestic or trivial situations. I would cook at a party, grill the food, and sometimes even wash the dishes. I also offered to babysit often simply because helping others came naturally to me. At this time, my supervisor took note of my behavior. He decided to help me advance further in my career. He provided the materials I needed to study and encouraged me to use my energy to grow. In the end, I did it and loved it. Immediately after I passed the exam, I started working as a leading Patrolman for the Law Enforcement. I loved it when people called our desk because they had locked themselves out of their car in the base and the desk sergeant would deploy me to that location. I remember taking my vehicle lockout kit, showing up at the scene, and unlocking their car within two minutes. These were all, in hindsight, opportunities I grabbed.

Another incident pops into my mind. When I was stationed in England in 2000, at Raf Alconbury, a mother had locked herself out of the car and her child was in the car and crying. It was raining heavily. Though I was off duty, I knew she needed my help. It never mattered that I was off duty to me because the situation supersedes everything. Before me, a patrolman was trying to help her, albeit unsuccessfully. I gave him his space and time to see if he could manage it all by himself. When I realized that he was struggling even after five minutes, I came in. On realizing that I was with the force, he smiled at me and asked me to help. The situation kept getting worse as the rain increased because the baby kept crying and we were soaking wet. When I parked my car next to them, the patrolman said "Oh man! I'm glad I saw you because I know you can help me with this car." I got out. It was around February in England and was freezing. I told him we have to do the passenger side doors first. I slid and worked the slim Jim into the passenger side; 60 seconds into it, and boom, the door was unlocked. All of us were relieved. I mention this incident because it was a mini success in my day. And these mini-successes that occur every day become powerful motivators.

So far I've only mentioned the opportunities I seized. Now I'll talk about something I did not and continue to regret it even today. I was in Iraq and my Public Health Officer, Captain Foster, saw how I loved my job. I kept asking questions and making phone calls on how to improve our programs. We were focusing on improving vector-born surveillance, and I was responsible for coordinating and setting up traps for mosquitoes, collecting the samples, and shipping them to Germany. I loved these tasks, and the Captain hinted that I could also do amazingly well if I applied this energy and enthusiasm at the schoolhouse at Wright Patterson Air Force, Ohio. He asked me to apply for an instructor position at the school, and said he would take care of the rest. I did not. I did not seize this opportunity, and I regret it today. It would have helped me gather the experience I needed. It would have prepared me sooner for the coaching career I subsequently embarked upon.

Optimism

"Optimism is the faith that leads to achievement.
Nothing can be done without hope and confidence."

Helen Keller

Let's talk about the final aspect: Optimism. The power and force of optimism cannot be underestimated. Your personal development and growth depend on it. When you can see the positive in every situation, you are better equipped to recognize and take advantage of opportunities that come your way. In other words, you are more able to spring into positive action in the face of life's challenges. Research, too, indicates that optimism plays a significant role in higher achievement and success rates.

How you do anything is how you do everything. I wasn't mindful before. But when you deploy mindfulness and observe people, ask yourself these questions: Will you let that person work or provide service to your customers? Is there a hidden gem and untapped potential? Does this person have a high teachability index? Now, I'll tell you how we can gauge this. We have to pay attention to their communication, tone, body language, posture, gestures, and facial expressions. More importantly, see how you react and be self-aware.

One of my co-workers, a young airman, who was under my supervision when I was assigned in the Occupational Health section, once told me, "Oh, yay! I'm glad to see you back from leave. You always make our section such a pleasant environment and have such a great sense of humor. I feel so comfortable with you and don't hesitate before telling you anything." Another colleague Master Sergeant Hammonds once remarked, "You sleep for only 3-4 hours while working on your business, but you manage to come to work with a smile. And you're always charged, even during these tiresome events. Man, let me have some of that energy." So how I did manage this? How were my colleagues impressed by me easily? It's simply this: I was optimistic. Optimism also goes hand in hand with 'service before self'. Without optimism, you may be serving others, but you may be loaded with self-doubt. You may say something like "I love doing what I do and helping others here, but this is all I know, and I'm probably going to get stuck here doing this because I can't and I'm not good at doing other stuff." What do you see in this statement? Can you observe the individual's mind-set? You can clearly see that he needs proper guidance.

Let me tell you a story, and you can record your perspective about it.

I have traveled to many cities in the world and have seen different janitors who exhibited different behaviors, despite having similar jobs. Some cheerful ones would sing as they sweep and mop, and then there were those who walked like zombies. When I asked them a few questions, it almost seemed as I woke them up from their dreams because they would seem oblivious. The cheerful ones greet you with a smile and sometimes even ask how you're doing and other general questions that keep the conversation going. I realized when they did this, I was impacted positively and it inspired me. That is why I smile at work even though I'm functioning with three hours of sleep. I know things will be okay, and others might feel happier when I smile.

In order to keep my optimistic spirit going, I start my day with a smile. Next, I write down things, or sometimes record, about what I'm thankful for. These little acts help you spread the good and bring in positive energy. So, I start my day positively and influence those around me with a positive vibe. It's a great feeling! Now, as I continue to develop leadership and train more, I've learned to smile more as well. Previously, I was an optimistic person but I never smiled as much and as a result, I was often misjudged. Many well-wishers came to my aid and informed me that despite my positive outlook, I looked serious because I didn't smile. I decided to take this in the right spirit and started applying these changes to my character. Did it make a difference? You bet it did. It shifted my environment just like that. It is amazing how this simple trick can also change your day. This simple practice sets up my day to win, and you feel so lively and ready to take over the world.

So, that's it. Those were the three aspects I wanted to focus on and tell you about.

If there's something I want to end this chapter with, it is this: service before self should be one of your foundational attributes. If you're currently working on being more self-aware, this attitude will help you immensely. It can become your bridge in transforming and finding the purpose of life. It is almost like a magnetic force as it reveals others' personality defects and increases your mindfulness. This attitude eliminates entitlements because you have a purpose: of helping others succeed.

So what about me? What am I doing today? Well, I am transforming lives as a Physique Transformation Coach. Fitness and nutrition are my biggest passions. I love being able to help others achieve their fitness goal by transforming their physique and health through exercise and proper diet. To me, fitness is not only a hobby, but it is an art and a lifestyle. My calling in life is to help others see the happiness and joy that fitness, nutrition, and health can bring. I achieved a tremendous mind and body transformation, and I know you can too. Setting goals and achieving them through hard work is an incomparable feeling. Sometimes we need a little guidance in our fitness journey, and I can be your coach on your trek to greatness and happiness. Life gives us dreams for a reason. They exist in order for us to achieve it. Most people pass them off as impossible or something that they could never aspire to do, but those who can forge greatness out of the tools they are given are the ones who can achieve them. Having the body of your dreams is not impossible; it is just a matter of having the proper guidance and discipline. Stop procrastinating on getting a personal trainer or wasting your money on expensive sports supplements without contacting me first. If millions of people around the world can do it, despite tough circumstances, SO CAN YOU.

Venerando Cortez

Venerando Cortez is a physique transformation coach and the founder of Flexible Anabolic Nutrition LLC. He previously served in the US Air Force. As a coach, he has authored the book FAN Physique Transformation Diet, which has helped many. Venerando previously developed wellness programs for his clients in the military community. He is currently ready to help and improve your health and life. In the last four years, he has coached and transformed over 400 clients and is now training many others to become physique transformation specialists. As an Air Force Veteran, Venerando was deployed to Iraq and served as a medic for Expeditionary Medical Support Squadron. These experiences enriched this thinking and sharpened his intuition. Today, he specializes in talking about the idea 'service before self' and helps his clients achieve their goals and regain their balance. His philosophy focuses on lifelong learning. He has transformed the quality of life of many by charting guided fitness programs in a caring, fun, and dynamic environment.

Contact Information

Website: www.fanptusa.com
Email: venerando@fanptacademy.com
Facebook: https://www.facebook.com/
messages/t/venerando.cortez
Instagram: @ven.cortez

THE SECRET POWERS OF MULTIPLE PASSIONS

TRANSFORM YOUR LIFE AND HAVE TIME TO DO IT ALL!

VIKKI COOMBES

I'm sitting in my mother's lounge in New Zealand with tears streaming down my face while sobbing "What is wrong with me" as my Mum is saying "nothing, nothing." It is eight weeks since my husband of seven years ended our marriage over the phone. I have lost so much weight in that brief time that my clothes are falling off me. I had flown back from the United Kingdom to spend two months with family and long-time friends. I wanted to reconnect with my beginnings and ground myself before returning to London. After all, moving to the United Kingdom had been MY dream.

In the years my husband and I were together, I had held five jobs across three careers; we had moved homes four times (including moving from one end of the planet to the other), and my passions had led us a merry dance of new beginnings, ideas, and friendships. This also meant there had been endings and goodbyes. We had struggled and flourished financially. At the time he ended our relationship, we were in the middle of another move—from England to Scotland, from one career to another (for me), and from one home to another new 'home'.

Now, I am a person driven by multiple passions—someone for whom variety and change are as required as breathing to live a life I love. With the benefit of hindsight, I understand that for him these were challenging times. Yes, there was excitement, but he was more comfortable making only a few changes in his life, every now and then. When we were together, he had one career across three jobs, and he only switched his employers because we moved cities.

So, no, there was nothing 'wrong' with me. Rather, we were people with very different energy and approaches in life. He was a steady flame rooted in what he enjoyed all of his life, while I am like a hummingbird, flitting from one flower to another and sipping the wide range of nectars I need to thrive.

Fifteen years have passed since that heartfelt moment in my mother's living room. I experienced major highs and lows as I opened my Self up to continuously learning who I am and the responsibility I have for how I interact with this world. It was only in September 2016 that I truly began accepting the secret powers of my 'difference' from conventionally accepted expectations of the 'choices adults make' (e.g., one career, marriage, kids, house, 'settling down,' etc.). I was listening to a talk by Elizabeth Gilbert, of *Eat, Pray, Love* fame, and she spoke of those people who rather than having 'the one thing' have a totally different approach to living life. For the first time, I heard the metaphor of the 'hummingbird' applied to people who are driven by their curiosity to pursue ever-changing multiple passions. This resonated so strongly with me that I literally leapt out of my chair and cried out loud "this is me!"

So, was I born a person with multiple passions and driven by curiosity? Yes. And my nurturing years honed this aspect of my Self. Having explored the realities of people with multiple passions by communicating globally with thousands of other people who identify with this way of living life, I began to explore the science behind the personality. I googled and discovered that all studies in this field start from the point that there are five 'BIG' personality spectrums. Upon further reading and reflection, I have come to believe that the people I call 'Hummingbirds' fall under **openness to new experience** rather than those who are dogmatic and closed to new experiences; whereas, I think that we could be anywhere in the other four personality spectrums. We could be an introvert or extrovert, collaborative or competitive, conscientious or spontaneous, and emotionally stable or neurotic.

Openness to new experiences is the defining personality characteristic of those I call Hummingbirds.
So, what might the life of a Hummingbird resemble? Fly upside down with me to discover how my experience unfolds.

* I am born in Kawakawa, New Zealand. My parents had migrated from England two years ago and taught at the local secondary school. It is a small rural town where the railway line goes up the center of the road. Everywhere we go, people know my parents. I am 14 months old, and my parents bring home my sister. She spends much of her first months with her legs in plaster while they

sort out her dislocated hips. We soon move homes to live in the new house my parents build. I am 41 months old and my parents bring home my brother. Plans begin for us all to go back to England to 'visit' for a year.

* I am four-and-a-half years old when we arrive in England; it is the middle of winter and I start school in Leeds, the city where my mother grew up. The classroom has a little playhouse inside. On my first day, I am allowed to play in it whilst the other children are doing a lesson. After a while, I am bored and look out of the small window at the other children in the classroom. I am unable to open the door from the inside. I spend the time watching the others, and I make no noise. At the end of the day, when the other children are sitting on the mat in front of her for final storytime, the teacher suddenly asks them where I am. Everyone turns to look at me in the little house. I wave.

* I am six-and-a-half years old, and we are back in New Zealand, living in Hawke's Bay. I am starting my fourth school because we have just changed towns again to live in a bigger house in a more vibrant location. Having started school eight months earlier than other Kiwi children, my parents are trying to convince the school that I should be placed a year ahead of my 'age' year because of the amount of education I've already completed and excelled in. The other two schools I have attended in our time back in New Zealand had accommodated this request, and I have been going from strength to strength in my learning. However, this new school refuses, and the only concession they make is

allowing me to source books from what everyone called the 'big kids library'. I repeat an educational year and start cruising intellectually.

* I am eight years old and sitting in the headmaster's office in tears. I've been sent to his office for being rude to my teacher. The headmaster says to me "If you don't stop crying, you'll stay here all afternoon" and I instantly stop. My parents are in Wellington and have been for weeks. My father came home from a hockey game feeling unwell. He was rushed to the hospital and is now in another city, which is 5 hours away, undergoing open-heart surgery. My siblings and I have been farmed out to family and friends for the duration. It turns out my father has a genetic syndrome called 'Marfan,' which is a connective tissue disorder. Because there is a 50:50 chance each time a child is born the child would have inherited the syndrome, the three of us are examined by a cardiologist. We all lucked into the side with the genetic mutation, and we start the roller coaster of constantly learning something new about this genetic syndrome.

* I am ten years old and am flying up from Brownies to Guides. I was a sixer at Brownies. My mother and sister are at the ceremony. I feel so proud. I love Girl Guides because we are always learning something new and do a wide range of activities every time we go. So far, my other interests have included swimming and gymnastics. The latter only lasted a few weeks. My non-school days are filled with walking the dog with my siblings (somewhere different every time), playing made

up games in our garden, exploring the local region with my family, and reading—lots of reading. I remember one time we were spending a day visiting family friends who had two children similar ages to my siblings and me. My mother hunted me down in the quiet spot I had found to read, removed the book from my hands, and turfed me outside with the admonition "Go and PLAY."

* I am fourteen years old. We moved to Auckland (the largest city in New Zealand) a year ago, and it is the end of my first year at secondary school. I am standing on a slope between two blocks of classrooms. It is lunchtime. Throughout the year, I have painfully learned that the social strata of the school are built around cliques of similar minded young people—the rugby heads, the athletes, the goths, the metallers, the geeks, etc. I belong to none of these groups. I circulate during breaks speaking with each of my friends who are scattered across a wide range of interests. However, at this moment, I am having an epiphany. I have a crush on Matthew, who is two years ahead of me, and I am incredibly shy about it. I suddenly realize that if I am going to be liked by people, I need to be outgoing. My world shifts on its axle.

* I am sixteen years old, and we are staying for the weekend with our cousins. It is Saturday night, and I am talking with Nicola, who is a year younger than me. She and my sister have spent the evening sharing stories with each other about all the parties and fun they have been enjoying in our separate towns. I just listened. I am outside the high-school party scene. I say to Nicola, "There is a part of me that wants to do what you guys do, but mostly I want to be me. And I like different things." Even in the midst of the angst of being a teenager and the peer pressure to 'fit in,' I wanted to do my own thing—fly swiftly from one interest to another while learning and trying out new experiences all the time.

*   I am seventeen years old, and it is the end of the first day of my final year at secondary school. I will be finishing my seventh school this year. I am at the bus stop waiting to go home and am talking animatedly with other students I know from the church youth group I co-lead. My siblings are there, too. We are laughing and joking around whilst we wait. I find out twelve years later that this moment was absolutely pivotal to a young woman who was sitting in the bus stop at the end of her very first day at secondary school. She had an epiphany that if she was going to be successful in life, she needed to be more like this whirling friendly red-headed dervish who had leapt to life in her space on a day filled with new experiences.

*   I am eighteen years old and am taking a gap year between secondary school and University to earn money to pay for my fees. I work as a teller in a bank, specifically choosing a role that I know will have no long-term interest for me. It serves as an introduction to professionalism, work bullying, work friendships, building customer relationships, and sexual harassment. A third of the way through the year, I get glandular fever and it wipes me out for six weeks. I am burning my candle at both ends and in the middle. Outside of work, I am co-leading two youth groups across a wide range of activities. My evenings and weekends are full.

* I am nineteen years old when I move out of my parents' place to go to University in Hamilton (a 2-hour drive away). Throughout secondary school, I had changed my mind and my courses to fit in with different career options. First, I was going to be a teacher. Next, an interpreter. Then, a travel agent. And finally, having observed a court in session, I decided to become a lawyer. I choose Waikato Law School because it is brand new. I am a founding student. The few people I know on campus are now a year ahead of me at University. I sit quietly outside the building clutching the bright red pre-read material. A woman introduces herself to me. Her name is Beth-Anne, and she was born and raised in Panama to parents of English and New Zealand descent. She moved to New Zealand when she was fifteen years old. We are inseparable for four years at law school.

* I am twenty-two years old, and it is the final year of my bachelor's degree. I was released from the hospital the day before after an overnight stay because my heart had gone out of rhythm. I have worked through the night completing an essay that is due now. The telephone goes. It is my family to tell me that my father is dying from complications related to Marfan Syndrome. My world tilts sideways. I struggle to hold on as my friends rally. Tamie, who has been one of my closest friends at university and comes from the same area of

Auckland, arrives to drive me at speed straight to be with my family who are two hours away. The next year is something of a blur as we all grieve in our own ways. I change churches to receive support from those who know what loss is. My nephew is born. In the darkness, he is a blazing ray of light. I continue to work part-time, be involved in a vast array of activities, and focus on my study. Somehow through the love and support of Beth-Anne and Benesia, the women in my university study group who become my life-long friends, I complete my Bachelor Degree in Laws.

*   I've just had my twenty-fifth birthday. I am standing in a courtroom. I am dressed in a black cape with a white wig on my head. I am being sworn in as a Barrister & Solicitor of the High Court of New Zealand. Jono is the solicitor standing as my witness. My mother, sister, and nephew are in the public gallery. My eighteen-month-old nephew gets to hold the gammel. There is an emptiness, like a gaping hole within my life, where my father should be. I am living in Auckland with a group of friends in a run-down house. I am studying for a Master's in Social Work (MSW). I am working part-time as a waitress. Beth-Anne has moved to Panama. Tamie has moved to Australia. Benesia has moved to Wellington. My future opportunities lie brightly before me on the horizon. There is no hiding it now—having attended seven schools and two universities, lived in fourteen homes across six urban centers, worked in six jobs, and pursued multiple interests…

I am an adult, I am a Hummingbird.

What have I already learnt about the secret powers of multiple passions?

* Being open to new experiences often means we look at the wider picture. We are highly skilled at taking in a lot of complex and messy information, recognizing patterns, and simplifying it for others to support their understanding.

* Being rampantly curious, we love learning. And we often prefer 'freestyle' learning because when the learning environment is too formal, we feel constrained. We love exploring new ideas, skills, and concepts, and we love considering how they interconnect with everything else we already have within our knowledge and experience bases.

So, I am on my way—or am I? I already know that I have no desire to become a high-flying lawyer in the adversarial legal system that so many countries around the world practice, which I believe adds no value to the well-being and connectivity of our societies. However, I also find that intellectual stimulation keeps me on my toes. My horizons are bright. And there are a whole range of opportunities before me. With so many options, what is a Hummingbird to do? Start flitting from one interest to another, of course!

* I am twenty-seven years old and am dressed in my suit with a briefcase in hand with a fifteen-year-old client by my side. We are about to appear before a Board of Trustees for his school to present the case for lifting his suspension for smoking. I am working for a human rights organization. I am still studying for an MSW. I am leading a Ranger Guide unit. I am doing some waitressing for additional money. I am just back from my honeymoon in Fiji—my first international trip since I was five. It is a daunting task to face down a room full of upper-middle-class white men who lead a Boy's Grammar School. But, we win.

* I am twenty-eight years old, and I am standing in front of a room of high-risk offenders, launching a 72-hour course on cognitive skills. I start by welcoming them in Te Reo Maori, the language of the indigenous peoples of New Zealand. I am a Probation Officer. I am attending the ALPHA course at the church where I was a youth group leader a decade ago, so that my husband, a self-proclaimed agnostic, and I can discuss concepts in depth. I have recently dropped out of my MSW because I feel that I have learnt all that I need from it. I am currently fascinated by the Enneagram to the point of creating a complex website with multitudes of pages detailing everything I am learning. I am struggling with expectations placed upon me by friends within my wider social circle. I am in the midst of planning all that needs to be done to move to the United Kingdom in a year.

* I am twenty-nine years old and am standing on the edge of Bryce's Canyon, Utah. I am in awe at the sight before me. My husband takes photos that are unable to capture but only hint at nature's magnitude. And then we seek help from an elderly couple because our car has broken down, and we have no cell phone. We have been on our road trip as we travel from New Zealand to the United Kingdom for a month now. I have been grieving for twenty-six days as my brother unexpectedly died from complications related to Marfan Syndrome only three days after we left the country. I made the choice to honor his love for life by continuing our trip of a lifetime. Our next stops will take in Death Valley, Yosemite, and San Francisco before we fly to Panama to spend a fortnight with Beth-Anne.

* I am thirty-one years old and preparing to move to London. We've spent the last year living in Nottingham, England where my husband had a contract before we even arrived in the country. It has all been rather surreal living among strangers trying to build a new life whilst grieving the loss of my brother. We are moving because I have finally landed employment in the new career I've decided to pursue—learning and development. I am just completing 12 months studying for my CIPD Certificate in Training Practice. My new job is for a local authority.

* I am thirty-two years old, and I have just been promoted. I am building a team of learning professionals, and we are making a real difference in how social workers and housing officers develop in their roles. My commute is on the Underground for 90 minutes each way. I spend two days every month traveling to Scotland to pursue further studies in Personnel Development. I have just returned from a weekend in Brussels with two girlfriends. My husband and I have a full social life with friends from many nationalities, who live in diverse areas of London. We are going to Venice for Christmas.

* I am thirty-three years old, and I am standing on Carlton Hill in Edinburgh, Scotland where I have been living for the last six months after deciding that it was time to live in a city that has always held my heart. My ten-year-old nephew is with me, and we are cheering as the New Year's Eve fireworks are soaring into the sky from five different hills around us. It is an amazing display and completely awe-inspiring. My heart is devastated. It is four weeks since my husband ended our marriage. My nephew and I explore the Scottish Highlands. When we stop for lunch, he tells me I must eat more. I force myself to take another mouthful. Following my two months reconnecting in New Zealand, I return to London, England to start rebuilding my life and my dream of living in the depths of history whilst traveling the world.

* I am thirty-four years old, and the weather is dark and wet as we are in the midst of my fifth winter in the United Kingdom. I am moving into a new flat with one of the women I've been house-sharing with and we decided we wanted a place for just the two of us. I am an independent consultant in learning and development. My current client is PwC, and I am leading the design and implementation of the learning strategy for one of their business units. Through significant support from friends, my healing from the personal devastation of my divorce is almost complete. One friend tells me that I "no longer look gaunt." I play my guitar quietly in my bedroom in celebration of all that I have learned and experienced so far.

*   I am thirty-five years old, and it is a new year. I had a lovely evening out the night before when a friend took me to the theatre. I've just completed reviewing a friend's essay for her Master's degree in Environmental Sustainability. I am sitting on the stairs in my flat all by myself. I am in floods of tears. My contracts have all dried up. I have had hundreds of job interviews and no job offers so far. My savings have gone after six months of careful shepherding. One friend has just declined to allow me to stay with him whilst I get my Self back on my feet because "no one would do what you ask Vikki." As I am sitting here in this state, all that I learnt through completing my practitioner's certification in Neurolinguistic Programming over the last four months floods through me. I am 100% responsible for every decision that I have made that has led me to this place. It is time to be at cause and own that every decision I make is mine. The world changes. I move into a new flat with a friend of a friend who becomes my friend. I am offered a job as a management consultant with Accenture. My first assignment is in Newcastle in northern England where, during the week, I share a flat with another person who becomes a friend. Doors open and life changes.

I have come through fire and ice to become a self-aware Hummingbird!

I have now uncovered another secret power of being a person with multiple passions.

* Being super fast processors, we assimilate learning and information faster than the average person. This is incredibly helpful in both work and education. There is a rule of thumb that for something to land, you need to be told/shown a minimum of three times. However, I've often found that once is enough. If it is particularly complex perhaps, 1.5 times. I rarely need three times. This means I am agile and adaptable in a wide range of roles, projects, and challenging situations.

Now that I am self-aware, that will be the end of trials and tribulations. Obviously. Or perhaps, it is because I now accept that I am 100% responsible for how I continue evolving as a human becoming that means that I experience life in a different way? Only time will tell.

* I am thirty-six years old. I am lying in a hospital room listening to a pharmacist tell me that I am no longer allowed cranberries and trying not to laugh as Tamie,

who moved to England five years ago and is my main support at the moment, quickly sweeps the bottle of cranberry juice I had just been drinking out of sight. We then have a highly amusing conversation:

Pharmacist: To keep your levels balanced, if you drink alcohol, you should have one glass a day.

Me: So, I need to drink more alcohol then?
Pharmacist: No, I'm not telling you to drink more alcohol.

Me: Yes, you are. I currently only have two to three glasses a week. If I have one glass a day, that adds up to seven glasses a week.

Pharmacist: No, I am not telling you to drink more alcohol.

It is 4 days since I had open-heart surgery where my mitral valve was replaced with a mechanical one. This is a necessity due to Marfan's Syndrome. In two days, I get to go home again. But then, I am not allowed to open doors or cook for myself for a few weeks as I rebuild my strength. This is the first time in my life that I have gracefully asked others for help and have been blessed with many people who lined up to be put on the roster.

* I am thirty-eight years old and running around like a headless chicken. Due to the economic circumstances, I am, what is known in the management consultancy world as, 'on the bench.' This means that I am currently on non-chargeable projects. And I am busier than I ever was when working on client projects. Although flattering to be in such demand, I need to learn to say 'no' as gracefully as I have learned to say 'help'. One of the senior leaders gives me some tips. I try them, and they work. Life becomes more manageable.

* I am thirty-nine years old and sitting in wonder as I listen to my trainer for my 'Master Practitioner in Neurolinguistic Programming' course read aloud from Deepak Chopra's *Way of the Wizard*. I am working for a niche consultancy after deciding that being a small cog in Accenture's corporate machine was the wrong fit for me. I am single, following a year-long on-and-off relationship with a gentleman I refer to as my 'learning curve'. I reflect as I imbibe deeper NLP understandings that if someone had said to me before I started that relationship that I would allow myself to be emotionally manipulated in such a way, I would have laughed at them. And yet, I had sunk into this place until I found the inner strength and respect for my Self to say "No, enough" and walked away.

* I am forty years old, soaking up the sun whilst swimming in a pool at a luxury villa in Florida. I am on a one-week retreat for life coaching from Matthew Hussey. I know by investing this time and money into me, my life will change exponentially. I am sharing the week with fourteen others and we go deep. The challenges and moments of AWE are real. I learn to say YES when opportunity knocks only if it aligns with how I truly, really, and deeply am. I also prepare myself to experience my upcoming open-heart surgery to replace my aortic valve with a mechanical one in a very different way than last time. And I do. Only six weeks post-surgery, I am dancing at a friend's wedding.

* I am forty-two years old and signing documents for a holding deposit to purchase a house off-plan. Sitting next to me is Gareth, who I have been dating for four months. On the drive over here, I was explaining to him how frustrating I found the whole house buying experience in England. I had been looking for over eighteen months. Usually, I make decisions quickly. For instance, when I bought my car, I went to the lot, looked at three, test drove one, bought it, and drove away three hours later. Job done. As we arrived at this estate, its history and majesty capture my imagination immediately. Three hours later, I have purchased a 2-bed, 2-bath townhouse.

* I am forty-three years old, and I'm sitting on the back of a big, yellow truck bouncing my way across the Serengeti. I have just sat for fifteen minutes making eye contact with a leopard lounging in a tree. I am on a three-month sabbatical from my work having realized that buying a house 'off-plan' meant waiting at least twelve to eighteen months. Waiting has never been a strong point. And I was ready to make a move in my professional journey and a significant one at that. But I had to stay where I was to get a mortgage. So, I decided to retain my mental health by doing something I had always dreamed of experiencing. This whole adulting malarkey is less than it is cracked up to be. I am deepening my understanding of my Self as an introvert as I share this truck with between 15–25 other people over 11 weeks.

* I am forty-four years old and I'm standing hand-in-hand with Gareth as we use our brand new key to open the front door of the house we have now bought together. Five days later, more than one hundred of our family and friends arrive from across the globe to celebrate with us. They join us in our celebration of love and commitment as evidenced through our joint mortgage. I have been in a high-stress mode for the last two months as completion on the house dragged for nine months longer than the initial due date. Our big party, our 'not wedding', is happening in our new home. The afternoon is a picnic with games for the children whilst the adults appreciate the match being played on the historical cricket pitch across the driveway from our brand new front door. The evening is a spit roast for our family and friends without children. Many silly photos are taken in a special photo booth. Overall, a fabulous celebration!

* I am forty-five years old, standing in the front of a room launching my new business, which has three strands of income generation—transformational coaching, leadership consulting and mBraining learning. There are sixty people from across all the different areas of my life celebrating with me. My mother is here from New Zealand; Beth-Anne has flown in from Panama and is with her mother who has also arrived from New Zealand; Deeti, my longest-serving friend here in England, has catered the event; Elinor, who used to be a consulting client, is playing background music with her quartet; and Gareth is here as my life and business partner. Collaborators, service providers, friends, clients, and peers. This is a diverse group of people with multiple perspectives on life—all connecting and conversing with each other. An amazing evening of celebrating all of who I am as I weave my multiple passions into a life I love.

I choose to be an empowered Hummingbird.

I have learnt two further secret powers that those of us with multiple passions have.

* Being passionate across multiple creative and analytical fields leads us to meet people with wide-ranging specialisms and interests. We stand in the intersections of our varied passions and invite these people to connect with one another, to share perspectives, to innovate together, and creating something new.

* Being fast and agile, we draw upon all of our other secret powers to offer innovative problem-solving opportunities within our work and wider communities. In our current fast-moving society, we are the talent that businesses are seeking.

Now I am empowered with my core confidence, evolving resilience, and buoyant existentialism to dance through the reality of all that life throws at me. I live my life to the fullest—ever-changing and ever-varied. I am weaving my multiple passions into a life I love, where I have time to do it all. And, having reviewed all the tools and techniques I have applied in my own life, there is one that stands out as having made a significant difference to me as a Hummingbird. Following this technique was the key to taking responsibility for the decisions I make and to consciously shape the way that I experience life in all its nuances.

What is the technique? **Uncovering your Patterns!** As people with multiple passions, Hummingbirds, are never going to have 'one thing', 'the true passion', or 'the purpose'. Instead, we have underlying Patterns that weave throughout our lives. When we take a moment to consider the 'why' behind the choices we have made, we will uncover them. By recognizing and accepting our Patterns, we will understand how our ever-changing passions fit together into an exquisite, ever-evolving pattern of flight.

How to uncover your Patterns:

* Get a HUGE piece of paper and a range of large colored marker pens. Split the paper into three sections:
  • Section 1: Birth to three years ago
  • Section 2: 3 years ago to now
  • Section 3: Now into your future
* In each section, be as creative as you want (writing, drawing, collaging, etc.), and set down all the passions, interests, experiences, jobs, courses, achievements, and moments you've lived through. In Section 3, note down everything you either already know you're planning or things that you've always wanted to learn, experience, and achieve.
* Now, highlight those that you truly, really, and deeply loved at the time you were doing them—those that have showed up over and over again in your life in multiple ways. Also, note those that you disliked or were only in

your life for a brief period of time or you did because, for whatever reason, you 'had to.'

* Once you've completed doing this, go away for at least thirty minutes. Go for a walk outside, drink a liter of water, or connect with a loved one.
* Upon your return, place the paper on the floor and stand over it. Notice any connections that exist, and draw lines between them as you deem appropriate. As you start identifying these, ask yourself: What is common here? Why do these light me up? What truly matters to me about these ones? What are the underlying patterns?
* You will find that you have two or three patterns that stand out for you. They shine like golden flight paths through your life.

How did this show up in my life? The first time I did this exercise, I was purely considering my professional journey. It was when I made the move from New Zealand to England and a recruitment agent looking at my Curriculum Vitae told me it was 'interesting' that I took a step back and looked at my résumé. I was wondering what she was missing because it all made perfect sense to me. It was then that I identified my patterns as 'people' and 'change.'. Everything I have chosen to do that has lit me up is about guiding people to grow, evolve, and become all that they have the potential to be within who they truly, really, deeply are.

In recent years as I have been growing my business, coaching Hummingbirds around the world, and talking with thousands of others, I have re-visited this exercise and understood that 'people' and 'change' are patterns across all aspects of my life— professional, social, and personal. What difference has knowing this made to my life? When something new and shiny appears on my horizon, I will immediately ask myself: how does this fit in with my patterns? How does it add to all that I already have experienced and learnt? What value will this bring to me and to those who matter to me? I have stopped ricocheting from one thing to another without sparing a thought for the consequences. I have taken responsibility for how my multiple passions are woven together so that I am living the life I love.

I share meaningful moments with my partner, my family, my friends, my social network, my peers, and my colleagues. I make a difference for my clients through my wide-ranging perspectives and the relationships I nurture. I travel far and wide while experiencing places, people, and activities that I have dreamed of for a lifetime. I am open to what else my life evolves into as I continue to pursue my passions so that they are fulfilling me as they align with my underlying patterns. And, I am excited about where my life may yet lead me!

You, too, may have time to do it all as you weave your multiple passions into a life you love. Join me in flying upside down by connecting with me so that you may make a difference by using your multiple passions' secret powers!

Vikki Coombes

Vikki Coombes is a transformational coach, leadership consultant, mBraining trainer, public speaker, and author. As discussed in appearances on Sky 203's 'The Chrissy B Show' and 'Womanars Podcasts' and featured articles in 'London Business Magazine' and 'New Zealand Business Women's Network,' Vikki has never had 'one thing'. She always had lots of different passions and has leapt from one to another. On one hand, this was a lot of fun. On the other hand, there were times when she had no money or friends and felt that she would never finish anything. People kept saying "Just make a choice and stick to it," "Choose a career if you want to succeed," and "When are you going to settle down?," which made her feel like there was something wrong with her.

One day, a friend said "You are really inspiring." Then, she realized that all her learning in twenty jobs across five careers, studying for more than 10 qualifications, and traveling the world pursuing her ever-changing multiple passions through hard and great times had led her to a life she loves. Now, she has taken control of how she weaves her multiple passions into a lifestyle that works for her. She is rewarded and valued for her diverse expertise and experiences. She has a wide range of inspiring, fun people in her life and she remains incredibly proud of all the different things that she achieves.

Contact Information

Website: www.vikkicoombes.com
Facebook: @VikkiCoombes
Twitter: @VikkiCoombes
Instagram: @vikki.coombes